LITERATURE IN STONE

The Hundred Year History of Pennsylvania's State Capitol

PENNSYLVANIA CAPITOL PRESERVATION COMMITTEE

Literature In Stone:
The Hundred Year History of Pennsylvania's State Capitol

PENNSYLVANIA CAPITOL PRESERVATION COMMITTEE
© 2006 by The Pennsylvania Capitol Preservation Committee
Room 630 Main Capitol Building
Harrisburg, PA 17120
Web: http://cpc.state.pa.us
ISBN Number 0-9643048-8-0

All rights reserved. No part of this book may be reproduced or transmitted in any form or by any means, electronic or mechanical, including photocopying, recording, or by any information storage or retrieval system without written permission from the committee, or its agent, except for inclusion of brief quotations in a review.

Printed by Integra Graphics, Harrisburg, Pennsylvania
Book Design by Amanda J. DeLorenzo
Editors, Ruthann Hubbert-Kemper and Jason L. Wilson
Capitol Preservation Committee
Printed in the United States of America

Table of Contents

Capitol Preservation Committee Members and Administrative Staff — v
Foreword — vii
Preface — xii
Acknowledgments — xiv

INTRODUCTION
Our Legacy from William Penn — 16

CHAPTER I
Pennsylvania's Early Capitols — 22

CHAPTER II
The Cobb Capitol — 66

CHAPTER III
The Huston Capitol: Inspiration, Design, and Construction — 84

CHAPTER IV
Capitol Dedication: October 4, 1906 — 124

CHAPTER V
The Capitol Graft Scandal — 164

CHAPTER VI
The Capitol's Fine and Decorative Arts — 196

CHAPTER VII
The Capitol Complex and the City Beautiful Movement — 250

CHAPTER VIII
The People's Building: A Preservation Journey — 286

Notes — 346
Appendices — 353
Bibliography — 369
Index — 376
Photographic Credits — 383

Paul I. Clymer John R. Bowie Thomas B. Darr David G. Argall Louis J. Appell, Jr.

Gibson E. Armstrong Fred Belardi James P. Creedon Barbara Franco Beatrice Garvan

Michael A. O'Pake P. Michael Sturla Patricia Vance John N. Wozniak Ruthann Hubbert-Kemper

LITERATURE IN STONE: THE HUNDRED YEAR HISTORY OF THE PENNSYLVANIA STATE CAPITOL

Committee Members

CHAIRMAN
Representative Paul I. Clymer

VICE CHAIRMAN
John R. Bowie
Governor's Appointee

SECRETARY
Thomas B. Darr
Supreme Court Appointee

TREASURER
David G. Argall
Pennsylvania House of Representatives

Louis J. Appell, Jr.
Governor's Appointee

Gibson E. Armstrong
Pennsylvania Senate

Fred Belardi
Pennsylvania House of Representatives

James P. Creedon
Secretary, Department of General Services

Barbara Franco
Executive Director, Historical & Museum Commission

Beatrice Garvan
Governor's Appointee

Michael A. O'Pake
Pennsylvania Senate

P. Michael Sturla
Pennsylvania House of Representatives

Patricia Vance
Pennsylvania Senate

John N. Wozniak
Pennsylvania Senate

Administrative Staff

EXECUTIVE DIRECTOR
Ruthann Hubbert-Kemper

CONTROLLER/PERSONNEL SUPERVISOR
Sue A. Ellison

PRESERVATION PROJECT MANAGERS
David L. Craig
Christopher R. Ellis

RESEARCH HISTORIAN
Jason L. Wilson

COMMUNICATIONS SPECIALIST
Richard E. Saiers

COMPUTER SYSTEMS ADMINISTRATOR
Daniel E. Markle

GRAPHIC DESIGNER
Amanda J. DeLorenzo

ADMINISTRATIVE SUPPORT STAFF
John Blessing
Tara A. Pyle
Carla E. Wright

RESEARCH INTERNS
Matthew Gundy
Christina Huffman
Brenda Niemeyer

THIS PAGE: *Top, Huston Capitol, February 1906; Bottom left, Joseph M. Huston's Capitol competition submission, 1902; Bottom right, Huston's Capitol competition entry, 1897.*

OPPOSITE PAGE: *Speaker K. Leroy Irvis at the House podium, 1984.*

LITERATURE IN STONE: THE HUNDRED YEAR HISTORY OF THE PENNSYLVANIA STATE CAPITOL

FOREWORD *The Spirit of Pennsylvania*

The Honorable K. Leroy Irvis
Speaker of the House, 1977-78; 1983-88
PENNSYLVANIA HOUSE OF REPRESENTATIVES

In 1958 I won a seat in the Pennsylvania House of Representatives. I was a young man, born and raised in Albany, New York, who had made a new home in Pittsburgh. I ran for office because I believed I could do some good for my neighborhood and my community. I did not know what was in store for me—the journey that would take me to the Speaker's podium. The Pennsylvania Capitol, my new office building, provided the first hint of the monumental task ahead of me.

The first time I walked into the House Chamber, I was awestruck. I had never been in such a building or such a room before. Here I was, just a back-bencher. I had not thought of the tradition and the great leaders who preceded me. I had not considered my place in setting policy that would determine the future of a Commonwealth. But I walked into this huge chamber, and it was all laid out before me, in the paintings and the windows, the desks and the chairs. I was with another newly elected member from Allegheny County, Jim Clarke, and we could hardly speak. I just said, "Good God." Jim said, "Do you think we got the right place?" And I said, "It's the right place, but where are we going to fit in here?"

How could I fit in? How could I fill this vast space? Somehow, it hardly seemed right that I could belong in a building that meant so much to so many people. The importance of our jobs was carved into the very walls, ceilings, and floors of this magnificent place.

That is exactly what the Pennsylvania Capitol was meant to do. From its first days, this building proclaimed the glory of the people of Pennsylvania and their willingness to strive for higher ideals, even as they sought prosperity and pursued the American dream. "You may enjoy what you do," this building seemed to say to lawmakers, "but you are not here to play games.

There is a grand design at work, and your role is finding your place in moving it forward."

With slow and sure steps, I did begin to find my place. The powerhouses of industry and politics had their assured positions at the policy-making table, but I sought a seat for an easily forgotten player—the people of Pennsylvania. I devoted my legislative career to a range of reforms in education, welfare, the environment, housing, justice, civil rights, and economic development. Those reforms centered around citizen representation in government. The people have the most important voice in government, and their Capitol should amplify that voice.

The Capitol of Pennsylvania found that confident voice at the start, but it got a little hoarse over the years. I did not notice at first, as awestruck as I was by the magnificence around me. But as I began to feel more sure of myself and my place in the legislature, I started to look at my physical surroundings. I noticed the boxy cubicles, the drab colors, and the dropped ceilings and paneled walls that probably hid great works of art from our eyes. This was not the building that the people of Pennsylvania deserved. A building reflects the people who put it there. Where you're satisfied to live and work tells much about you. Here we were in a "Palace of Art," doing the work of government, but we were being unfair to the very people we were meant to represent. It didn't matter whether or not they would ever see the Capitol. They paid for this building, and it was a reflection of their character. We had a responsibility to maintain it, but any visitor who saw its terrible state could only feel that we must not think very much of ourselves.

As I noticed the degradation of the building, I happened to mention it to Matt Ryan. His response? "When did you learn about this? Yesterday?" Matt's eyes had always been open to the indignities heaped upon the Capitol, and now, I was beginning to see them. Matt and I shared our vision of what a capitol should look like when people first saw it. It shouldn't look like a dirty, grimy building that no one was caring for, we agreed. It should shine, inside and out. The trees around it should be trimmed. The dome should gleam. The interior spaces should reflect pride in the state it represents.

We talked often about what we could do, and fortunately, we both achieved positions to make those things come true. I became Speaker of the House first, but the credit for Capitol preservation really goes to Matt Ryan. When he pushed for something, I could help by moving it along.

THIS PAGE: *Speaker K. Leroy Irvis portrait, South hyphen corridor.*

OPPOSITE PAGE: *Matthew J. Ryan and K. Leroy Irvis, 1984.*

Many others began to join the cause, and when we finally started to clean things up, it seemed as if a new world was appearing. When you came up those broad steps, it was amazing to see what happened when the sun shone on that magnificent building. It made you proud, and that was a major change. As a whole, the Capitol projected majesty. In its individual parts—through its murals, tiles, and statues—it gave us pieces of wisdom to ponder. The meaning of Pennsylvania and its Capitol is clear in the prescient words of William Penn that circle the rotunda. He envisioned the outcome of his Holy Experiment, this common wealth, and declared, "My God will make it the seed of a nation. That an example may be set up to the nations. That we may do the thing that is truly wise and just."

The seed of a nation. Pennsylvania did contribute new and radical concepts to a young United States—ideas of religious liberty, self-determination, equality under the law. The people of this Commonwealth made those high-flown concepts real, and the Capitol replicates, in stone and paint, their spirit. Most of all, it reflects their independence. Nobody owns Pennsylvania. Some have tried to own it, but it has never worked. It did not work in the past, and it won't work today. Pennsylvanians are independent.

Those independent souls have a Capitol that mirrors their soaring ideals, bright ideas, powerful industries, lofty ambitions, love for natural and man-made beauty, and stubborn insistence on their God-given rights. They are awestruck by the beauty of the building, and that is the important thing. When the people of Pennsylvania see their Capitol, in all its restored glory and its vision of a bright future, they see themselves. φ

Judge Patricia H. Jenkins
1993-Present
Delaware County Court of Common Pleas

One day, when Matt Ryan was a young lawmaker, he walked by a dumpster on his way into the Capitol. There, he saw a sight that sickened him. A beautiful marble fireplace had been carved up and discarded, actually butchered, because it didn't fit into some legislator's decorating scheme. The act was thoughtless. Matt knew it would leave a permanent scar, and he vowed that if he ever reached House leadership, he would use his power to preserve this beautiful Capitol. The Capitol did not belong to individual legislators, administration officials, or staffers, he believed. It belonged to the people of

Matt saw the building and the work as intertwined. Under his watch, even Capitol interns had to get acquainted with the space they occupied. I know, because I was one of them in 1973, and even though Matt was not Speaker of the House yet, he encouraged all of the interns to tour the Capitol because it was so beautiful. Sadly, though, only parts of it were beautiful then. He also pointed out the contrast between the spaces that were marvelous and those that weren't. Rooms were divided. Offices were carved out of closets and storage rooms. Artwork was crumbling. The impact of our responsibilities resonated across the state, but our workspace did not reflect that.

In those days, when the beauty of the Capitol was not respected institutionally, Matt found a sympathetic soul in Leroy Irvis. That was fortuitous, because both rose to preside over the House of Representatives. During their terms in the Speaker's office, they gave Capitol preservation a place in state law and created a legal entity, the Capitol Preservation Committee, responsible for restoring the building to its past glory. Perhaps more importantly, they provided leadership that changed minds, convincing legislators and other Capitol occupants that their offices were not their individual domains but part of a broader legacy. In a place where countless conflicting issues fight for their place on the agenda, Matt and Lee made Capitol preservation a policy priority.

Pennsylvania, and their children and grandchildren. They trusted their elected officials to guard its treasures, but the desecrations he witnessed showed that their trust was misplaced.

My husband, Matt Ryan, believed passionately in the beauty and meaning of the Pennsylvania Capitol. He loved what this building said about Pennsylvania. Matt was famous for the years he devoted to the House of Representatives, and for the love he showed the institution, but above all, he loved Pennsylvania. He loved its diversity. Every person represented something in the ideal that is the Commonwealth of Pennsylvania. Sometimes, driving home from Harrisburg, he would take back roads instead of highways, because he could see people at home, at school, at work. He believed that the policies created in Harrisburg made a difference in so many lives, and he wanted the building to reflect the importance of that task. He wanted it to be something very special for all Pennsylvanians to enjoy.

Matt had tremendous pride in the building—not for anything he did himself, but for the work of the people who first built the building, and those who restored it. The restoration process and the beauties it uncovered never ceased to amaze him. Some evenings when artisans were in the hallway outside the Speaker's office, painstakingly restoring gold leaf in the ceilings, that's where he'd be. He liked to talk to the restorers and ask about their procedures, and he would bring me to see what they were doing.

That was the hallmark of Matt Ryan's love for this building—his passion for showing the world the wonders at our feet and above our heads. When he wasn't working in the Speaker's office, he left the door open so anyone standing in the hallway, waiting for the elevator, could peek into that glorious room. After all, it belonged to them as much as it did to him.

If Matt were still here, I think he would have been both proud and embarrassed at the praise for his work as a champion of preservation. He did not feel that he was doing anything extraordinary. He was doing something that interested him, for a cause he believed in.

If he took pride in his work for the Capitol at all, it was in the difference it made for the institutions he loved, the House of Representatives and the Pennsylvania General Assembly. The members of the Pennsylvania Legislature joined him in preserving their magnificent building. They have a greater measure of self-respect because their space reflects the magnitude of the job they are doing.

Among the things Matt kept in his district office desk was a page from a 1999 House journal, when a House member applauded the building's transformation and Matt's role:

"I have been here when they butchered this building with cheap wood paneling, drop ceilings and cheap lights," the member said. *"I'm glad to see, through Matt Ryan and the Capitol preservation program that we have changed that direction, and that we have gone through the historic preservation program to keep the integrity of these buildings for others to follow. Thank you, Mr. Speaker."*

That was all the thanks Matt Ryan ever needed. His memory still lives in a building that has been restored to its original glory, and in the Capitol annex, renamed in his honor. More importantly, his memory lives in the seed of an idea that he planted—that the Pennsylvania Capitol belongs to the people of a brilliant, diverse, energetic, and resilient state. If the men and women who work there every day sometimes pause and look around them, in awe of the building and the tremendous things that happen there, then Matt is smiling. With the help of many others, he did what he set out to do—to make the Pennsylvania Capitol worthy of the wonderful people of this Commonwealth.

THIS PAGE: *Speaker Matthew J. Ryan portrait, South hyphen corridor.*

OPPOSITE PAGE: *Speaker Matthew J. Ryan speaking at the Victorian Society of America awards ceremony, May 10, 2000.*

Preface

It was a fortuitous combination of events that turned Harrisburg, Pennsylvania, from a small river crossing and trading town into the capital city of Pennsylvania. To most Americans, especially those who have not traveled through the city, it may be just a dot on the map. With certainty, it's one of those state capitals that is most likely glossed over or missed in trivia games and fourth grade capital quizzes in favor of the former capital—Philadelphia.

There were many reasons why Harrisburg became favored as the capital city as early as 1785, not the least of which were free land, a localized population center, and its potential as a transportation hub. For these reasons in 1810 the legislature moved the capital to its current site. As the nineteenth century wore on, railroads, iron,

coal, and petroleum all contributed to Pennsylvania's dominance as the nation's industrial powerhouse. Harrisburg evolved into a crossroads of the state, with both the river and railroads allowing commerce in all directions. By 1900 the city would have many industrial and manufacturing jobs available for its citizens.

Many of these citizens were there to stare in awe in 1897, when Pennsylvania's first red brick Capitol caught fire and burned beyond repair. A year and a half later, citizens could look at the Commonwealth's new Capitol—an unsightly brick structure hastily built for $500 thousand stood in its place. It took four years for state lawmakers to muster the financial resources to build a structure befitting the Commonwealth's industrial and commercial might at the turn-of-the-century. In 1901 the legislature appropriated $4.5 million for the building's construction. All told, by 1906 the General Assembly would spend $13 million to produce a monument for all Pennsylvanians—an architectural and artistic gem worthy as their seat of government.

Of course there was a scandal, (there almost had to be—after all, political factions in Pennsylvania were as old as Independence Hall) and the investigation would last until 1911. However, those Pennsylvanians who had a chance to visit the new building had never seen anything like it in America, most probably paid little mind to the $13 million price tag ($542 million today, factoring inflation).

Visitors could stand in awe in the rotunda that soared upward 272 feet, replete with gold leaf, hues of reds, greens, and blues, all contrasting with stark white marble against the myriad of colors in the clay-tiled floor. They did not have to leave the state to feel like they were in Rome, Paris, or Athens—places most could only read and dream about. All of that had suddenly appeared right here, in their home state, on the banks of the Susquehanna. There, in the middle of the rotunda, at the very center of the architectural representation of balanced houses and democratic power, they could simply stare up and think, "Only in Pennsylvania." φ

THIS PAGE:
A. *Stephen Hills Capitol, ca. 1880.*
B. *Henry Ives Cobb Capitol, 1898.*
C. *Joseph Miller Huston Capitol, 1905.*

OPPOSITE PAGE: *Capitol showing East Wing and Complex buildings, 1996.*

Acknowledgments

"Who Made A Difference" was the title for one of the covers on the publication *Smithsonian*. Articles filled the magazine on people from all walks of life whose talents and dreams inspired achievements in the sciences and arts, on the beauty of nature, on society's problems, and on human progress. In many ways the Commonwealth of Pennsylvania began with an individual who also listened to an inner voice and who started a spiritual journey that would forever change the multitudes. William Penn had a vision that would chart a course of events and transform his colony to "make it the seed of a nation."

This publication is likewise recognizing those people "who made a difference." As we celebrate the one-hundredth anniversary of the State Capitol we have come to know artisans and tradespeople who have helped to restore the building and who, as they labored, came to appreciate more and more the intricate design and the beauty that had been constructed a century ago. Alongside these talented artisans we would like to thank farsighted legislative members who championed the preservation course. It was Speaker Matt Ryan who twenty-five years ago charted the course that would begin the restoration journey for the Capitol that had gone from a shining "Palace of Art" in 1906, to a sad state of deterioration in 1981 when the Capitol Preservation Committee was first implemented.

As the Committee began the restoration and uncovered the first of many inscriptions that were left for us by the talented craftsmen many years ago, we came to appreciate and understand that each one of them was putting into this Capitol a piece of themselves—leaving their own mark. Joseph Huston knew that without art a building such as this would be only a finely featured face devoid of expression. It is to Joseph Huston and all artisans, past and present, that we are indebted. We hope that this compilation will in a small part pay homage to all those who have helped to construct and preserve Pennsylvania's amazing State Capitol Building.

Over the course of the past twenty-five years literally thousands of contractors and their workmen have helped to restore the building as closely as possible to its original splendor. There are simply too many to list here, but we sincerely appreciate all the work that they have contributed in restoring the Capitol. Likewise, *Literature in Stone* contains a multitude of photographs from many institutions and individuals too numerous to list. We thank all those listed in our credits for their contributions to this book, along with the photographers who documented the projects over the years. Numerous hands were involved in the research and compilation of this Capitol history, which is the culmination of several years of research, writing, and design.

Special appreciation is extended to all past and present Capitol Preservation Committee members who spent many hours reviewing and evaluating proposed projects. Of

THIS PAGE: *Art conservator, Lucy Moran at work in the House Chamber, 1989.*

OPPOSITE PAGE: *Committee Members and Staff*
A. *Full-Committee Meeting, June 2004.*
B. *From left: David Craig and Christopher Ellis.*
C. *From left: Ruthann Hubbert-Kemper, Carla Wright, Sue Ellison, Tara Pyle, and Daniel Markle.*
D. *From left: Jason Wilson, Amanda DeLorenzo, and Richard Saiers.*

singular importance is the support from legislative, executive, and judicial branches of government who are honoring the long-range preservation commitment so vital to preserving the splendor and integrity of the Commonwealth's Capitol and its associated historic complex buildings.

For specific contributions to the success of this publication, we would first like to thank Jason Wilson, Committee Research Historian for his methodical research, writing, and preliminary editing of the text. Richard Saiers, Committee Communications Specialist for his help in design consultation and editing of the manuscript. For research and editing assistance on many of the chapters, we thank our summer interns over the course of the past several years, Matthew Gundy, Christina Huffman, and Brenda Niemeyer. Our Committee administrative staff, Tara Pyle, Executive Secretary and Carla Wright, Administrative Assistant contributed to the compilation of the appendices. Finally, for producing a most visually-appealing publication, we thank Amanda DeLorenzo, Committee Graphic Designer for her talents in design and layout of *Literature in Stone.*

We would also like to thank Ken Frew for his human interest finds in newspapers about the Capitol and Doris Dorwart for her critique and final editing of the text.

Without the diligence, attentiveness to detail, and labor of the above people, this publication—truly a collaborative effort—would never have come to fruition. May this book stand as a lasting testament to the grandeur of Pennsylvania's State Capitol and the talented artists and craftspeople who took part in its creation and restoration.

"**HISTORY** no longer shall be a dull book, **IT SHALL WALK INCARNATE** in every **JUST AND WISE** man." —*Ralph Waldo Emerson*

Representative Paul I. Clymer
Chairman
PENNSYLVANIA CAPITOL PRESERVATION COMMITTEE

Ruthann Hubbert-Kemper
Executive Director
PENNSYLVANIA CAPITOL PRESERVATION COMMITTEE

INTRODUCTION *featuring William Penn*

OUR LEGACY FROM WILLIAM PENN

William Penn was born in London in 1644 near the tower where he would later be held prisoner for his religious beliefs. During his youth, England was going through a tumultuous period of civil war, religious dissention, and social unrest. Penn was four, and probably still living in London, when Charles I was beheaded; nine when Oliver Cromwell became Lord Protector; sixteen when the monarchy was restored; twenty-one when London had a devastating plague; and twenty-two when London suffered from the "Great Fire" that changed its face forever. Little wonder that he had his first serious religious experience at twelve.[1] Penn's father became a captain in the parliamentary navy the year that his son was born, and rose rapidly in rank, eventually becoming an admiral. He easily made the political shifts needed to facilitate his career, and was knighted for his service to the crown after the monarchy was restored. As a result of his profession, he was frequently away while his son was growing up. The world the young Penn lived in posed two competing ways of going forward, and as a young man he was deeply conflicted about the proper course to take in his life: he could try to follow in his father's kind of career path, or he could choose a route determined by his spiritual experiences.

We can watch this contest being played out when he went to Oxford but was expelled for heretical religious ideas. He was sent to France to acquire social graces and connections (which according to Samuel Pepys he definitely did), but while there he also went to Saumur to study with a famous Protestant theologian. He enjoyed being a political emissary for his father and working on the family estates in Ireland. While in Ireland he even engaged in military action (there is an early portrait of him wearing armor), but that is also where he met Thomas Loe and was

THIS PAGE: Penn's Vision, *Violet Oakley, 1906, Governor's Reception Room.*

OPPOSITE PAGE: *William Penn as depicted in Edwin Austin Abbey's* Apotheosis of Pennsylvania, *1911, House Chamber.*

converted to Quakerism. And despite furious quarrels with his father about this choice, he cast his lot with George Fox and the Quakers, and soon became an important Quaker polemicist—an activity that landed him in the Tower of London in 1668. He was twenty-four.

These several strains can be followed throughout his life. Penn was deeply committed to the Friends' beliefs, and their principles were most emphatically his principles. He believed in the light within, and the right to give voice to religious ideas and inspiration. He believed with Friends in a fundamental equality before God, and therefore would not use titles or engage in acts of deference to those of higher station—not even to the king. Penn believed in peace and rejected the sword. He was prepared to suffer for what he believed. And he was also prepared to resist those who put obstacles in his way, and to work hard to make his kind of religious activity legal.

A notable early example of resistance was his preaching at a Quaker meeting for which he was arrested under the Conventicle Act of 1670, an act that outlawed such religious meetings on the grounds that they caused public disturbances. In the resulting trial, he convinced the jury that his speaking did not offend against the law because, he said, the Friends' meetings were peaceful. When the judge tried to strong-arm the jury, the jury held out for its verdict and rejected the judge's instruction. The case became a landmark in the history of trial by jury and the jury's right to make independent decisions.[2] However, his father's example and ambitions for him also bore fruit. Although he dressed in plain style, he always strove to live like a gentleman.

Penn was very interested in politics, especially as a means of acquiring freedom of religion for Friends. And he was able to shift from the Whig party—a party that sought protections for parliamentary government and was a system he really believed in—to support King James II, a Roman Catholic, because he believed the king was interested in religious tolerance. During this Whig period, he went electioneering for the most radical of Whigs, Algernon Sydney, and he was equally articulate in defense of the most conservative of kings. But if in some ways he was like his father, his visions were larger than his father's. He was prepared to take on a huge territory, design its government, and use it for asylum of the persecuted. Interestingly, rather late in his life, he even devised a plan for a European council, a league of nations, that would keep the peace and prevent war, and war had been his father's path to success.[3]

He BELIEVED... in a FUNDAMENTAL EQUALITY before GOD, and therefore would not use titles or engage in acts of deference TO THOSE OF HIGHER STATION— not even to the king.

It is perfectly understandable why Penn sought the charter to Pennsylvania. He saw the colonies as a place where religious dissidents who were persecuted in England could live and work peacefully. His efforts to convince the English Parliament to grant religious tolerance to Friends had not been successful. He had been involved in the West New Jersey settlement, and certainly heard reports from the Friends who traveled to America to give witness. He was in debt because he poured his resources into defense of persecuted Friends, into publication of his tracts and books (he published at least 135 titles), and efforts to change the laws. The colonies undoubtedly felt like a wonderful opportunity. It is a little less clear why Charles II granted the charter in a period when the Lords of Trade were tightening control of the colonies. The public reason given was that the crown owed Penn's deceased father money, and the charter was in payment of that debt. It has been speculated that Charles took an opportunity to get rid of Friends, who were troublesome. It is certain that Penn had many powerful allies who could help him. For whatever reason, Penn received a charter and his colony received a name—Pennsylvania. He immediately plunged into the business of creating a colony.

Taking first things first, he wrote to the small number of Europeans who had already settled there, assuring them that they would "be govern'd by laws of yr own making, & live a free…People."[4]

And for the Native American population he proposed what was unusual in American settlements. In the conditions he laid out for those who first purchased land in Pennsylvania, he set forth numerous protections for Native Americans: protection against cheating in trade and abuse by settlers; guarantees of justice, with adjudication in disputes by juries of twelve (six planters and six Indians); and promises of liberty to improve their holdings. He wanted, he said, Indians and planters to "Live friendly Together, and as much as in us Lyeth, Prevent all Occassions of Heart Burnings and Mischeifes."[5] In a letter to the "Kings" of the Indians, he made assurances directly to them.[6] And while he was alive he made good on those promises.

Next, if Pennsylvania was to be a haven for the oppressed, and turn a profit for the proprietor, he had to convince people that they should come, buy land, and settle down to a peaceful life. Penn had excellent connections with Friends all over the British Isles, and he had also traveled to Holland and Germany in 1671 and again in 1677. He advertised extensively, offering attractive land deals as incentives, and freedom of religion to the persecuted. For the time, William Penn brought an unusually diverse population to his colony. In addition to the Finns and Swedes who were already in residence, there soon came English, Irish, Welsh, Dutch, and German settlers. Some were Jews. Origins were not important to Penn.

The form of government Pennsylvania would take was also important to him. Numerous drafts stand testimony to the care and concern Penn gave to the task of designing a constitution, and the number of advisors he consulted.[7]

The final Frame of Government and Laws Agreed Upon in England, while not as liberal as his very first draft, was still daringly experimental and sought to correct what he saw as the weaknesses of the English unwritten constitution. In his first draft, he came close to popular sovereignty; in the final version, he created a two-house system in which the lower house, or General Assembly, had only the right to approve or reject laws, and the upper house, or Provincial Council, composed of men of substance, had the exclusive power to propose legislation. Some of his father was still in him. On the other hand, somewhat limited authority was reserved for the governor or proprietor; this was by no means an autocratic government.

It is particularly interesting to note that Penn's several experiences of imprisonment, and his knowledge of the suffering of fellow Friends, led to a penal code that was innovative in important ways. Trial by jury was guaranteed. Capital crimes were limited to murder and treason (in England there was a long list of crimes that could result in execution). Some attention was given to innocent victims—some of a debtor's property could be saved for his children, and in cases of capital crime, one-third of the criminal's estate was to go to the victim's family, the rest to the criminal's heirs. Prisons were to be free, which was not the case in England, and lawyer's fees controlled.

Another of Penn's values was public education. The Frame of Government delegated to the Provincial Council authority to establish schools, and the importance of schooling was reiterated in the Laws Agreed Upon in England. He wanted the youth of the colony to acquire useful knowledge—knowledge of the arts, and knowledge of useful trades. This was consistent with the Friends' educational values, that is, they did not want children to receive religious education that would interfere with freedom of religion, nor were they interested in classical educations that were part of the elite educational structure.

But the great achievement for Penn and the persecuted people who came to Pennsylvania was freedom of conscience or religion. A walk through the eighteenth century section of Philadelphia tells the story of the successful application of this principle. We find Quaker meetings and churches of all types including German Lutheran, Swedish Lutheran, Methodist, Presbyterian, Anglican or Episcopal, Roman Catholic, and the AME church founded by Richard Allen. There remains a Jewish cemetery. No other city in the colonies had such religious diversity.

In addition, Penn gave great attention to the design of the city of Philadelphia. He intended a town laid out on a grid, neat and orderly, with large squares set aside for open space. These parts of the plan are still in evidence. However, he also wanted each householder to have a large enough plot so that the house could be surrounded by gardens. The plague and fire of his youth, and the rebuilding of London, certainly inspired him. The settlers, however, preferred to huddle together, and the lot owners were happy to make profits, so they soon cut up the spacious lots with alleys and small houses, recreating conditions for fire and health hazards. A significant innovation for a colonial town was the absence of fortifications.[8]

THIS PAGE: Top, *William Penn Portrait, Governor's Office;* Bottom, *Penn as Law Giver,* Violet Oakley, 1927, Supreme Court Chamber.

OPPOSITE PAGE: King Charles II signs the Charter of Pennsylvania, *Violet Oakley, 1906, Governor's Reception Room.*

The early years of Penn's proprietorship were happy ones, with good collaboration between the founder and settlers, grateful for their escape from Europe. However, Penn soon had to return to England to protect the colony from Lord Baltimore who was trying to expand the borders of Maryland at the expense of Pennsylvania, and then dark days followed. Penn supported James II, and after the Glorious Revolution of 1688, had to go in to hiding. By the time he restored his reputation, he was once again deeply in debt. He was also in serious difficulty with his colonists over taxes, and over the role of the lower house of the legislature, which was unhappy with its limited powers. Penn returned briefly to Pennsylvania, and when he had to leave yet again to save the colony, this time from

THIS PAGE: *Top*, Penn's First Sight of the Promised Land, *Inset*, Penn Writing in Prison; *Violet Oakley, 1906, Governor's Reception Room.*

OPPOSITE PAGE: Penn's Treaty, *Edwin Austin Abbey, 1911, House Chamber.*

seizure by the crown, he submitted to the will of the General Assembly, and signed The Charter of Liberties.⁹

Penn's original Frame of Government had a complicated history, and the colonists who were political activists protested that it was no longer in force. Penn did not like to agree, but he was also anxious to grant a charter that would protect the colony if it were taken over by the royal government. Therefore he signed The Charter of Liberties, a document that became the base of Pennsylvania's government and freedoms for seventy-five years. It created a unicameral legislature, unique in America, with powers closely modeled on those held by the English Parliament. It stipulated freedom of religion, and Penn bound himself and his heirs to protect the liberties granted in the charter and do nothing to infringe upon or break them. The Charter retained Penn's penal code, but dropped the secret ballot (Pennsylvania had been the first place in the English speaking world to use it).

And so Penn left, never to return. Despite the granting of the charter they wanted, and another charter to protect their land holdings, he left behind a people who no longer looked upon him as a savior, and who were anxious to be left to govern themselves. Penn, who was dispirited, hopelessly in debt to his steward, and headed for debtor's prison, was forced to mortgage his colony. He eventually came to some resolution of his quarrels with the colonists, but in 1712 he suffered a severe stroke that brought an end to his public life.

Penn's legacy is an important one, and he may be underappreciated today. It is an American truism that an important reason for the settlement of the American colonies by the English was the search for freedom to practice one's religion in peace. But that did not always mean that the settlers were prepared to offer that freedom to others. It was William Penn who made it a matter of policy, a constitutional right. He was opposed to the creation of a state religion, and looked forward to the separation of church and state. Because of persecution, he became a penal code reformer. Because of Quakerism, he accepted the equality before God of all humans. Even though he was unable to surrender all of the trappings of his class, he devoted himself and his fortune, unselfishly and energetically, to right the wrongs done to his co-religionists, and to change the laws that led to persecution. He was a civil rights activist par excellence. He had human failings—for example, he was not good at managing money and he did not make good appointments—but he was a man of honor and integrity. Pennsylvanians are fortunate that he was the source of our Commonwealth's beginnings.

Contributing Writer **Mary Maples Dunn**
Co-Executive Officer
AMERICAN PHILOSOPHICAL SOCIETY

The Hills Capitol, L.C. Allison, early 1890s.

C·H·A·P·T·E·R
ONE

Pennsylvania's Early Capitols

WHEN William Penn first established the colony of Pennsylvania there was no fixed location for a permanent seat of colonial government. The day after landing at New Castle on the Delaware on October 27, 1682, Penn traveled to Upland, which was then a Swedish settlement. Penn ordered that its name be changed to Chester after the English town of the same name. It was at Chester on October 28 that Penn called the first meeting of a general assembly in the colony of Pennsylvania, stating that it would meet on December 4, 1682 in the newly-named town. Just three days later on December 7, the "Great Law" was enacted, this first governmental framework for the colony of Pennsylvania.

Penn's first General Assembly was just that—any freeman who wanted to attend the meeting was permitted to do so, making it a pure democracy. However, Penn stipulated some rules to maintain his power as governor. Therefore, the members had no powers of initiation or debate, and they could only agree or disagree on the proposed measures. Over ninety laws were voted on, sixty-one of which were included in what became known as the "Great Law" of the new colony. In 1683 Penn ordered a general election for members of the Provincial Assembly and directed the General Assembly to meet at Philadelphia. There were from this period until 1701 fifty-four delegates to the Assembly, which meant that a

gathering place was needed, especially since the Assembly after 1683 was divided into two houses.[1]

In the early days the General and Provincial Assemblies had no regularly established house in which to meet. They would meet at irregular intervals upon the call of Penn or his colonial manager in several suitable locations in or around Philadelphia. The Assembly would often gather in Quaker meeting houses or private residences in the area. The Bank Meeting House was used initially as a gathering place and the Friends' Meeting House from 1684–1695. For a period of five years, the Assembly met in the homes of wealthy Philadelphians, and after that period began to meet at a schoolhouse, known as Makin's. No one is sure how long or how frequently the Assembly met at Makin's, but in 1728 they began to meet at the house of Captain Anthony Morris. During the course of the next session after approximately forty-seven years of roving sessions, assembling at meeting houses, to residences, and finally schools, the Assembly decided that it must have a permanent location of its own. On May 1, 1729, they appropriated £30 thousand for the construction of a proper meeting place. The commission to oversee the building of this structure consisted of Speaker Andrew Hamilton, Thomas Lawrence, and Dr. John Kearsley, all of whom were Assemblymen.

1643 *Johan Printz establishes the capital of New Sweden at Tinicum Island on the Delaware River. It is the first permanent establishment in the future colony of Pennsylvania.*

1647 *George Fox founds the Society of Friends, which comes to be known as the Quakers.*

1691 *Germantown, the first German settlement in Pennsylvania, is established.*

1701 *William Penn's Charter of Privileges is enacted; It will remain the governing document of the colony until 1776.*

THIS PAGE: Friends Meeting House and Old Courthouse, *William L. Breton, undated.*

OPPOSITE PAGE: Top, *A view of the Bank Meeting House, Front Street, Benjamin R. Evans;* Bottom, *The Building in Which the First Assembly was Convened by Penn at Chester, 1682, William L. Breton.*

CHAPTER ONE • *Pennsylvania's Early Capitols*

This structure was built between Fifth, Sixth, and Chestnut Streets in Philadelphia, and at the time of its construction was one of the largest buildings in the American colonies. The original architect of the structure was Edmund Woolley, and construction began in 1732, with the Assembly first using the building in 1735. In 1751 a bell tower was added, and Hamilton requested that a large bell be cast in England for installation in the new tower. Hamilton stipulated that the bell was to be lettered with a passage from the book of Leviticus, in honor of the fiftieth anniversary of William Penn's 1701 Charter of Privileges. The verse "Proclaim Liberty throughout all the Land unto all the Inhabitants thereof" is the famous passage engraved on the Liberty Bell. The first time the bell was rung it cracked, and the Philadelphia foundry of Pass and Stowe was requested to melt the bell and re-alloy it to make it stronger. In addition, citizens in the town were

not happy with the dull tone that the bell gave upon ringing. Pass and Stowe remelted the bell but the tone was no different. The citizens of Philadelphia were forced to settle on the tone of the recast bell, which was rung for important occasions of colonial and later national significance. It rang in the bell tower for the battles of Lexington and Concord, and later with the first public reading of the Declaration of Independence on July 8, 1776. The bell purportedly rang last on Washington's Birthday in 1846, when a fissure in the bell widened rendering the bell unringable. Since that time the Liberty Bell has been displayed at prominent locations of national significance, most notably the nation's centennial and bicentennial celebrations, and also at the 1904 St. Louis World's Fair.

The Liberty Bell was not the only nationally significant item to come from Pennsylvania's first state house. The Declaration of Independence, Articles of Confederation, and the

THIS PAGE: *Top, Back of the State House, Philadelphia, drawn, engraved and published by William Birch and Son, 1799; Bottom, Independence Hall, west transverse section.*

OPPOSITE PAGE: Building the Cradle of Liberty, *Jean Leon Gerome Ferris; Andrew Hamilton pictured at center.*

CHAPTER ONE • *Pennsylvania's Early Capitols*

Constitution were all debated and signed within its halls. The location of the building within the colonies and its size made Independence Hall the most logical site for meetings of the Continental Congress.

HARRISBURG:

"high, airy, healthy, and pleasant; the soil rich, and the water wholesome; there is clay for brick, stone for building, and fuel in the greatest abundance..."

However, by the 1790s, with both the State Assembly and the National Assembly meeting in Philadelphia, the area was becoming cramped. The Commonwealth's General Assembly began in earnest to debate a move westward. When the state legislature moved to Lancaster in 1799, they left the building for the use of Congress, (who would move to New York City the very next year). The Assembly retained control of the building, and in 1802 rented the upstairs to famed artist Charles Willson Peale for use as a museum. Later, the state legislature sold the building to the city of Philadelphia for the sum of $70 thousand, largely to finance the building of the new state Capitol at Harrisburg.

Harrisburg has remained Pennsylvania's capital city since 1812, despite several attempts to dislodge the center of state government and relocate it elsewhere. The beautiful and artistically magnificent Capitol building that currently stands watch over John Harris' eighteenth-century ferry route was yet unimagined. For the first seventy-five years of the capital's existence in Harrisburg, a different, more rustic Capitol building dominated the agrarian landscape at Harris' river city. The Hills Capitol, or old red brick Capitol, as it is sometimes called, was Pennsylvania's first official Capitol building. It was exceptionally significant architecturally, because it was the first U.S. state house to represent through its form, the new democratic virtues embodied in the early republic through the use of balanced houses.[2] It served the Commonwealth through numerous legislative battles, welcomed various dignitaries to its halls, and lasted the vast majority of the nineteenth century.

Philadelphia, the Commonwealth's cosmopolitan metropolis of the eighteenth century, was the natural choice for the colonial capital of the state. With an erudite and learned citizenry, Philadelphia was without a doubt the largest and most scientifically-advanced city in the colonies by the late 1700s. Not only was its location key, as the center between the northern and southern colonies, but its colonial state house was one of the larger in the American colonies.

Almost as soon as the war for independence had been won, the debate over removing the governmental center from Philadelphia began. Now that the

THIS PAGE: *"Harris Mansion" taken from View of Harrisburg, Pennsylvania, daguerreotype by J. Thomas Williams, 1855.*

OPPOSITE PAGE: *A map of Philadelphia and parts adjacent with a perspective view of the State House, Nicholas Scull and G. Heap, ca. 1752.*

CHAPTER ONE • *Pennsylvania's Early Capitols*

prolonged conflict had secured the nation's future, development of the interior sections of the nation and of the Commonwealth were a certainty. The main impetus for the move from Philadelphia was eastern Pennsylvania's decline as the population center. In addition, fears that city politics might dominate those of the state, cramped quarters for both Congress and the General Assembly, rampant disease, and the oppressive summer heat prompted the General Assembly to debate relocation of the capital further to the west.[3]

In 1784 a commission comprising Philadelphian David Rittenhouse and two other delegates reported to the legislature that John Harris, Jr., of Harris' Ferry on the Susquehanna, had offered to lay out a town. Harris would provide two hundred quarter-acre lots, a courthouse and jail, and in addition, convey an area of approximately four acres to be held in perpetuity for any use the Commonwealth might deem fitting. The

Rittenhouse commission praised the site, terming it, "high, airy, healthy, and pleasant; the soil rich, and the water wholesome; there is clay for brick, stone for building, and fuel in the greatest abundance."[4] The legislature approved the Rittenhouse commission's report, seeing the site as a favorable location for the eventual seat of government, and through their actions set in motion several measures to ensure that Harris' offer did not go to waste.

The next year, 1785, the Assembly formed Dauphin County, with its seat at Louisburg, as Harrisburg was then known, until incorporated as a borough in 1791. The Supreme Executive Council chose both the county and town names in honor of French King Louis XVI.[5]

In 1789 the Assembly resolved that Philadelphia was "an unfortunate location" and that the capital should be located at Harrisburg, but there was no bill passed to move the governmental seat. In the years from 1790–1799 there were several votes taken and petitions filed by Pennsylvania towns, all vying to be considered as locations for the new capital. Carlisle, Lancaster, Reading, Harrisburg, and Wright's Ferry on the Susquehanna were among the sites considered. None of the

THIS PAGE: *Top, "Dauphin County Prison" taken from* View of Harrisburg, Pennsylvania, *daguerreotype by J. Thomas Williams, 1855; Bottom, Governor Thomas Mifflin portrait, Governor's Office.*

OPPOSITE PAGE: *Lancaster County Courthouse, 1799.*

proposed cities garnered enough votes to pass both houses of the Assembly.

THE MOVE TO LANCASTER

In April 1799, due to agreements reached by both eastern and western legislators, the General Assembly mustered the necessary votes to remove the capital from Philadelphia. A resolution was made by Richard Martin of Lycoming County and Jacob Strickler of Lancaster County. It stated that movement of the population had rendered Philadelphia unacceptable and that it was necessary to move the seat of government somewhere nearer to the population center of the Commonwealth. In addition, it added that, "as of late a disease called the yellow fever had raged at particular periods so as to render it dangerous for the members of the legislature to meet."[6]

Governor Thomas Mifflin approved a joint Act of the House and Senate to move the capital to Lancaster. The government was to have completed its move by the first Tuesday of November 1799. On December 3 the Assembly met for the first time in Lancaster's new brick courthouse, an expanded version of the building in which they had met after fleeing Philadelphia during the revolution. The Red Rose City was bustling with activity and optimism, and the spirit of westward expansion was already evident. However, the move to Lancaster did little to quell discussion over a permanent location for the state capital. Most Assembly delegates knew that the move to Lancaster was only temporary.

CHAPTER ONE • *Pennsylvania's Early Capitols*

One delegate, a Mr. Dorsey, claimed that he doubted the capital would return to Philadelphia, but was in favor of any other town, aside from remaining in Lancaster.[7]

By 1801 there were already debates on whether to transfer the capital to the Susquehanna, where John Harris' four-acre tract was still waiting. Among the delegates to the Assembly, it was generally agreed upon that the Susquehanna Valley was the optimal place in Pennsylvania for the seat of government. In the debates of 1801–1803, several Lancaster citizens sought to donate land for the Commonwealth's use in an effort to retain the government at Lancaster, thereby answering Harris' offer of free land at Harrisburg. The Assembly could not agree on the proposals of the Lancaster citizenry and all motions were tabled.

It was several years until the issue of removal was once again brought before the legislature, and this time it came in the form of a serious petition from the citizens of Northumberland, Pennsylvania. In January 1809 they petitioned the Senate, stating what a fine town theirs would be for the capital city, and the debate once again raged. This time, perhaps seeing the handwriting on the wall, every town or borough that had ever entertained even the most remote thoughts of becoming the capital entered a plea for consideration.

Lancaster, Philadelphia, Pittsburgh, Harrisburg, Middletown, Northumberland, Bellefonte, Carlisle, Columbia, Reading, and Sunbury were all locations proposed and voted on during the debates. Senators and Representatives who had extreme distances to travel to get to Lancaster were the most avid supporters of the move, but eastern representatives who agreed that a more centrally located capital city would better represent the people of the state also agreed with another move. The votes were counted, and on February 21, 1810, Governor Simon Snyder signed the act moving the Commonwealth's seat of government one more time. The measure was to take effect in October 1812, and in that month the General Assembly would convene at Harrisburg for the first time.

Along the Susquehanna

There are indications very early on that William Penn himself thought a location on the river "Susquehannagh" would be beneficial as a possible sister city to Philadelphia. John Harris, Sr., father of the founder of Harrisburg, knew the Penn family and was granted permission by them to trade with the Indians around 1717, several years before he established a trading post. John Harris ultimately chose the site and was granted the land because both he and the Penns knew it would be an optimum location for a town. It was the elder Harris who first believed that, "the seat of government of Pennsylvania will some day be located here."[8] With that possibility in mind, John Harris, Jr.'s grant of four acres of "the publick ground" was held in the eventuality that the state would deem the location suitable as the capital, and also as a carrot to assist in the decision-making process. This of course was contingent upon the fact that the small town needed to grow, and from the time of its establishment in 1785, prominent Harrisburg residents sought to construct more permanent brick structures to entice the General Assembly.

With the decision to move to Harrisburg in 1810, the area deeded by Harris for five shillings was now the property of the state. The legislature bought ten more acres of ground at $100 per acre from U.S. Senator William Maclay, which was located north of the Harris tract. The Senator and the Commonwealth had agreed that the Capitol, when built, would sit atop this rising piece of ground, facing the Susquehanna to the west.

When constructed, the center line of the building would run parallel to a new street, which the senator was to create toward the river, to be called "State Street."[9] Maclay also purchased five lots, which had divided the original Harris tract and his own, so that the state's land would be contiguous. The state also purchased five more individual lots, which brought the total amount of land owned to fifteen acres. This was the beginning of the original Capitol Park and the grounds that would house the first state buildings.

With the passage of the Act of 1810 that successfully moved the capital city, provisions to move and house the different branches and offices of government in Harrisburg began. Robert Harris, George Hoyer, and George Zeigler were appointed as commissioners to supervise the move of books, records, papers, and furniture from Lancaster to Harrisburg with an appropriation of $2 thousand to cover expenses. Among the original items to make the trip from Philadelphia to Lancaster and then Harrisburg were articles associated with both the Declaration of Independence and the Constitution, such as the Rising Sun Chair, Philip Syng's inkwell, and the original signers' table. At this time, the act also stipulated that any furniture too worn or antiquated was to be sold at auction, with proceeds returned to the state's coffers.[10]

Section 6 of the Act of 1810 also provided $30 thousand for the construction of two fireproof buildings to house the offices of the state, but the legislature had to find another suitable location to meet while these were being constructed. Harris, Hoyer, and Zeigler made arrangements for the Dauphin County Courthouse to serve as legislative chambers, while the county courts would meet on Market Street at a building known as White Hall.

The old Dauphin County Courthouse would serve as the Capitol of the state for ten years, but several modifications were needed to outfit the building for the legislature's use. The House met in the court chamber, and the Senate met in a large meeting room on the second floor. The structure stood two stories high, with

Top, "View of Bridgeport, Susquehanna River & Harrisburg from the South" taken from View of Harrisburg, Pennsylvania, *daguerreotype by J. Thomas Williams, 1855; Bottom, Governor Simon Snyder portrait, Governor's Office.*

CHAPTER ONE • *Pennsylvania's Early Capitols*

View of Harrisburg, Pennsylvania, *daguerreotype by J. Thomas Williams, 1855.*

LITERATURE IN STONE: THE HUNDRED YEAR HISTORY OF THE PENNSYLVANIA STATE CAPITOL

CHAPTER ONE • *Pennsylvania's Early Capitols*

1722 — The Pennsylvania Supreme Court is established by the General Assembly.

1727 — From this year on, the pace of German emigration to Pennsylvania increases dramatically. By the time of the Revolution in 1775, German immigrants would comprise a third of the populace.

1730s — Inventions arise in the Pennsylvania German population: The Pennsylvania long rifle becomes one of the most replicated firearms in the new colonies and is eventually produced in Virginia, Tennessee, and Kentucky, where it is renamed the Kentucky long rifle. The Conestoga wagon comes into being. Named for a creek in Lancaster County, it will eventually transform much of the nation as it evolves into a smaller lighter wagon known as "the prairie schooner."

1754 — Colonel George Washington is defeated at Fort Necessity in western Pennsylvania. The opening battle of the French and Indian War would lay the groundwork for the British conquest of North America and the American Revolution.

1776 — The Declaration of Independence is signed in Philadelphia's Independence Hall, listing the abuses of England's King George III and declaring separation of the American colonies from Great Britain.

1780 — Pennsylvania became the first colony in the struggling nation to pass a law for the gradual abolition of slavery.

two side wings and a wooden cupola containing a bell. The state added a semi-rotunda at the front, and several additions were added to the courthouse to accommodate government offices. To undertake the alterations to the courthouse, and also to build two fireproof state office buildings, the commission sought the services of local builder Stephen Hills.

Stephen Hills

Hills was a native of Ashford, Kent, England. He had emigrated to the United States in the 1790s, and his Boston carpentry shop had grown swiftly in a few short years. By the early 1800s he had relocated to Lancaster where his reputation as a skilled and talented craftsman grew. When the legislature moved to Harrisburg in 1810 Stephen Hills, the well-known housewright from Lancaster, was asked by the commissioners to erect and modify new state buildings. Hills relocated his family to Harrisburg in 1811. While finishing the modifications to the Dauphin County Courthouse and constructing the old north and south Capitol executive buildings, he also began to construct houses in the city. One such home was that of Commissioner Robert Harris, one of the men that had supervised the move to Harrisburg. A master builder was someone then in high demand in Harrisburg—a town of 2,200 inhabitants with some 800 houses, a third of which were brick.

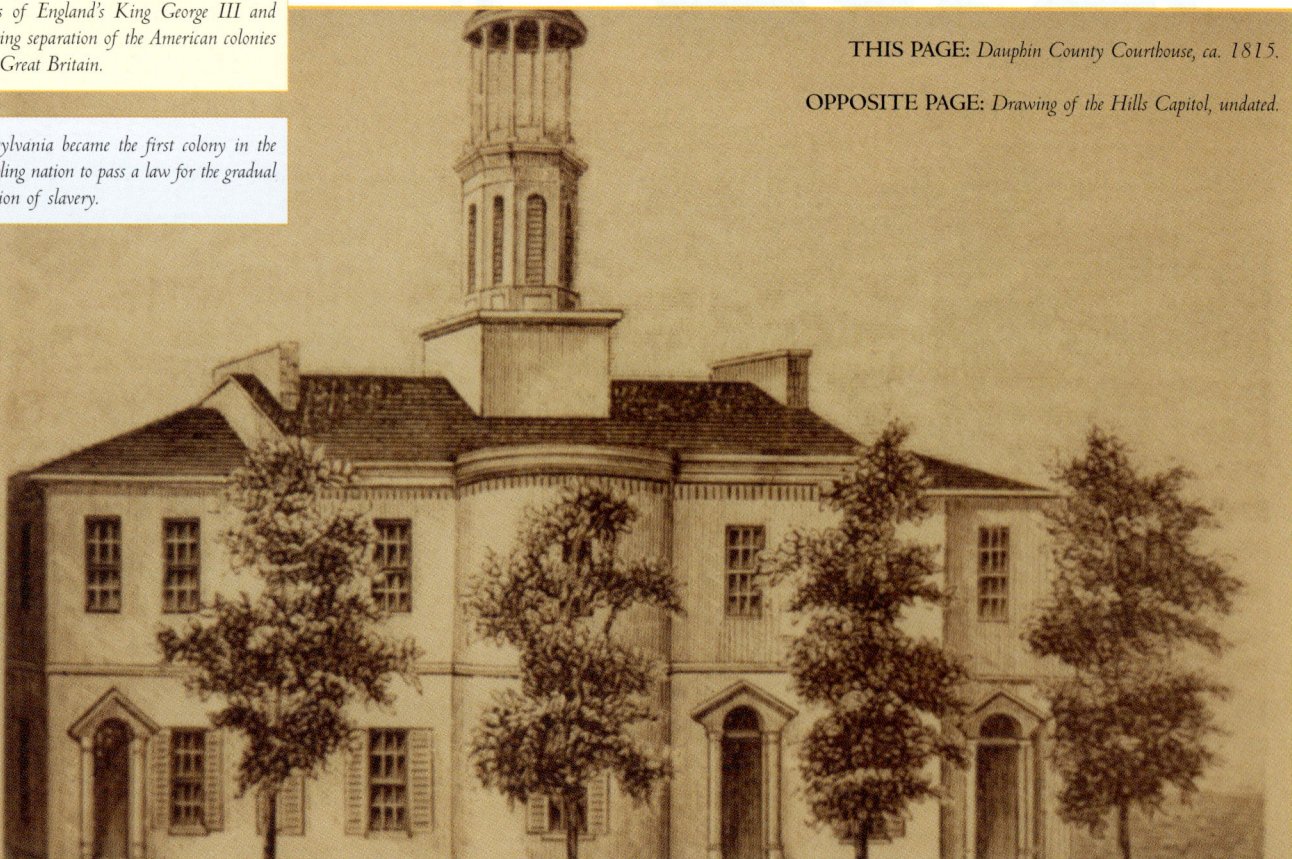

THIS PAGE: *Dauphin County Courthouse, ca. 1815.*

OPPOSITE PAGE: *Drawing of the Hills Capitol, undated.*

There seemed to be no question of Hills' ability, given the rapid nature in which he finished the first two state office buildings.

Hills had earlier developed a theme for both of his state office buildings—identical, two story, five-by-three-bay structures situated 325 feet apart on the "publick ground"—which was largely the old William Maclay tract. As stipulated by Section 6 of the 1810 act for the removal of the seat of government to Harrisburg, these two buildings were to be fireproof, or in the terminology of the time, made of brick. The initial appropriation of $30 thousand was to be sufficient for their construction, but it took another $43 thousand to finish and furnish the buildings.[11] This last appropriation was to pay for counters, shelves, and other necessary furniture for all of the state offices. The office buildings were to accommodate the secretary of the Commonwealth, the secretary of the land office, the surveyor general, the auditor general, and the treasurer, along with one empty office for future expansion. For his part in the erection of the buildings, the supervising of workmen, and the procuring of supplies, Stephen Hills received $3,572. Though he was considered by many as a master builder, he was listed on the supply ledger as simply, "carpenter."[12]

After the construction of the two state buildings, which were then known as the North and South Executive Buildings, Hills submitted a proposal for a "Main Capitol" building, which would be arranged between these office buildings, its center axis running perpendicular to the newly created State Street.[13] According to William Seale and Henry-Russell Hitchcock, Hills seems to have laid out construction of all the buildings in 1810 in a complete and unified theme, much like Robert Mills did in a rendering that he submitted to the Commonwealth. There was no formal architectural competition held at this time, and Hills and Mills probably submitted their renderings as a result of advertisements soliciting bid estimates for the eventual work.[14]

Regardless of the submission of plans, Hills was the man already on the job. The construction on the two office buildings progressed so rapidly, both as an expedient to avoid another vote to move the capital, and as a matter of necessity, that the General Assembly passed a supplement to the 1810 act and moved to Harrisburg in April of 1812. The original act had stipulated that the move be made in October.[15] Despite Hills' 1810 proposal for a large central capitol to dominate the hill and house the General Assembly, that body itself had not made any provisions for constructing a structure in which it could meet, most likely a result of the War of 1812.

It is believed that this competition was the FIRST FORMALIZED CONTEST EVER HELD to determine the design of an American statehouse.

It was not until March 11, 1816, that the legislature finally began to move toward constructing a new building by agreeing to the sale of the old state house (Independence Hall) to the city of Philadelphia for $70 thousand, and using the proceeds toward building a newer, more modern capitol building in Harrisburg.[16] One week later, Governor Snyder signed an act providing for the erection of a state capitol.

Though Hills was the logical choice for architect, having completed the two Capitol office buildings and having submitted a proposal for a "Main Capitol," political pressures compelled the Commonwealth to hold a design competition to select the winner. To this end the governor, in keeping with the legislative mandate, cancelled any agreements with Hills and advertised for architects to submit their plans. It is believed that this competition was the first formalized contest ever held to determine the design of an American statehouse.[17]

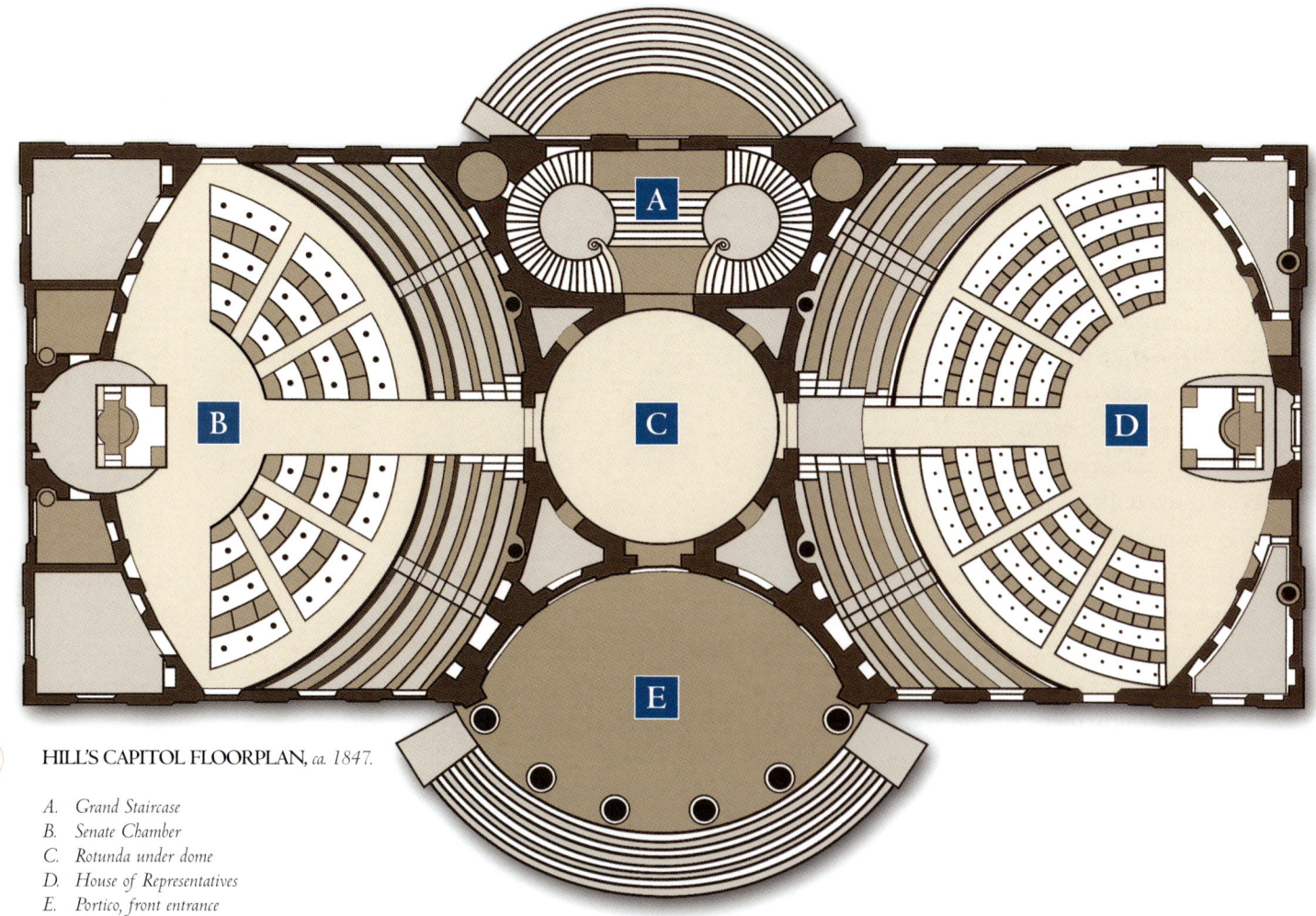

HILL'S CAPITOL FLOORPLAN, ca. 1847.

A. Grand Staircase
B. Senate Chamber
C. Rotunda under dome
D. House of Representatives
E. Portico, front entrance

LITERATURE IN STONE: THE HUNDRED YEAR HISTORY OF THE PENNSYLVANIA STATE CAPITOL

The legislative act governing the competition stipulated that the governor publicize the competition in two Philadelphia papers, along with Lancaster, Harrisburg, and Pittsburgh papers.[18] Only four of the entrants who submitted designs in answer to the 1816 competition are known: William Strickland, Robert Mills, James C. Lavelier, and Stephen Hills. Little information exists on the submitted plans, but it is known that Strickland's estimate of cost was around $300 thousand, while Lavelier's was less elaborate but more expensive at $330 thousand.[19] Most likely all the proposals are some variant on Hills' original theme, since the 1811–1812 buildings dictated the general nature of the center building's design. Regardless of the submissions, none of the architects' plans were accepted, not necessarily because of lack of merit, but a lack of money on the Commonwealth's part. The state had only $70 thousand—the money available from the sale of the old state house—and they further postponed the project until more funds could be raised.[20]

Despite the failure of the act of 1816 to produce either a suitable architect or plan, the act did allow the state to begin procuring materials for the actual construction. The legislature appropriated $50 thousand toward gathering construction materials, fencing and improving the public ground, and also appointing an agent of the state to procure the goods. Though it would be seen as a conflict of interest today, none other than Stephen Hills was the man selected as the state's purchasing agent. Hills had already built two buildings for the state and knew the prices, locations, and amounts of material that would be needed, when the contract was finally let. By gathering $25,641 worth of materials together on Capitol Hill, Stephen Hills was certainly in a better position to calculate with increased accuracy what his bid for the new building would be, whenever the next architectural competition occurred.

The gathering of materials for a building as large as that envisioned by Hills was not a small feat in the early nineteenth century. Harrisburg had yet to become a center of commerce or industry and the transportation network that would serve the Commonwealth's extremities was nonexistent. Neither canal nor rail service was available to transport any of the goods and raw materials for the Capitol. All wood, brick, shale, slate, and iron was hauled from the east, ferried from the west, or floated from the north—a laborious and time-consuming task. River stone, sandstone, limestone, and other materials were hauled over the Susquehanna River on Oglesby's Ferry, the price—$2 per wagon. Fifty thousand feet of white pine lumber came to the site via the Susquehanna. Hills and his assistant Erasmus Lindy piled the materials on Capitol Hill and built a shed to protect them from the elements. Other than that, no construction on the building was begun.

THIS PAGE: *Governor William Findlay portrait, Governor's Office.*

1787 — On December 12 Pennsylvania became the second state in the nation (Delaware being the first) to ratify the new constitution, which was also debated at Independence Hall.

1813 — Commodore Oliver Hazzard Perry defeats the British in the Battle of Lake Erie. Pivotal in the War of 1812, the victory secured the northwest territories for the United States and raised morale.

1826 — Pennsylvania launches a massive canal building campaign under the new "Main Line of Public Works." The Pennsylvania Canal, linking various smaller canals and railroads is completed from Philadelphia to Pittsburgh by 1834.

1834 — Pennsylvania passes the Free School Act, becoming one of the first in the nation to ensure a free education for all children.

1846 — The Pennsylvania Railroad is chartered. By 1852 the railroad had connected Philadelphia to Pittsburgh and by 1860 would have a monopoly of all rail traffic from Chicago through Pennsylvania.

1855 — An act was passed by the General Assembly for the founding of the Farmer's High School of Pennsylvania in Centre County. In 1862 it is changed to the Agricultural College of Pennsylvania and in 1863 selected to be the Commonwealth's sole land-grant college. The name changes again to the Pennsylvania State College in 1875 but it is not until 1953 that the name was finally changed to the Pennsylvania State University.

THIS PAGE: Architectural drawing of the Hills Capitol.

OPPOSITE PAGE: Top, Hills Capitol with North and South Office Buildings, Thos. B. Cochran, 1896; Bottom, House of Representatives, undated.

> [The Hills Capitol] was the first…to represent, through its form, the new democratic virtues embodied in the early republic through the use of balanced houses.

In the interim period, while the legislature wrangled with allocating money for the Capitol, Hills was contracted to construct the first state arsenal near the corner of Third and Walnut Streets in Harrisburg. The structure was brick and was used by the Commonwealth until 1873, when the second state arsenal was constructed at Eighteenth and Herr Streets. The original wrought-iron fence surrounding the first arsenal was moved to Eighteenth and Herr, and one section was placed around the grave of founder John Harris on Front Street.

By May 26, 1817, Hills wrote the secretary of Commonwealth and auditor general explaining to them that he had paused in his procurement of materials for the building, largely because it would be unwise to keep stockpiling materials, given the fact that there was no assurance that they would ever be put to good use. In the interim, he would direct his efforts to the construction of homes in the city.

By December 1818 in a message to the Senate and House, Governor Findlay seemed to agree with Hills, stating:

> Many of the materials that have been collected for the erection of the Capitol at Harrisburg, may be injured by time; and with all the vigilance that has been exercised for their preservation, they have been gradually wasting. I would therefore, with deference to the judgment of the legislature, recommend their being applied to the object for which they were originally intended.[21]

The governor's message was not lost upon the Assembly. They responded with a supplement to the Act of 1816, in late January of 1819, which provided for a second architectural competition, coupled

Literature in Stone: The Hundred Year History of the Pennsylvania State Capitol

with an extra $70 thousand for construction. Requests for proposals were published in Boston, Washington, New York, Baltimore, Philadelphia, and Harrisburg. Four hundred dollars was to be offered to the winner, with $200 going to the runner-up. Five commissioners selected the winning design and were to supervise construction: Governor William Findlay; Auditor General George Bryan; State Treasurer Richard M. Crain; John Bannister Gibson, Associate Judge of the Pennsylvania Supreme Court; and William Graydon, a Harrisburg attorney.[22]

Seventeen proposals were received, and though all were identified by number, only the names of the winner and second-place entrants are known. Baltimore's Robert Mills won the $200 second prize with entry number seventeen. Though entry number eight had reached the commissioners only on April 18, the next day the five men assembled and announced that local master builder, Stephen Hills, had submitted the winning design. Hills signed the contract naming him Capitol architect on that day, April 19, 1819.

Design of the Hills Capitol

The drawings that Hills prepared for the 1819 competition no longer exist, though several published drawings and sketches of the building from that time period do.[23] Hills' design called for a uniform and harmonious structure with outer walls of brick set in Flemish bond, partition walls of limestone, stone facing around the foundation, and a large portico facing State Street. Hills' description is as follows:

> *[The building is] 180 feet front and 80 feet deep, two stories high. The lower story is designed for the accommodation of both branches of the legislature, and the second for committee rooms, library, etc., with a portico in front to correspond with those of the wings [the office buildings], and a dome on top of the roof. The great westerly entrance is a circular portico the whole height of the building, composed of six Ionic columns, 4 feet in diameter and 56 feet high, and recessing 37 feet to a circular wall...*[24]

THIS PAGE: *State Capitol Grand March Music Cover, lithograph, J. R. Smith, undated.*

OPPOSITE PAGE: *Discovery of Hills Capitol cornerstone, 1898.*

CHAPTER ONE • *Pennsylvania's Early Capitols*

Interior of the House of Representatives in 1851, Harrisburg.

THIS PAGE: *Top, House of Representatives, Hills Capitol, 1880s; Bottom, "House of Representatives" taken from* View of Harrisburg, Pennsylvania, *daguerreotype by J. Thomas Williams, 1855.*

OPPOSITE PAGE: *Reproduction of the Hills Capitol of the House of Representatives, lithograph, P. S. Duval, 1851.*

HOUSE OF REPRESENTATIVES

CHAPTER ONE • *Pennsylvania's Early Capitols*

Interior of the Senate Chamber in 1844, Harrisburg.

PRINTED BY S. T. WILLIAMS & CO.

THIS PAGE: Top, *Senate Chamber, Hills Capitol, Reproduced from Art Work of Harrisburg, William Henry Egle, 1892;* Bottom, *"Senate Chamber" taken from* View of Harrisburg, Pennsylvania, *daguerreotype by J. Thomas Williams, 1855.*

OPPOSITE PAGE: *Reproduction of the Hills Capitol Senate Chamber, lithograph, 1844.*

Senate of Pennsylvania

CHAPTER ONE • *Pennsylvania's Early Capitols*

The dome of the building was forty feet in diameter with the rotunda measuring thirty-four feet across. To the left upon entering the building was the Senate Chamber, seventy-five by fifty-seven feet; to the right, the House Chamber, measuring seventy-five by sixty-eight feet. Both rooms were twenty-one feet high, and each had a gallery able to seat 180 people. The desks in each chamber were arranged in concentric semi-circles, with the Senate seating thirty-six members at the time and the House 108.

On the second floor a corridor twelve feet wide and twenty-one feet high ran the length of the building. Along this corridor were three committee rooms, the joint legislative library, and another four committee rooms. All interior spaces were stipulated to be finished in plaster, except for the rotunda where additional ornamentation was planned. All woodwork was to receive three good coats of paint, as stipulated in Hills' writings.[25]

Groundbreaking for the new building began immediately and the cornerstone was laid on May 31, 1819. Once the process was finally sanctioned by the legislature it progressed fairly rapidly, given the time period. Hills had already assembled numerous skilled and specialized workers—masons, blacksmiths, and carpenters—to assist in the construction. Despite various pitfalls and stoppages for bad weather, the work was finished in less than two-and-a-half years. The total cost for the new Capitol itself including furnishings was $160 thousand. For the Capitol and office buildings the price was $233 thousand.[26]

Dedication of the First Capitol

It was an "unusually favorable" day in Harrisburg on January 2, 1822 when state officials, clergy, workmen, architect, and citizens of Harrisburg gathered adjacent to the old Dauphin County Courthouse for the procession to the new building. Hills led the group followed by eighty of his workmen. They were followed by Dickinson College President John Mason and the Reverend Dr. George Lochman of Harrisburg. Governor Joseph Hiester, heads of state departments and officers, the Speaker[27] and members of the Senate, the Speaker and members of the House, and finally the judiciary followed. The mayor and city council were next and last followed the citizens of Harrisburg, who numbered around a thousand.[28]

When the procession neared the front of the edifice, Hills signaled his workmen to part, and they formed two separate lines to allow the procession to pass through their ranks. Hills inserted the large key into the door under the massive front portico and as it was opened, guns and muskets boomed in celebration. The new House Chamber was full as Reverends Mason and Lochman addressed the assembled crowd. Finally the Commonwealth of Pennsylvania had its new state house, some twelve years in the making. The speakers thanked the architect and prayed blessings upon the glorious Commonwealth, the assembly, and the building. They further asked that the Almighty would guide the minds of those whose work would shortly be carried on within. Local and state papers covered the event with interest.

Immediately following the dedication, the legislature began its business in the building. The Capitol required approximately $7 thousand for more furnishings, and Stephen Hills was still owed $3 thousand by the Commonwealth for his work on the building. Subsequent appropriations in the few years after the building's construction raised the final estimate of cost for the "Main" Capitol and fringing structures to $244,500, aside from of any improvements to the Capitol's grounds, which included fences, trees, and walkways.

There were numerous occurrences, significant legislation, and notable figures that visited the Hills Capitol over the course of its seventy-five year history. The first famed visitor was the Marquis de Lafayette. The soldier/statesman had returned to the country in 1824 to begin a tour of the states. He would eventually make it to all twenty-four states. In 1825 he stopped at the Capitol in Harrisburg. Lafayette was held in high

THIS PAGE: *Pennsylvania State House from stand pipe, 1890s.*

OPPOSITE PAGE: *Hills Capitol Building, undated.*

esteem by Americans for the service he and his country had provided during the war for independence. Americans realized that without French assistance—for which the Marquis was in large part responsible—the fledgling colonies could never have succeeded in gaining independence from Great Britain.

In 1843 author Charles Dickens visited Harrisburg. In his *American Notes*, he mentions the legislature, the old Camelback Bridge, and the beauty of the Susquehanna River Valley. From Harrisburg, Dickens took the Pennsylvania Canal over the Alleghenies to Pittsburgh.[29] Edward, the Prince of Wales also visited the Capitol in 1860. In 1906 when the current Capitol was dedicated, he would be King Edward VII. Abraham Lincoln came through Harrisburg in March of 1861 on his way to the inauguration in Washington. He was ushered out of Harrisburg and through Baltimore to thwart an attempted assassination plot. In 1865, following the successful attempt on his life, the President's funeral train stopped in Harrisburg, as it did in many northern towns. Lincoln's catafalque laid in state in the House Chamber before the remainder of the journey back to Springfield, Illinois. All told, six U.S. Presidents had been within the walls of the Hills Capitol, and famed orator Daniel Webster had spoken from its Senate

Numerous bills of STATE AND NATIONAL IMPORTANCE were passed within the chambers of the Hills Capitol.

THIS PAGE: *Left, David Wilmot portrait, lithograph, Morris H. Traubel, ca. 1888; Right, President Lincoln's catafalque lying in state in House Chamber, 1865.*

LITERATURE IN STONE: THE HUNDRED YEAR HISTORY OF THE PENNSYLVANIA STATE CAPITOL

A. Pennsylvania Railroad broadside, lithograph, ca. 1874.
B. "Train view, West Philadelphia," Pennsylvania Railroad, ca. 1874.
C. "Depot at Harrisburg," Pennsylvania Railroad, ca. 1874.
D. Pennsylvania State Lunatic Asylum, from daguerreotype by J. Thomas Williams, 1855.

CHAPTER ONE • *Pennsylvania's Early Capitols*

1859 *First commercial oil well is established in Titusville, Pennsylvania.*

1861 *Pennsylvanians join the Union war effort in record numbers. Over the duration of the Civil War almost 350,000 Pennsylvania's will serve, either in one of the state's 215 regiments, or in the U.S. Navy.*

1863 *The Union Army led by George G. Meade repulses the second Confederate of the north at the battle of Gettysburg in south central Pennsylvania. Numerous regiments from Commonwealth distinguished themselves fighting for the first time on their home soil.*

1876 *Famed suffragette Susan B. Anthony read her "Declaration of Rights for Women" in front of Independence Hall in Philadelphia. Other early feminists such as Lucretia Mott, Ann Davies, and Emma Guffey Miller were highly active in the long battle that would culminate in women receiving the right to vote in 1920.*

THIS PAGE: *Pennsylvania State House, 1880.*

Chamber. In addition, throughout its history, numerous bills of state and national importance were passed within the chambers of the Hills Capitol.

Perhaps the first significant piece of legislation was the creation of Pennsylvania's Main Line of Public Works launched in 1828. This was a progressive measure in determining funding of statewide projects, such as railroads and canals, in an effort to keep Pennsylvania in commercial competition with the 1825 Erie Canal in New York. The School Act of 1834 mandated publicly funded education for all Pennsylvania children. In that same year, the government completed the Philadelphia and Columbia Railroad, the first in the nation built by a state government, and the forerunner of the Pennsylvania Railroad. Measures were passed in the 1840s and 1850s dealing with the scourge of slavery. Harrisburg was a stop on the Underground Railroad[30] and many Pennsylvanians, including David Wilmot of Bradford County, were averse to the return of fugitive slaves to their masters. In 1847 the state forbade the use of its jails for the internment of fugitive slaves. The state also passed measures within the Hills Capitol dealing with prisons and the mentally ill, progressive measures at the time they were initiated.

During the Civil War the state formed numerous regiments for the war, second only to New York in the numbers of those who served. Men were mustered into regiments just up the street from the Capitol at Harrisburg's Camp Curtin, the largest mustering camp in the north. In the early days of the war some of the soldiers enlisted for three months of service had been mustered out and returned to the

I·N·S·I·G·H·T

George & Washington the Lost Portrait

In 1849 a portrait of President George Washington was produced for the Senate Chamber of the Hills Capitol by artist Cornelius T. Hinckley. The work is believed to have been copied by an artist such as Stuart or Peale in a primitive style. The portrait, shown at left, is a full length view of Washington in a black suit with gold trim. He is wearing the ribbon of the Cincinnati, with his right hand on a desk and his left holding a sword.

Lost! At some point, most likely following one the renovations of the chamber either in 1858 or 1895, the painting left the chamber and its subsequent location for years remained unknown. In 1981 the painting was donated to the State Museum with the oral history that it had once hung in the old Capitol Building in Harrisburg. Documentation comes from the engraving below, which dates to 1855. The image of Washington, bearing the same pose as the painting is evident on the northeast wall of the Chamber. φ

1870s *Through the next two decades the growing conflict between labor and management becomes increasingly evident with the rise of unions and strikes. Two of the worst episodes in this time period are the arrest and execution of the Molly Maguires and the Great Railroad strike of 1877.*

1876 *Philadelphia, Pennsylvania hosts the Centennial Exposition of 1876. Visitors witness the first elevated monorail system along with many other inventions.*

Alexander Graham Bell displays the telephone.

Thomas Edison demonstrates the automatic telegraph system, which he called the "electric pen."

1879 *Thomas Edison invents incandescent light. The City Hotel in Sunbury, Pennsylvania, is the first building to be lit with Edison's patented three-wire system.*

THIS PAGE: *Top, House Chamber, Hills Capitol, undated; Bottom, Hills North Executive Building, ca. 1901. (Notice the Cobb Capitol building in the background.)*

OPPOSITE PAGE: *Top, House of Representatives, Hills Capitol, Reproduced from* Art Work of Harrisburg, *William Henry Egle, 1892; Bottom, Senate Chamber, Hills Capitol, ca. 1892.*

LITERATURE IN STONE: THE HUNDRED YEAR HISTORY OF THE PENNSYLVANIA STATE CAPITOL

state. These troops bunked several days in the Capitol or on its grounds, and later threatened to riot when pay due to them was late in coming.

Both Capitol Park and the Main Capitol saw numerous changes and upgrades over the course of the nineteenth century. In 1825 an effort was made to try to extend the Capitol grounds westward along State Street to the Susquehanna River. This attempt would include buying all of the property in the little village that was known as Maclaysburg, named after deceased U.S. Senator William Maclay Sr., but the purchase of this ground never came to fruition. The cost for all the area was not to exceed $2 thousand, but many of the owners were unwilling to sell and the proposal was quickly abandoned.

While efforts were made to expand Capitol Park, the new Hills Capitol itself did not last long without additions and modifications. In 1858 local historian George Morgan noted that a large amount of money was spent in the preceding

CHAPTER ONE • *Pennsylvania's Early Capitols*

year on refitting the interior of the Capitol. The floors of both chambers were covered with Brussels carpet, and the rotunda was refloored with tile. The walls and ceilings of the chambers were frescoed, and the building was furnished throughout with large gas-lit bronze and crystal chandeliers.[31] Perhaps the most important addition came in 1864 when money was allotted to erect an eastern "wing" from the central axis of the Capitol. A sum of $50 thousand was allotted for the construction, though the new fireproof wing eventually cost nearer to $90 thousand. The upper portion of the new extension was to be used as the State Library, and as a result the entire new wing was known as the library extension.[32] In 1868 the legislature appropriated money to build the Mexican War monument next to the Capitol.

LITERATURE IN STONE: THE HUNDRED YEAR HISTORY OF THE PENNSYLVANIA STATE CAPITOL

Both Capitol Park and the Main Capitol SAW NUMEROUS CHANGES AND UPGRADES over the course of the nineteenth century.

In 1877 Philadelphia architect James Hamilton Windrim was given a commission by the state to add a one-story extension to the House side of the Hills Capitol. The addition was to add space for the new members of the General Assembly, which had grown over the course of the nineteenth century. Again in 1893 the legislature voted money to build a new Executive, Library, and Museum Building, adjacent to the Hills structure. They also appropriated $125 thousand for remodeling the former library in the Capitol's center wing, along with any other alterations that were deemed necessary. The new structure, designed and built by John Torrey Windrim, the son of James Hamilton Windrim, was to house the state's archives and historical artifacts, its library, the Civil War battle flag collection, and records from the early Department of State. The new structure would also provide

THIS PAGE: *Hills Capitol with John T. Windrim alterations, ca. 1894.*

OPPOSITE PAGE: *Top, Interior of the Senate Library, Herman Miller seated on the left; Bottom, Interior of Hills Capitol Library and Museum Room located in center east addition, undated.*

1879 — *Women lawyers are permitted to argue cases before the Supreme Court.*

1892 — *Workers at steel magnate Andrew Carnegie's Homestead Plant find themselves locked out of the mill at the end of a three-year contract between management and the steelworkers. Expecting the worst, superintendent Henry Clay Frick asks for 300 armed Pinkertons. By the end of the strike, 10 men were killed and 30 wounded, and the state's National Guard had broken the strike. Workers were forced to return to a non-union shop amid fears that their families would either freeze or starve.*

1895 — *Pennsylvania Superior Court is created.*

THIS PAGE: *Top, Executive, Library and Museum Building, ca. 1895; Bottom, Interior of Executive, Library, and Museum Building, ca. 1895.*

OPPOSITE PAGE: *Scenes from Capitol Park, 1892, Reproduced from* Art Work of Harrisburg, *William Henry Egle, 1892.*

BOTH PAGES: *Views of the Hills Capitol during and after the fire, 1897.*

A PIECE OF HISTORY FALLS:

The Hills Capitol Fire

LITERATURE IN STONE: THE HUNDRED YEAR HISTORY OF THE PENNSYLVANIA STATE CAPITOL

offices for the Governor, who up until this time had a private office in the Hills Capitol, but no official receiving room in which to greet guests and dignitaries.[33] The *Harrisburg Telegraph* stated that from 1895–1897 many alterations and upgrades to the private offices and interiors of the building had been undertaken and further estimated that the cost of work approached the sum of $200 thousand. There were also numerous appropriations made toward the end of the century for refitting the building with newer furniture and desks for the Assembly.

The Capitol Fire

As the new century approached, one final event occurred within the Hills Capitol that would change the look of Harrisburg's streetscapes forever. The following several pages are distilled primarily from Robert M. Houseal, Jr.'s highly-detailed account of the Pennsylvania State House fire, one of the best accounts of what happened on that fateful day.

Both the House and Senate were in session. It was approximately 10:30 on the morning of February 2, 1897, when Senator John C. Grady noticed a slight smell of wood smoke in the chamber. He summoned a page to check on the odor. The page quickly returned saying that he could find no evidence of any trouble. By 11:15 A.M. the Senator asked another page to check on the smoky smell, which had become more pronounced. The second page was also unable to find anything out of the ordinary. Just slightly after noon, President Pro Tempore Samuel J. M. McCarrell recessed the body with instructions to return at 1:00 P.M. The Senate had an important vote that afternoon on whether to hold hearings and audit alleged misappropriations within the Treasury Department.

While several Senators milled about discussing the upcoming bill for the afternoon, they all agreed that the smell of smoke had become more acrid and decided to investigate. Senator Saylor and Senate Librarian Herman Miller went upstairs to the corridor overtop of the Chamber to see if they could locate its source.

Several senators returned with buckets and began fighting the fire when the ceiling of an adjacent room collapsed.

They found smoke wafting from underneath the door to the Lieutenant Governor's office.

Upon gaining entrance, Senator Henry D. Saylor chopped through a partition from which smoke was billowing. Almost immediately flames jumped out of the interior wall and, at about the same time, from a wall on the other side of the room. Miller and Saylor fled the room and sounded a general alarm, and a bucket brigade was formed. Several senators returned with buckets and began fighting the fire when the ceiling of an adjacent room collapsed. The senators determined that the fire was definitely out of their immediate control and they fled the upstairs. Miller then ran into the library and pulled the fire alarm. The time was half past noon.

Harrisburg's Fire Companies recorded the box alarm at 12:30 P.M. As the companies received the call, the Senate Chamber became a crescendo of chaos. Everyone who was in the building, from Senators to pages, messengers, transcribers, folders, and others, grabbed anything they could remove as the fire quickly began to spread.

Harrisburg's fire companies responded to the blaze, but the dry wood and NATURE OF THE FIRE made it impossible from the start for the FIRE COMPANY to do anything to combat the fire.

However, the House, which was also in session, remained fairly sedentary compared to the flurry in the Senate. When first told that the rooms above the Senate were aflame, several representatives on the floor of the House laughed incredulously, as though the building were impervious to fire. Several minutes later, the Speaker received another message, and the House was swiftly adjourned. Representative Charles Voorhees was apparently the last man out of the House Chamber. Just as he left, flames were beginning to streak across the ceiling of the large room, an indication of the fire's rapid spread. Immediately following his exit, an explosion occurred in the dome, most likely caused by a buildup of gases from pitch, pine tar, and other combustible substances.

Several of Harrisburg's fire companies had some confusion in getting to the scene. Either an incorrect box had rung, or the location was misinterpreted.

Whatever the cause, some companies responded to Seventh and Reily Streets—thinking the fire was at the Pennsylvania Railroad shops. Since several companies responded to the same location, perhaps a malfunction in the system could have occurred, despite an accurate test of it after the fire. Regardless, these companies made their way as quickly as possible to the Capitol building, now visibly aflame.

Despite all the additions to the building, there had been no hydrants added to the Capitol grounds, so the companies fringing the building had to run their hose lines much farther than normal. The February weather also hindered the firemen's ability to combat the blaze. Snow, sleet, and rain in the face of a driving northwest wind, coupled with the twenty-nine-degree temperature, helped to fan flames that were now slightly protruding from the roof of the Senate.

Overall seven pumpers along with numerous accoutrements and devices from all eleven of Harrisburg's fire companies responded to the blaze, but the dry wood and nature of the fire made it impossible from the start for the fire companies to do anything to combat the fire. While fighting the fire, numerous hose lines burst due to the cold weather conditions. All the while people were rushing in and out of the Capitol, removing furniture, records, and valuables, while timbers, bricks, and debris fell from the burning building. Just after 1:00 P.M., the dome clock became engulfed in flames. At 1:19 the American flag atop the dome slowly descended into the now raging sea of flames. The crowd that had gathered outside of the main entrance quickly moved down the steps to Third Street. Shortly after, with a boom that echoed throughout the city, the remnants of the Capitol dome came crashing down. The fire now threatened to ignite the adjacent Executive, Library, and Museum Building. So the firemen, knowing that the inferno was untamable, trained their hoses on the nearby structures, and by 2:00 P.M.

THIS PAGE: *Hills Capitol interior after being destroyed by fire, 1897.*

OPPOSITE PAGE: *Hills Capitol rotunda after fire, 1897.*

CHAPTER ONE • *Pennsylvania's Early Capitols*

all were declared safe. By 4:00 P.M. that same afternoon the old Hills Capitol was a smoldering mass of debris. However it was 3:30 the next afternoon until the last company was ordered to retire from the still smoldering ruins.[34]

Overall the Capitol was an entire loss, though there were areas that had not burned completely, where items were in fact salvaged. Many old bills from the House and Senate dating back to colonial times were lost, along with furniture, personal effects, and records, not to mention the $70 thousand put into the restoration of the House of Representatives for new decorations, furniture, and a frieze.

There was much loss of state property, but thankfully no loss of human life. Several people, including firemen and police officers, were injured in the fire, but no one was killed—a rather remarkable statistic. The devastating fire left a feeling of loss for the citizens of Harrisburg and uncertainty as to whether the legislature would remain in the city.

For most people there was a nostalgia; perhaps the romance of bygone days that was embodied

FOR MOST PEOPLE there was a nostalgia; *perhaps the romance of bygone days* that was embodied in the old Hills Capitol… IT REPRESENTED THE LOSS OF SOMETHING intrinsically symbolic of the Commonwealth.

LITERATURE IN STONE: THE HUNDRED YEAR HISTORY OF THE PENNSYLVANIA STATE CAPITOL

in the old Hills Capitol, especially indicated through editorials sent to the newspapers at the time. Harrisburg had changed much since the Capitol's construction. As the legislators and citizens of the Commonwealth watched the stunning immolation, there were those in the throng that wept openly.[35] It represented the loss of something intrinsically symbolic of the Commonwealth. Those citizens who had seen nothing but the dome crowning the landscape for years could not reconcile in their minds that it was indeed gone.

For exactly seventy-five years and one month, the Ionic porticoed Hills Capitol had served the Commonwealth. It saw the passing of the state from an agrarian society—with neither transportation routes, nor massive interstate commerce—to an industrial giant—producing seventy percent of the nation's coal, sixty percent of its steel, and a large amount of its oil by the late 1800s. Its transportation network was second to none, and the Commonwealth was at its commercial and industrial zenith.

The assembled mass that stood outside at 1:19 P.M. February 2, 1897, silently watching the flag atop the dome sink, knew that the "old red brick" Capitol was gone, but did not know what to expect in its place. What they received within the next few years would appall some and infuriate others. For the citizens of Harrisburg and Pennsylvanians alike, it would be several years into the next century until something rivaling the old Capitol would start to take shape, rising from the ashes on Capitol Hill.

THIS PAGE: *Hills Capitol west facade after fire, 1897.*

OPPOSITE PAGE: *Top, Burnt out Hills Capitol, 1897; Bottom, Citizens stand on the Capitol steps watching the devastating fire, 1897.*

CHAPTER ONE • *Pennsylvania's Early Capitols*

Completed Cobb Capitol, 1898.

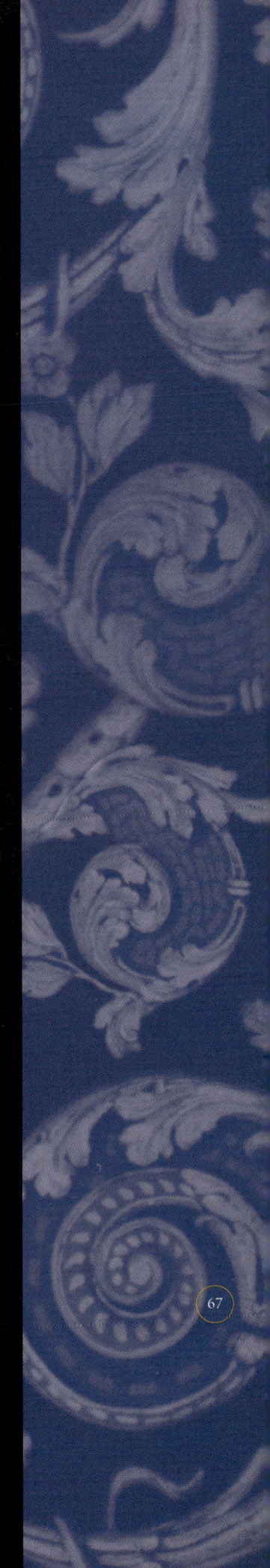

C·H·A·P·T·E·R
TWO

THE COBB CAPITOL

BEFORE the last horse-drawn engine left the smoldering Hills Capitol, Governor Daniel Hastings, assuming his role as head of the Board of Commissioners of Public Grounds and Buildings, was meeting with the Senate President Pro Tempore, Samuel J. M. McCarrell of Dauphin County and Speaker of the House Henry K. Boyer to determine what to do about the current legislative session. This meeting took place around five o'clock February 2, the evening of the fire. The next day the governor announced that the legislature would meet the following Monday, February 8, at Grace Methodist Episcopal Church, located on State Street across from the burned-out shell of the Hills Capitol. On February 3, contracts were awarded to several Harrisburg contractors to refit the church for the legislature's use. The church allowed the Commonwealth the use of its building for as long as the state deemed necessary. The House would meet in the downstairs "auditorium," and the Senate upstairs, with the smaller rooms reserved for caucus and committees. In the meantime, parishioners of the church would meet at the Harrisburg Opera House. For their inconvenience, the state paid the congregation $20 thousand in addition to covering the costs incurred through the installation of electric lights and new carpets.[1]

The interim Capitol of Pennsylvania was in the church from February 8, 1897, until December 31, 1898. As expected,

"The [Hills] Capitol is now what it has long appeared to be—an antiquated ruin."

the legislature's biggest task while there was to determine what to do about creating a suitable building in which to meet.

While they debated how to create a new Capitol building, they also sought answers as to what had caused the Hills Capitol fire. Indeed the cause of the fire was a question of increased speculation for years after its occurrence. Charges were first leveled that the fire had been deliberately set to force the legislature out at a time when they were considering a crucial vote on investigating fraud within the Treasury Department.

Another supposed cause was a defective flue, but this was also ruled out because all the flues had been inspected and cleaned just six months prior. Ultimately, the majority of suspicions subsided, and the final cause was determined to be an unattended fire left burning in Lieutenant Governor Walter Lyon's private office. Theory held that an ember had exploded in the fireplace and dropped through a floor crack onto the dust-covered floor joists beneath. All morning long on February 2 the dry beams beneath the building's second floor had been slowly burning.[2]

An uncanny coincidence helped to further heighten the atmosphere of suspicion surrounding the Hills Capitol fire. On February 3, 1897, one day after the building burned, the old north Capitol building, which predated the Hills Capitol by ten years, caught fire and was almost lost. At noon on February 3 it was discovered that the chimney of the old North Office was aflame. Fortunately, several of Harrisburg's fire companies were still on site and were able to extinguish the flames before they spread to other areas of the building. Damage to the structure was slight, but in saving the structure, the firefighters also saved the records of numerous departments. These included the State Zoological Department and most importantly the Adjutant generals' records, having in it at the time the records of Pennsylvania soldiers predating the Revolutionary War.[3]

Following the fires, the debate again quickly opened in favor of returning the state's seat of government to Philadelphia. Senator C. Wesley Thomas and a faction of Philadelphia politicians supported the measure to move the capital, but the state Constitution stipulated that a majority vote obtained by a statewide referendum of the people would be needed to move the capital to anywhere but Harrisburg.

THIS PAGE: *A temporary office in the Grace Methodist Episcopal Church, ca. 1898.*

OPPOSITE PAGE: *Interior of the Grace Methodist Episcopal Church, ca. 1898.*

CHAPTER TWO • *The Cobb Capitol*

The building…would be fireproof in nature and constructed in what was then termed, "THE COLONIAL STYLE OF ARCHITECTURE." Its design would be able to sufficiently harmonize with the construction of future state buildings, and Hastings indicated that THE SUM OF $550 THOUSAND SHOULD BE SUFFICIENT to produce this structure, furnishings and all…

Political interests outside the legislature were also acting to either move or retain the capital in Harrisburg.

On the evening of the fire, Philadelphia Mayor Charles F. Warwick called Governor Hastings to assure him that the legislature could meet in the City Council chambers for as long as they needed. That same evening back in Harrisburg, Mayor John D. Patterson told a crowd of concerned citizens that he felt immediate action had to be taken by the people of Harrisburg, "to retain the legislative sessions in this city."[4]

Another debate that quickly came to the forefront was whether to rebuild the Hills Capitol or create a new building. The shell of the Hills Capitol was determined sound, including the drum of the dome. Some members such as Speaker Henry Boyer and House Appropriations Chair W. T. Marshall supported the rebuilding of the Hills Capitol.[5]

Not only would this avenue save the Commonwealth considerable money, but also, as the *Harrisburg Telegraph* indicated, would preserve what architects at the time stated was "the only pure specimen of a colonial style capitol left in the country."[6]

Editorials written to various Harrisburg papers supported the fact that many citizens felt very strongly about seeing the old Capitol rebuilt.

The *Harrisburg Patriot* at the time was not convinced of this necessity, asserting that, "The Capitol is now what it has long appeared to be—an antiquated ruin."[7] There was wide support for this side of the debate. In addition, the Hills Capitol was seventy-five years old when it burned, and the state's bureaucratic mechanism and size of the legislature had outgrown its small confines. Lieutenant Governor Walter Lyon wanted to see a new Capitol built, as did Superintendent of Public Grounds and Buildings John Delaney, stating to the *Patriot*, "I believe it will be necessary to put up a new building."[8] However, the question of how to finance a new structure was one that would underlie the ongoing debate.

Governor Daniel H. Hastings portrait, Governor's Office.

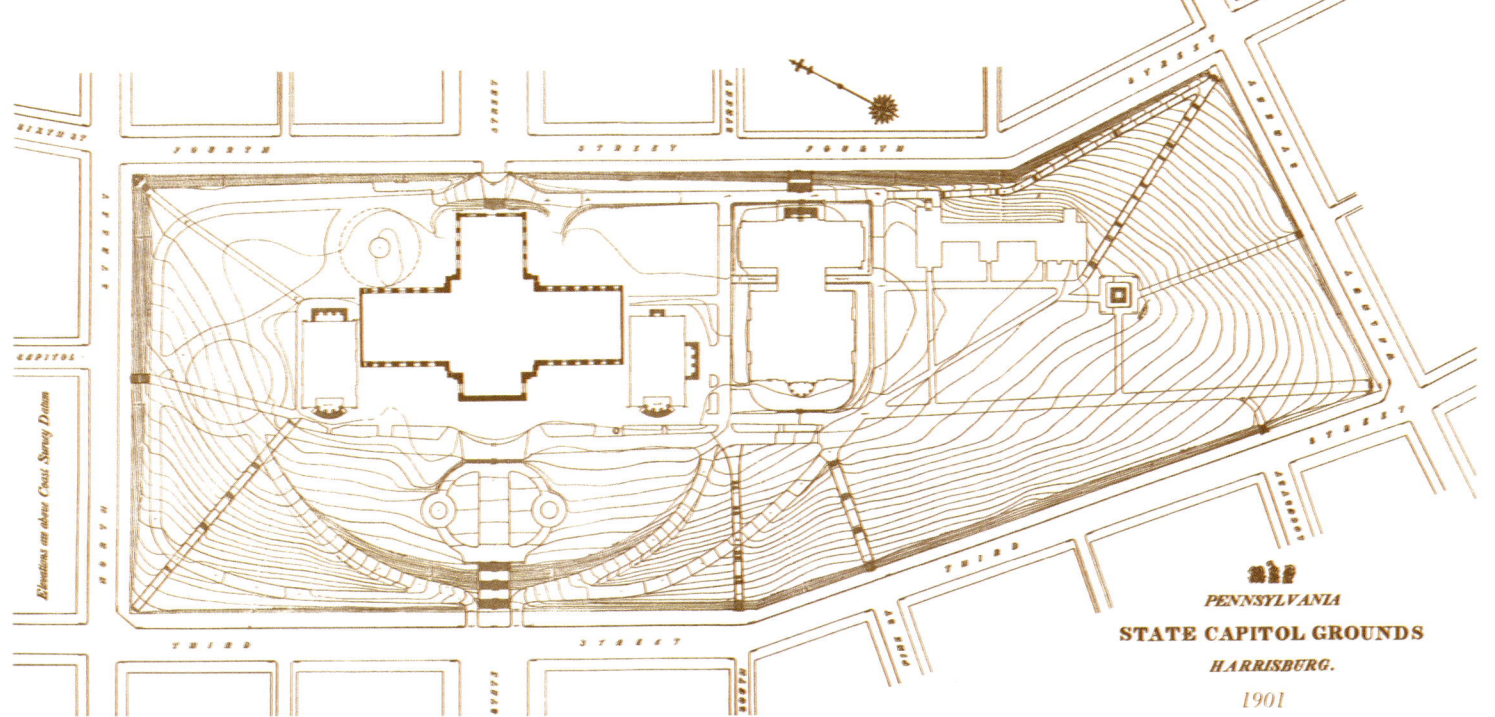

PENNSYLVANIA STATE CAPITOL GROUNDS HARRISBURG. 1901

Though many legislators supported the idea of a new State Capitol, some felt a single large structure was impossible for the Commonwealth to afford since the state's total revenues for 1897–1898 were not expected to exceed twenty million dollars. Making a five million dollar appropriation—the suggested price for a new and completely furnished building—was out of the question. In addition, a clause in the state's Constitution of 1873 forbade the Commonwealth from going into aggregate debt of over one million dollars, save for the most dire of situations, such as the defense of the Commonwealth. Instead it was concluded that the new building, if it were approved, would have to be based on a tight budget, or multiple annual appropriations.

Governor Daniel Hastings wanted his administration to leave office without creating any new debt for the state. To this end, he wanted a pay-as-you-go policy for the new building. He argued that a small legislative building be constructed and as successive years wore on, subsequent state office buildings could surround this structure to house the other government offices. This would allow the annual budget to absorb some of the costs of the building over an increased length of time. The state had received $200 thousand for the loss of the Hills building, which was grossly underinsured at the time of the fire. The remaining loss was estimated at $300 thousand, a sum that state officials felt they could cover.

The debate over whether or not to build a new Capitol took place against this fiscally conservative backdrop, but the debate was largely resolved when a resolution was passed on April 14, 1897, allowing the governor to solicit designs for a new building. Hastings, resolution in hand, sought the professional assistance of Warren P. Laird, professor of architecture at the University of Pennsylvania. The governor and Laird reviewed the options and decided that the best possible plan would be to create a building for the General Assembly, one that would be larger than the old Capitol, but not large enough to house all the departments of state. The building, they determined, would be fireproof in nature and constructed in what was then termed, "the colonial style of architecture." Its design would be able to sufficiently harmonize with the construction of future state buildings, and Hastings thought that the sum of $550 thousand should be sufficient to produce this structure, furnishings and all.

Both the House and Senate passed bills for a new Capitol building. The Senate had little debate over the bill, but the House debated for five days. Several provisions were suggested, which included changing the Capitol Building Commission from five to seven members,

CHAPTER TWO • *The Cobb Capitol*

· PENNSYLVANIA · STATE · CAPITOL · COMPETITION ·

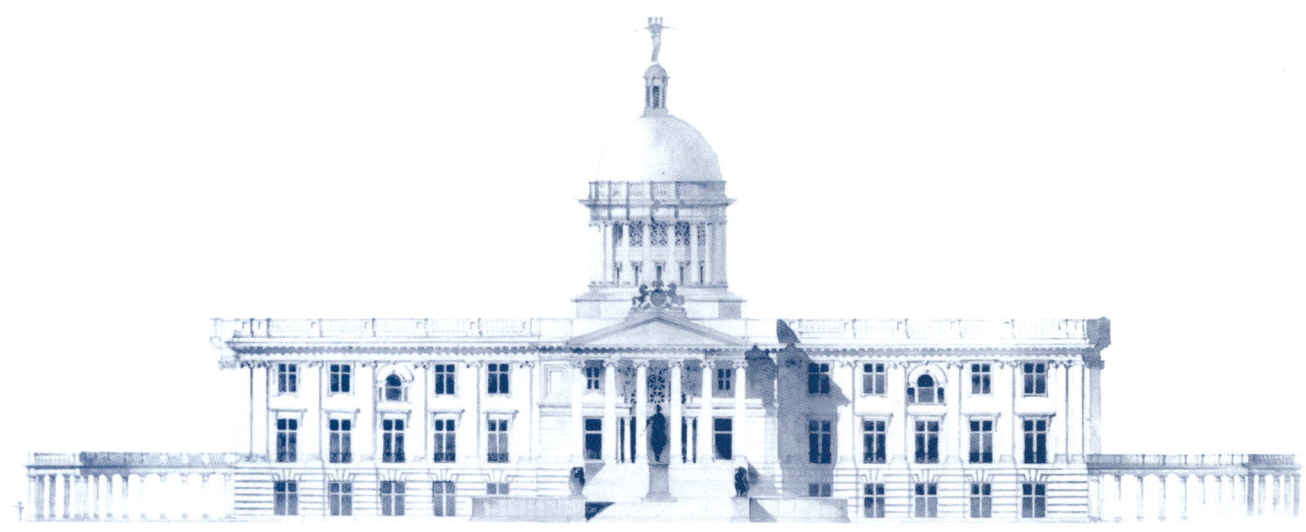

· WEST · ELEVATION ·
SCALE 1/8 = 1'0"

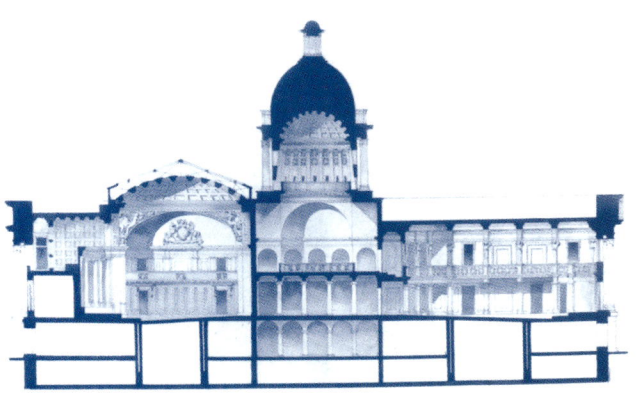

· LONGITUDINAL · SECTION ·

· END · ELEVATIONS ·

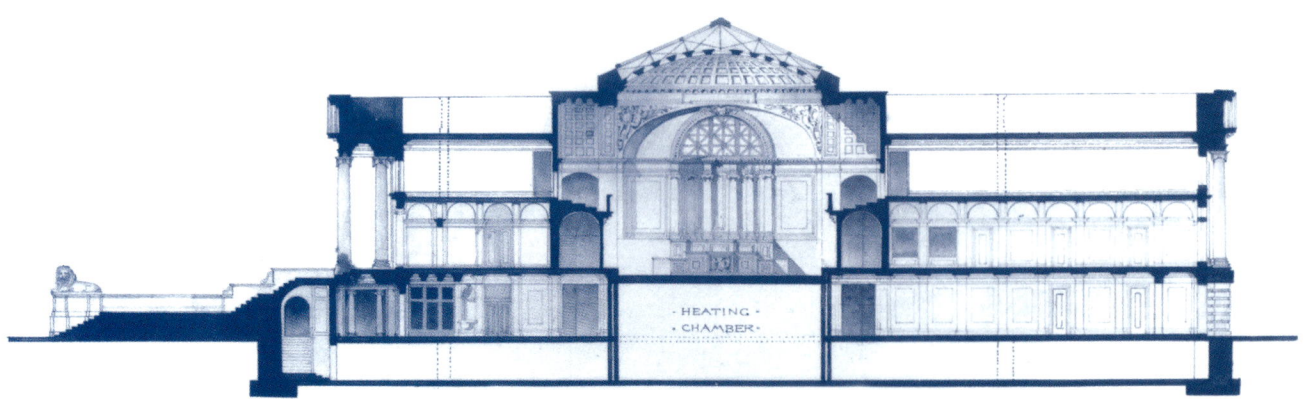

· TRANSVERSE · SECTION ·
· THROUGH · PORTICO · VESTIBULE ·
· SENATE · CHAMBER · AND · WING ·

A portion of the 1897 Competition sketches entered by Joseph M. Huston, Architect.

LITERATURE IN STONE: THE HUNDRED YEAR HISTORY OF THE PENNSYLVANIA STATE CAPITOL

adding a power and light plant for the building, and including members of the minority party to the commission. All the measures were defeated, although some House members expressed a concern that the money appropriated was too little to completely construct the new building. Regardless of the debates, the House passed its bill on April 13 by a vote of 149 to 39.

There were also strict guidelines for what the drawings themselves should include, and these rules were strictly enforced.

Governor Daniel Hastings signed the bill the following day and appointed a five-member Capitol Building Commission to oversee the construction. The commission consisted of Hastings, State Treasurer Benjamin Haywood, Auditor General Amos Mylin, Senate President Pro Tempore McCarrell, and House Speaker Boyer. This commission was charged with producing a building for the General Assembly with the least possible delay. The new Capitol was to be completed and ready for occupancy by January 1, 1899.[9] Although they were not required to do so, the commission did hold a competition to select an architect for the new structure. The design competition was open to all American architects held in good standing, but there were firms that were especially invited to participate: Alden and Harlow of Pittsburgh; Cope and Stewardson and Furness and Evans, both from Philadelphia; Harding and Gooch of New York; Peabody and Stearns of Boston; and James H. Warner of Lancaster.[10] Each firm was promised $1,000 for their participation in the competition.

A three-member board of experts was also selected to evaluate the proposals. The board consisted of Warren P. Laird, John M. Carrere, and Walter Cook of H. B. Marshall. Laird stipulated that all designs must include a "campus" of state buildings, lettered A through E. Building "A" was to be the new Capitol building, situated directly on the foundation of the old Hills Capitol. Although only the main building was to be constructed at the time, Laird and the commission felt that the harmony between the proposed buildings was very important. Since the primary building would only house the legislature and associated departments, future auxiliary buildings were a certainty. Professor Laird also sought to curtail political favoritism and to ensure fairness to all entrants by ensuring anonymity. All shipped entries were delivered unlabeled, with no return address. Each entry was double wrapped, and a small white inner envelope was to contain the name and address of the firm. All envelopes were to be numbered by the board and delivered to their custodian, Judge John W. Simonton of the Dauphin County Court of Common Pleas. There were also strict guidelines for what the drawings themselves should include, and these rules were strictly enforced. Several entries were disqualified—one for being framed and signed, another for showing trees, and another for improper use of colors. In all there were thirty-one entries received, and twenty-eight of these were accepted. The board first narrowed the selection process down to eight entries—one which was singularly the best, two that were nearly as good,

Cobb Capitol
Floor Plan

THIS PAGE: *Proposed Competition sketches entered by Henry I. Cobb, Architect, 1897.*

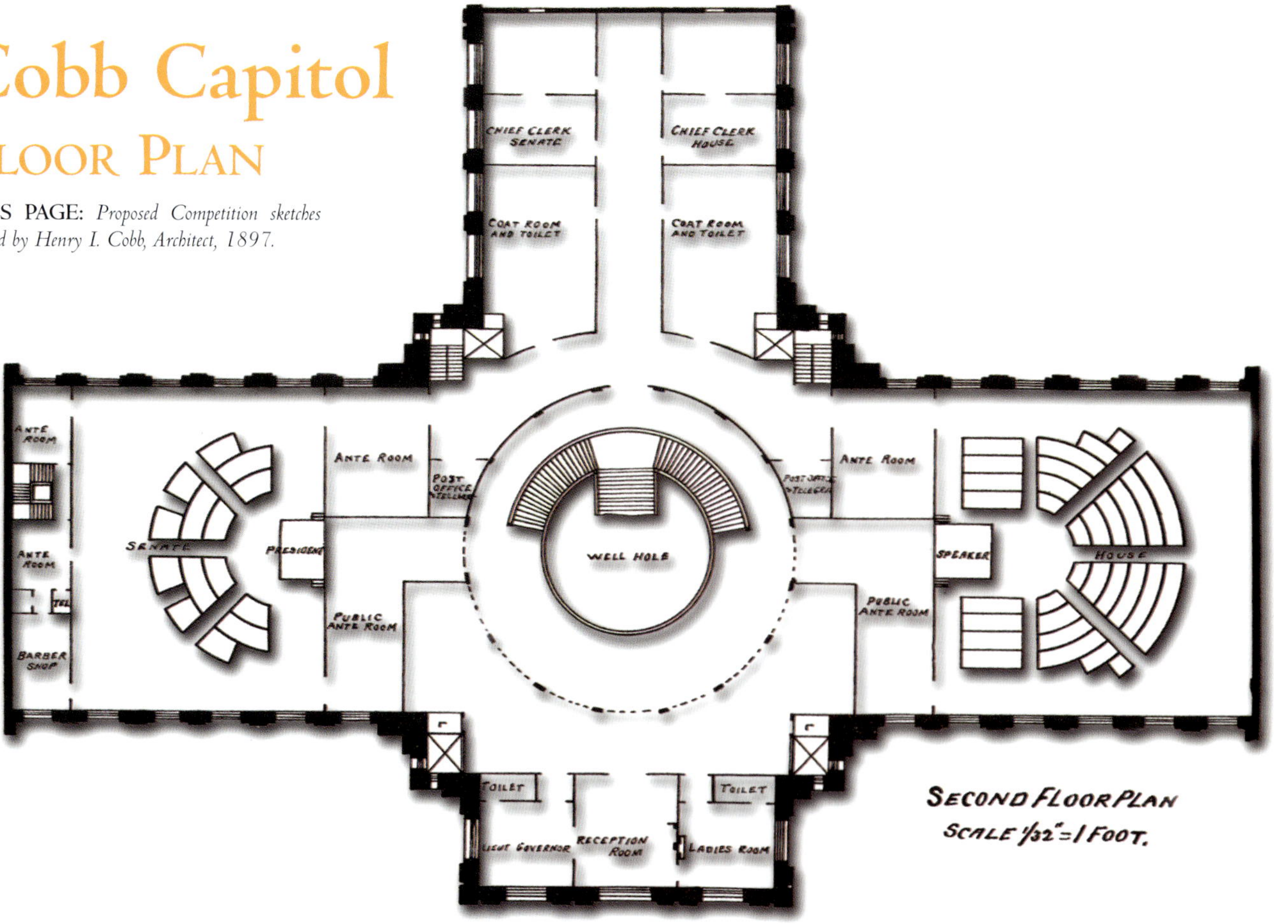

and five that were of lesser quality but superior to the twenty that were rejected.

The experts seemed to reach their conclusions rather easily, and they chose entry number twenty-four as the one that best met the parameters stipulated in the competition, stating in their final assessment to the board that, "the treatment of the whole design seems to indicate imagination, skill, and training. We think it indicates a special capacity in its author for dealing with this special problem. The design would suffer less by necessary modifications than any of the others."

Henry Ives Cobb, undated.

Though COBB'S renderings and designs depict an AMAZINGLY ornamented and completed Main Capitol Building, THE REALITY of what he was forced to provide WAS FAR FROM HIS VISION.

The Capitol Building Commission met on August 12, 1897, to discuss the recommendations of the experts. Despite the seeming ease with which the review board picked entry twenty-four, the commission had several reservations. For one, the legislative chambers were lit only from the ceiling. This, they believed, would not work well. The commission also noted that none of the accepted drawings could be produced without modification for $550 thousand. Though the submitting architects claimed they could complete the buildings under budget with no modification, the commission was certain that costly changes would be necessary. They felt that these modifications after awarding the contract would violate the terms of the competition. Lastly, the commission thought two of the disqualified entries were rejected for trivial reasons. Needless to say, the commission was not completely satisfied.

Following the meeting and a story in the Philadelphia *North American*, which stated that the selected firm assured that it could modify its design to meet the $550 thousand price tag, Philadelphia architect Frank Furness was angered and protested to Governor Hastings. Furness argued that in submitting his design he was governed strictly by the monetary ceiling and in awarding the commission to any firm that went over the stipulated budget, the experts and Capitol Building Commission would violate the terms of the competition. He went so far as to hire an attorney and continued protesting to the Commonwealth. Furness also learned that it was his color entry that had been disqualified for not being rendered in monotone, which only exacerbated his protests.

The designs that were approved by the board were placed in Grace Methodist Episcopal Church. Somehow a clever newspaper correspondent gained access to

CHAPTER TWO • *The Cobb Capitol*

Digging the foundation for the Cobb Capitol, June 10, 1898.

them and took photographs of two of the plans, which accounts for the publication of James Warner's design in several Pennsylvania papers. Frank Furness continued his protests, asking why the experts could disqualify entries for coloring but ignore the cost stipulation. The Building Commission agreed with Furness, approving a resolution that rejected the board of experts, blaming them for ignoring the cost ceiling and for eliminating two entries for no real reason. The Board approved the resolution by a four-to-one vote, and Governor Hastings, apparently disgusted with all of the debate, immediately turned over the chairmanship to Boyer and left the meeting. He took no further role in the commission's deliberations.

Following Hastings' hasty retreat, the commission approved several other measures and returned all entries to their original submitters, with instructions to modify and resubmit them by September 29, 1897. As a result of this action and the commissioners' disapproval of the experts, Professor Laird promptly resigned. The ensuing debacle involving the competition prompted lawsuits from architects and condemnation from the American Institute of Architects. James Warner, who had been identified through the Philadelphia *North American* as the winner of the competition, obtained a temporary injunction that prevented the commission from

The commission announced HENRY IVES COBB AS THE WINNER OF THE COMPETITION... Stating in their final assessment to the board that, *"the treatment of the whole design seems to indicate IMAGINATION, SKILL, AND TRAINING. We think it indicates a special capacity in its author for dealing with this special problem. The design would suffer less by necessary modifications than any of the others."*

choosing any design not among the original eight chosen by the experts. Other architects filed similar lawsuits.

Despite all the legal wrangling, the commission went ahead with its review on September 29, as planned. In October five finalists were asked to appear in person to further explain their designs. Furness, Evans and Company, Harding and Gooch, and Henry Ives Cobb of Chicago were first. Later in the month Baker and Dallett and J. M. Huston and Company followed. On October 22, 1897, one day after hearing the last of the architects' presentations, the commission announced Chicago architect Henry Ives Cobb as the winner of the competition. The lawsuits slowly died down, helped in part by the Commonwealth's Supreme Court, dismissing a case brought by Cope and Stewardson. As a result, on November 24 Cobb signed his contract.

Design and Construction of the Cobb Capitol

Architect Henry Ives Cobb was born in 1859 in Brookline, Massachusetts, and had graduated in 1881 with a bachelor of science degree from Lawrence Scientific School. The school was a joint program between the Massachusetts Institute of Technology and Harvard University. After graduation, Cobb, like many Ivy League graduates at the time, went to Europe to travel and study. Upon his return in late 1881 he began his career with the Boston architectural firm of Peabody and Stearns. While working for the firm, Cobb entered a competition for a new Union Club Building in Chicago.

He won the competition and moved to Chicago in 1882. Cobb joined with Charles S. Frost, and this architectural partnership lasted until 1889. During this time period Cobb and Frost were responsible for a number of outstanding commissions in Chicago, including the Historical Society Building, Newberry Library, and numerous buildings on the campus of the University of Chicago. After the partnership dissolved, Cobb went on to design the Horticultural Hall and the Fisheries Buildings at the World's Columbian Exposition in 1893. Cobb's most important Chicago commission was the new Federal Building, which was completed between 1898 and 1905. While engaged in this commission Cobb also entered and won the design for the new Pennsylvania Capitol Building.

Cobb designed his building as a single large structure, instead of five independent buildings. He explained that this was to avoid both constriction imposed by State

---

1889 — Flood in Johnstown, Pennsylvania kills 2,300 people.

1890s — Peak of lumber production in northern Pennsylvania.

1893 — In Hawaii, Queen Liliuokalani's government is overthrown. The territory of Hawaii becomes a U.S. protectorate despite President Grover Cleveland's opposition.

1894 — Jacob N. Hershey founds the Hershey Creamery in Hershey, Pennsylvania.

1895 — Citing the Sherman Anti-Trust Act, the Supreme Court upholds an injunction against striking railway workers, claiming that the strike impedes interstate commerce. The decision is a major upset for proponents of organized labor.

1896 — At Koster and Bial's Music Hall in New York, the public sees its first movie. The movie was very short and came at the end of a vaudeville show. Thomas Edison premiered the short silent film on his projector called the vitrascope.

1896 — The case of Plessy vs. Ferguson is argued before the United States Supreme Court. The idea that the practice of segregation (via Jim Crow laws) conflicted with the thirteenth and fourteenth amendments is denied by the Court which defends its decision by articulating the doctrine of "separate but equal." This idea will stand until the 1954 Brown vs. Board of Education decision by the court.

Four miners discover placer gold deposits in Canada's remote Yukon territory along the banks of the Klondike River. It takes the news nearly a year to reach the United States but almost immediately people begin traveling to the territory to stake their claim. By 1900, over 100,000 people had journeyed to the gold fields, though few struck it rich.

CHAPTER TWO • *The Cobb Capitol*

BOTH PAGES: *Excavation for the cellar for the new Capitol building, May and June 1898.*

Cobb knew he was in an exceedingly tight fiscal situation, and he stated that as a result the building would be
"a plain brick building, devoid of all ornamentation..."

and Capitol Streets, and also the ruining of Capitol Park, which would have been accomplished by placing numerous small buildings on the grounds. However, to stay within the guidelines of the competition, Cobb had to design a five-part scheme, as stipulated by the commissioners. Cobb knew that the $550 thousand was too little to finish all five parts of the building. In fact he thought it would only be enough for the central wing, which was to run east to west, parallel with State Street. Yet this wing could not stand alone, so Cobb increased his scope of work to include the two north and south flanking wings. Although not originally planned as such by Cobb, these were now to contain the House and Senate Chambers. Cobb knew that constructing three sections would cost more than the appropriation, but he likewise believed that the legislature by then would provide more money to continue construction. Cobb's design was criticized by several architects, some of whom were personally antagonistic to him, and some who had nothing to gain. One critic, Chicago architect John Clifford, stated that Cobb totally lacked the qualifications necessary for the Pennsylvania Capitol, and he took it upon himself to write to Governor Daniel Hastings, expressing his disdain.[11]

Though Cobb's renderings and designs depict an amazingly ornamented and completed Main Capitol Building, the reality of what he was forced to provide was far from his vision. The "completed" structure, if it could be called that, did not include north or south transverse wings paralleling the center one, or even a dome. Instead, there was a wooden trussed roof that was covered with boards, tarred felt, and gravel.[12]

CHAPTER TWO • *The Cobb Capitol*

Cornerstone dedication for the Cobb Capitol, 1898.

On February 4, 1898, Attorney General Henry C. McCormick filed suit in the Dauphin County Court of Common Pleas in an effort to restrain the Commission from making any contract for the building according to the specifications, because it would not produce a complete building. Both that court and the state's Supreme Court refused to issue injunctions, and Cobb began collecting bids for the work.

Since Cobb knew that there was no possible way his intended building could be created, he modified his original plans and reduced, even further, the scope of construction. All exterior marble, which Cobb had planned to sheath the porticoes, was excluded, and rubble stone masonry was substituted for the brick masonry in the foundation. Cobb knew he was in an exceedingly tight fiscal situation, and he stated that as a result the building would be "a plain brick building, devoid of all ornamentation..."[13] The construction of the new building now progressed rapidly. On April 18, 1898, contractor Allen B. Rorke of Philadelphia bid on the general construction of the building. His bid of $325 thousand, the lowest received, was approved, and the Commonwealth entered into contract with him on that same afternoon. On April 29 the commission appointed Philip H. Johnson, also of Philadelphia, to serve as its construction superintendent on the project, in an effort to ensure that the work was completed as quickly as possible. James A. Palmer was selected to prepare the heating, lighting, ventilating, and plumbing systems within the building. Palmer died shortly after accepting the responsibilities, and Robert G. Clarkson assumed these duties. Clarkson would also prepare the contract documents for the electrical system, after the resignation of Frederick W. Darlington.

Ground was broken for the new Capitol on May 2, 1898, and by August 10 the cornerstone-laying was held. A Masonic ritual was held with Grandmaster William J. Kelley presiding. Governor Hastings delivered an address, and Alexander K. McClure, editor of the *Philadelphia Times*, delivered the keynote speech. Three citizens who witnessed the laying of the old Capitol cornerstone—Abraham T. Erb, John C. Clyde, and Charles Schwartz—were also present for the Cobb building's ceremony. The old Hills Capitol cornerstone was reused for the new building.[14] The old documents from the cornerstone were inspected and replaced in the box along with items, newspapers, coins, stamps, and documents dealing with the authorization of the new Capitol, which were also placed inside before it was reburied.

All parties associated with the building were pleased with the speed at which it was erected, and of those Cobb may have been most pleased, stating that "the work had to be done in a little over eight months. Mr. Rorke took hold at once and responded to the emergency, accomplishing one of the greatest building feats on record. It would have been impossible to get the building ready had the contract happened to fall to any ordinary builder."[15]

Though there were delays in the shipment of steel to the building site during the summer of 1898, the outer brick façade of the new Capitol began to take shape as fall progressed into winter. Although Allen Rorke did not entirely complete the contracts for shelving, plastering, varnishing, painting, glazing, and decorating work for the Cobb Capitol by January 1, 1899, the General Assembly was still able to occupy the building by this date. They met on January 3, 1899, in the new building to hear Governor Daniel Hastings' final annual address to the joint session.

The ultimate question in the minds of many of the legislators was, "was this building, in fact, complete?" The four men active on the building commission deemed that the structure was complete, in keeping with the act of April 14, 1897. They stated as strongly as they could that they felt the building met any strictures imposed by the legislature and though they could not state it publicly, felt that if the legislature was unhappy with the result, they alone had the means to appropriate the necessary funds to remedy the situation.[16] Despite the Commissions' assertions, public and private reactions to the new structure were lukewarm to outright hostile. As early as June 1898 an English writer, truly tongue-in-cheek stated, "that extraordinary building by itself will be almost enough to deter the English people from an alliance with the United States."[17] Domestic criticism was sharper and less sarcastic. Some termed it a "barn," and assuredly people felt that many Pennsylvania buildings bested it. Others called it a "sugar factory." Henry Ives Cobb himself termed it simply "ugly." Governor Hastings was perhaps the angriest and most outspoken critic of the new building, and although a member of the Commission, would not place his signature on its final report:

> The structure in which you are assembling today is unworthy of your honorable bodies and is a disgrace to the Commonwealth. In its present condition it is hardly fit for human habitation, much less the official abode of the representatives of the great Commonwealth. This structure bears no more resemblance to Colonial architecture than does the Egyptian Sphinx. There are a score of farmers' barns in Pennsylvania more attractive in appearance than this building. It is made of cheap mortar, looks like a hastily erected factory building and is repulsive to the eye.[18]

1897

William McKinley is inaugurated as president, and elected to a second term in 1900. In 1901, while attending the Pan-American Exposition in Buffalo, New York, McKinley is shot twice by deranged anarchist Leon Czolgosz. He dies eight days later of infection and his Vice-President Theodore Roosevelt succeeds McKinley for the remainder of his term.

Backing away from earlier pro-management decisions, the Supreme Court votes 5 to 4 that railroads are subject to the Sherman Anti-Trust Act, meaning that no one railroad can hold a monopoly over the others.

1898

The explosion and sinking of the battleship Maine in Havana harbor results in 260 deaths, leading to the battle slogan "Remember the Maine!" and the beginning of the Spanish-American War.

Assistant Secretary of the Navy Theodore Roosevelt sends the Pacific fleet to the Philippines.

The Spanish-American War ends with the Treaty of Paris; the U.S. purchases the Philippines from Spain for $20 million.

1899

At New York's Sing Sing prison, Martha M. Place becomes the first woman executed in an electric chair, despite pleas to New York's Governor Theodore Roosevelt to issue a pardon.

1900

The American League of Professional Baseball Clubs is organized in Philadelphia. Pennsylvania enters 8 founding teams.

Wielding a hatchet, noted temperance fighter and member of the Women's Christian Temperance Union, Carrie Nation, demolishes 25 saloons in Medicine Lodge, Kansas.

Temperance pins, 1890s.

He saved his harshest words, however, for the members of the commission, claiming that in approving the modifications to the design submitted by Cobb, and deciding to build three wings instead of just housing the General Assembly, the commissioners had violated the law and the act of 1897, which created the commission and set forth the appropriation.

"THE STRUCTURE in which you are assembling today is unworthy of your honorable bodies and is a DISGRACE to the Commonwealth. IN ITS PRESENT CONDITION IT IS HARDLY FIT FOR HUMAN HABITATION… This structure bears no more resemblance to Colonial architecture than does the Egyptian Sphinx."

In the end, any fault for the building's "ugly" façade was not that of architect Henry Ives Cobb. Cobb took his orders from the commission—a commission that was created by the legislature. Though he chose to go the route of constructing three of the "wings" of his conceived building, this was more from necessity than his own imposed will. Furthermore, his plan was approved by the commissioned representatives of the state. For Cobb, to have constructed a small, completely unusable legislative office space

LITERATURE IN STONE: THE HUNDRED YEAR HISTORY OF THE PENNSYLVANIA STATE CAPITOL

"There are a SCORE of farmers' barns in Pennsylvania MORE ATTRACTIVE IN APPEARANCE than this building."

would have been even more of a disservice to the Commonwealth than fully understanding that the expenditure was too small and modifying the designs. Cobb viewed his structure as a significant beginning to his grand scheme for an entire campus of government buildings, and though he took much of the blame, he could do little more with the strict adherence to funding imposed upon him.

As soon as it was complete, the legislature was able to meet in the "finished" structure, though the roof leaked and the ornamentation was lacking. It was not what they or the citizens of the Commonwealth had expected. However, Cobb expected to be given every opportunity to finish the construction of his proposed Capitol building in line with his original plans, just as soon as subsequent budgets were passed. Unfortunately for Cobb, 1899 brought a new administration and new members of the Assembly to Harrisburg, all with differing opinions about how to finish what was already started. Despite his desire to finish his building, the politics of the time dictated that Henry Ives Cobb would not be included in the upcoming commission.

THIS PAGE: *Interior of the Senate Chamber, Cobb Capitol Building, ca. 1901.*

OPPOSITE PAGE: *Left, Campaign button for future Governor Stone bearing the competition sketch for the Cobb Capitol, ca. 1898; Right, Harrisburg celebrates the dedication of the Cobb Capitol, Summer 1899.*

CHAPTER TWO • *The Cobb Capitol*

Large marble sections being set into place on the Capitol's exterior; Joseph Huston at far left.

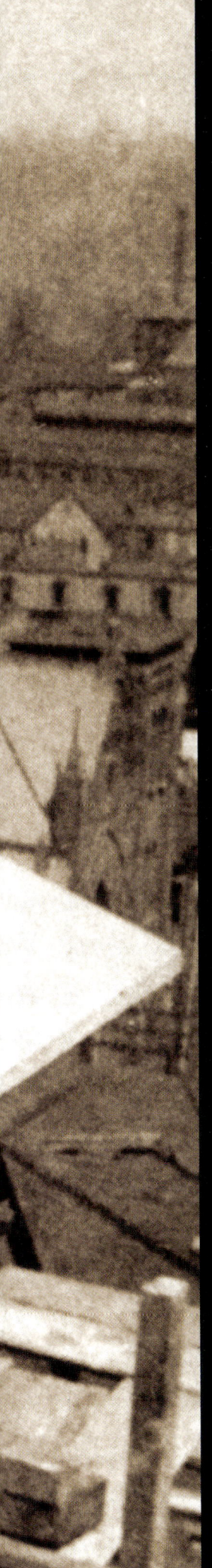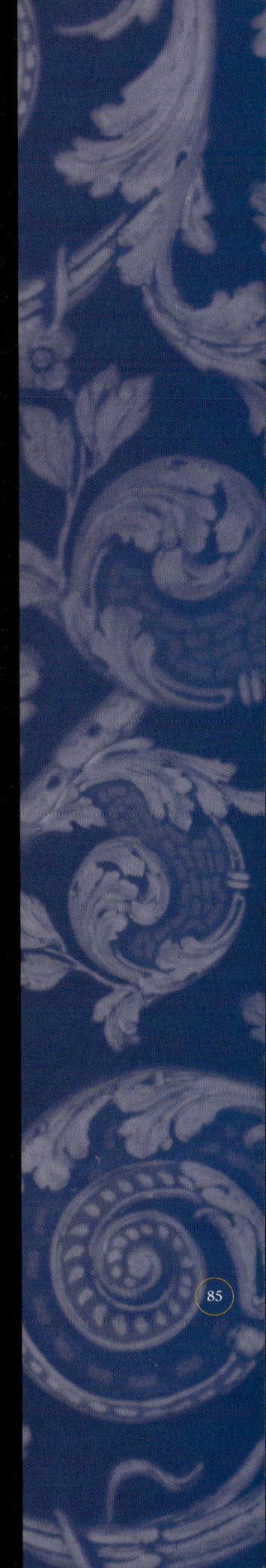

C·H·A·P·T·E·R
THREE

The Huston Capitol Inspiration, design, & Construction

JANUARY 17, 1899, was inauguration day in Pennsylvania. William A. Stone, a lawyer from Pittsburgh and a Tioga County native, was the new chief executive of the Commonwealth. Stone was a bit more even-tempered than Hastings regarding the red brick shell on Capitol Hill. This building, he felt, was a substantial beginning, and the necessary monies to complete it should be somehow raised or appropriated. Stone stated that the building "is a structure which is of sufficient stable foundation to warrant a further appropriation for its completion... and cannot now be regarded as a wasteful expenditure. The problem now to be dealt with is the completion of this structure."[1]

In the interim, while the new administration became situated within Harrisburg, both houses of the General Assembly mulled legislation to complete the start that Henry Ives Cobb had provided. HR-277 would have led to the reappointment of Cobb as architect and the appropriation of the $4 million amount Cobb estimated as necessary to complete his structure. Several measures, all dealing with various amounts of money, were debated but none were passed, and the issue faded for two years.

In 1901, with no legislation having been enacted to finish the Cobb building, Representative Charles E. Voorhees proposed a bill to return the capital to Philadelphia. Once

1900
60% of U.S. steel production came from Pennsylvania. The state also led the nation in textile production and was 4th in lumber production.

1902
The Pennsylvania anthracite coal strike of 1902, in which President Theodore Roosevelt intervened, set the pattern for non-violent arbitration in labor relations.

An explosion at the Rolling Mill Mine in Johnstown kills 112 miners. The tragedy was blamed on firedamp, a methane buildup in the mine that is highly flammable. It is estimated that during this time period an average of 500 miners a year lost their lives.

Willis Carrier designs first air conditioning system.

1903
Cuba leases Guantanamo Bay to the U.S. "in perpetuity."

Morris Michtom and his wife Rose introduce the first teddy bear to the United States.

Orville Wright flies the first powered aircraft at Kitty Hawk, North Carolina in the first documented heavier-than-air flight.

First debut of Crayola Crayons by Binney and Smith of Easton, Pennsylvania.

THIS PAGE: *Governor William A. Stone portrait, Governor's Office.*

OPPOSITE PAGE: *Library of Congress, 1888, Smithmeyer and Pelz.*

---

again, this measure was debated at great length, and various riders and provisions were attached to the bill. In the end, however, the cost of moving the capital city and a strong feeling against returning the seat of government to Philadelphia prevailed. The bill was defeated, but only by a vote of 103 to 75.[2]

The issue of moving the seat of government may have been the impetus for action to finish the Capitol building. After consulting with Cobb to determine the amount needed to adequately complete the building, Senator John Fox of Dauphin County introduced legislation at the start of the 1901 session, which would authorize $5 million for that task. This time, the main controversy in the bill was who exactly was going to serve on the Capitol Building Commission and how that body would operate. Fox stipulated that the new Commission would not be bound by any rules governing or actions taken by the 1897 Commission. Therefore, the new Commission would have to decide whether to reappoint Cobb as architect. The Fox bill was defeated on April 17, 1901, but Fox then added an amendment to allow the governor to appoint the entire Commission. On May 1 his bill passed the Senate.

Meanwhile, the House was introducing its own bills for a new Commission. HR-647 was similar in nature to Senator Fox's bill, except that it required the

"The exterior or outer walls of the building ARE TO BE of granite of the best quality, and in so far as practicable the interior decoration, finish, and style of the Congressional Library at Washington will be taken as TYPE, SCHEME, OR MODEL…"

construction of a heating and power plant for the building and stipulated the employment of a Pennsylvania architect, a statement that would later cause much controversy. On June 6 it was amended to lower the appropriation from $5 million to $4 million, and on June 11 the bill passed the House by a vote of 139 to 39. The two bills were reconciled in a joint House-Senate conference committee, with the committee adopting the House's version. The bill repealed the act of April 14, 1897, pushed the completion date for the building back to 1906, and placed a ceiling of $800 thousand upon annual appropriations for the Capitol, unless a surplus was to be had. The total cost of construction, including all architectural fees, could not exceed $4 million.[3] Both chambers approved the compromise bill on June 27, the last day of the session, and Governor Stone signed the act on July 18, 1901. A new third Capitol was indeed going to be built in Harrisburg.

Governor Stone quickly named the new members of the Commission. They were to be: Nathan C. Shaeffer of Lancaster, the state superintendent of public instruction; William H. Graham, congressman from Pittsburgh; William P. Snyder, Senate president pro tempore; and Edward Bailey, a banker from Harrisburg. The Commission organized in August, naming Stone

The Institute went even further, advising all architects in Pennsylvania not to participate in the competition, because of its poor planning, favoritism, and injustice.

1904

A great fire in Baltimore, Maryland destroys over 1,500 buildings in 30 hours.

Cy Young of the Boston Americans pitches the first perfect game in modern baseball against the Philadelphia Athletics.

Lincoln Steffens' The Shame of the Cities *is published, highlighting urban blight.*

Ida Tarbell, a native of Erie County, Pennsylvania, publishes The History of Standard Oil Company.

BOTH PAGES: *1902 Capitol Competition Sketches submitted by Joseph M. Huston.*

as president and Bailey as treasurer. Robert K. Young of Wellsboro was named as legal counsel. Edgar C. Gerwig, Stone's personal secretary, was appointed secretary for the Commission, and Thomas L. Eyre, superintendent of public grounds and buildings was named the Commission's superintendent.

The first order of business was to approve a new design competition. However this Commission, anxious to get the process in motion, seemed to do so rather hastily. Unlike the 1897 competition, which rigorously stipulated what could and could not be submitted, there was no detailed program for the new competition. Having no architectural advisor as of yet, the members of the Commission simply placed announcements in Pennsylvania newspapers and ordered Gerwig to run them throughout the month of September in nine specific Pennsylvania papers.

The notice called for interested Pennsylvania architects to submit designs for a new Capitol of the Commonwealth on or before November 30, 1901. The cost ceiling of $4 million was repeated, and it was noted that under no terms shall the price rise above that cost. The notice in the papers also gave the completion date— January 1, 1906. The Commission did stipulate what the inner and outer finishes would be made of, stating, "The exterior or outer walls of the building are to be of granite of the best quality, and in so far as practicable the interior decoration, finish, and style of the Congressional Library at Washington will be taken as type, scheme or model..."[4] The Capitol would be built according to the winning design selected by the Commission, and the top five runners-up would receive $1 thousand for their efforts.

By October the Commission was becoming concerned. They had received few entries, and many of the state's most qualified architects had not taken part. This may have been a result of the debacle with the 1897 design competition, with architects reluctant to enter into a competition that would involve lengthy litigation and professional discredit. To entice more submissions, the Commission ordered copies of the newspaper notice, topographical plan of Capitol Park, a floor plan of the Cobb building, and a statement of space requirements mailed to all Pennsylvania members of the American Institute of Architects (AIA). In addition, it hired Professor William H. Ware of the Columbia University School of Architecture as its consulting architect.

As the month of October wore on, the Commission became more concerned with the lack of entries and considered canceling the competition entirely. Ware was outraged at this notion, stating that regardless of how many entries they received, it was still a legally binding agreement with the men who had submitted designs. Ware balked at the politics surrounding the competition. He had agreed to serve as consultant, then resigned in disgust at the Commission's discussion over canceling it. He then wrote a letter to Edward Bailey, stating that he would serve in a limited role on the Commission and that he would make his colleagues in the profession aware of his role. All the vacillating on the part of Ware did little to bring more entrants and in fact further alienated architects and the AIA.

The architectural community became even more galvanized against this competition than in 1897, with the AIA issuing a resolution of condemnation. The AIA stated that the program was "loosely drawn and offered little promise that designs would be considered on their merits."[5] They went on to mention Ware's indecisiveness in serving and that there was a recognized method already in use by the Federal government and recognized by the AIA, which stipulated how architectural competitions were to be conducted. The Institute went even further, advising all architects in Pennsylvania not to participate in the competition, because of its poor planning, favoritism, and injustice. (It would later inform its members that participation constituted unprofessional conduct.)

After an informal vote they chose ENTRY NUMBER ONE, which **when uncovered read, "J. M. Huston, Philadelphia."**

In answer to the charges of political favoritism, the Capitol Building Commission met in mid-November and decided to issue a statement, which dictated that upon receipt of the entries, Professor Ware had promised to review all of them, without knowing names of the submitters. As planned the competition ended on November 20, 1901. In all, the Commission had received nine entries. The names of the seven known entrants were: William C. Hays, Joseph M. Huston, Addison Hutton, Herman Miller, Fred J. Osterling, Trimble and Stevens, and James H. Warner.

Both Warner and Huston had entered the 1897 competition, with Warner as an invited guest architect of the Commission and Huston as one of the finalists. Gerwig opened them, only to seal the names and number them one through nine. He gave them to Ware who evaluated them and issued his report at the end of December 1901. On December 28, Ware went before the Commission to verbally discuss his conclusions. He stated that he had commented on each plan by number. He did not, however, rank any of the plans, but selected four that were superior, three that were lesser, and two that should not even be considered because they were distinctly poorer than the rest.

Of the top four numbers that Ware had selected, numbers one, three, four, and seven were those that impressed him most. He talked at great length about the merits of number four, and apparently this was the one he thought best, though he did not specifically say so to the Commission. He stated that the Commission would be justified in selecting any of the first four designs, and reiterated that his evaluations had been made without knowing any of the names of the architects. Upon Ware's evaluation, the Commission members confined their debate to the selected plans.

THIS PAGE: *Italian print purchased by Huston, undated.*

OPPOSITE PAGE: *Early rendering by Huston of the House Chamber, 1901.*

Following the signing of his contract in January 1902, HUSTON would quickly set out to turn his vision of Pennsylvania's Capitol into a REALITY.

However, the plans, which Ware had mailed from New York two days prior, had not yet made it to Harrisburg because of heavy express traffic over the Christmas holiday. The Commission adjourned until 3:30 P.M. the same day, December 28, 1901.

During the interim, the plans arrived, and they were arranged for the Commission's inspection. There was a period of general reviewing, and then the members proceeded to debate the four that Ware had suggested. After a period of time they narrowed the field to numbers four and one. The Commission asked Ware if they would be justified in selecting either entry, and he replied in the affirmative, if the authors were of known reputation.

Finally, the Commission was ready to vote on the plans, but they asked Ware one last question as to whether they should cancel the competition altogether and begin anew. Ware stated that he thought this would be counterproductive, wasteful of time and money, and most likely would not provide entries any better than the ones already in hand. Following this assertion, the Commission voted. After an informal vote they chose entry number one, which when uncovered read, "J. M. Huston, Philadelphia." Discussion then ensued, followed by Senator Snyder moving for adoption of a motion:

> *Resolved: That J. M. Huston be selected as architect of the new Capitol building, provided he can satisfy the Commission that the building proposed by him will not exceed in cost the amount appropriated…on the roll call being called, all members voted in the affirmative.*[6]

Joseph Miller Huston, the selected architect, was a thirty-five-year-old resident of Germantown, Pennsylvania. He had grand ideas, but little experience within the field, and certainly he had never attempted anything as large as the scale of his plans for the Capitol.

Almost immediately controversy arose over his appointment. Some papers, such as the *Harrisburg Telegraph*, praised the selection of Huston and attributed his success to his hard work and attention to detail. Certain newspapers, however, were not convinced that Huston had been randomly selected on the merits of his plans. There were other rumors regarding a rigged selection process, but none of which could be corroborated through any type of conclusive evidence.

CHAPTER THREE • *The Huston Capitol: Inspiration, Design, & Construction*

Literature in Stone: The Hundred Year History of the Pennsylvania State Capitol

All of the conjecture, articles, and editorials were enough to make Herman Miller, one of the disappointed runners-up, call for an investigation of the selection process. The *Philadelphia Press* editorialized that the Commission should make public all its documentation of the competition, but the members refused. In 1907, when the impending Capitol graft scandal came to light, those who remembered the 1901 competition would derisively point fingers and say that the fraud was present from the very beginning with the selection of the architect. Regardless, it remains troublesome for history to try to pinpoint or uncover with any degree of accuracy the inner workings of a process cloaked and veiled in secrecy. Certainly Professor Ware, despite his reluctance at judging the entries, did commend Huston's design to the Commission. Later, insinuation on the part of other entrants in the competition would indicate, largely without proof, that some members of the Commission knew beforehand which entry to choose. There has been no evidence found to prove any of these allegations leveled by architects unhappy that they had lost the competition.

In the long term, the structure that Joseph Huston's vision would create in Harrisburg over the next four years did much to bolster his supporters, silence his critics, and make the people of the Commonwealth forget how the Capitol's architect was selected. Following the signing of his contract in January 1902, Huston would quickly set out to turn his vision of Pennsylvania's Capitol into a reality.

Joseph Miller Huston

Architect Joseph Miller Huston was a man who, from a very early age, was determined to make his mark in the world of architecture. Joseph Huston was born in 1866 in Philadelphia the fifth of six children. He was the son of Irish immigrants and a gifted young man of high standing in his church and community. He was known even then to have high artistic visions. By 1880, he completed public school, which at the time was eighth grade. He went to work with John B. Ellison and Sons, a well-known Philadelphia businessman. At age seventeen, he joined the architectural firm of Furness and Sons for a period of five years. While with the firm he studied Greek, Latin, and mathematics with a tutor. His self-eduction progressed so rapidly that he gained admittance to Princeton University in September 1888. At Princeton, Huston was an honors student and a member of several artistic and literary societies. At college Huston had the good fortune to meet numerous artists and architects who would remain his friends for life. Between the summer of his freshman and sophomore years he traveled to Europe with fellow Princetonians, Frank Hays, Edward Redfield, and Alexander Calder. The three men and Huston made a sketching tour of Ireland, England, Belgium, and France. Upon his return to school in September, Huston was awarded the Sophomore Medal, an award given to the Freshman at the top of their class. The next summer Huston produced a bird's-eye view of the entrance of the Reading Railroad into Philadelphia for A. A. McLeod, president of the Reading line. In large part is was his years and associations at Princeton that molded Huston's desire to do something great in the world of architecture. During his senior year of college, he had won three gold medals for oratory and began to make note of the people he met and their impact upon him.

After graduating in 1892, Huston returned to the firm of Furness and Sons,[7] during which time he

THIS PAGE: *Joseph M. Huston, ca. 1906.*

OPPOSITE PAGE: HUSTON'S EARLY CAREER

A. *The Philadelphia Building at the Charleston Exposition was designed by Joseph Huston to resemble Independence Hall, 1902.*
B. *The completed Library of the University of Pennsylvania, which Huston delineated early in his career, 1888.*
C. *John B. Ellison & Sons Building, Philadelphia, ca. 1898, Huston's first employer.*
D. *Witherspoon Building, 1901. Inset, Huston at work inside the building, undated.*

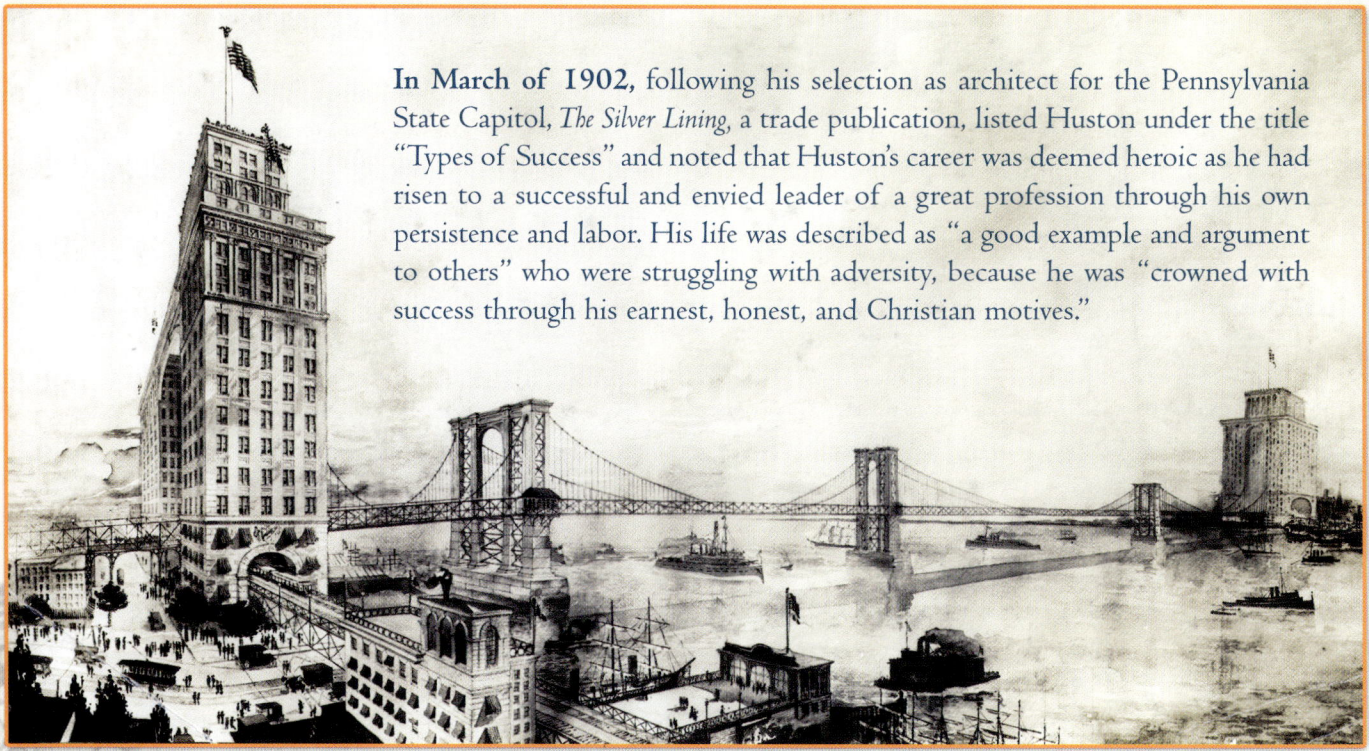

In March of 1902, following his selection as architect for the Pennsylvania State Capitol, *The Silver Lining,* a trade publication, listed Huston under the title "Types of Success" and noted that Huston's career was deemed heroic as he had risen to a successful and envied leader of a great profession through his own persistence and labor. His life was described as "a good example and argument to others" who were struggling with adversity, because he was "crowned with success through his earnest, honest, and Christian motives."

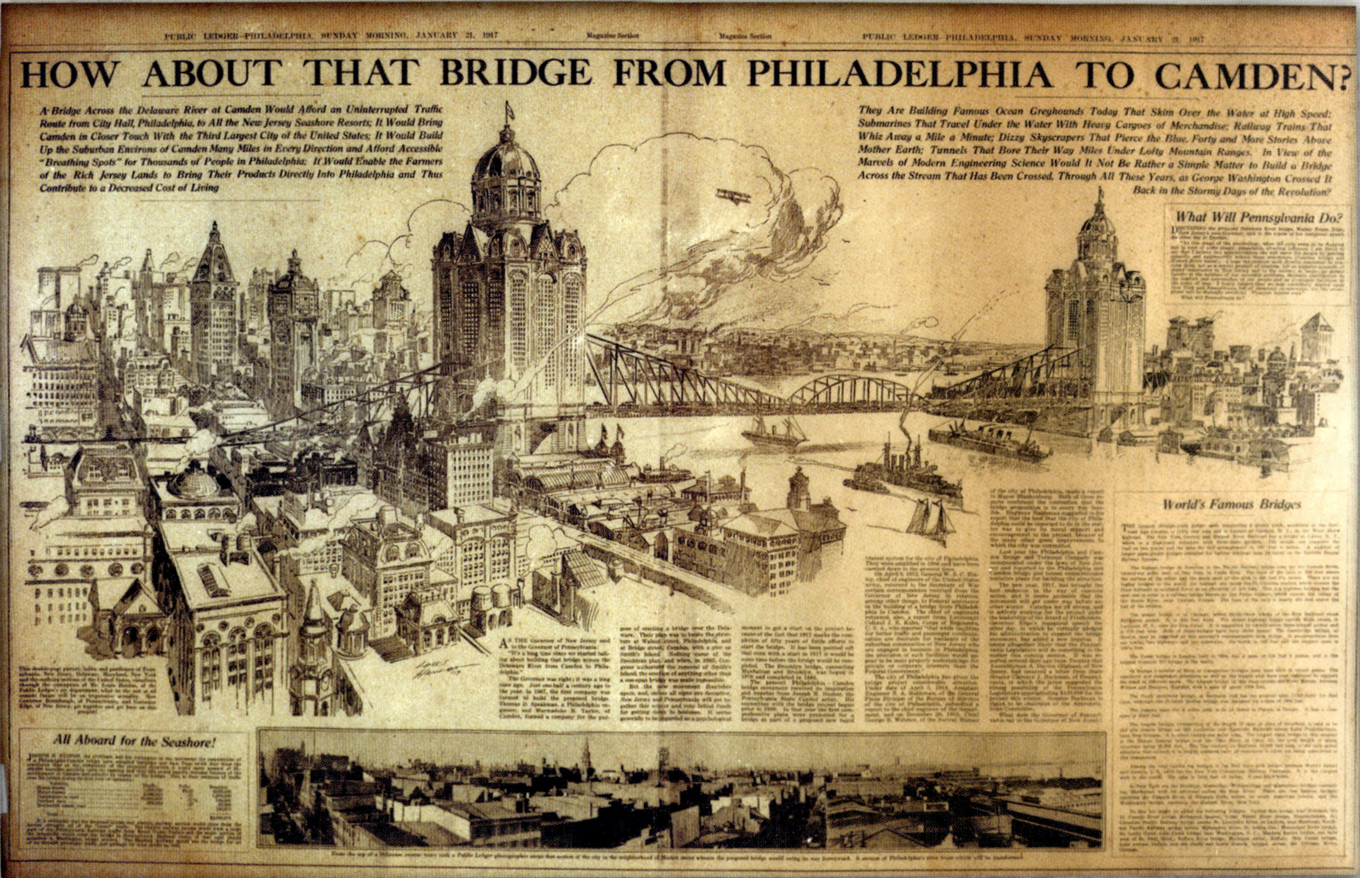

THIS PAGE: *Top, Early sketch of Huston's proposed suspension bridge in Philadelphia, 1913; Bottom, Newspaper showing Huston's proposal for a bridge spanning from Philadelphia to Camden (the future Benjamin Franklin bridge), January 21, 1917.*

OPPOSITE PAGE: *Elevation drawing comparing the architecture of St. Peter's Basilica to that of the Pennsylvania State Capitol.*

PUBLIC LEDGER—PHILADELPHIA, SUNDAY MORNING, JANUARY 21, 1917 Magazine Section

Magazine Section PUBLIC LEDGER—PHILADELPHIA, SUNDAY MORNING, JANUARY 21, 1917

HOW ABOUT THAT BRIDGE FROM PHILADELPHIA TO CAMDEN?

A Bridge Across the Delaware River at Camden Would Afford an Uninterrupted Traffic Route from City Hall, Philadelphia, to All the New Jersey Seashore Resorts; It Would Bring Camden in Closer Touch With the Third Largest City of the United States; It Would Build Up the Suburban Environs of Camden Many Miles in Every Direction and Afford Accessible "Breathing Spots" for Thousands of People in Philadelphia; It Would Enable the Farmers of the Rich Jersey Lands to Bring Their Products Directly Into Philadelphia and Thus Contribute to a Decreased Cost of Living

They Are Building Famous Ocean Greyhounds Today That Skim Over the Water at High Speed; Submarines That Travel Under the Water With Heavy Cargoes of Merchandise; Railway Trains That Whiz Away a Mile a Minute; Dizzy Skyscrapers That Pierce the Blue, Forty and More Stories Above Mother Earth; Tunnels That Bore Their Way Miles Under Lofty Mountain Ranges. In View of the Marvels of Modern Engineering Science Would It Not Be Rather a Simple Matter to Build a Bridge Across the Stream That Has Been Crossed, Through All These Years, as George Washington Crossed It Back in the Stormy Days of the Revolution?

What Will Pennsylvania Do?

World's Famous Bridges

All Aboard for the Seashore!

worked on the design for the Pennsylvania Railroad's Broad Street Station in Philadelphia. In 1895 Huston set up his own firm and spent the next two years working on the design of the Witherspoon Building at Juniper and Walnut Streets in Philadelphia. In 1897 Huston moved his personal office into the newly completed building. Huston was also a member of several civic and professional organizations such as the Presbyterian Social Union, the Union League, the University Masons Lodge 610, F.&A.M. (Free and Accepted Masons), the T-Square Club, the Merion and Germantown Cricket Clubs, and the Princeton Club of Philadelphia, among others.

Huston had met a young architect named Stanford B. Lewis during his time at Furness and Sons. Huston hired Lewis, a native of Charlottesville, Virginia, as his partner. Together Huston and Lewis would enter the 1897 Pennsylvania Capitol Design Competition, losing to Henry Ives Cobb. In 1899 Huston and Lewis produced the design for the Court of Honor in Philadelphia, through which President McKinley would pass during the celebratory Peace Jubilee. This Beaux-Arts style arch was declared by critics to have revolutionized the architecture of pageantry in the United States and to have given birth to decorative arches to follow, such as the Dewey Arch in New York. Throughout this time and even following the creation of the Capitol, Huston and Lewis would produce designs for numerous private residences in the Philadelphia area. It was Huston who in 1913 suggested the idea of a suspension bridge between Camden and Philadelphia. Though Huston was never awarded the commission, the Benjamin Franklin bridge was built in the mid-1920s.

In 1898 Huston and his older brother Samuel would depart on an around the world tour to see the great art and architecture of Europe, Arabia, and Asia. While Samuel was sick (he nearly died from appendicitis suffered while in Rome) Huston would travel the city with sketchbook in hand making copies and drawings of the art and architecture of St. Peter's basilica and other Italian works of art. It really was this European sojourn that planted the idea of designing monumental public buildings firmly in Huston's mind. It was Rome and Paris, those two amazing European cities, which confirmed for Huston that America, to be a lasting world power, had to have monumental architecture like the great societies of antiquity.[8]

CHAPTER THREE • *The Huston Capitol: Inspiration, Design, & Construction*

A

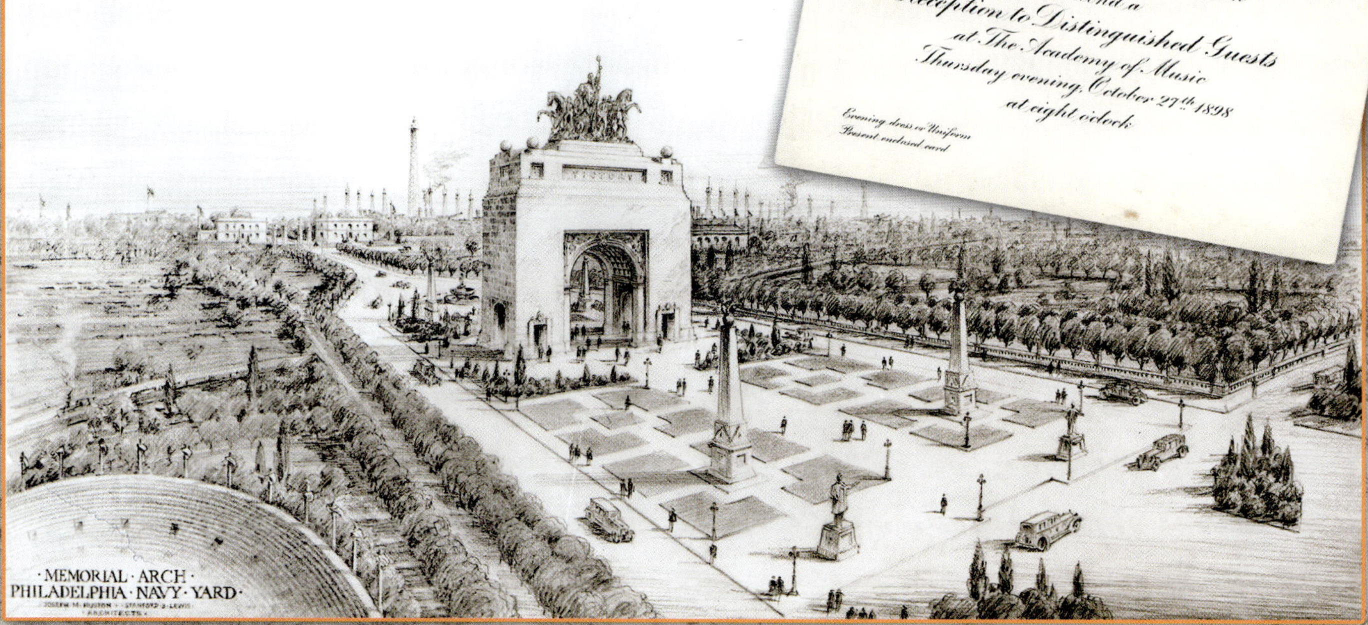

·MEMORIAL·ARCH·
PHILADELPHIA·NAVY·YARD·
ARCHITECTS

B

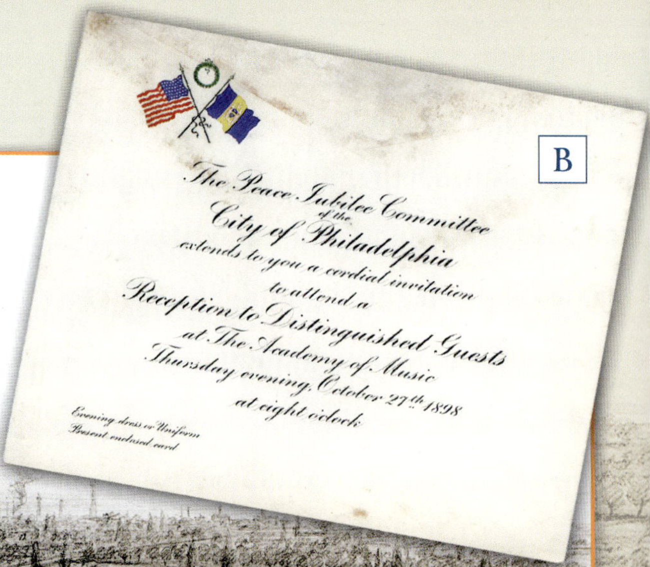

The Peace Jubilee Committee
of the
City of Philadelphia
extends to you a cordial invitation
to attend a
Reception to Distinguished Guests
at The Academy of Music
Thursday evening, October 27th 1898
at eight o'clock

Evening dress or Uniform
Present enclosed card

C

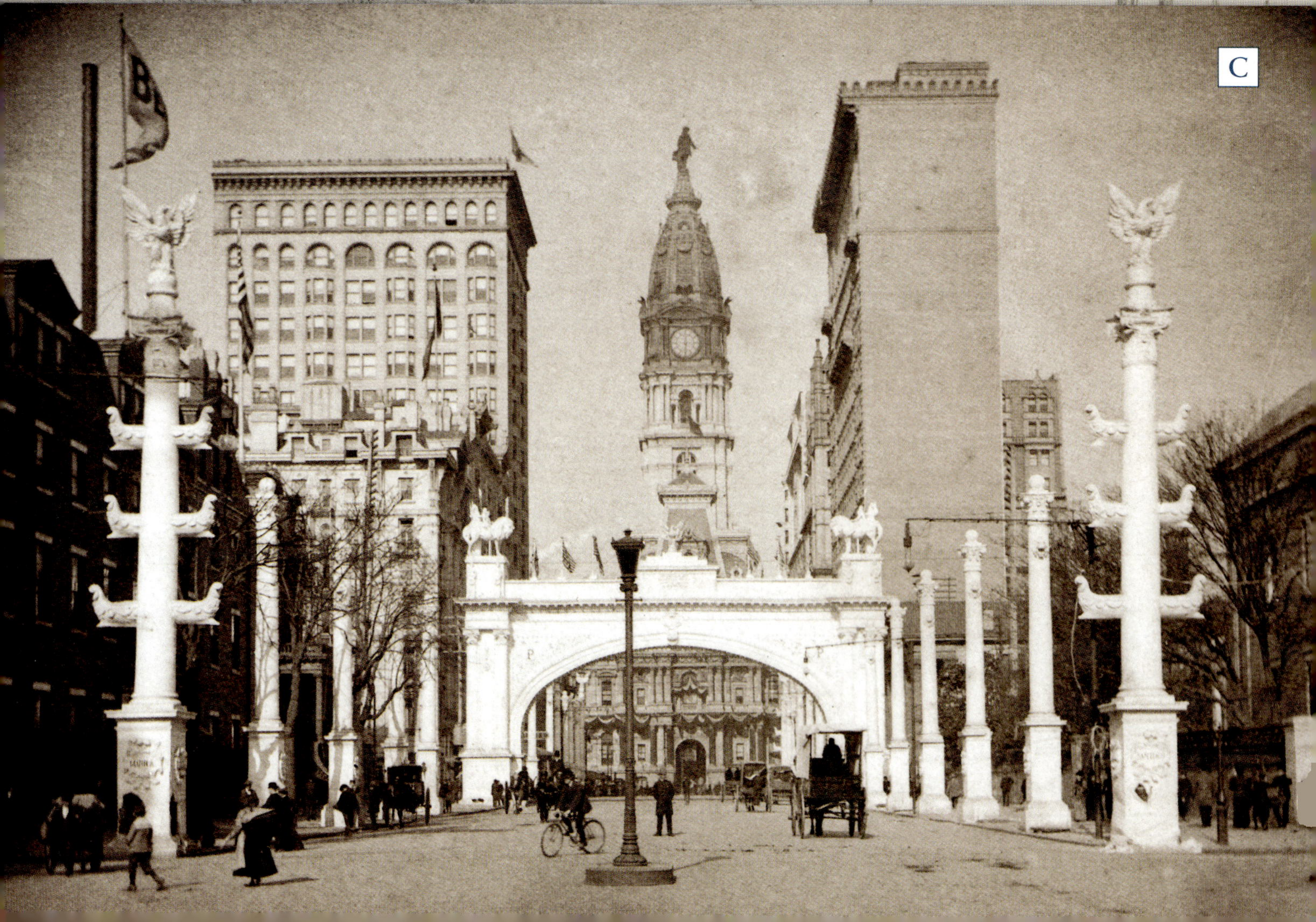

A STUPENDOUS EXPOSITION!
From Philadelphia to Atlantic City! The Twentieth Century Dream!

Other Works by Joseph Huston.

THIS PAGE: *Top, Newspaper page from the* Philadelphia Press *showing Huston's proposal for a bridge spanning from Philadelphia to Atlantic City, March 10, 1901; Bottom, Joseph M. Huston, by famed Philadelphia photographer Frederick Gutekunst, undated.*

OPPOSITE PAGE:

A. *Memorial Arch for the Navy Yard, designed by Joseph M. Huston, 1898.*

B. *Huston's invitation for Peace Jubilee reception, 1898.*

C. *Court of Honor at the Peace Jubilee, designed by Joseph M. Huston, 1898. This was the first monument honoring the Spanish-American War.*

CHAPTER THREE • *The Huston Capitol: Inspiration, Design, & Construction*

Though Huston and Lewis' 1897 plan was not chosen, their firm still chose to enter the 1901 Capitol design competition, which was restricted to only Pennsylvania architects and firms. Upon the decision to enter the competition, it was those European motifs and ideas that Huston remembered with extreme vividness, so much so that they became incorporated into the new building's design.

For the dome, Huston chose a one-half scale replica of the dome of St. Peter's Basilica in Rome. When it came to the magnificent backdrop of the central rotunda, only a replica of the grand staircase and triple arcaded gallery from Charles Garnier's 1868 Paris Opera would suffice. The House Chamber would be adorned in Italian Renaissance style, the Senate Chamber in French Renaissance. The Supreme Court Chamber would be Greek and Roman in design, and the Governor's Reception Room would be Tudor. The Ladies' Lounge would be adorned in the style of Louis XV.

After having won the competition, Huston set about paying attention to every minute detail of the new building's construction.

He, Lewis, and several employees would design almost every feature for the Capitol, from the decorative arts to custom clocks, to escutcheon plates and doorknobs, ornate bronze railings, chandeliers, torchieres, painted finishes, and specially-designed furniture. Huston's attention to detail was exceptionally meticulous—everything down to the last rosette, acanthus leaf, types of columns, pediments, and Greek keys would be designed, drawn, and implemented in just the location that Huston envisioned.

Professor Ware, as consultant to the Commission, did issue a caveat regarding Huston's selection, primarily based on his youth and inexperience as an architect undertaking a project as large as the Capitol. Ware stated, "In case the choice should fall upon a design the author of which, by reason of youth or inexperience, or for any other cause, an unsuitable person to be entrusted with the sole charge of so important a work, he shall be called upon to associate with someone more experienced..."[9] Ware's advice was followed only loosely by the Commission. Though they never officially asked Huston to choose a consulting architect, the Commission hired Bernard R. Green, the former superintendent at the Library of Congress, to serve as clerk-of-the-works for the Capitol. Joseph Huston received a congratulatory letter from William Ware on December 30, 1901, informing him of his selection. From early January until mid-July 1902, Governor Stone, William Ware, Bernard Green, and Huston debated over changes and modifications that each wanted in the building, with Huston maintaining adherence to his original plans in most cases. After

THIS PAGE: *Huston competition sketch showing rotunda elevation, 1901.*

OPPOSITE PAGE: *Top, Stanford B. Lewis, ca. 1906; Bottom, William R. Ware, ca. 1906.*

his contract was signed in January 1902, Huston set to work designing electrical and mechanical system plans for the building.

Huston's working plans, all dated July 1, 1902, were submitted to the Commission on July 9. Huston asked the Building Commission to allow four weeks for contractors to prepare bids for the various work. Though the Commission approved his plans, they also sent them on to Bernard Green for comment.

Green in turn prepared a thirty-four page report detailing various changes, mainly in terms of the engineering of the building and not the art or architecture proposed. He suggested numerous clarifications and improvements, specifically on the proposed telephone and electrical systems, which he stated were "hastily written."[10] Though Green had several other items with which he had problems, he thought that all of these were relatively minor to what he termed the "ruling question"—could the building be created within the $4 million budget; Green believed, given the specifications, ornamentation, and artwork, that it could not.

Whether Huston or the Commission adopted many of Green's changes is unknown. Throughout the Capitol's construction, there existed several modified sets of blueprints. One important revision, that may have come at Green's suggestion, was that Huston's revised July 1902 specifications show no quadriga (four horsemen with a

HARRISBURG, PA., THURSDAY EVENING, JUNE 9, 1904

Stanford Lewis' Son Drowned in Millrace

Little Stanford Huston Lewis, a son of Stanford B. Lewis, assistant architect on the new Capitol, was drowned in a millrace at Telford on Tuesday morning. Mr. Lewis had left home to come to Harrisburg with Architect Huston to attend the opening of the bids for State supplies, and did not learn of his son's death until he returned home in the evening.

The little fellow had gone to a millrace near his father's residence, and was standing on a bridge across the race throwing pebbles in the water. He lost his balance on the slimy, moss-covered boards and fell into the water. His mother missed him and intuitively felt that he had fallen into the race.

The race was shut off and the stream dragged, and the little boy's body found. Mr. Lewis only left Philadelphia for his country place last Saturday. The little boy was an exceptionally bright lad, giving every promise of a bright future.

CHAPTER THREE • *The Huston Capitol: Inspiration, Design, & Construction*

Joseph Huston's CAPITOL Vision

1901 Capitol Renderings

A. Vestibule.
B. West entry bronze doors.
C. North corridor, first floor.

C

Huston's attention to detail was exceptionally meticulous—
everything down to the last rosette and acanthus leaf, types of columns, and pediments would
be designed, drawn, and implemented in just the location that Huston envisioned.

CHAPTER THREE • *The Huston Capitol: Inspiration, Design, & Construction*

THE ·TRIUMPHANT·
QUADRIGA

NEVER EXECUTED

chariot), on the center roof area, no tympanums (bas relief triangular sculpture above porticoes), nor sculptural groups at the north and south wing entrances. Huston cut these from his original competition sketch due to budget constraints, and in addition, he lessened the amount of sculpture to be placed at the center or main entrance. Still Green was skeptical about Huston's construction estimates and asked two other firms to give their evaluations of probable cost.

Regardless of the disagreements between Green and Huston, bid opening was scheduled for September 6, 1902, at twelve noon with numerous construction firms bidding. Both Huston and Green concurred on the issue that when all the bids were examined, George F. Payne and Company had submitted the lowest proposal. In late September, Payne and Company was awarded the general contract for the Capitol's construction.

The month of October saw Payne conducting preliminary work before he could begin construction of the Capitol. Onsite activity actually began mid-October with the demolition of some of the Cobb Capitol's interior walls.

THE CONSTRUCTION

The official groundbreaking ceremony for the new building took place on November 2, 1902. Joseph Huston marked the outline of a Masonic Cross on the ground where excavation of the south wing was to begin. The event was not a large ceremony; only Huston, Payne, Wetter, Superintendent of Construction Owen Roberts, Huston's partner Stanford Lewis, and a few other public figures were present. It was not until December 3 that workers from Payne and Company were able to begin demolition of the 1811–1812 Hills north and south Capitol offices.[11] On December 11, Stanford B. Lewis, reported in his daily log that one hundred twenty-five men and approximately sixty carts were engaged in tearing down the old buildings.[12]

New construction on the Capitol actually began in January 1903, despite the winter weather. Payne enlisted Joseph Bechtel as the masonry contractor, and on January 5 Huston arrived from Philadelphia to inspect the progress on the dome pier footings. On the same day Huston, with his brother Samuel and partner Stanford Lewis, placed a small sealed bottle containing a copy of the New Latin Testament and his speech *Literature in Stone* into one of the basement pier footings for the dome. Stanford Lewis carefully recorded the location of the private ceremony in his daily journal.[13] January was a busy month, with both the inauguration of Governor-elect Samuel Pennypacker and the meeting of the 1903 General Assembly. Both the 1903 and 1905 Assembly were to hold session in the Capitol, even as it was being built. Despite the fact that the presence of the legislature greatly slowed construction, both sessions did sit in the building, as stipulated in the specifications.[14]

Over the winter months, Green, Huston, and Payne debated the type of granite to be used on the exterior of the building. By March 18 the pool of potential granite types had been narrowed, and Huston, Green, and several other Commission members took a trip to Vermont, to examine the quality of the granite. After their return, the Commission voted and decided that either Barre or Woodbury granite would suffice.

1904
The first underground line of the New York City Subway opens.

1905
THE U.S. IN THE YEAR 1905…
- The American flag had 45 stars.
- There were 8,000 cars in the country and only 144 miles of paved roads; Common maximum city speed limit was 10 MPH.
- Over 95% of all births occurred in the home.
- Average life expectancy was 47 years.
- Five leading causes of death were:
    1. Pneumonia and influenza
    2. Tuberculosis
    3. Dysentery
    4. Heart disease
    5. Stroke
- 6% of all Americans graduated from high school.
- 90% of all doctors had no college education.
- 20% of adults could not read or write.
- Average wage was 22¢ per hour; Average worker made between $200 and $1,400 per year.
- Sugar cost 4¢ a pound; eggs were 14¢ a dozen; coffee was 15¢ a pound; A three-minute call from Denver to New York City cost $11.
- 8% of homes had a telephone.

President Theodore Roosevelt was inaugurated for his first full term in office, having succeeded the slain William McKinley in 1901.

Albert Einstein continues work on the special theory of relativity as well as the theory of Brownian motion.

The first all-motion-picture theater in the world was opened on Smithfield Street in Pittsburgh by John P. Harris and Harry Davis. The term "nickelodeon" is coined there. The Warner brothers begin their careers in western Pennsylvania.

With the help of President Roosevelt, Japan and Russia make peace, ending the Russo-Japanese War.

Britain produces the HMS Dreadnought naval ship, revolutionizing battleship design and triggering a naval arms race.

The Hershey Chocolate Company built its first factory in Hershey and the H. J. Heinz Company was formed.

Literature in Stone: The Hundred Year History of the Pennsylvania State Capitol

Huston Capitol
CONSTRUCTION 1•9•0•4

1. Large pieces of stone are winched into place.
2. View of the southwest wing, showing brickwork, steel skeleton, and completed first floor granite facing.
3. Work on the granite facing overtop of the existing Cobb building progresses rapidly.
4. Wing construction May 17, 1904.
5. Workmen laboring on the drum of the dome and center wing roof in April 1904.
6. A large piece of stone is hoisted into the building through the window.

THIS PAGE: *East facade of the Capitol during its construction, looking west from Pennsylvania Railroad, April 1, 1904.*

CHAPTER THREE • *The Huston Capitol: Inspiration, Design, & Construction*

I·N·S·I·G·H·T
George Payne
General Contractor

Little is known about George F. Payne as a child and a young man. It is known that he was a member of the Washington Grays, serving with that Philadelphia artillery corps during the infamous railroad strike at Pittsburgh in 1877. How this experience affected Payne's attitude toward organized labor is unknown. After his departure from the Washington Grays, he apprenticed with a carpenter and, when he had finished, went into business for himself.

Payne and Charles G. Wetter together founded the Philadelphia construction firm of George F. Payne and Company in 1881. While most of their work was done in and around Philadelphia, they also served as contractors in State College, Pennsylvania; Newport, Rhode Island; and Spring Lake, New Jersey.

A listing of the Philadelphia buildings that were erected by Payne and Company is quite impressive: the Bullitt building at 133–137 South Fourth Street, the Crozer building at 1420 Chestnut Street, the United Gas Improvement Company building at Broad and Arch Streets, a professional building at 1831–1833 Chestnut Street, the Perry Building at 16th and Chestnut Streets, the Loraine Hotel at Broad Street and Fairmount Avenue, the Academy of Natural Sciences at 19th and Race Streets, Widener Memorial Home on York Road above Logan, the Wistar Institute at 36th and Spruce Streets, and St. Joseph's Academy in Chestnut Hill. Other buildings of note outside Philadelphia include the Carnegie Library; a dormitory and an agricultural building in State College; residences for Peter A. B. Widener and

Chas. G. Wetter   Jos. M. Huston   Owen Roberts   Geo. F. Payne   Stanford B. Lewis

William L. Elkins in Ashbourne, Pennsylvania; and three Newport, Rhode Island residences.

Payne was the successful bidder for the Capitol contract over five other contractors. His firm also became a subcontractor to John H. Sanderson, the Capitol special furnishings contractor, as the Capitol project progressed.

Payne and Company was implicated in the Capitol graft scandal, and Payne, himself, was subsequently indicted for conspiracy to defraud the Commonwealth. Payne retreated to Mount Clemens, Michigan in 1907, during the investigation by the Capitol Investigation Commission.

His health gradually failed and he died there during the latter part of 1907. His estate was not listed among the parties paying restitution to the Commonwealth for the Capitol graft.[15] φ

THIS PAGE: *Top, Groundbreaking ceremony on November 7, 1902; Bottom, George F. Payne, ca. 1906.*

OPPOSITE PAGE: *Ground excavation beginning in January 1903.*

Throughout the Capitol's construction, there existed several modified sets of blueprints.

Payne and Company chose the Woodbury Granite Company of Hardwick, Vermont, to quarry, cut, and ship the granite to Harrisburg via rail.

Throughout the spring of 1903 Huston and the other members of the Commission had difficulty in getting George Payne to submit a complete list of his subcontractors, and as late as August, the Commission's attorney, Robert K. Young, was still asking for the list. Payne and Company had their fair share of problems and setbacks in the first year of the construction. Delays in granite and steel continued into June, and a strike at the quarry further prolonged shipments. Bricklayers went on strike from the middle of May through mid-June. On May 25 Payne's construction superintendent, Owen Roberts, was killed when a wall that was being demolished collapsed onto him. As a result, George Payne was forced to personally supervise the onsite work for a number of months, until a replacement construction superintendent could be found.

Joseph Huston sailed to Europe in June 1903 to check on the progress of artists George Grey Barnard and Edwin Austin Abbey, both of whom were producing their Capitol artwork abroad.

By mid-summer Payne was moving forward, attempting to replace the time that was lost through the strikes and delays of the spring. He reported to the *Harrisburg Telegraph* that five hundred men were onsite and that the workforce would be doubled within a month.[16] Soon after this time Payne named Samuel B. Rambo as the new construction superintendent.

Throughout the summer the delinquent steel and granite shipments began to arrive in larger numbers and more frequently. The American Bridge Company of New York supplied the steel from its Pencoyd, Pennsylvania mill, and the Etter Erecting Company of Philadelphia was in charge of setting the granite. By September granite shipments averaged approximately one carload per day for the first time all summer. While the pace of work was quickening, Huston and the Commission's rapport was lessening.

The Commission was not always happy with Huston, because both he and George Payne seemed all too willing to conduct business on their own without contacting the Commission, or Clerk-of-the-Works Bernard Green, when requested. In addition Huston complained to Governor Pennypacker that the Building Commission did not have sufficient funds to complete the approaches to the building, along with numerous other items, which Huston was forced to drop from his original plan. Huston stated, "The work of the Capitol Building Commission is at an end so far as entering into any more contracts is concerned."[17] The Commission had no authority other than to construct the building—furnishing it was a separate matter entirely. For this reason, and probably to maintain the unity that was in

THIS PAGE: *Elevation of rotunda by Joseph M. Huston, 1901.*

OPPOSITE PAGE: *Top, Miniature plaster model of frieze for Capitol's tympanum, undated; Bottom, Fountain located in Capitol Park, undated.*

Hardwick, Vermont
Granite Quarry

THIS PAGE:
A. Brickwork continues on the building's exterior, ca. 1903.
B. Marble columns and capitals are loaded onto flatbeds in preparation for shipping, ca. 1903.
C. Train car awaiting transport to Harrisburg, July 10, 1903.
D. Workers use a system of ladders to manuveur the steep quarry landscape, 1903.

OPPSOITE PAGE: Rock cutters take a break from the laborious quarry work, 1903.

Huston's original plan, the Board of Commissioners of Public Grounds and Buildings resolved to hire Huston to design the furnishings for the building.[18] This contract, completely separate from the contract for the Capitol, had no stipulation or ceiling over the amount that could be spent. This section would later come back to haunt both commissions during the Capitol graft scandal, but at the time it seemed a logical decision.

Throughout the fall and into December granite, steel, and brick came with more frequency to the jobsite and were installed quite rapidly. Huston told the bricklayers to work beyond the level of the granite facing, in an attempt to get as much of the building as possible covered before winter. This, however, was not able to be accomplished to the height that Huston wanted for fear of making the walls unstable. Work came almost to a standstill from January until March 1904, because of the cold winter weather. Warmer weather allowed the pace of construction to again speed up and Huston noted that sixty thousand bricks had been laid in the week prior to March 9. In April, areas of the building were sufficiently complete to allow the Department of Public Grounds and Buildings and the Department of Public Instruction to move into the structure. On May 5, 1904, the cornerstone of the building was laid at a ceremony which, unlike the Capitol's groundbreaking, drew a large crowd.[19]

1906

The PA Department of Health records vital statistics, such as births and deaths, for the first time. The state's population at the time is 7,133,500 people.

The Pennsylvania Elks State Association is founded in Philadelphia.

More than 500,000 coal miners walked off their jobs seeking higher wages. The American Federation of Labor met with President Roosevelt demanding an eight hour workday.

Mt. Vesuvius erupts in Italy.

A major earthquake estimated at a magnitude of nearly 8.0 decimates the city of San Francisco killing from 700 to 3,000 people.

CHAPTER THREE • *The Huston Capitol: Inspiration, Design, & Construction*

I·N·S·I·G·H·T

1904 Labor Union Protests

Merritt and Company 1024–1030 Ridge Avenue, Philadelphia was one of the "Associated Expanded Metal Companies," which manufactured products sold by the individual member companies. Merritt furnished and installed the steel lath throughout the Capitol. The firm was considered by organized labor to be a nonunion firm and was one of the subjects of the labor union protests of 1904.[20]

David A. MacGregor and Brother of 212 South 13th Street, Philadelphia was a family firm of decorators who supplied glass and performed decorating work and painting under subcontracts both to Payne and Company and with John S. Sanderson. Considered an "old established firm," according to a Capitol handbook of 1906, the company had previously traded under the name of D. R. MacGregor and Sons, when the artist, Donald R. MacGregor, managed it. Two sons, David A. and Norman R., joined him in the business, and shortly after 1901, the name of the firm was changed. Announcement in June 1904 of the company's contract to decorate the Capitol provoked a labor dispute, due to its reputation among organized labor as an anti-union firm.[21] ϕ

Workers begin the arch that will support a small dome on a wing of the Capitol when complete, 1904.

Joseph Huston poses for the camera while inspecting construction progress, 1903.

Pennypacker, Huston, and Payne were all present, and each delivered several short speeches. The stone was placed at an area to the right of the main entrance portico. Numerous state documents, several Pennsylvania newspapers, a copy of Penn's *No Cross, No Crown*, coins of the period, and a Saint Louis Exposition silver dollar were all placed in a bronze box, which was laid in the stone. Governor Pennypacker, Huston, and Payne then each ceremoniously cemented on the capstone and workmen lowered it into place.

Prior to the laying of the cornerstone, Huston had been making numerous drawings for decorative work, lighting fixtures, metal filing cases, and improvements for Capitol Park. Bids for the special furnishings contract were opened on June 7, 1904, and Philadelphian John H. Sanderson presented the lowest bid and was subsequently awarded the contract.

During the summer and autumn of 1904 attention turned to getting the building sufficiently completed for the upcoming legislative session starting in January 1905. Huston assured the Commission and the governor that the rooms would be ready on time. However, as the construction progressed, it became evident that the chambers and meeting rooms would not be finished at the very beginning of the session, due to back orders of supplies. The *Harrisburg Telegraph* reported that the legislature would meet on January 3, 1905, adjourn until January 15, when it would elect a U.S. Senator, and then reconvene in the middle of February.

CHAPTER THREE • *The Huston Capitol: Inspiration, Design, & Construction*

Literature in Stone: The Hundred Year History of the Pennsylvania State Capitol

Huston Capitol
CONSTRUCTION 1•9•0•4

1. Scaffold lifts workers to proceed in setting mortar for the porticoes of the building despite harsh weather condions.
2. A granite column is set into place.
3. Henry-Bonnard Bronze Company light standard awaits placement in the Governor's Reception Room.
4. Eugene Aucaigne of the Henry Bonnard Bronze Company stands alongside a light standard for the Capitol's main entrance.
5. The 1905 skyline of Harrisburg from one of the smaller wing domes.

THIS PAGE: *Front west facade of the Capitol during its construction in 1905.*

Deaths During Construction

IN MEMORIAM:

William Campbell, mason's helper
Lucas A. Hoelle, laborer
George Johnson, laborer
Meyer Kauffman, roof tiler
Albert Lyter, steel setter
Owen Roberts, superintendent

Six fatal accidents and an unknown number of worker injuries occurred while the Capitol was under construction. The first took place on May 25, 1903, when Owen Roberts, the Capitol construction superintendent for Payne & Company, was killed when a large piece of terra cotta fell on his head, fracturing his skull. The accident occurred "at the very outset of the work," when workmen were "tearing out" the Cobb Capitol as part of the Capitol's transformation.[22]

On January 9, 1904 the *Harrisburg Independent* reported the death of William Campbell, a mason's helper, due to an accident on the job. Although the nature of his accident is not clear, Campbell's death led to a belated recognition of the danger inherent in the bricklaying and granite setting for the Capitol. The dangerous combination of high winds and the height of the dome had proven to be hazardous during the bricklaying process for the dome. Many construction delays and interruptions were attributed to bad weather.[23]

On September 10, 1904 several laborers were injured when a scaffold in the rotunda collapsed and fell twenty-seven feet to a hard wooden floor. The workers were hauling a 1,000-pound girder

from the Senate Chamber on the second floor across a heavy frame scaffold to a crane that would lower it to the first floor. The scaffold collapsed under the weight. The workers were pulled from the mass of broken timbers with three of the men in serious condition. George Johnson, a African-American laborer from Harrisburg, died as a result of the accident.

On April 12, 1904 steel setter Albert Lyter, of Philadelphia, fell to his death while working with an iron girder in the northern wing of the Capitol.[24] Again in November 1904, laborer Lucas A. Hoelle was killed when he fell twenty-six feet through an opening in the Senate floor. In August 1905, Meyer Kauffman of Pittsburgh, was preparing to tile the inside of the dome when he fell through an empty elevator shaft that was to hoist him to the base of the dome.

The Final Count: Although the deaths of these men were mourned within the Capitol community and beyond, the six fatal accidents during the Capitol's

construction were considered to be "the smallest number of accidents that ever happened on the erection of a building the size of the Capitol."[25] Builders at the time ordinarily estimated one worker fatality for each $200 thousand of contract price. According to this scenario, an estimated eighteen deaths could have been anticipated during the Capitol's construction.[26]

THIS PAGE: *Top, A worker straddles metal rafters that will support the new structure; Bottom, Two laborers pause from granite work atop the Capitol dome.*

OPPOSITE PAGE: *Two workers sit atop the Capitol's enormous dome ribs.*

Left, George Payne and Stanford Lewis talk amidst the construction site, 1905; Right, The cornerstone laying ceremony held on May 5, 1904.

BIDS for the SPECIAL FURNISHINGS CONTRACT were opened on June 7, 1904, **and Philadelphian JOHN H. SANDERSON…was** subsequently **awarded the contract.**

On October 5, 1904 the Board of Commissioners of Public Grounds and Buildings awarded a contract for the completion of the Capitol's fifth floor or attic. Five new departments of state government were to be created under the 1903 and 1905 sessions, and none of these were reflected in Huston's original plans. Huston was issued a change order for the attic design and engineering work. The construction contract was awarded to Payne and Company and their subcontractors. This additional contract would also extend the completion date for the Capitol. The problem that arose for Joseph Huston was that he had to set up walls with doors to allow the large turnbuckles for the House and Senate chandeliers, weighing three to four tons apiece, to be solidly attached to the beams above the attic.

The addition of a 6th or "attic" floor also created a design change for Joseph Huston. He had originally designed a large stained glass dome in the center of the House Chamber to help illuminate the large room with exterior light. The floor above the chamber meant that his dome had to be eliminated. This left a twenty-four-foot circular void in the center of the room. Huston, in turn, wired Edwin Austin Abbey in England and asked if he could produce an additional mural to fill this

Commonwealth
ATOP THE CAPITOL DOME

Top, Workers set the bronze Commonwealth statue into place atop the dome in May of 1905; Inset, A closeup of the statue; Bottom, Coins placed underneath the statue during its installation.

CHAPTER THREE • *The Huston Capitol: Inspiration, Design, & Construction*

I·N·S·I·G·H·T
Samuel Rambo
Construction Supervisor

Samuel Rambo (1863–1930) was trained as a carpenter and served as superintendent of Capitol construction for George F. Payne and Company from 1903 until the completion of the Capitol in 1906. Afterwards, he made a career for himself as a respected member of the Commonwealth government. Rambo was a native of Elkton, Maryland and served an apprenticeship with a carpenter in Wilmington, Delaware. In 1884, at the age of twenty-one, he moved to Philadelphia and began employment with George F. Payne and Company. During the summer of 1903, Payne named Rambo to be superintendent of construction for the Capitol, replacing Owen Roberts who had been killed in an accident on the job.

In February 1907 Governor Edwin S. Stuart appointed him to succeed James M. Shumaker as Superintendent of Public Grounds and Buildings, a position he would hold for a decade. Later that year, Rambo served as a key witness during the hearings of the Capitol Investigation Commission. As superintendent, he successfully oversaw the first Capitol Park extension from 1911 to 1916. In 1915 Rambo, together with Harrisburg architect Charles A. Keyworth, proposed the enlargement of the Capitol in an extension eastward which would have doubled its size, but his plan was rejected. Rambo was appointed Deputy Secretary of the Department of Property and Supplies in 1923 and served in that capacity until his resignation in 1919. During the course of his final governmental tenure, he collected extensive files documenting both the Capitol's construction and its artwork.[28] φ

THIS PAGE: *Capitol Grounds, 1917; Inset, Samuel Rambo, ca. 1906.*

space on the ceiling. The concept that Abbey developed was the *Hours* mural that was placed on the House Chamber ceiling.

The work on the Capitol's second through fourth floor areas would largely cease during the legislative session of 1905, but in May the Department of Public Grounds and Buildings and the Department of Public Instruction were already housed in their permanent offices on the Entresol Floor, and the Adjutant General's Department was expected to be in by summer. Also in May the statue of *Commonwealth* was hoisted onto the top of the nearly completed dome. One of the workers present on that day in May placed three Indian Head pennies under the base of the statue.[27]

"THE WORK of the Capitol Building Commission IS AT AN END so far as entering into any more contracts is concerned."

By summer the Capitol Building Commission began to look forward to the completion of the building, and Huston assured them that construction was progressing as fast as possible. Huston, Payne, and Wetter (Payne's partner) disagreed about the exact date. Wetter claimed the building would be done by November 1, but Huston reported on September 11 that the building would not be done until January 1, 1906, the date that was stipulated in the original legislation. Former Governor Stone raised the subject of the penalty clause, which provided that the Commonwealth could reclaim $250 per day that Payne was over schedule. As the dome neared completion, it appeared to most everyone that the Capitol really would be completed by its due date of January 1, and at every meeting of the Commission the question was raised as to when the building would be done. It became obvious to Huston, and no doubt to Payne and Wetter, that the building, though mostly finished, would not be one hundred percent complete by January 1, 1906.

Huston issued the opinion that Payne and Company not be charged the $250 per day for not meeting the deadline, but suggested instead the state retain the contractor and withhold $75 thousand until all the work in the Capitol was complete. Although the Capitol Building Commission was by law scheduled to be abolished on January 1, Attorney General Hampton L. Carson stated that they could still meet to settle bills and expenditures, and also because the building was not fully complete. The Commission would continue to meet until the building was officially accepted by the Commonwealth in August 1906.

1906

Standard Oil Company is charged with stifling competition through intrigue and trickery.

France accepts a loan of $50 million from Pennsylvania railroads.

Harry K. Thaw is arrested for the fatal shooting of New York architect Stanford White. The shooting centered around Thaw's wife, White's former lover, Florence Evelyn Nesbit.

The first Pure Food and Drug Act becomes law largely because of Upton Sinclair's book, The Jungle, which exposed the filthy conditions of Chicago's meat packing houses.

Captain Alfred Dreyfus receives the Legion of Honor for his wrongful imprisonment on Devil's Island in the South Atlantic.

An earthquake in Chile kills 5,000 people and injures thousands more.

The interior of the House Chamber was temporarily setup for members to hold session during construction in 1905.

CHAPTER THREE • *The Huston Capitol: Inspiration, Design, & Construction*

1906

The Chicago White Sox beat the Chicago Cubs in the World Series after 6 games.

Pierre Samuel du Pont begins the creation of Longwood Gardens by saving an arboretum of trees near Philadelphia.

President Roosevelt returns to Washington after surveying progress at the Panama Canal.

The Building Commission took possession of the building and formally accepted the new Capitol in the name of the Commonwealth of Pennsylvania.

Late in 1905 Governor Pennypacker called for a special session in January of 1906, which further delayed the full completion of the building, especially since the majority of the work was on the interior. In actuality, the completion of the building would drag on well into 1906. As late as July 20, Bernard Green still found workmen laying wood floors in the House and Senate Chambers.

Huston presented his final certificate of July 27, 1906, to the Commission for approval. The Commission met for the last time on August 15, 1906, and accepted Huston's certificate. The Commission further resolved:

> *Whereas, the Architect and the Engineer have certified to the Capitol Building Commission that the Capitol Building is completed. Therefore, be it resolved, that the Board of Public Grounds and Buildings be notified of this fact and that it be requested to assume entire charge, custody and control of the building until the formal transfer to the Governor at the dedicatory ceremonies in October 1906, and that the Capitol Building Commission be relieved from all further responsibility in the custody and control of the building.[29]*

With this measure, the Commission took possession of the building from Payne and Company and formally accepted the new Capitol in the name of the Commonwealth of Pennsylvania.

THIS PAGE: *The unfinished Capitol as it appreared in late 1905.*

OPPOSITE PAGE: *Portrait of Joseph M. Huston, by Horace W. Snyder, ca. 1930s.*

CHAPTER THREE • *The Huston Capitol: Inspiration, Design, & Construction*

President Roosevelt speaks at the Capitol's dedication, 1906.

CHAPTER FOUR

Capitol Dedication: October 4, 1906

THE excitement was almost tangible throughout Harrisburg, as preparations were finalized and dedication day grew closer. The exterior of the Capitol building had been complete since late 1905, but the special legislative session in 1906 had pushed the dedication date back to Thursday October 4, 1906. Final arrangements for the entertainment of Harrisburg's numerous guests were made at a meeting of Harrisburg's General Committee at the Board of Trade on the Tuesday preceding the dedication. The various committees made their reports to the General Committee and from all indications, Thursday's celebration promised to be the most successful ever hosted by the city of Harrisburg.

Requests had been issued to the railroad companies serving the city asking that special excursion trains carry the crowds to and from Harrisburg for the ceremonies. The Transportation Committee made arrangements with the Pennsylvania, Northern Central, Reading, and Cumberland Valley railroads to run special trains out of Harrisburg to all points starting at 10:30 A.M. and continuing until the crowds had dispersed. Excursions were run from all points in the state and orders called for all special trains to leave their various starting points in time to arrive in the city at or before 10:30 A.M. on Dedication Day. In the evening special trains, large enough to handle the massive crowds, were scheduled to leave the city at 10:30 P.M.. The Reading Railroad had promised to run a train long enough to accommodate all of its patrons as far as Norristown, while the

Pennsylvania, Northern Central, and Cumberland Valley railroads had offered to run as many special trains as necessary to get the visitors from Harrisburg back to their homes or to temporary lodging outside of the city.[1]

Harrisburg's Publicity Committee, chaired by local resident J. Horace McFarland, reported that 35,000 brochures outlining points of interest in Harrisburg and the program of the day's events had been printed and would be distributed to the visitors by special guides. These brochures gave details of the events of the day, the program for the dedicatory ceremonies, fireworks, and every other important feature that was planned over the course of the day. Traction companies had even included trolley schedules making the brochure an invaluable guide for out-of-town visitors.

A committee of approximately four hundred men was selected from fraternal societies in the city to distribute these brochures and to direct the visitors who would visit the city during the day. Each guide wore the button or emblem of his order and a handsome badge furnished by the Publicity Committee. Each was instructed to take special care in showing visitors around the city.

Refreshments and food for the visitors during the day had been carefully planned and the General Committee had asked all hotels and boarding houses to make special preparations for hasty lunches and quick meals. The ladies of the Sacred Heart Catholic Church secured the large room formerly occupied by C. S. Weakley and Company on Market Square and prepared to serve meals and quick lunches for thousands of visitors during the afternoon. Eating places were opened throughout the city and everything possible was done to make the trip to Harrisburg a memorable one for all the visitors.

The Music Committee, through its chairman John Fox Weiss, planned a concert on the eve of Dedication Day to entertain the thousands of visitors who would likely be in the city at that time. The Commonwealth Band was scheduled to play

I·N·S·I·G·H·T

Dedication Reception Committee Badge

Special Souvenirs: Each member of the Reception committee wore a handsome souvenir badge suspended from the buttonhole of the left lapel of his coat for the Capitol dedication. These badges were duplicates of the solid gold one presented to President Roosevelt by Governor Pennypacker on behalf of the state.

The Fob: The badge was a silk trimmed watch fob, which is a decorative ornament designed to hang on a vest pocket. The charm, a circle of gold about the size of a half-dollar, dangled from a ring. The obverse illustrates the Capitol in bas relief with this inscription: Harrisburg, Oct. 4th, 1906. The reverse is charged with the coat of arms of the Commonwealth, also in bas relief with "Dedicatory Ceremonies" on the border. In addition to being equipped with the catch for a watch, the fobs had a button at the top, the intention being for them to be worn from the lapel during the ceremonies, after which the button could easily be detached and the ornament used as a fob. The badge made one of the handsomest souvenirs of the day. President Roosevelt's medal was made of solid gold, while other dignitaries were gold-plated. All the medals for the occasion were produced by Dreka of Philadelphia.[2] φ

THIS PAGE: *Dreka Medal, 1906.*

OPPOSITE PAGE: *Reproduction of the railroad broadside advertising excursion trains traveling to the Capitol to view Violet Oakley's murals, 1906.*

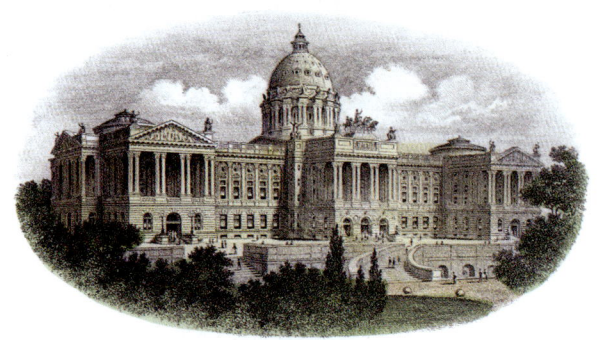

*The Governor of the Commonwealth
and the
Dedication Commission
request the honour of your presence at the
Dedicatory Ceremonies of the Capitol of Pennsylvania
in Harrisburg
on Thursday the fourth of October
nineteen hundred and six*

Thomas J. Lynch
Thomas M. Jones
Secretaries
Harrisburg, Pa.

Samuel W. Pennypacker Governor
William C. Sproul   Henry F. Walton
John E. Fox   William P. Snyder
         William H. Berry
         Dedication Commission

THIS PAGE: *Top, Grandstand tickets for the big event, 1906; Bottom, The Grand Opera House welcomes the Capitol dedication, 1906.*

OPPOSITE PAGE: *Top, Harrisburg festooned, ca. 1906; Bottom, Capitol Dedication Invitation, 1906.*

beneath the Venetian canopy on Market Square between the hours of seven and ten thirty.

Probably the best news came from the Finance Committee. William Jennings, chairman of the committee, reported that Harrisburg residents had responded generously to the call for contributions to meet the expenses incurred for the city's celebration ceremonies and that enough money had been pledged to cover all the expenses so far incurred by all of the special committees.

During this meeting, Harrisburg's Mayor Edward Z. Gross expressed his concern that he had secured all the rope that Philadelphia could send, but the city was still ten thousand feet short of the amount needed to adequately rope off all the streets, which had to be kept clear during President Roosevelt's tour through the city. To meet the emergency, Mayor Gross had to order an additional ten thousand feet of rope to be used during Dedication Day; he justified the additional expenditure by explaining that he would save it for other police purposes afterwards.[3]

Prominent African-American citizens organized the Colored Citizens' Reception Committee for the purpose of entertaining the hundreds of African-Americans who would come to Harrisburg for the dedication. Charles H. Thompson, chairman of the committee consisting of over one hundred people, had secured the Chestnut Street Hall for entertainment purposes. The hall would be opened for visitors at 1:00 P.M. on Thursday afternoon and all visitors were received and entertained until 2:00 A.M. Friday

CHAPTER FOUR • *Capitol Dedication: October 4, 1906*

Literature in Stone: The Hundred Year History of the Pennsylvania State Capitol

morning. There would be music by the symphony orchestra and lunch was to be served to all who cared to take their meals at the hall.

Not only was the new Capitol building sparkling, but so was the city of Harrisburg. The city was in gala dress and most of the businesses were covered with red, white, and blue bunting. Decorators had been working hard and their labors were almost finished. Even the streets were in the finest condition for this special event. All over the city, mortar beds, and other impediments were removed from the streets under orders from Harrisburg's Building Inspector Ferree and Highway Commissioner Lynch. Paving companies had made necessary repairs and a large work force of men, under orders from Commissioner Lynch, swabbed down the asphalt streets with long hoses and sprayers. A group of men with brooms followed the nozzles, scrubbing the asphalt until it gleamed.

Those residents in the vicinity of Third and State Streets, in entrepreneurial spirit, took the opportunity to cash in on their fortunate location. One merchant, who had a store at the corner of these streets, in the Brady House directly opposite the grandstand, prepared three tiers of seats. He offered seats on the lower tier, just a little above the level of the sidewalk, at $5 per person, with seats on the higher tiers costing $10 apiece. Seats on the balcony of the building were also sold at $10 each.[4]

While the fireworks would be the principal attraction along the riverfront on the evening following the dedication, much of the beauty of the scene would be due to the number of boats on the water. Great plans were made for a light show on the Susquehanna called "Lights on the Water." Rivermen had rented all their rowboats weeks in advance and a hundred or more canoes were expected to be afloat. Steam tugboats had been reserved to transport eager viewers with their chairs to the sand flats in the river shortly before the fireworks started. Some of these boats had been chartered for the entertainment of private parties and others would provide public transportation at nominal sums. Every person with a boat was encouraged to

INSIDE THE CAPITOL
DEDICATION 1•9•0•6

A. ROOM 184: Health Department.
B. ROOM 187: Department of Public Buildings and Grounds.
C. ROOM 640: Highway Department Drafting Room.
D. ROOM 353: Dairy and Food Bureau.

THIS PAGE: *Top, Dreka dedication ribbon pin; Bottom left, Mirror Capitol souvenir; Bottom right, Metal souvenir pin; All souvenirs ca. 1906.*

CHAPTER FOUR • *Capitol Dedication: October 4, 1906*

Capitol Park looked like a dreamland, with colored arrangements of orange globe lanterns and colored cups containing candles. **They were strung all over the park, hidden in flower beds, festooned from the monuments,** fastened to the big palm vases, and placed on the buttresses in front of the Capitol. **Soon after, all of the lights in the new Capitol building were ablaze. Harrisburg had never hosted such a gala affair…**

decorate his craft with some type of light so that the reflection on the water would add beauty and life to the scene. Harrisburg was duly prepared for the onslaught of visitors expected for Dedication Day.

Part II: Dedication Eve

They packed Market Street and Market Square; they filed down Third and Fourth Streets and flocked all of Front Street. State Street was one continuous mass of curious people, all streaming toward one common destination—the glistening new Capitol building. Visitors began pouring into the city for the celebration on the Wednesday before the dedication. Suppers were hastily finished and people began to flock from all parts of the city and from the suburbs toward the imposing dome of the State Capitol. Barely had dusk settled into night before the dome was illuminated.[5]

Every car, open or closed, of the Central Pennsylvania Traction Company was put into service with cars running over the principal city and Steelton lines at all hours. A new powerhouse had been running for several weeks and all the power the company could command was turned out for Dedication Day. Extra cars were placed on the principal city routes as necessity required and the schedule of the suburban cars was changed so that cars would run at much shorter intervals.

The dome was lighted, but many of the departments of the building were still

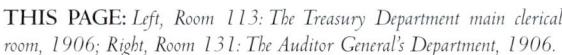

THIS PAGE: *Left, Room 113: The Treasury Department main clerical room, 1906; Right, Room 131: The Auditor General's Department, 1906.*

OPPOSITE PAGE: *Capitol postcard, ca. 1906.*

N 43 Pennsylvania State Capitol, Harrisburg, Pa.

locked. In an effort to placate the disappointed crowd, estimated at around 5,000 people, State Treasurer Berry and Auditor General Snyder opened up their departments to allow the throngs to stream through. Several other areas of the building were open and there was no attempt made to keep visitors out. The doors were merely propped open and the sightseers allowed to stream in one door and out the other at will.[6]

Trolley cars ran to Hummelstown every half-hour, or every fifteen minutes as the crowds demanded, with the last car scheduled to Market Square at midnight. The same schedule was provided for both Middletown and Rockville, with a half-hour schedule provided for Linglestown. All-night trolley service was provided for various parts of Harrisburg. Every half hour a car left the central part of the city for Allison Hill, Fourth or Sixth Streets by way of Second, going as far as Emerald Street. An all-night system also went into effect to and from Steelton. Cars ran once an hour after midnight, leaving Market Square on the hour.[7]

The congestion to the entrances of the Capitol was at times dangerous. Crowded conditions existed when many visitors wanted to get out and just as many wanted to get in. Fortunately, there were no reports of injuries throughout the evening.[8]

Meanwhile, down on Market Square, visitors mingled and waited in anticipation of the band concert. The Venetian Canopy, designed by architect Huston, had been completed only the day before and the visitors were eager for the illumination long before twilight. Approximately six hundred small electric lights, with two hundred of those lights situated on the bell at the top, decorated the temporary structure. The canopy was unique, for nothing like it had ever before, or since, been utilized in the decoration of Harrisburg.[9]

The canopy and the festoons of lights in the square and along the second block of Market Street were turned on at 6:30 P.M. and soon after that the other festoons throughout the city were lighted. Between eight and nine thousand lights on the festoons along

CHAPTER FOUR • *Capitol Dedication: October 4, 1906*

HOUSE OF REPRESENTATIVES

1. Justice, *Stained glass window by William Brantley Van Ingen.*
2. Abundance, *Stained glass window.*
3. Bronze Light Standard, *1906.*
4. House Chamber showing gallery, *1906.*
5. House Ceiling, *1906.*
6. Commerce, *Stained glass window.*

the streets added to the magical effect. Private persons and business firms had erected decorations of their own, which in some cases included electric lights.[10]

A few minutes after the clock had stuck seven, the searchlights on the Union Trust, the Mt. Pleasant Press building, and Allison Hill began to flash ribbons of light across the city that added to the excitement until midnight. Workmen attended to the task of lighting the candles in the fairy lamps and lanterns in Capitol Park and on the State Street grass plots. Capitol Park looked like a dreamland, with colored arrangements of orange globe lanterns and colored cups containing candles. They were strung all over the park, hidden in flower beds, festooned from the monuments, fastened to the big palm vases, and placed on the buttresses in front of the Capitol. Soon after, all of the lights in the new Capitol building were ablaze. Harrisburg had never hosted such a gala affair before.[11]

The decorating of the grandstand was finished at midnight. Sections were lettered and the seats numbered. As *The Star Independent*, one of Harrisburg's daily newspapers, reported, "The legislative committee on decorations, with a stubbornness that cannot be accounted for, insisted that a stairway be erected in the rear of the stand, as they considered that it would be undignified for their august personages to take seats on

THIS PAGE: *Capitol facade and grandstand at the dedication, 1906.*

OPPOSITE PAGE: *House Chamber, 1906.*

CHAPTER FOUR • *Capitol Dedication: October 4, 1906*

I·N·S·I·G·H·T

Edward Klingerman
Dedication Fatality

Edward Klingerman of Tamaqua was thirty-two years of age when he visited Harrisburg to witness the festivities in connection with the dedication of the Capitol. He was watching the dedication day parade and while standing under a small balcony over a doorway of a house on Sixth near Briggs Streets, a large stone from the balcony dislodged and fell on him. The stone weighed about 150 pounds and the man's skull was fractured. Klingerman was taken into a nearby doctor's office and after temporary aid had been rendered he was removed to the Harrisburg Hospital, where it was found that the fracture was more serious than at first suspected. Klingerman never regained consciousness and died on October 7, 1906.[12] Of the large crowd visiting Harrisburg during dedication, Klingerman's was the only reported fatality—a tragic and truly odd circumstance. φ

Dedication grandstand during speeches, 1906.

Handbook of the Capitol
By Charles H. Caffin

Originally printed in 1906 when the Capitol was first presented to the public, this helpful handbook guided guests around the building while highlighting the charms of the elaborate architecture and artwork.

Author Charles H. Caffin sought to bring people to a higher understanding of the building's purpose and the ideals that it embodied. The handbook includes photographs, floorplans, and extremely detailed descriptions of the Capitol enabling it to remain one of the best resources available on the architecture of the state building.

A. Special leather-bound copy of the handbook made for Governor Pennypacker.
B. Original cover for the handbook.
C. Inscription from Architect Joseph M. Huston taken from inside cover of Governor Pennypacker's handbook.
D. Sample pages from inside the original handbook.

CHAPTER FOUR • *Capitol Dedication: October 4, 1906*

THIS PAGE: *A military troop marches through Harrisburg in honor of the Capitol's dedication, October 4, 1906.*

OPPOSITE PAGE: *Souvenir minature German stein bearing the words "New Pennsylvania Capitol, Harrisburg, PA, 1906."*

the grandstand through the regular passageway. It made a whole lot of extra work and expense and men had to labor until far into the night to accommodate their royal highnesses."[13]

And so Harrisburg was ready for the big day. Many people had gotten a sneak peak of the cause of celebration and their enthusiasm was contagious. Everyone looked forward to a beautifully sunny October day, with the autumn hues complementing the statuesque building that they came to dedicate. Unfortunately, Mother Nature had other plans.

Part III: Dedication Day

Forecasters had predicted a clear October day for the dedication. Rain had not fallen on October 4 during the past seven years and everyone hoped that this tradition would continue, but rain began falling at approximately 2:00 A.M. Sightseers who had remained on the streets late Wednesday evening watched as the moon, which had shone brightly between the clouds during the evening, became obscured. Around midnight the moon was completely covered by the gathering clouds.[14]

And so dedication day dawned with a rainy forecast. Instead of the bright sunshine of the day before, the skies provided a penetrating rain. The downpour kept up until after daybreak, but ceased about 8:00 A.M. This was considered a hopeful sign but the respite was brief, and the rain soon began at a steady rate once more. The decorations in Capitol Park were wind-torn and water-soaked. And yet, despite the dampness of the day and the tri-colored drops that were dripping from the bunting on the buildings, nothing could dampen the spirits of those who came to see the new Capitol building.

From 9:00 A.M. on there was a continual hustling of the sightseers as all sought the place which, to his or her particular mind, offered the best advantages for witnessing the arrival of the President and subsequent events on the program. Railroad cars and trolleys brought visitors to Harrisburg and all of the regular and special cars were crowded to capacity.[15]

> **Despite the dampness of the day** and the tri-colored drops that were dripping from the bunting on the buildings, nothing could dampen the spirits of those who came to see the new Capitol building.

Stationary awnings offered shelter from the rain and crowds were under these at all times. All of the souvenir shops did a booming business, profiting by the sales of both souvenirs and umbrellas. The rain also drove from the streets those souvenir peddlers who had eluded the police and were crying their wares along the curb.[16] The business establishments in Harrisburg had closed their offices from 10:30 A.M. to 3:00 P.M. to assure that no one would miss the festivities.

Harrisburg's Chief of Police Joseph B. Hutchison was on the alert, mounted on a dapple-gray steed moving through the crowds, seeing that his own men and the newly created State Police were maintaining

CHAPTER FOUR • *Capitol Dedication: October 4, 1906*

adequate crowd control. The city police department had completed all arrangements for handling the great crowds, clearing the streets and guarding the public against pickpockets and crooks.[17]

At 10:00 A.M. the Capitol Building Commission, the Capitol Dedication Commission, and Justices of the Supreme Court, with other distinguished citizens met in the Governor's office, where the members of the two commissions were given the handsome memorial medals to adorn the lapels of their coats. The good humor and suppressed excitement of the day was not reserved just for visitors out on the street. A half-hour later, members of the Dedication Commission left in horse-drawn carriages for the train station. They drove down Fourth Street to Market, to the railroad station where they prepared to meet the orator of the day—President Theodore Roosevelt.

The crowd within the train station was filled with people who were eager to catch a glimpse of the nation's Chief Executive at the earliest possible moment. Presidential security was tight with Secret Service agents scattered among the crowds at the station and in other parts of the city. A few of these men wore official looking badges on their left breast, but most of them were without any distinguishing marks. Crowd control utilized the most modern technology—ropes. A rope ran down the north side of Market Street, crossed the street at Aberdeen Alley, and was secured at the Hotel Russ. The rope on the opposite side of Market Street turned in toward the entrance to Union Station plaza. Another rope was stretched in the middle of the plaza, from the wall of the station over to the fence at Grace Alley. This gave access to the station from Market Street and all other points through the two alleys. Vigilant police kept the crowds from surging through the entrance and into the plaza.[18]

While the eager crowd was waiting, a loud boom came from the arsenal at 18TH and Herr Streets. At 10:18 A.M. the first of twenty-one guns constituting a presidential salute, boomed out at the arsenal. The whole city and countryside within earshot knew that Theodore Roosevelt's train was nearing Harrisburg.

Barely had the salute been finished when the Presidential Special came steaming up Mulberry Street and around the curve into the station. When the special train had first entered the station, a State Police bugler had drawn all of his comrades to "Attention!" with one sharp blast on his bugle.[19] The chimes of Zion Lutheran Church began to ring *America* and then *The Star Spangled Banner,* under the operation of Ed Kepner.

Governor Pennypacker was the first man to climb the steps of the railroad car to meet the President. All of the committeemen, attired in conventional dress for men on such ceremonial occasions—light trousers, frock coat, and silk hat—entered the car and there was a brief informal reception with introductions all around. Governor Pennypacker presented President Roosevelt with the gold medal that the state had made for him. Mayor Edward Gross, representing

THIS PAGE: *Left, Sheet music for* The Star Spangled Banner *by Francis S. Key; Right, Train engine pulling President Roosevelt's special train, ca. 1903.*

OPPOSITE PAGE: *Top, Ribboned badge worn by a member of the Dedicatory Committee, 1906; Bottom, Ribbon souvenir pin, ca. 1906.*

the city, presented him with the solid gold medal that the Citizens' Committee had cast especially for him.[20]

When Roosevelt disembarked from his train car, the crowd began to cheer all through the crowded station and along the passageway to the waiting carriages. The President with his unshakable nerve and energetic verve made his way through the railroad station, rain hat in hand, bowing and smiling to the cheering thousands. Crowds had gathered at the ropes along the streets that were to be traversed by the Presidential cortège.[21] As a result, the distinguished visitor saw nothing but a seemingly endless mass of cheering Pennsylvanians.

Governor Pennypacker led the way to the new Capitol, where he hosted a hurried inspection of the

CHAPTER FOUR • *Capitol Dedication: October 4, 1906*

Senate of Pennsylvania

1. *Architecture,* Stained glass window by William Brantley Van Ingen.
2. *Senate Chamber,* 1906.
3. *Senate Ceiling,* 1906.
4. *Railroads,* Stained glass window.
5. *Glass Blowing,* Stained glass window.

THIS PAGE: *The dedication grandstand during President Roosevelt's speech, 1906.*

OPPOSITE PAGE: *Top, Capitol souvenir plate, ca. 1906; Bottom, Governor Samuel Pennypacker portrait, Governor's Office.*

"This is the handsomest state capitol I have ever seen," said President Roosevelt, "and I don't believe there is a finer on earth."

building. The President visited the Governor's office, the legislative chambers of the Senate and the House, and witnessed the beauty of the building and the handsome decorations. Roosevelt personally congratulated architect Joseph Huston on the splendid edifice he had designed and successfully carried to a finish. The President found all of the clerks and state employees at work in the several departments for it was not an official state holiday. Roosevelt's admiration was boundless and he proclaimed the new Capitol "the handsomest state capitol I have ever seen."[22]

In the meantime, the water-soaked First Brigade Band was performing in front of the Capitol. They had started off with the *Washington Post March* with the rain pattering down on their faces and running in little streams down their collars. A great crowd had gathered in the vicinity of the grandstand in front of the Capitol as eleven o'clock drew near. By eleven, when the ceremonies were scheduled to begin, every possible vantage point was crowded with human beings. Roofs, windows, trees, even the rim of the great dome of the Capitol itself had its quota, as seen in numerous photographs of the ceremonies.[23]

The band had persevered for forty-five minutes in the rain when they were finally able to play the inspiring notes of *Hail to the Chief* announcing that the guest orators for the dedication were about to take center stage. As the band played a patriotic anthem,[24] Governor Pennypacker, as president of the dedication committee, stood up and motioned with his hand for silence.

John H. Dillingham, a member of the Society of Friends or Quakers, read the scriptures. He was a modest gentleman, dressed with no sign of ostentation. He addressed the crowd:

I will read brief selections from the Holy Scriptures, trusting that it is in the heart of not a few of us in coming here, to dedicate both in this temple of government, and in our bodies as temples of the Holy Spirit, only whatsoever things are honorable, whatsoever things are just, whatsoever things are pure, whatsoever things are lovely, whatsoever things are of good report; if there be any virtue, and if there be any praise, and to think of these things."[25]

Governor Pennypacker introduced former Governor William A. Stone, president of the Capitol Building Commission. Stone held the gold key of the Capitol presented by architect Huston. Governor Stone spoke briefly about the 1901 Act of Assembly, which appropriated four million dollars for the removal of the old state buildings and the construction of the new, the plan for choosing an architect, the architectural competition, the execution of the contracts, the Capitol Commission, and the payments made. He ended with the following words:

This occasion does not justify me in making any extended remarks. Having briefly made a report of our work, my mission is now ended. And now, in behalf of the Commission, I tender to you, sir, as Governor of the State, the building, and hope that it will not only meet with your approval, but with the approval of all the people of our State.[26]

Governor Pennypacker received the Capitol and accepted the key on behalf of the Commonwealth, and addressed the crowd. Pennypacker concluded his dedicatory oration with the following statement: "On behalf of the Commonwealth, as its Chief Executive, I accept this Capitol and now, with pride, with faith, and with hope, I dedicate it to the public use and to the purposes for which it was designed and constructed." Governor Pennypacker's voice carried fairly well and he received warm applause. As he finished and turned to present President Roosevelt, the vast audience gave him absolute

CHAPTER FOUR • *Capitol Dedication: October 4, 1906*

Literature in Stone: The Hundred Year History of the Pennsylvania State Capitol

Inside the Capitol

DEDICATION 1•9•0•6

A. ROOM 224: Governor's Private Office.
B. ROOM 229: Governor's Reception Room.
C. ROOM 202: Lieutenant Governor's Reception Room.
D. ROOM 200: Lieutenant Governor's Private Office.

CHAPTER FOUR • *Capitol Dedication: October 4, 1906*

I·N·S·I·G·H·T
President & Roosevelt the Dedication

Riding Into Harrisburg: Senators Penrose and Knox accompanied President Roosevelt from Washington on his special train. As they came into Harrisburg, President Roosevelt performed one of those gracious acts which went so far to endear him with lighthearted men. The President had been informed that lying in the hospital just outside the city were two boys who were crying their hearts out because broken limbs had laid them up and prevented them from seeing the President. One of them was Ralph Hartzell, son of Rev. Dr. Hartzell, of the Factory Inspector's office. The other was six-year-old Hale Jenkins. "Have them near a window and I will see if they can't get a look at me," was the word the President sent when he heard of the plight of the two little boys. As the train passed the hospital the President went out on the rear platform in a driving rain to make a military salute to the little sufferers.[27] President Roosevelt showed his love for children during the dedicatory ceremony when he saw Speaker Walton's little grandsons on the grandstand, and was told who they were. "Tell them to come down here," he remarked, and when the two little fellows heard this, they were delighted. They clambered over the rail and in a moment were both hanging on to the President's hand.

Roosevelt Makes a Veteran Happy: Teddy Roosevelt had not spoken more than a hundred words along the way of his prepared manuscript, when he left it for a sentence to address an interpolation to a man in the audience. There was an old graybeard about ten rows back who wore on the lapel of his faded blue suit the little bronze button of the Grand Army of the Republic. The President had been speaking of the steadfastness of Pennsylvania during historical crises and mentioned the time when the preservation of the Union was the issue.

"The time," he suddenly exclaimed, departing from his written lines, "when you, my friend down there, with

> "We can show that the past is with us, A LIVING FORCE, only by the way in which we handle ourselves in the present, and each of us can best show his devotion to his own state by making evident his paramount devotion to that Union which includes all the States."

the button—you and your comrades saved the Union." The veteran's face beamed with joy. Tears of pride stood in his gray eyes. He grabbed off his wide felt hat and raised it aloft. A minute later the President was telling how it was on Pennsylvania's soil, at Gettysburg, when the tide of battle turned. He was still gesturing toward the veteran. The latter could no longer keep silent. "You bet it did!" he shouted. "Hurrah!" The crowd joined in the cheer and before the speech was finished, all of the audience was as enthusiastic as the veteran. φ

THIS PAGE: *Top, President Roosevelt, 1904; Bottom, Stereograph of President Roosevelt addressing the dedication crowds, 1906.*

OPPOSITE PAGE: *President Roosevelt speaking at the dedication, 1906.*

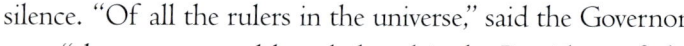

silence. "Of all the rulers in the universe," said the Governor, "the greatest and best beloved is the President of the United States. We have him with us today and I now present him to you."[28]

President Roosevelt arose, bowed right and left, and raised his hand for silence. Then, in ringing voice, he plunged into his speech, following closely the printed notes that he held in his hands. Aside from the president's commendation of prominent Pennsylvanians and praise of the record of the legislature in extraordinary session, the leading features of the President Roosevelt's address at the dedication of the new Capitol were his advocacy of increased power of the Federal government and a recital of what the Federal government had accomplished in the past few years. He refrained from saying anything that could have been distorted into approval or even acknowledgement of the corrupt state political machine at the turn of the twentieth century.[29]

The President expressed his support of interpreting the constitution in broad and liberal fashion so that the federal government could exercise greater and surer control of corporations. Roosevelt felt that the subject was worthy of the consideration of the people as a whole; the subject was far too important to be left to the decision and determination of a few men. The President's address as a whole was made to the entire country, not just to the people of Pennsylvania. His allusions to Pennsylvanians were gratifying and his laudation of Justice James Wilson as one of Pennsylvania's greatest sons was especially pleasing to the crowd. In addition, Attorney General Knox was honored when the President hailed him as the leader in the movement for Federal control of the predatory corporations.

His concluding words recommended that all men be guided by "a sense of honorable obligation to their fellows that will bind them as by bands of steel, to refrain…from doing aught to any man which can not be blazoned under the noonday sun."[30] Perhaps he was hoping that this advice would be taken to heart by some Pennsylvanians who occupied high official positions.

The Right Reverend James Henry Darlington, bishop of Harrisburg, concluded the dedication ceremony with the benediction. According to newspaper accounts, Reverend Darlington advanced to the front of the stand and with uplifted hands invoked the divine benediction, bringing the ceremony to a solemn and impressive close:

May the Heavenly Father, the Creator of all men, grant His blessing upon this structure now dedicated to the use of the Commonwealth of Pennsylvania. May all who enact or execute the

THIS PAGE: *A rendering of President Theodore Roosevelt, undated.*

OPPOSITE PAGE: *Left, Ribboned dedication souvenir pin, ca. 1906; Right, Two presidential campaign buttons for President Roosevelt, ca. 1903.*

CHAPTER FOUR • *Capitol Dedication: October 4, 1906*

[Roosevelt] recommended that all men be guided by "a sense of honorable obligation to their fellows that will bind them as by bands of steel, to refrain...from doing aught to any man which can not be blazoned under the noonday sun."

law remember the words of the Holy Scripture, "the powers that be are ordained of God," and that the representatives of the people must be men of Godly life and purpose.

As the founders of this colony called it "A Holy Experiment" may it continue Holy forever. Bless our colleges, our public and private schools, our churches, societies and charities, bless soldier and citizen, black and white, stranger and native born. May the toleration of varying beliefs, which was the first principle of our past, be also the motto of the future, and as this State was perhaps more favored than any other in furthering the Revolutionary cause, so may she ever be ready in the years to come to offer herself and her sons a sacrifice for the good of the nation, of which she is a part...

Called rightly the "Keystone State," may she ever value that truth and uprightness which is keystone of religion and all virtue...[31]

As the rain continued, the vast concourse resumed their seats and a signal was given from far down the street. The sharp notes of a bugle ordered the advance of the parade and the word "Forward!" sounded along the line. The President and Governor stood to review the procession as the head of the column merged.

First came a detail of the State Police, taking the place of the Harrisburg police platoon that from time immemorial had headed all state parades in Harrisburg. The Harrisburg platoon was busy with other official duties during this busy day. The Commonwealth Band followed and then came the six color sergeants who bore the United States and Pennsylvania flags. Grand Marshall Marlin E. Olmsted, congressman from Philadelphia, followed next and gave a stately salute to which the President and Governor responded by raising their hats. Chief of Staff Colonel William F. Richardson headed a staff of a hundred orderlies and aides, all of who saluted the Presidential party as they rode by on handsome horses.

The military units came next, headed by that staunch old veteran of two wars, Major General John P. S. Gobin, with his staff, and the people on the grandstand gave them an ovation. Next came brigades composed of veterans of the Spanish American War. As each officer passed the

THIS PAGE: *Capitol dedication souvenir plate, vase, creamer, and cup, ca. 1906.*

OPPOSITE PAGE: *A crowded Third Street during the dedication ceremonies, 1906.*

CHAPTER FOUR • *Capitol Dedication: October 4, 1906*

reviewing stand, he raised his sword in official salute, which was acknowledged by the President and Governor.

The State College Cadets under the command of Captain H. H. Hoy followed the National Guard. Their excellent marching and neat appearance drew applause all along the route and the President remarked that they looked like "West Pointers."

The cadets from the Carlisle Indian School came next, and were met with cheers and prolonged applause. President Roosevelt remarked, "Fine, and a credit to the nation that cared for them and the school where they are being educated."

The little "chappies" from the Scotland Soldiers' Orphans School followed, and were also greeted with great applause. "What a wonderful state is Pennsylvania to care for the children of its old soldiers," remarked the President as he watched the littlest fellows toddling along carrying guns as big as themselves. According to the *Star Independent*, "the boys didn't mind the fatigue of the march, their bearing was fine and they stepped like veterans."[32]

Four companies of mounted State Police under the command of Captain Groome concluded the procession. They had been doing police duty up to 11:00 A.M. and had hastily mounted and taken their place in line. The four companies were acknowledged to be the finest looking set of men that ever marched through the streets of Harrisburg. Every man had been chosen not only for his physical, but also for his educational qualifications and for having seen military service before he entered the police force. Their helmets were patterned after the Irish constabulary and their olive colored uniforms were patterned after those of the officers of the United States Army, and every one of them was in "fine fettle." The crowd approved and applauded enthusiastically. The Governor was particularly pleased with his police, and the President joined in the applause that greeted them.

President Roosevelt and his entourage departed from Harrisburg about three o'clock to return to Washington, D.C. Although Harrisburg was enshrouded with gloomy clouds, the light spirits of the visitors still

LITERATURE IN STONE: THE HUNDRED YEAR HISTORY OF THE PENNSYLVANIA STATE CAPITOL

I·N·S·I·G·H·T
Dedication Emergency Hospital

Early in the morning of Dedication Day, the State Board of Health asked the staff at Harrisburg Hospital if it could furnish a doctor and a few nurses for a first aid station at the Capitol. Miss Jones, the superintendent, soon had everything ready for an emergency hospital and Dr. G. B. Stoll, one of the residents at the hospital, was placed in charge. With him were sent Miss Shaneman, operating room nurse and Miss Edith Yingel, a student nurse.

The emergency hospital was opened about 11:00 A.M. in the north wing on the first floor of the building at the office of State Superintendent of Health Dr. Samuel Dixon. Dr. F. C. Johnson, chief medical inspector, and Wilbur Morse, private secretary of Dr. Dixon, rendered valuable aid during the day. The hospital had a store of smelling salts, adhesive plaster and heart stimulants. Very few cases were treated but most of the cases were due to the crushes in various parts of the building. Several women grew faint during the afternoon, but were soon brought about in the emergency hospital. One or two men also came to the room for aid but their maladies were not disclosed.[33]

THIS PAGE: *Patriotic women of the early twentieth century, ca. 1906.*

OPPOSITE PAGE: *Capitol memorabilia, from the Capitol dedication and other events, ca. 1906; President Roosevelt at the ceremony, 1906.*

prevailed. It had been a memorable day. Roosevelt had been duly impressed with the new Capitol of the Commonwealth of Pennsylvania and considered the dedication a great event, highly creditable to all concerned, and long to be remembered.

Due to the continuing downpour of rain, no attempt was made to carry out the program of evening events. The proposed display of fireworks and the band concerts were postponed until the following night. Despite the weather, the Harrisburg streets were brilliantly illuminated until midnight. But the crowd, for the most part, was kept indoors by the rain until it finally ceased about eleven o'clock in the evening. By that time most of the visitors had departed for home. For those who were fortunate to spend another day in the capital city, there was something to look forward to the next day.

Part IV: The Following Day

And so, the new Capitol building had been dedicated to the citizens of Pennsylvania with a great deal of fanfare and excitement. The professional decorators who had dressed the principal buildings of the city in holiday attire for dedication week began to remove the bunting and other trimmings from the fronts of buildings and the Harrisburg Light, Heat, and Power Company put a force of men at work taking down the cables that carried the thousands of small incandescent lights.[34]

The Venetian canopy in Market Square continued to stand for a few days but it was not long before that too disappeared. Most of the visitors had returned home via railcar or trolley. A few of the visitors still lingered in the city, but most were persons who had come here to visit friends and who had intended to stay a little longer.

The decorations had been stripped from Capitol Park and the grandstand was a thing of the past. The orange colored Chinese lanterns in Capitol Park had been ruined by the rain and were piled in a mass under a tree. Vandals, unable to carry away anything from the interior of the new Capitol, had swiped the small illuminating lanterns suspended by wires from the trees. There were none left in the park the following morning.[35] But not all of the festivities were over. Several thousand people gathered at Union Square near the railroad station on Friday afternoon to witness the display of Japanese day fireworks, which had been postponed from Dedication Day. Henry McCormick, Jr., who supervised the firing, assisted by his brother, James McCormick, and by Leroy J. Wolfe, provided the pyrotechnic entertainment. A lusty-lunged man with a megaphone announced the figures to be displayed just as the fuses were lighted.[36]

The fireworks consisted of a bomb that was projected skyward and exploded when about five hundred feet in the air. A parachute liberated by the explosion displayed some sort of decorative figure made of picturesque party-colored Japanese paper—a different figure to each piece. Spectators jockeyed their positions among the crowd as they attempted to catch the figures as they floated earthward.[37]

As evening approached, all of Harrisburg and thousands of remaining visitors turned out along the riverfront to view the massive display of fireworks, the crowning feature of the dedication of the Capitol. It was the largest crowd that ever congregated at nighttime in the city, so large that thousands of people filled the parks, pavements, grassy slopes, steps, windows, and even the rooftops. The crowd stretched from Vine Street to the city limits, several miles northward, although the

greatest crowd was concentrated along the high bank between Market and Harris Streets—a distance just equal to a mile.[38]

Thousands of visitors who had come to Harrisburg for the dedication extended their visits so they would not miss the fireworks. Men and women, some carrying their suitcases, went to the park searching for a vantage point for this grand event. Nimble boys and men climbed trees hoping to secure a clear line of vision. Hundreds of benches and campstools and chairs were carried for blocks to Front Street; carriages and automobiles formed a continuous line for blocks while all of the suburban trains and trolley cars carried capacity crowds to the city.

It was almost eight o'clock when large balloons were launched upward, one after the other until ten had come sailing across the river. Everyone for miles around could see the beginning of the display. Each balloon had a red light pendant that dropped, unfolding a line of colored balls. Long fiery reflections were cast across the water and the visitors were awestruck.

The salute then followed. Twenty-one time bombs were sent into the air and exploded. There was no illumination, simply a loud explosion that reverberated down the Cumberland Valley and caused the noise to echo across the Susquehanna. Since there were no bright balls of fire sailing through the air when the salute was fired, many of the crowd assumed that the fireworks had been dampened during Thursday's rain and many believed that the bombs were just sizzling in their dampness. Just as the crowd was expressing their

THIS PAGE: *Souvenir postcards: Top, Capitol facade, undated; Bottom, Capitol Park, ca. 1906.*

OPPOSITE PAGE: *Glass cobalt basket and shoe souvenirs bearing the Capitol's image, 1906.*

CHAPTER FOUR • *Capitol Dedication: October 4, 1906*

THE CAPITOL AS SEEN AT NIGHT, HARRISBURG, PA.

disappointment with a loud collective sigh, a dozen or more bombs that had "more than gunpowder" inside were sent up into the heavens and broke into a thousand red, green, and blue sparks.[39]

SIZZ! BOOM! AND BANG!

Sizz, boom, and bang went a score or more sky rockets, each one trying to chase the other into the higher altitudes. Hargest's Island (now City Island) was then illuminated with low lights. For many hundreds of feet, white and green lights were ignited and these changed to red and blue. Above in the clouds of smoke that were being wafted towards the city by a western breeze, the searchlight from the Union Trust Building was piercing holes in the dark sky. There was a flash and a hundred fiery snakes shot up from the island, hissed, illuminated the great hanging clouds of smoke, and died away. Many more fireworks followed, each giving the picture a different color effect and turning the river into a mass of color. Some of the fireworks contained electric effects. A mad riot of color dazzled the eyes of the spectators and then would be followed by a succession of small explosions and bright flashes that would almost blind those looking squarely at the lights.

The lower pieces were greatly enjoyed by those who had front seats. Cries of "Down in front!" and "Hats off!" had no effect upon the front-liners. Those behind stretched their necks and saw what they could. Displays of the President and the Governor in fire were quite large on the island but a half a mile away on the riverbank their heads looked small. The Capitol was displayed in fiery white lines with a gold top on the dome, representing the statue *Commonwealth*. This and the other pieces were greeted with loud applause. A representation of Niagara Falls,

A MAD RIOT of color dazzled the EYES of the spectators…

probably two city blocks in length, also caused applause. The Coat of Arms of the Commonwealth was one of the most impressive and the set pieces and giant pinwheels that revolved amid showers of silvery sparks greatly pleased the children, of which there were thousands. It was reported that baby carriages by the hundreds were everywhere.

One of the finest places for observing the fireworks was on the Walnut Street Bridge. It was filled, and hundreds stood on the Market Street viaduct. The wall at the filter plant was topped with people and many were in boats on the Susquehanna. Big boats and little boats carried lights and the effect of the water when the lights were not drowned by the glare from the bursting fireworks must have been dramatic. Sand flats were decorated with lanterns and carried scores of people, providing front row seats from the water.

During the entire evening three bands provided music for the promenading crowds: the Steelton band played at Pine Street; the Commonwealth Band played at Forster; while the West End band enlivened things at Harris Street. The concerts consisted of patriotic airs and other lively music and were enjoyed by the passersby and those located near them for the evening.[40]

With the last explosion, the official dedication celebration was over. The *Harrisburg Patriot* newspaper extended congratulations to everyone involved in the Capitol dedicatory ceremony on the perfect success of the ceremonies, in the face of weather conditions that could hardly have been more unfavorable and disagreeable. The arrangements for the dedication, by the State Commission and Harrisburg's Citizens

THIS PAGE: *A patriotic child celebrates, ca. 1906; Sheet music for patriotic and popular songs of the day, 1906.*

OPPOSITE PAGE: *Capitol postcard, ca. 1906.*

CHAPTER FOUR • Capitol Dedication: October 4, 1906

The *Harrisburg Patriot* newspaper extended CONGRATULATIONS to everyone involved in the CAPITOL DEDICATORY CEREMONY on the perfect SUCCESS of the ceremonies, in the face of weather conditions that could hardly have been more unfavorable and disagreeable.

Committee, the mayor and police force; the escort by the Governor's Troop commanded by Captain Ott and the great military parade marshaled by Congressman Olmsted, had all been admirably carried out.[41] Notwithstanding the rain that fell steadily, the dedication of the new Capitol had been successfully conducted.

The Capitol's dedication was ultimately a glorious celebration of the majesty of the new structure gracing the city, yet even prior to the ceremonies, stories in newspapers and word-of-mouth rumors about misappropriations were starting to buzz. The next several years would bring numerous attempts to defame the new structure, and in the end those rumors would fuel a full-fledged scandal that would reach to some of the highest officials in the Commonwealth.

THIS PAGE: *Dedication Aide ribbon, souvenir pin, and collectible plate, ca. 1906.*

OPPOSITE PAGE: *Picture from a postcard (bottom left) taken on the roof of the Capitol during the dedication activities, 1906; Bottom right, Souvenir aluminum medal, 1906. (Notice the same medal is being worn by a child in the photograph.)*

LITERATURE IN STONE: THE HUNDRED YEAR HISTORY OF THE PENNSYLVANIA STATE CAPITOL

CHAPTER FOUR • *Capitol Dedication: October 4, 1906*

The infamous bootblack stand cited as an exorbitant cost in the Capitol graft trial.

CHAPTER FIVE

Palace of Art Temple of Graft
Capitol Graft Scandal

THE completion of Pennsylvania's Capitol in 1906 was an important event in the Commonwealth's history for several reasons. For the first time it exposed to the entire state, and in some cases a national audience, the inner-workings of the long-running, well-entrenched statewide political machine. After its conclusion, it provided an effective push toward political reform in Pennsylvania during the Progressive Era, and it forced the state to upgrade an antiquated purchasing system which had permitted such a scandal to occur.

The graft scandal is best understood from an examination of the state's Republican party machine in the decades from the Civil War to shortly after the turn of the twentieth century. The statewide machine was led by party boss, U.S. Senator Matthew Stanley Quay, until his death in 1904, and afterward by U.S. Senator Boies Penrose. Quay had once stated sarcastically, "I can sometimes do without a Governor, but I always need a Treasurer."[1] Behind this statement lay more than a generation of controversial frauds perpetrated against the Commonwealth by insiders in the State Treasury Department on behalf of politicians and interests around the state, usually intricately linked to party boss Penrose, Quay, and or even to their predecessor Simon Cameron. An early response to some of these frauds was the provision in the Constitution of 1874 for the election of a State Treasurer, an attempt to afford a safe distance for the office from corrupt party machine. Instead, the mechanics of the frauds were only slightly altered, and they continued largely unimpeded. As an example, in 1879 Former State Treasurer William H. Kemble and other colleagues were implicated in a scandal involving the addition of $4 million to a bogus bill to pay for the 1877 railroad riots.[2]

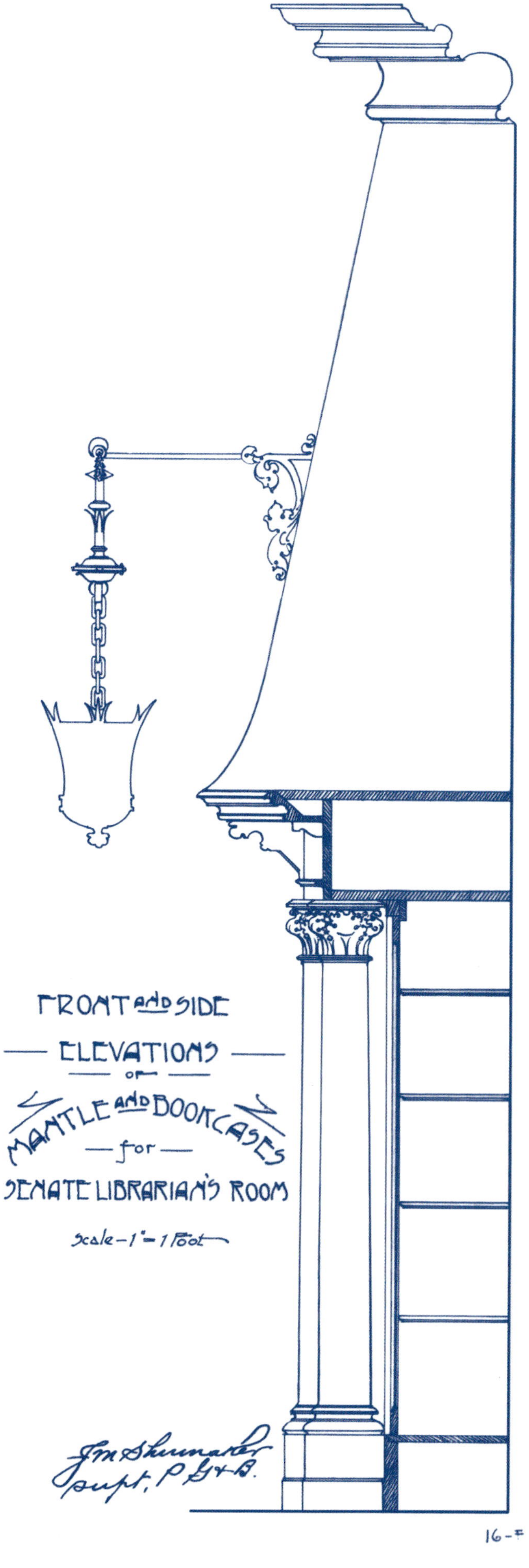

However, by 1901 there were hopeful signs, including the holding of a second architectural competition, that the new Pennsylvania Capitol Building could be completed without the political intrigue that had dogged other state-sponsored projects. Within Pennsylvania's newspapers, which at the time were much more politicized than today, three themes were generally common: praise for the building's magnificent design; satisfaction that it would be completed on time; and a strong belief that it could be completed within the budgeted appropriation.[3]

No payoffs to politicians or bureaucrats were ever proven in the graft scandal; a point that Governor Pennypacker used extensively in claiming that there was no Capitol graft—at least of which he was aware. Contrary to most of Pennsylvania's

The Leaders of the Republican Party Machine

treasury scandals, which involved bank frauds with payoffs to politicians or officials, the Capitol graft scandal revealed the abuse of the state's woefully outdated and confusing purchasing system.[4] In essence, the real disparity comes between the appropriation for the building's construction and what was ultimately spent to furnish it. The construction of the Capitol was indeed within the $4 million appropriation. On the other hand the furnishing of the building, excluding the artwork, doubled that figure, which is where the roots of the graft scandal lie.

In order to understand the complexity of this scandal, it is essential to be aware of the underlying causes and interrelations between the issues. Two distinct bodies were responsible for the completion of the Capitol. The Capitol Building Commission was created by an act of July 18, 1901, with power to construct a new State Capitol within an appropriation of $4 million. However, there was no provision in this act for furniture, equipment, or decoration of the building.

THIS PAGE: *Left, Boies Penrose, 1906; Right, Statue of Matthew Stanley Quay, Installed 1909, Rotunda.*

OPPOSITE PAGE: *Left, Side elevation of mantle for Senate Librarian's Room; Right, Simon Cameron ca. 1863.*

CHAPTER FIVE • *The Capitol Graft Scandal*

Political Campaigning of the 1900s

Featuring the Republican Party and Samuel W. Pennypacker

Campaign Memorabilia from the Gubernatorial ELECTION OF 1902

A. Ribbon endorsing Pennypacker for Governor.

B. Various campaign buttons for Pennypacker

C. Official State Seal and Governor Post Card.

D. Governor Pennypacker leading the National Guard at President Theodore Roosevelt's Inauguration on March 4, 1905.

E. Celebratory Republican ribbon lauding Roosevelt and Pennypacker.

CHAPTER FIVE • *The Capitol Graft Scandal*

grounds and buildings, including the furnishing and refurnishing of the same."[6]

Furthermore, the General Appropriation Act of 1903 authorized the State Treasurer to pay out any monies not otherwise appropriated, such sums as are required for repair and furnishing of state government buildings.[7] This act also placed a cap on the amount of money that could be spent on an annual basis. The act also set specific requirements to govern competitive bidding. Each item in the schedule was to be accompanied by a maximum price, and bids were to be expressed as percentages subtracted from the maximum. Bidders were required to furnish bonds in amounts established by the board, as assurance of their ability to complete the work. Awards were to be made to the lowest responsible bidder on each item, and bidders could bid on single items without prejudice.[8] This provision did not affect the existing powers of the Board of Public Grounds and Buildings under the Act of 1895.

As a result the Building Commission had no power to provide any type of furnishings for the building. This act was intended by the legislature to ensure that the actual cost of the new Capitol would be kept within budget.[5]

Furnishing of the Capitol was left to the second body—the Commonwealth's Board of Public Grounds and Buildings—consisting of the Governor, the State Treasurer, and the Auditor General, and their deputies, which was established by an act of March 26, 1895. Under this act, the board was given "entire control and supervision of the public grounds and buildings . . . all repairs, alterations, and improvements made, and all work done or expenses incurred in and about such

The Board also resolved that in all cases where requisitions were approved and articles ordered, the bids accepted did not authorize the payment of more than the cash price or market value for the articles, supplies, or work. Although the bidder may have been the lowest, if his bid was higher than the average cash price or market price of the article, supply, or work at the time ordered, he could not be paid more than such average cash or market price.[9] This provision would ensure that the state would not be billed exorbitant rates above the commonly accepted prices of the day.

THIS PAGE: *Left, Front of Senate President's chair, from blueprint, 1902; Right, Side view of the House Speaker's chair, from blueprint, 1902.*

OPPOSITE PAGE: *Top, Capitol two-arm light sconce; Bottom, State Treasurer's Office, 1906.*

LITERATURE IN STONE: THE HUNDRED YEAR HISTORY OF THE PENNSYLVANIA STATE CAPITOL

The Commonwealth's Purchasing System

Pennsylvania had developed an overly-elaborate system for ordering and purchasing supplies, equipment, furnishings, landscaping state grounds, and altering or improving state-owned buildings. In 1896 the use of unit prices based on feet and pounds was instituted. Therefore, some items in the listing for competitive bidding of supplies and materials were bid on the basis of a price "per foot" or "per pound." Use of this system of measurement became known as the "per-foot rule."[10] The per-foot rule, which was begun with only a tiny portion of the schedule, was gradually extended to cover an increasing number of items throughout the coming years.

The per-foot rule was subject to abuse or misunderstanding unless rigorously controlled, which it was not. Articles contracted for under the per-pound basis must have their maximum weights specified; articles contracted for under the per-foot basis must have a regular and well-defined system for taking measurements. Failure to rigorously observe either of these requirements could open the door to excessive overcharges by contractors. In the Capitol graft scandal, the Commonwealth of Pennsylvania learned this lesson painfully.

The Board of Public Grounds and Buildings was receptive to architect Joseph Huston's desire to achieve

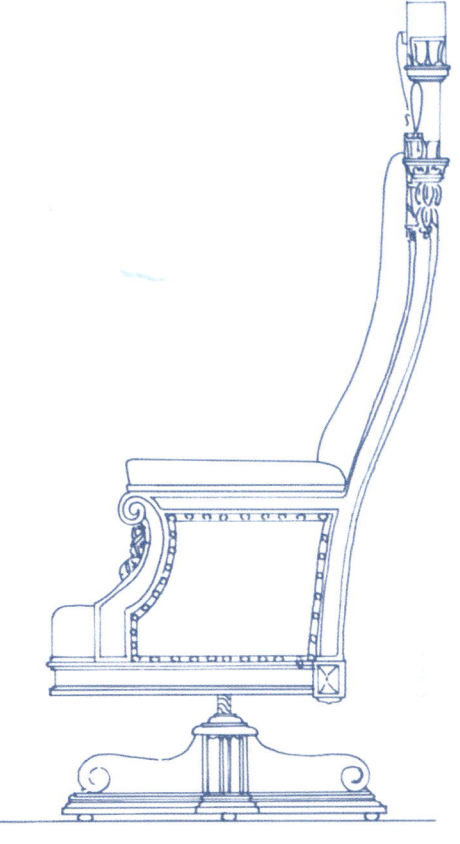

· FRONT · VIEW ·   · SIDE · VIEW ·
· ROTARY · CHAIRS ·
· SUPREME · COURT ·

According to Huston, the selection of a single contractor to provide all the furnishings simplified coordination aimed at producing a harmonious result.

aesthetic harmony and unity in the furnishing and equipping of the Capitol. Accordingly, in October 1903 the Board hired Huston to design the decorations, furnishings, and metal cases for the building. The Board preferred to rely on the same contractors for the four consecutive years of the construction and furnishing of the Capitol; however, this conflicted with the state system of issuing annual contracts. According to Huston, the selection of a single contractor to provide all the furnishings simplified coordination aimed at producing a harmonious result.[11] The Board of Commissioners of Public Grounds and Buildings also chose to extend the state's per-foot rule for bidding to cover Capitol furniture. This system, though in use in Europe at the time, was not a commonly understood practice in the purchase of furniture in the United States and it caused a great deal of confusion for most competitive bidders.

In actuality, a single contractor had won every annual contract for furniture since 1896.[12] He was John H. Sanderson, a furniture dealer from Philadelphia whose family had been in the furniture business since 1810. As the customary furniture supplier to the state, Sanderson evidently expected to provide the Capitol furniture under his annual contract to furnish the several departments of the state. Sanderson began collaborating on furniture designs with Huston's staff in 1904. When the schedule for bidding was published, Sanderson's detailed knowledge of what was required provided him a tremendous advantage over any other potential bidder. He won the bidding easily and was the only contractor to bid on every item of the special schedule.[13]

Sanderson's prior experience with the state bidding process provided him unfair advantages over other competitive bidders. Specifications were brief and vague,

CHAPTER FIVE • *The Capitol Graft Scandal*

"LOST IN ADMIRATION." Philadelphia Press, *October 9, 1906*

and did not provide a standard procedure for taking measurements of items that were to be invoiced by the foot. There were no estimates of quantities required for any of the items in the special schedule, no estimates of the number of feet needed for each of the items ordered by the foot, and no restriction upon maximum weights for those items ordered by the pound. Strawbridge and Clothier, a well-known Philadelphia furnishings retailer, entered a bid on the furniture portion of the schedule, but found both the schedule and specifications "unintelligible." Since they were unable to understand the per-foot system, they bid their furniture by the piece, which ultimately placed them a higher bidder.[14]

The Scandal Breaks in the Press

During the time of the Capitol's construction, a reform movement in Philadelphia, known as the "City Party," began fighting the Republican party machine.[15] In some elections it ran "fusion tickets" of Democrats and reformist Republicans. For this reason, in 1905, Democrat William H. Berry gained election as State Treasurer on a fusion ticket, allowing him to be one of the only Democrats in a wholly Republican administration. In fact Berry was the only Democrat elected to a state office between the years of 1895 and 1934. Governor Samuel Pennypacker termed Berry's election a "freak of ill fortune."[16] This upset victory clearly affected the individuals involved in the ongoing Capitol graft scheme. Although it was not discovered until later in the investigation, Sanderson sought rushed approval and payment of his invoices from Public Works before the start of Berry's term. Between Election Day 1905 and May 2, 1906, Sanderson pushed through more than $2 million in billings, nearly forty percent of his total payments from the state. Expenditures during this period totaled nearly $3 million. During the last week before Berry's inauguration, at least $950 thousand in payments were rushed through, some of it for work not

> ## "Yes, the State Capitol cost nearer twelve millions than ten!"
> ### Treasurer William H. Berry, 1906

SIZE LIMITED ONLY BY BERRY'S WIND.

Berry went so far as to use state monies to publish postcards with the prices of Capitol furnishings and items, such as the infamous bootblack stand that had purportedly cost the state $1,619.20. Berry later admitted that this type of defamation may have been going too far.

yet completed, for Sanderson and others knew that change would come under Berry's term of office.[17]

As expected, when Berry took office on May 6, 1906, he immediately began investigating Capitol expenditures. He became the whistle-blower, playing the central role in bringing the Capitol fraud to light. The last of Sanderson's invoices, totaling $108,879, went unpaid because Berry flatly refused payment.[18]

"SIZE LIMITED ONLY BY BERRY'S WIND," Harrisburg Telegraph, September 21, 1906.

CHAPTER FIVE • The Capitol Graft Scandal

Collapse of the House of Cards

"COLLAPSE OF THE HOUSE OF CARDS," Harrisburg Telegraph, *October 29, 1906.*

Berry's first significant discovery was that the posting of the books in his department was far in arrears. He soon learned that the payments made for furnishing the Capitol totaled far more than the $4 million figure that was fixed in the public mind.[19] To this end in September of 1906, less than a month before the dedication of the Capitol, Treasurer Berry, with perhaps more enjoyment than he should have found in the process, teasingly tossed details to the press. During a visit to Erie he stated publicly that, "It will surprise the taxpayers to know that their Capitol cost nearer ten million than four." Within a week, he was telling a huge crowd at Reading, "Yes, the State Capitol cost nearer twelve millions than ten!"[20] It was through William Berry that the graft scandal was broken, through the use of newspapers that were often critical of the administration, to the general public. Around the time of the October 4 dedication, Berry announced that he was refusing all payment of any further invoices for Capitol construction and furnishings.

Headlines at the time now proclaimed the Capitol as the "Palace of Graft."[21] Governor Pennypacker, always willing to comment, said: "I know of no graft. I do not believe there has been any. I do not like the term."[22] On September 26, 1906, about a week before the dedication, Pennypacker and Auditor General William P. Snyder issued a five-page report outlining the costs of the building, and explaining why it had cost so much, possibly an attempt to control damage from Berry's accusations. The total amount for both construction and furnishings approached $12.5 million. If the initial construction of the Cobb structure was included with this cost, that figure rose above $13 million.[23] However, it was not graft they insisted but merely disparity in the construction and furnishings budget, which they claimed Berry did not fully comprehend.

Berry continued to probe, and though he had no concrete proof for all his accusations, he listed Governor Pennypacker, Auditor General William P. Snyder, former State Treasurer William L. Mathues, ex-State Treasurer Frank G. Harris, the Superintendent of Public Grounds and Buildings James M. Shumaker, contractors George F. Payne and John H. Sanderson, and architect Joseph M. Huston as culprits in the emerging scandal.[24]

"I KNOW OF NO GRAFT. I do not believe there has been any. I do not like the term."

Sam¹ W. Pennypacker
Oct 4ᵗʰ 1906

In assessing Berry's fervent pursuit and exposure of the Capitol scandal, one wonders if he was playing the part of loyal public servant, or merely throwing jabs at the dominant Republican administration. Berry went so far as to use state monies to publish postcards with the prices of Capitol furnishings and items, such as the infamous bootblack stand that had purportedly cost the state $1,619.20. Berry later admitted that this type of defamation may have reached too far.[25]

CHAPTER FIVE • *The Capitol Graft Scandal*

The Audit Company found the minutes to be "indefinite," with reports OMITTED and containing a number of ambiguities.

Attorney General Hampton L. Carson, under pressure from both Berry and the press, probed into the scandal and compiled a book-length report in 1907. His method of investigation consisted merely of studying the evidence within the contract documents and board minutes, and addressing written inquiries to the individuals involved. He called no witnesses, nor took testimony under oath. When the suspected grafters wrote exculpatory replies, Carson accepted them at face value, but this was not enough for the over-zealous Berry who criticized Carson's means of investigation. Huston, Sanderson, and other accused grafters looked upon Carson's process as a friendly inquisition, and therefore cooperated with Carson. However, they did not cooperate as genuinely with the subsequent legislative investigation.[26]

Governor Pennypacker, as chairman of the Board of Public Grounds and Buildings, had not evaded responsibility for the work of decorating and furnishing the Capitol. He was proud of the new building and earnestly believed there had been no fraud or graft. He pointed to baseless charges, the high professional standing of the architect, the extraordinary efforts to eliminate fraud, the unequaled result for the cost, and he stated that probabilities were all in favor of the Capitol—not against it. He compared the cost of the State Capitol to other contemporary buildings of similar scale. The Capitol's cost per cubic foot of contents, which is the usual architectural system of estimation, was $1.04, inclusive of the furnishing and decorating. The National Capitol in Washington was $1.10; New York's

CAPITOL Furniture

BLUEPRINTS

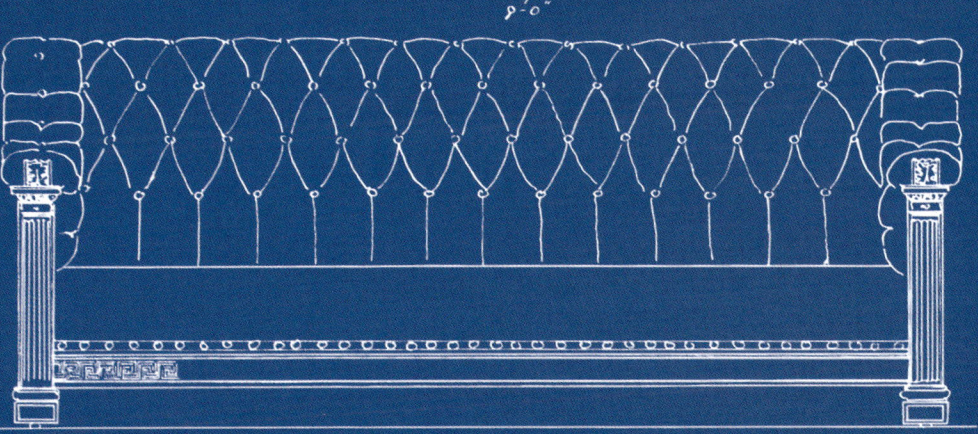

8'-0"
FRONT ELEVATION.

Front and side view of sofa for Public and Private Senate Anterooms.

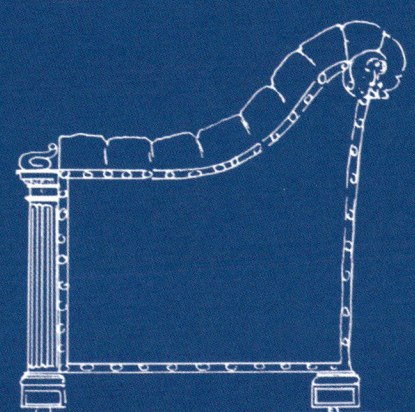

SIDE ELEVATION

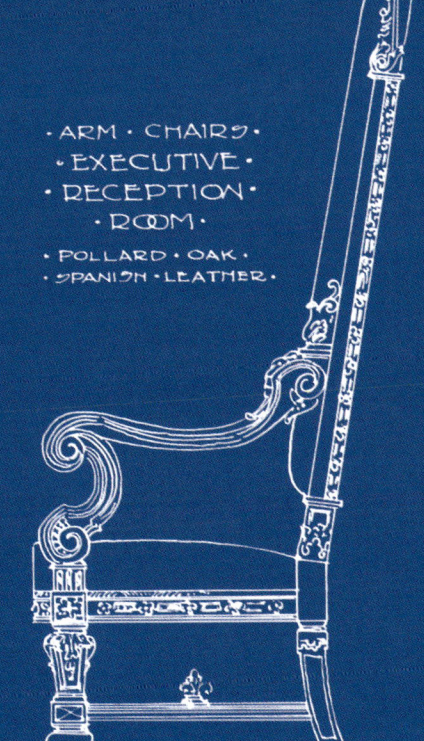

· ARM · CHAIRS ·
· EXECUTIVE ·
· RECEPTION ·
· ROOM ·
· POLLARD · OAK ·
· SPANISH · LEATHER ·
· SIDE · VIEW ·

CLOCK DIAL
MARBLE
MARBLE
ELEVATION.

Plan for mantle in Room 230.

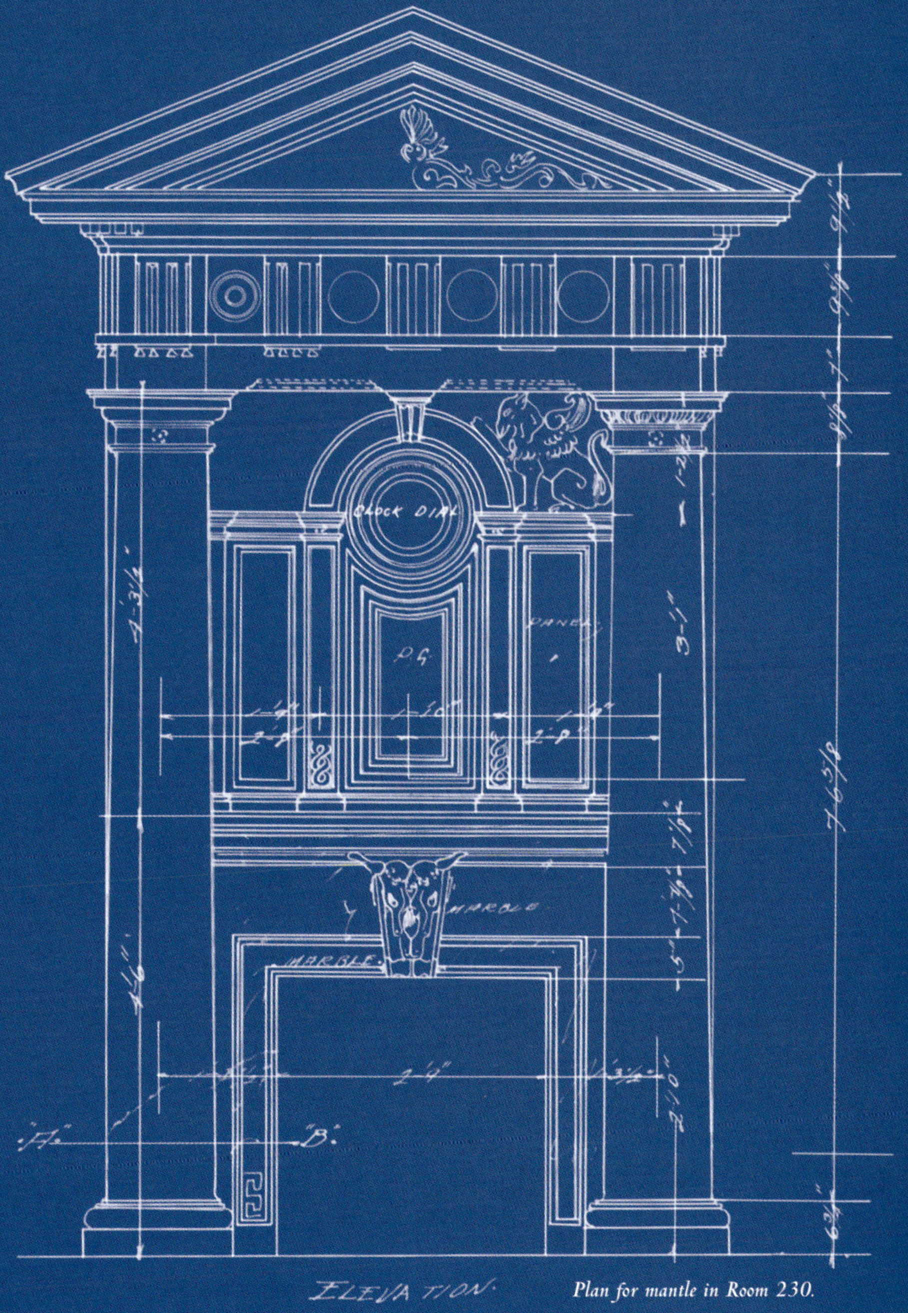

Top, The Governor in his private office, 1906; Bottom, Attorney General Hampton L. Carson, 1906.

Capitol at Albany, $2.00; William C. Whitney's residence, $2.55; the Knickerbocker Trust Company, New York, $1.30; and the Hotel St. Regis, $1.10.[27]

THE CAPITOL INVESTIGATION COMMISSION

In January 1907 Harrisburg witnessed the inauguration of a new governor, Edwin S. Stuart, and the beginning of a new legislative biennium. Thorough investigation of the Capitol graft had been an important campaign promise from Stuart, and with the support of the legislature, he moved quickly to carry it out by creating a commission with the sole purpose of investigating the alleged graft. The Capitol Investigation Commission met for the first time on February 4, 1907, and Governor Stuart named the Audit Company of New York to be the Commission's accountants and auditors.[28]

Waiting for Information

PENN—"Willie Berry, Come Right in and Attend to Business."

"WAITING FOR INFORMATION." Harrisburg Telegraph, *1906.*

CHAPTER FIVE • *The Capitol Graft Scandal*

The Audit Company's report to the Capitol Investigation Committee confirmed what Berry had found the previous year—that **more than $12.5 million had been spent to construct, equip, and furnish the Capitol.** It also found that **more than $5 million, had been fraudulently overcharged.**

The initial findings of The Audit Company showed that the Capitol Building Commission had overpaid Huston by $663 but when the mural and sculptural contracts were completed, the architect would still be owed a net of $895. However, a more serious matter was the minute books of the Capitol Building Commission. The Audit Company found the minutes to be "indefinite," with reports omitted and containing a number of ambiguities.[29]

Another area of concern was that the Capitol Building Commission had ignored conflicts between architect Huston and Clerk-of-the-Works Bernard Green, whom the Commission had hired to oversee Huston's performance. Much of their disagreement concerned matters of professional judgment. For example, Huston and Green differed sharply on the quality of the Capitol's construction, especially with the granite work. This disparity may have come from the fact that Green's background was as a construction engineer, and he was therefore more focused on quality of materials, than on matters of design. As a result, Green consistently maintained that the granite work was not of the quality specified in the contract and was not in the interest and integrity of the building. Green forced Huston to admit to the Capitol Investigation Commission that he had approved some compromises in the granite work, "as a matter of generalship" to keep construction on schedule. However, this was completely within Huston's right, and was no proof of scandal.[30]

The reputation of the Capitol Building Commission was damaged when the report of the Audit Company showed that the commissioners knew that the Board of Commissioners of Public Grounds and Buildings was involved with the Capitol construction,

Governor Edwin Stuart, ca. 1906.

1906 Capitol Graft Postcards
1. ROOM 226: Anteroom Governor's Office.
2. ROOM 227: Passageway to Governor's Office.
3. ROOM 200: Desk located in Lieutenant Governor's Office.

and simply ignored this misapplication of power.³¹ As an example, in November 1904 commission member William P. Snyder reported that the Board of Commissioners of Public Grounds and Buildings, on which he also served, had awarded a contract to Complete the attic or fifth floor, despite legal prohibitions against its doing so.³² In addition, the following month Huston reported that the Board of Public Grounds had changed the wood floors that were to be placed in the building, an even more clearly illegal act. Yet, the Building Commission had made no protest to the Board.

The Audit Company's report to the Capitol Investigation Committee confirmed what Berry had found the previous year—that more than $12.5 million had been spent to construct, equip, and furnish the Capitol. It also found that more than $5 million, had been fraudulently overcharged. The overpayments came from three sources: (1) inflated invoices from John H. Sanderson, (2) fraudulent bills for metallic furniture, and (3) exaggerated commissions demanded by Huston.³³

MIXING IT UP.

The Capitol Investigation Hearings

On March 11, 1907 the Capitol Investigation Commission launched the public hearing phase of its investigation, making the front page in nearly every major paper in the country. The hearings were held in a paneled committee room on the fourth floor of the Capitol. Sometimes the newsmen were admitted; other times they waited in the dark hallways outside. During the succeeding three-and-a-half months, the Commission heard testimony on thirty-seven separate days, examined 188

THIS PAGE: *"Mixing It Up,"* Harrisburg Telegraph, *1906.*

OPPOSITE PAGE: *"Furnishings; That's All!,"* Philadelphia Press, *October 1, 1906.*

THE CAPITOL INVESTIGATION HEARINGS

witnesses, 159 of whom testified publicly, and produced a transcript of more than 3,500 pages.[34]

The Commonwealth's poor record keeping was a significant factor in the investigation. Many documents important to the commission's work simply could not be found, and in terms of auditing and accounting the Commonwealth still operated on a single-entry system.[35] Since most of the graft centered on the special furnishing contract awarded to Sanderson, the hearings focused a great deal of attention upon that subject. Sanderson chose not to attend the investigative hearings but testimony proceeded regardless.[36]

Finally, the Capitol Investigation Commission issued its report on August 17, 1907 to Governor Stuart and to the press. The report concluded that the contracts awarded by the Board of Commissioners of Public Grounds and Buildings to John H. Sanderson, George F. Payne & Company, and to the Pennsylvania Construction Company were illegal. It found that Joseph M. Huston, John H. Sanderson, James M. Shumaker, H. Burd Cassel, and Charles G. Wetter made false certificates and fraudulent invoices. It had been the intention of the architect, interior decorator, and the contractors to "cheat and defraud the state" through "false certificates and fraudulent invoices upon which warrants were issued." The Commission also found the Capitol Building Commission blameworthy for allowing the Board of

A. William L. Mathues
B. H. Burd Cassel
C. Charles G. Wetter

All portraits ca. 1906.

HARRISBURG, PA., WEDNESDAY EVENING, MARCH 6, 1907

MICE SET FIRE TO THE NEW CAPITOL

Rodents Ignited Matches by Gnawing at Them

LOSS ESTIMATED AT $1,000

Smoke Attracted Watchman Householder's Attention

Mice and matches formed the combination that early this morning set fire to a desk in the office of State Registrar Batt, in the Department of Health at the new State capitol. Night Watchman E. M. Householder was parading through the corridor in the north wing of the capitol when he smelled smoke. It was about 1 o'clock and he knew there was no necessity for a fire at that hour, and he began an investigation, which resulted in the discovery of the fire in Dr. Batt's office.

Alarm Sent In.

Watchman Householder quickly gave the alarm to State Health Commissioner Dixon, Private Secretary Morse and Clerk Nelson, who were still in the main office of the department, and the quartette quickly unreeled the hand hose kept for fire purposes and breaking in the door of the office soon had a stream on that destroyed the fire microbes, the conflagration germs and the flame bacteria. An alarm was sent out but when the firemen arrived they were informed that their services were not needed as the fire had been extinguished.

An Investigation Was Made.

Investigation showed that the fire had started in a drawer in a desk in which matches were kept, and the mice in making a square meal of match heads had ignited them and the fire followed. The flames ate downward and then communicated to the other wood work in the room, all of which was badly extinguished. The furniture of the room was also blistered so that it must be replaced. The loss will amount to $1,000. Superintendent Rambo at once set men to work to straighten matters out, and the room will be ready for occupancy in a short time.

Mouse Was Cremated.

Swift justice followed the incendiary act of the mouse that nibbled the matches and set the desk on fire. In clearing away the debris the incinerated remains of the incendiary were found, the fire fiend being cremated in his attempt to set fire to the capitol. Nothing remained of the mouse but a charcoal and a scorched tail. A gross of mouse traps have been ordered by Superintendent Rambo.

"STUNG!" *Harrisburg Telegraph, October 27, 1906.*

CHAPTER FIVE • *The Capitol Graft Scandal*

Commissioners of Public Grounds and Buildings to "interfere with its contracts and duties… because, having the power, it could have prevented such interference, and in failing to exercise its power, opened the way for the frauds perpetrated upon the State."[37]

The Attorney General was instructed to "institute such criminal and civil proceedings as may, in his judgment, be warranted by the law and the facts found by the commission against any and all persons concerned in the fraudulent transactions… to the end that the money unlawfully taken from the State may be recovered and punishment meted out to all the offenders."[38] In May 1907 Attorney General Todd had announced that civil and criminal actions would be taken against those involved in the scandal. In the aftermath of the commission report, attention was focused on two items: (1) the prosecution of the men named by the commission, and (2) recovery of money owed to the Commonwealth.

Former Governor Pennypacker rebutted, saying that the State had gotten something very fine in exchange for its money. Pennypacker later wrote: "The work of the Investigation Commission…entirely failed to discover… that the building and equipment had been paid for without withdrawing the balance in the treasury."[39] The work of the Capitol Investigation Committee also failed to discover who benefited from the graft. Although rumors were rampant, it was never clearly substantiated whether any graft was paid out by contractors to an unknown number of politicians.

Indictments and Arrests

Warrants for the arrest of fourteen men were issued on September 18, 1907. They included Huston; Sanderson; Shumaker; Snyder; Mathues; Cassel; Payne and his partner Charles G. Wetter; Huston's partner Stanford B. Lewis; Sanderson's partners in the Pennsylvania Bronze Company Charles F. Kinsman, Wallis Boileau, John G. Neiderer and Charles K. Storm; and Frank Irvine, an employee who was responsible for auditing the Capitol invoices under Auditor General Snyder.[40]

Some of the defendants made appearances in Dauphin County Court the same day. The principal defendants, including Cassel, Huston, Sanderson, Shumaker, Snyder, and Mathues, each posted bail through their sureties. Not arrested were former State Treasurer Frank G. Harris and former Auditor General E. B. Hardenbergh, who escaped legal accountability for their actions through the state's prevailing two-year statute of limitations. On September 19 Sanderson announced in Philadelphia that "if it could be shown that the material used in the building was not up to specifications he would make restitution to the State." The September 19, 1907 edition of the *New York Times* quoted Sanderson as saying, "Much of the clamor…is due to the newspapers, and I am made to suffer for the shortcomings of others. If there is faulty material in the Capitol it was not put there with my knowledge." All of the defendants were arraigned on October 9 and a trial date was set for January 27, 1908.

The Trials

On January 27, 1908 the trial of Huston, Sanderson, Shumaker, Snyder, and Mathues opened in Dauphin County Court of Common Pleas, presided over by President Judge George Kunkel. When the trial opened, Huston asked for and received a severance—an acknowledgement that he would testify for the prosecution.[41] The attorneys for Shumaker, Sanderson, Snyder, and Mathues also requested severance, but Huston was the only one granted the exception. Huston's

> **Pennypacker later wrote:** "The work of the Investigation Commission… ENTIRELY FAILED TO DISCOVER… that the building and equipment HAD BEEN PAID FOR WITHOUT WITHDRAWING the balance in the treasury."

cooperation meant that his partner, Stanford Lewis, would also testify for the prosecution.

Huston and his brother, the Reverend Samuel C. Huston, testified that Huston had been out of the country when the furniture had been delivered, and thus was not present to certify that Sanderson was due all of the money. Even greater blame was placed on Sanderson for falsely procuring a blank certificate which Huston had signed before his departure and left in the possession of his brother. The defense counsel put Pennypacker and Snyder on the stand as major witnesses, resting its case on February 27, one month after the opening of the trial. The jury convicted all of the defendants, handing down the verdict on March 12, 1908.[42] Each of the four men, Sanderson, Shumaker, Snyder and Mathues, was given the maximum sentence allowed for conspiracy under Pennsylvania law: two years in the Eastern State Penitentiary in Philadelphia and a $500 fine.[43]

Through a lengthy series of motions for new trials, bail respites, and continuances, Huston's attorneys were able to postpone his trial. Meanwhile, the circumstances of Huston's pending trial continued to change. Several of the defendants who could have testified against him had died or were soon to die. George F. Payne, a potentially devastating witness against Huston, had died in 1907. Sam Matt Fridy, a deputy under Auditor General Snyder, died the same year. Mathues died of pneumonia in his home on December 30, 1908. And Sanderson himself, who had moved from Philadelphia to New York City, became gravely ill.[44]

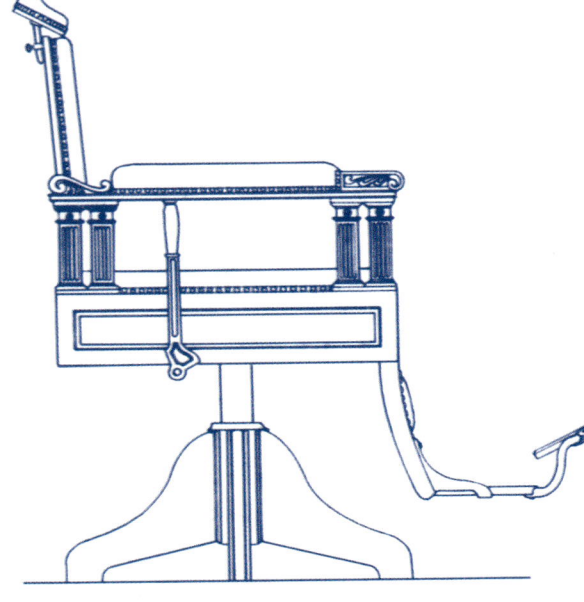

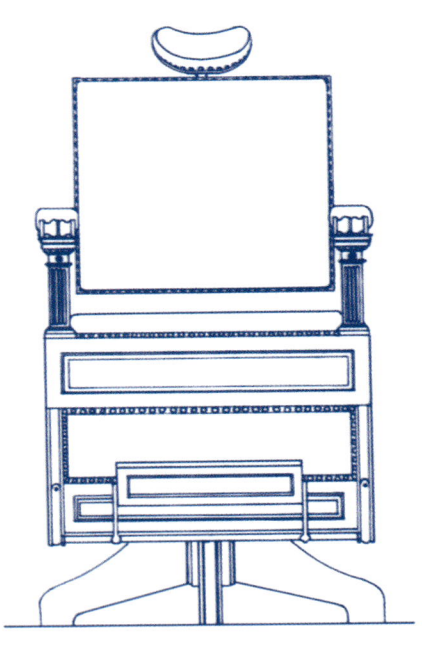

Left, A Pumpkin Ball light fixture like those located throughout the Capitol; *Right,* Side and front view line drawings of a Capitol barber's chair.

1906 Capitol Graft Postcards
1. ROOM 156: Senate Caucus Room.
2. ROOM 224: Governor's Private Office.
3. ROOM 254: Umbrella Stand located in Senate Anteroom and Post Office.

SEEING ONLY ONE SIDE OF THE EXHIBIT

Top, George F. Payne, undated; Bottom, Deputy Auditor General Sam Matthew Fridy, ca. 1906.

Before his appearance in court on January 24, 1910 Huston issued a letter to several newspapers saying, "The cost of the Capitol furnishings exceeded my expectations and those of the members of the board. But wherever the money has been expended it was in accordance with the law and in the only manner permitted by law. As a result of it all the State has got, by actual comparison, the cheapest, biggest and best building of its kind in the country or in the world."[45]

It is difficult to prove who was guilty and who was not. Most evidence points to John Sanderson as the most guilty party within the graft scandal, but it is uncertain whether Huston was completely unaware of the scandal or just so consumed with the Capitol project that he became oblivious to the overcharges. Huston was negligent in his oversight of financial matters concerning the construction, such as the stack of presigned certificates he left with his brother when he traveled to Europe. As a young architect undertaking a commission so large, he may have had less of the ultimate professionalism and experience that was demanded of the job. Yet it is uncertain that this negligence and inexperience constituted the charge of "conspiracy" that the courts handed down. Regardless of his plea of innocence and assurances that he had no knowledge of the over-expenditures, Joseph Huston became the ultimate scapegoat of the graft scandal.

He was convicted on April 29, 1910 on circumstantial evidence for failing to adequately carry out a duty (verifying measurements and prices of furnishings supplied by John Sanderson) that was not assigned to him under the contract.[46]

The final charge by the court was one of conspiracy to "cheat and defraud the Commonwealth." The actual dollar amount listed by the court amounted to twenty-three thousand dollars. He appealed this verdict and was sentenced on October 15, 1910, receiving six months to two years at Eastern State Penitentiary. This amount of time was the lowest sentence for

CHAPTER FIVE • *The Capitol Graft Scandal*

any of the accused conspirators. His final appeal was turned down by the Pennsylvania Supreme Court on May 24, 1911 and he was thereupon imprisoned. After learning that he must go to jail, Huston announced to the press: "The State Capitol stands as a monument to me—a monument to my straightforwardness and honesty. I have never committed an act of fraud or dishonesty in public or private life."[47] He further noted that "persecutions, malice, clamor convicted me—my monument will stand on Capitol Hill when my persecutors are dead, rotten and forgotten."[48] Joseph Huston was later paroled on December 20, 1911 having served just under seven months of his sentence.[49] Immediately after his time in jail, Huston and his brother Samuel visited the Capitol in January 1912. He discretely toured the building, paying particular attention to his first view of Abbey's completed House Chamber murals. His visit was brief and without fanfare, most likely due to his recent incarceration and alleged involvement in the graft scandal.[50]

Even today the Capitol graft scandal remains somewhat of an enigma. The sheer volume of documents and number of governmental and legal institutions involved make a thorough understanding of the scandal nebulous, at best. The old political cliché of "who knew what and when did they know it" seems especially applicable to the context. While it is assured that some knew more than others in the case, leveling accusations on a person-by-person context remains more difficult today than during the resulting trials. What is certain is that the guilt can certainly be spread around and was not only personalized, but in many cases, institutionalized. Individuals such as John Sanderson were without a doubt guilty, but it is hard to determine to what extent other individuals were involved. Difficulty lies in proving whether they were so transfixed upon the mammoth construction project that they cared little about the bills, so long as they were paid. Perhaps Joseph Huston's only real crime was his close attention to detail and granting responsibility to others in his absence. With certainty there were agencies of the Commonwealth that did not adequately do their jobs, such as the Board of Public Grounds and Buildings and the Capitol Building Commission.

In the end, whatever entities knew or did not know, or even those that just went along for the ride regardless of the outcome, will most likely remain shrouded as part of the lore of the Capitol's construction. At the time, most people only knew that there was a scandal, but learning specific details was left to those who followed the trials in the papers. As author Owen Wister stated during the scandal, he felt that Pennsylvania during the scandal was "a government by knaves at the expense of fools."[51]

As may be expected, there was no march on the Capitol by Pennsylvanians angry at the abuse of state money. Most at the time were still spending twelve- to fourteen-hour days laboring in coal mines, blast furnaces, fields, and lumber mills. Therefore, Pennsylvanians overall had little concern for the political, machine-dominated politics that largely made a scandal involving the new Capitol building inevitable. In fact, given awareness that the public of the time had to the scandals of the late nineteenth century and the dealings of Quay, Penrose, and other political bosses, the citizens of Pennsylvania may have been more surprised if there had never been a scandal at all.

OPPOSITE PAGE: *"Will it Work?,"* Philadelphia Record, *October 14, 1906.*

Even today the Capitol graft scandal remains somewhat of an ENIGMA. The sheer volume of documents and number of governmental and legal institutions involved MAKE A THOROUGH UNDERSTANDING OF THE SCANDAL NEBULOUS, AT BEST.

CHAPTER FIVE • *The Capitol Graft Scandal*

Burning of the Books at Oxford, *Violet Oakley, 1906, Governor's Reception Room.*

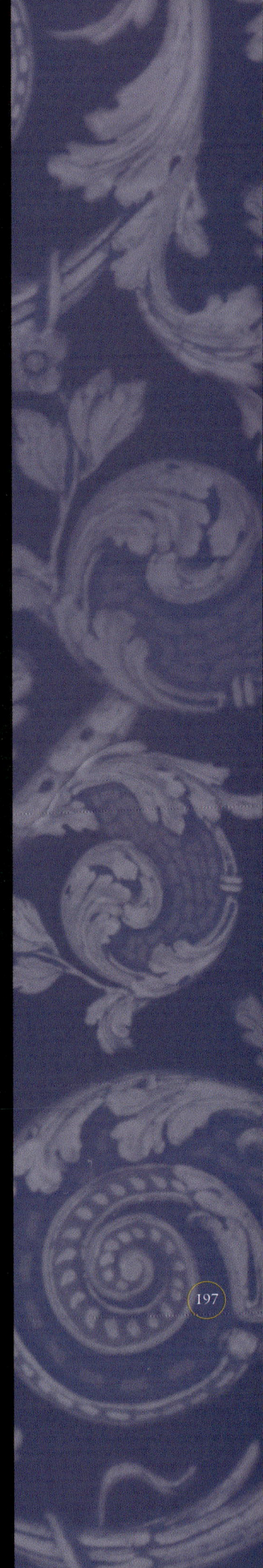

C·H·A·P·T·E·R
SIX

The Capitol's Fine & Decorative Arts

THE architecture and design of Pennsylvania's Capitol is breathtaking in its grandeur and elegance, but it is made complete only by the artwork that graces its halls and chambers. From plaster to paint, tile to glass, the level of artistry in the building was rendered at the pinnacle of twentieth century ingenuity. Even today the scale and overwhelming symbolic significance of works such as Edwin Austin Abbey's *Apotheosis* or Violet Oakley's *Unity* mural remains strong. The artwork of the Capitol has captured the idealism and character of the state and embodies a universal appeal recognizable to all generations. With proper care and preservation, these Pennsylvania treasures will continue to be a lasting testament to the spirit of Pennsylvania.

Despite the graft scandal surrounding the building's construction, there was little fault associated with the art commissions that were given to the highly talented artists who would decorate the Capitol. Artists such as Violet Oakley and George Grey Barnard from the very beginning requested that their contracts not be with John Sanderson. While the scandal was going on, they asserted that they had no knowledge of any kickbacks or payments to parties associated with the construction. The Capitol artists were exculpated from the scandal because only several pieces of artwork for the Capitol were completed before the building was dedicated in October of 1906.

Edwin Austin Abbey

CAPITOL WORK

ROTUNDA
- Science Revealing the Treasures of the Earth
- The Spirit of Light
- The Spirit of Vulcan
- The Spirit of Religious Liberty
- Art
- Science
- Law
- Religion

HOUSE CHAMBER
- The Hours
- Apotheosis of Pennsylvania
- Penn's Treaty
- Reading of the Declaration of Independence
- The Camp of the American Army at Valley Forge, February 1778

EDWIN AUSTIN ABBEY, 1852–1911

Joseph Huston was determined that the artwork for Pennsylvania's Capitol would be second to none, and he was fortunate to have a large number of Pennsylvania artists to choose from for his commissions. The first artistic choice he made was for the main rotunda and the three principal rooms—the Senate, House, and Supreme Court Chambers of the building. For this mammoth task, Huston requested the talents of noted muralist Edwin Austin Abbey.

Abbey was one of the most talented illustrators of his time. He was born in 1852 in Philadelphia and studied art at the Pennsylvania Academy of the Fine Arts under Christian Schuessele. Even before he was twenty years old, Abbey was a brilliant illustrator working for *Harper's Weekly*. He would remain an illustrator with *Harper's* from 1871–1874, but the company was so impressed with his work that he maintained an almost continual link with the publishers returning to it in 1876. He produced numerous sketches and illustrations for other magazines of note such as *Scribner's*.

In 1874 Abbey traveled to England, fell in love with the countryside, and became enamored with English culture. Though he always retained his U.S. citizenship, for all intents and purposes Abbey felt more English than American, and he made few trips back to the United States. During his time spent in England, Abbey became increasingly intrigued with historical drawings. However, in 1890, architect Charles Follen McKim, on the basis of advice from

sculptor Augustus Saint-Gaudens, recommended Abbey paint a frieze of murals for the Boston Public Library, which was designed by the famed architectural firm of McKim, Mead, and White. The frieze was to be titled *The Quest for the Holy Grail*. Abbey immediately went to work on the commission from his studio in England. Eleven years later the commission was completed and installed in the library, receiving numerous accolades within artistic and architectural communities. While working on this frieze, Abbey took a position as a staff artist with *Scribner's Magazine*.

It was while he was back in England, in 1901, that Joseph Huston telegraphed Abbey asking if he would be willing to undertake the massive mural commission for the Capitol in his native state. Knowing that this commission would be the largest and most time-consuming of his life, Abbey agreed and set to work immediately. He devoted most of his energies toward this project, which he viewed as a tribute to his native state of Pennsylvania.

It was six years until the eight murals for the lunettes and rondels of the Capitol rotunda were completed. These murals were sent to Harrisburg in early 1909. During the crossing the freighter that was carrying the murals was immersed in a fierce storm. The captain reported that the ship nearly capsized several times, which would have sent all the cargo, including the precious artwork to the bottom of the sea.

Upon their safe arrival in Harrisburg, the completed Abbey murals were hung in the rotunda, which up until that time had been adorned only with a decorative fleur-de-lis pattern to help detract from the bare plaster

THIS PAGE: The Camp of the American Army at Valley Forge, February, 1778, *1911, House Chamber.*

OPPOSITE PAGE: *Abbey at work in his studio, 1889.*

CHAPTER SIX • *The Capitol's Fine & Decorative Arts*

Abbey's Rotunda Murals

"Art deals with things forever incapable of definition, and that belong to love, beauty, joy and worship…"

THIS PAGE: *A.* Law; *B.* Religion; *C.* The Spirit of the Vulcan. *All rotunda murals were installed in 1909.*

OPPOSITE PAGE: The Apotheosis of Pennsylvania, *1911, House Chamber.*

walls of the lunettes. The large circular rondel murals, *Religion, Law, Science,* and *Art* respectively, each measure fourteen feet in diameter. The four crescent-shaped lunette murals measure thirty-eight feet in length by twenty-two feet in height.

During the period from 1902 until 1908 Abbey had also been at work on the murals for the House Chamber and had begun one for the Senate. Suddenly in 1911 Abbey became very ill and his work slowed dramatically. By the summer of that year, his studio assistant Ernest Board was at work on the unfinished *Reading of the Declaration of Independence* mural, with minimal supervision from the exhausted and often bed-ridden Abbey. In early August 1911 the art world was saddened when Edwin Austin Abbey passed away. Abbey had been fighting a losing battle with cancer for the majority of the year. His death left his remaining commission unfinished. Abbey's friend and neighbor John Singer Sargent supervised and assisted Board with the completion of the *Declaration* mural. Gertrude Abbey, Edwin's widow, oversaw the shipment and installation of her late husband's murals in the House

CHAPTER SIX • *The Capitol's Fine & Decorative Arts*

ABBEY'S ARTWORK

A. *The Reading of the Declaration of Independence,* Installed 1911, *House Chamber.*
B. *Art,* Installed 1909, *Rotunda.*
C. *The Spirit of Religious Liberty,* Installed 1909, *Rotunda.*

The Hours, *Edwin Austin Abbey, Installed 1911, House Chamber.*

Chamber. At the time of their installation in November 1911 it was decided that the only mural that had been completed for the Senate Chamber, *The Camp of the American Army at Valley Forge, February 1778*, would be removed from the Senate and installed on the north wall of the House Chamber. This would unify all of Abbey's completed work in two areas, the rotunda and the House of Representatives. The task of decorating the remaining two rooms would be given to famed Philadelphia artist Violet Oakley, and the themes and murals within them would be solely her design, from inception to completion.

Abbey also designed the decorative ceiling elements for both the House and Senate Chambers. In addition he produced two murals showing female figures holding garlanded wreaths for the spandrels of the Senate gallery arched entablature.

George Grey Barnard

CAPITOL WORK

NORTH GROUP
Love and Labor: The Unbroken Law
- Adam and Eve
- The Thinkers
- The Young Parents
- Two Brothers
- Prodigal Son
- The New Youth
- Baptism
- Philosopher - Teacher

SOUTH GROUP
The Burden of Life: The Broken Law
- Adam and Eve
- Angel of Consolation
- Burden Bearer
- Kneeling Youth
- Forsaken Mother
- Two Brothers
- Mourning Woman
- Despair and Hope

GEORGE GREY BARNARD, 1863–1938

The next area of artwork that Huston focused on was the building's exterior sculpture. For this task, Huston chose Pennsylvania native, George Grey Barnard. Barnard had been born in Bellefonte, Pennsylvania in 1863. Though by birthright a native of the state, his family moved west to Illinois when he was only three years old. From childhood Barnard manifested a determination and an aptitude for creating form with his hands. He worked as an engraver and later a taxidermist before entering the Art Institute of Chicago when he was nineteen. At the Institute, Barnard became enamored with the works of Italian master Michelangelo who he emulated throughout his lifetime. After his studies in Chicago, Barnard had made enough money from sculpting to travel to Paris to engage in advanced training. In Paris, Barnard was admitted to the prestigious École des Beaux-Arts for a four-year term of study. He truly lived the Bohemian lifestyle of an artist—reclusive, often penniless, and totally devoted to his art. His first large commission came from Alfred Corning Clark of the Singer Manufacturing Company. Clark's commission was for the famous *The Two Natures of Man*, now in the collection of the Metropolitan Museum of Art in New York City. Lauded for this

"The subjects, [bearings as they do on **Man's fulfilling** OR NOT FULFILLING the LAWS of God and nature] seemed to me peculiarly appropriate for the headquarters of a LEGISLATURE."

GEORGE GREY BARNARD

THIS PAGE: *Top, Barnard South Group,* The Burden of Life: The Broken Law; *Bottom, Portrait of George Grey Barnard, Anna Bilinska, 1890.*

OPPOSITE PAGE: *Barnard at work in studio, ca. 1930.*

CHAPTER SIX • *The Capitol's Fine & Decorative Arts*

creation, Barnard was relegated to financial hardship after the death of his patron in 1896. While he had several commissions that allowed him artistic survival, it was Joseph Huston's 1902 Capitol commission that again propelled Barnard to the forefront of the sculpting world.

The original sculptural commission for Barnard was much larger than what was actually produced for the building—another unfortunate side effect of monetary cutbacks in the construction costs. The original commission called for six sculptural groups, each to be situated on pedestals at all three of the Capitol's west entrances. Barnard set out immediately sketching and creating small models of his sculpture in clay. As soon as the first of these models was complete—those for the main entrance— Barnard set off for France to begin the creation of the twenty-seven heroic figures. During his time in France Barnard began collecting artwork from the Middle Ages in France as well as Gothic and Romanesque period pieces from his European travels. However, as he often said Barnard was no artist when it came to financial matters and, accordingly, it was widely known that he lived a bit beyond his means. To supplement his income, he was later forced to sell portions of his vast collection to wealthy American patrons to help pay for

> **Hippolyte LeFevre hailed Barnard as the "greatest artist of Amerca... Undoubtedly ONE OF THE GREATEST SCULPTORS OF THE WORLD."**

THIS PAGE: *Piccirilli Brothers at work carving the Barnard south statuary group, ca. 1907.*

OPPOSITE PAGE: *Top, Installation of the marble sculptures progresses, 1911; Bottom left, Barnard poses in his studio, undated; Bottom right, Sheet music written for the Barnard statuary dedication, 1911.*

Barnard Statuary
North Group
Love and Labor: The Unbroken Law

Top, Facing north; Bottom, Facing south.

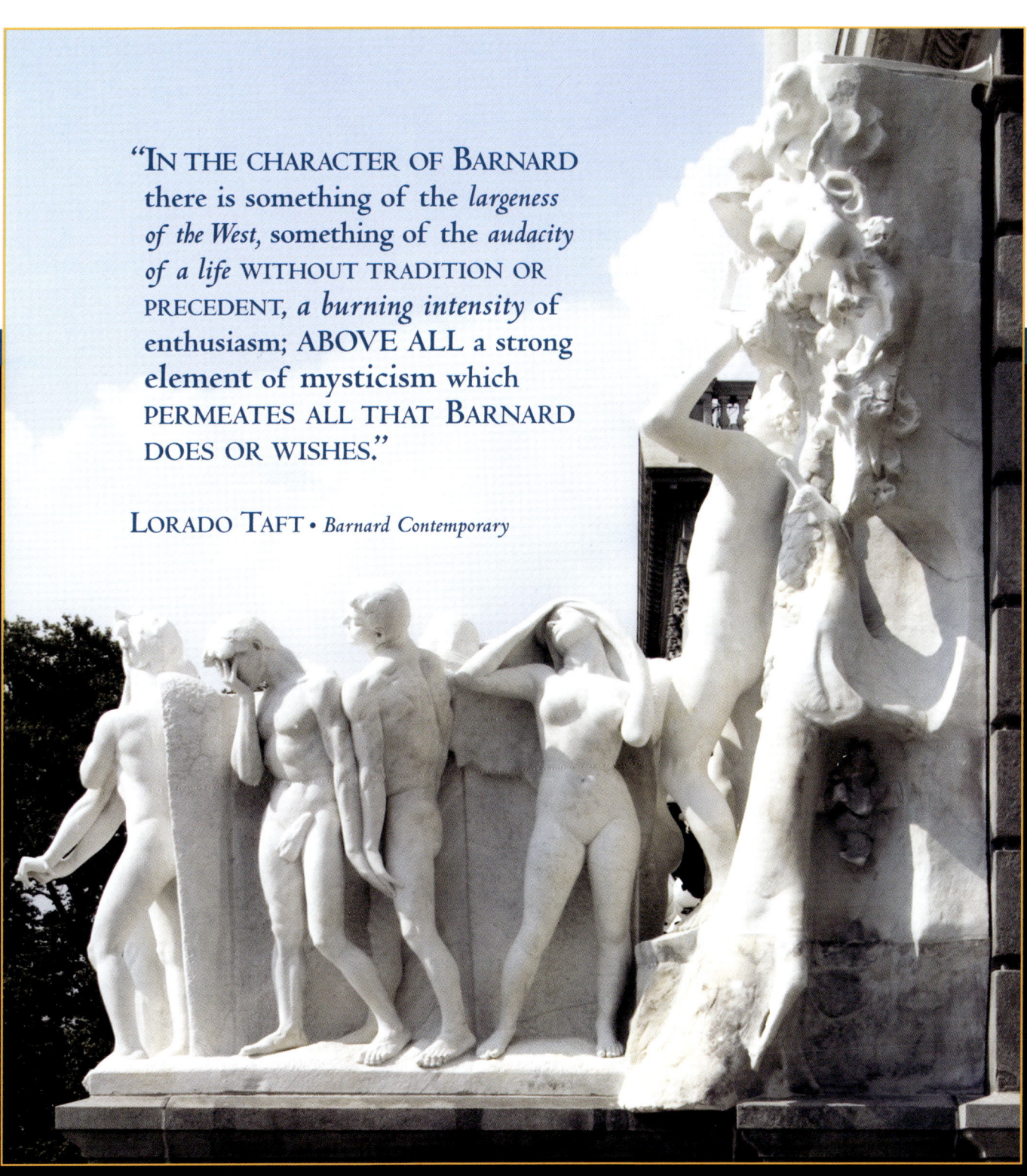

"IN THE CHARACTER OF BARNARD there is something of the *largeness of the West*, something of the *audacity of a life* WITHOUT TRADITION OR PRECEDENT, *a burning intensity* of enthusiasm; ABOVE ALL a strong element of mysticism which PERMEATES ALL THAT BARNARD DOES OR WISHES."

LORADO TAFT • *Barnard Contemporary*

South Group
The Burden of Life: The Broken Law

his workers and the marble casts of the Capitol groups.

In 1904 the original sculptural scheme along with other artwork within the building was scaled back, which allowed Barnard to focus on completion of the two groups for the main entrance. Barnard completed these two groups in 1910. They were titled *Love and Labor: The Unbroken Law*—the north group, and *The Burden of Life: The Broken Law*—the south group, respectively. The rough carving of these groups was done by the famed Piccirilli Brothers, a highly talented family of artists many of whom had emigrated from Italy to New York City. The Piccirillis were also contracted to install the statues in 1911, inspect them for damage in 1928, and clean them in 1935.

George Grey Barnard's finished groups were exhibited at the Paris Salon with praise from his contemporaries such as Auguste Rodin. President Roosevelt was returning from one of his African safaris and just happened to be in attendance at the Paris Salon. Upon seeing the statues he remarked that they were "ideal for a capitol." After their exhibition, the groups were disassembled and shipped to Harrisburg. Installed on October 4, 1911—a day that the legislature designated "Barnard Day"—the magnificent marble groups were dedicated in front of a crowd of five thousand people. Notable dignitaries included former Governors James A. Beaver and Samuel W. Pennypacker, and artist Violet Oakley.

In 1917 Barnard produced a huge statue of Abraham Lincoln. During this time Barnard continued his collecting of Romantic and Gothic works of art and assembled a massive collection at his home called "The Cloisters" in Washington Heights, New York. Barnard completed numerous other works of sculpture such as *The God Pan* located at Columbia University, *The Hewer* in Cairo, Illinois, and *Rising Woman* and *Adam and Eve* for the Rockefeller estate at Pocantico Hills, New York. He was at work on a massive project called the *Rainbow Arch* when he passed away in 1938. At his request, his body was moved to Harrisburg and he was buried in Harrisburg Cemetery, to be close to what he always considered his masterpiece.

Kneeling Youth, *George Grey Barnard, from south statuary group, ca. 1903.*

William Brantley Van Ingen

CAPITOL WORK

FIRST FLOOR MURALS
- Ephrata Community Spinning and Carding
- Scotch-Irish Teaching Theology
- Mennonite Foot-washing
- Brothers of Ephrata transcribing the Declaration of Independence
- Friends in Meeting
- German Immigrants from the Palantine on the Sarah Maria
- Rosicrucian Monk before the cave of Kelpius on the Wissahickon Creek
- Bonfire lit by the early settlers on Christmas Eve
- Moravian Sister preaching to the Indians
- Dunkards open air baptism
- Trombone Choir in the cupola of the Moravian Church at Bethlehem
- Old Swedes Church built in 1702
- Printing of the Bible on the Saur press at Germantown Press
- Pastorius circulating the first petition for the abolition of slavery

Van Ingen posing in front of a mural, ca. 1938.

WILLIAM BRANTLEY VAN INGEN, 1858–1955

The next art commission that Joseph Huston granted was two fold in nature—the completion of murals for the first floor south hyphen corridors and the stained glass windows for the House and Senate Chambers. For this task, he chose William Brantley Van Ingen. This multi-talented artist was born in Philadelphia, August 30, 1858, the son of William Henry and Sarah (Fairlamb) Van Ingen. He was a student of Thomas Eakins and Christian Schuessele at the Pennsylvania Academy of the Fine Arts. After finishing his studies at the Academy, he moved to New York where he apprenticed under John La Farge, Francis Lathrop, and Lewis Comfort Tiffany, three noted stained glass artists. However, Van Ingen's abilities were not restricted to stained glass alone. He was a brilliant muralist painter, a credit to his Parisian training under Leon Bonnát.

Religion

*Stained glass window by William Brantley Van Ingen, 1906.
Located in the House of Representatives.*

His fame as a muralist came with a commission for murals in the Library of Congress in Washington, D.C. and the U.S. Mint in Philadelphia. In addition, Van Ingen also produced sixteen panels depicting the industries of New Jersey for the State Capitol at Trenton; *Construction of the Canal*, five panels for the Panama Canal Administration Building in Balboa Heights, Panama; eight panels for the Federal Building in Chicago; and two panels for the Federal Building in Indianapolis, Indiana, along with a series of murals for the Gideon Hawley Library at the University of Albany, among other less mammoth commissions. Huston often relied on "Van," as he called him, for advice about art and artists. Huston commissioned Van Ingen for several other art commissions, including murals in the Witherspoon Building in Philadelphia, which Joseph Huston had also designed.

Van Ingen's 1902 commission for the Capitol was to design fourteen painted murals for the lunette spaces of the first floor south hyphen corridor on the House side of the Capitol building. In addition he was to design all of the stained glass windows for both the House and Senate Chambers. Van Ingen chose to represent the religious history of the Commonwealth within the south hyphen corridor. He selected groups that depicted Pennsylvania's religious diversity, including the Quakers, Mennonites, Rosicrucian monks, Moravians, Dunkards, Scots-Irish, Germans, and Swedes. For the ocular stained glass windows in the Chambers he chose industrial, commercial, technological subjects along with windows depicting peace, liberty, and religion that were symbolic of Pennsylvania's heritage. The stained glass windows were executed by Thomas Wright and John Calvin of the Decorative Stained Glass Company of New York. They were installed in time for the Capitol's dedication on October 4, 1906.[1] The murals for the south hyphen were installed in the lunette spaces in 1907.

William Van Ingen went on to produce art in the United States and abroad. He received a commission from New York financier Charles T. Yerkes to create a Japanese Room in his mansion. Van Ingen traveled to Japan to conduct research for his murals. He also painted murals for private residences in the Philadelphia area.

House
- Abundance
- Bridge Building
- Chemistry
- Commerce
- Education
- Electricity
- Justice
- Liberty
- Natural Gas
- Petroleum
- Printing Press
- Religion
- Steam Engineering
- Steel and Iron

Senate
- Architecture
- Foundries
- Glass Blowing
- History
- Legislature
- Militia
- Peace
- Railroads
- Temperance
- Weaving

He held memberships in the Society of Mural Painters and the Architectural League of New York, was a fellow at the Pennsylvania Academy of the Fine Arts, and was a member of the Artists Aid Society and Artists Fund Society of New York. Though best known as an artist, he also lectured on behalf of the preservation of New York's public parks, serving for a time as the president of the parks committee. Van Ingen spent the latter part of his life at the Masonic Home in Utica, New York, where after lingering from a long illness he passed away on February 6, 1955 at the age of ninety-six.

Brothers of Ephrata, William Brantley Van Ingen, South corridor.

Van Ingen's Stained Glass Windows

A. Liberty.
B. Steel and Iron.
C. Natural Gas.
D. Petroleum.
E. Steam Engineering.

South Corridor Lunette Murals by Van Ingen. *From Top:* Scotch-Irish Teaching Theology, *Located at Log College, birthplace of Princeton University;* Ephrata Community Spinning and Carding; Trombone Choir in the cupola of the Moravian Church at Bethlehem.

CHAPTER SIX • *The Capitol's Fine & Decorative Arts*

Portrait of Mercer, ca. 1898.

Henry Chapman Mercer

Henry Chapman Mercer, 1856–1930

In 1902, while commissions were being given out, Joseph Huston was approached by Henry Chapman Mercer of Doylestown, Pennsylvania. Since the late 1800s, Mercer had been making what he termed Moravian tile, for floors, fireplaces, and other decorative purposes. He suggested to Huston that his tile would better harmonize with the white marble Capitol walls, than the original marble floor that Huston had envisioned in his designs for the Capitol's first floor. Huston related to Mercer that he wanted picture designs within the floor. Huston recommended that Mercer develop drawings or cartoons for the floor and bring them back to Huston's office. Mercer decided that he would trace the history of the Commonwealth from prehistoric times to 1906 using mosaics grouted into the floor. The concept was approved by Huston, and Mercer went on to produce four hundred mosaics that would begin at the north wing entrance and continue chronologically through the building until they ended at the south wing entrance.

Apparently the idea impressed Huston enough that he agreed to allow Mercer to produce his tile for the Capitol building, resulting is the largest single piece of artwork in the Capitol.

Born in Doylestown, Pennsylvania in 1856, Mercer attended Harvard University and the University of Pennsylvania's Law School. Though he worked as a lawyer for a time, he later gave up the practice in favor of archaeology. After travels in Europe with his wealthy aunt Elizabeth Lawrence, who was very influential in Mercer's life, he returned home to the United States. In the early 1890s he was appointed Curator of American and Prehistoric Archaeology at the University of

Scythe, *floor mosaic, North corridor.*

CHAPTER SIX • *The Capitol's Fine & Decorative Arts*

Henry Chapman Mercer's
MOSAIC
FLOOR TILES

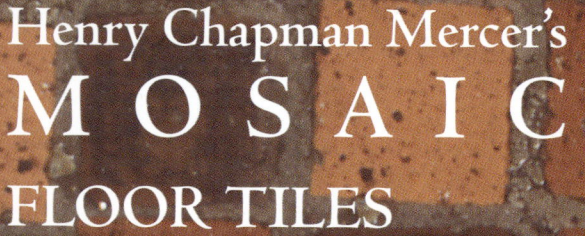

A. *The Elk*, *North corridor and rotunda.*

B. *The Grey Squirrel*, *North corridor and rotunda.*

C. *The Raccoon*, *North lobby.*

OPPOSITE PAGE: *Candle Dipper*, *North corridor.*

"IT IS THE LIFE OF THE PEOPLE that is sought to be expressed; THE BUILDING OF A COMMON-WEALTH economically GREAT, BY THE INDIVIDUAL WORK OF THOUSANDS OF HANDS, rather than by wars and legislatures…"

Henry C. Mercer

Pennsylvania's Museum. Mercer claimed later that, "Archaeology…turned me into a potter."[2] In 1897 Mercer became concerned with the destruction of early American society, which he saw being replaced by industrialism. Seeing a jumble of old agricultural tools and household utensils for sale, he realized very quickly that American pre-industrial history was being displaced. Mercer abandoned his job at the museum and began "rummaging the bake ovens, wagon houses, cellars, haylofts, smokehouses, garrets, and chimney corners" for what would later be known as Americana. He said of his collecting, "If we are going to collect old furniture, porcelain, and candlesticks," he wrote, "why not go a step further and gather hoes, axes, tin kitchens, scythes, forks, plows, and beehives?"[3]

At around the same time he also became interested in the pottery of Pennsylvania Germans. Concerned that this practice was dying out, he apprenticed himself to one of the few authentic potters left in the area to learn all that he could about early German pottery. In September of 1898 he founded the Moravian Pottery and Tile Works, which is still in existence in Doylestown.

The first tiles he produced were based on early German stove plates, which Mercer himself had collected. By 1900 Mercer was becoming an important artisan who was influenced by the Arts and Crafts movement in America. No doubt aware of the building contracts being sought for the State Capitol in 1902, Mercer made a point to suggest the idea of folk-art tile for the buildings floor. Huston accepted the idea of allowing both folk and fine art to coexist in the Capitol building, proving that he was interested in this art form, which he also installed in his private residence. In all, Mercer would produce thousands of clay field tiles for the floor of the Capitol—the most of any building containing his tiles. For the sixteen thousand square feet of tile they received, the Commonwealth was billed three dollars per square foot, or $48 thousand total.

Though the Capitol is the largest single collection of Mercer's tiles, it may not be the most famous. The casino at Monte Carlo, Rockefeller's New York estate in Pocantico Hills, and Grauman's Chinese Theater in Hollywood all boast Mercer tiles in quantity.

After the completion of the Capitol commission, Mercer went on to build his own unique house called Fonthill, located adjacent to his tile works. He also built his own museum to house the artifacts of Americana that he had collected. Today the Mercer Museum is home to over forty thousand artifacts of early American society, twenty-five thousand of which were in Henry Mercer's own collection.

THIS PAGE: *Left*, Blast Furnace, *South corridor; Right*, Automobile, *South vestibule*.

LITERATURE IN STONE: THE HUNDRED YEAR HISTORY OF THE PENNSYLVANIA STATE CAPITOL

A. Penn's Treaty, *Rotunda*.
B. Indian Paddling Canoe, *North vestibule*.
C. Shelling Corn, *South corridor*.
D. Milking the Cow, *Rotunda*.

Violet Oakley

VIOLET OAKLEY, 1874–1961

The first woman artist to receive a large commission for adorning a capitol building in the United States was Violet Oakley. Though it was not known at the time, Oakley would become the principal artist for the largest amount of murals in the Pennsylvania Capitol. In 1902, through the assistance of a mutual friend of hers and Huston's, architect John Irwin Bright, she was recommended as an artist for the building. Huston offered Oakley the commission to paint murals for the Governor's Reception Room because he felt it would "add interest to the building and act as an encouragement of women of the state."[4]

Oakley was actually born in Jersey City, New Jersey, though she lived the majority of her life in Philadelphia. She studied at the Art Students' League in New York and later at Drexel with famous

CAPITOL WORK

GOVERNOR'S RECEPTION ROOM:
The Founding of the State of Liberty Spiritual
- William Tyndale printing his Translation of the New Testament into English at Cologne 1525
- Smuggling the volumes into England 1526
- The Burning of the Books at Oxford 1526
- Execution of William Tyndale 1536
- Answer to Tyndale's Prayer: Henry VIII granting permission for the Bible to be read 1537
- Condemnation of Anne Askew for Heresy 1546
- Culmination of Intolerance & Persecution in Civil War: Rise of the Puritan Idea 1642
- George Fox on his Mount of Vision 1652
- William Penn, student at Christ Church, Oxford 1660
- He hears the Quaker-Preaching in the Fields 1662
- Admiral Sir William Penn Denouncing and Turning his Son from Home 1667
- Arrest while preaching at Meeting 1670
- Examination before the Lieutenant of the Tower of London
- Condemnation to imprisonment in Newgate, writing "The Great Case of Liberty of Conscience"
- After his own Liberation Penn seeks to free other Friends imprisoned
- Penn's Vision
- King Charles II signs the Charter of Pennsylvania 1681
- Penn's first sight of his Promised Land 1682

illustrator Howard Pyle. Oakley became part one of a triumvirate of three noted female illustrators of their time—Oakley, Elizabeth Shippen Green, and Jessie Wilcox Smith. From 1899 until 1901 these three illustrators lived together at the Red Rose Inn in Villanova, Pennsylvania, which was where Violet started her murals for the Governor's Reception Room, a frieze that she titled *The Founding of the State of Liberty Spiritual*.

Traveling to England, Oakley immediately set out to conduct research for her murals. Though both Governor Pennypacker and Huston gave her recommendations on topics for the room, Oakley persisted in depicting the story of William Penn, as the founder of

THIS PAGE: *The Legend of the Latchstring, 1919, Senate Chamber.*

OPPOSITE PAGE: *Oakley poses for a portrait, undated.*

SENATE CHAMBER:

The Creation and Preservation of the Union
- The Legend of the Latch-string
- The Legend of the Slave-ship
- Troops of the Revolution 1777
- Troops of the Civil War 1863
- Washington at the Constitutional Convention 1787
- Lincoln at Gettysburg 1863
- The Armies of the Earth, striving to take the Kingdom of Peace by Violence
- The Slaves of the Earth, driven forward and upward by their Slave-Drivers
- International Understanding and Unity: the End of Warfare, the End of Slavery. Supreme Manifestation of Enlightenment. Prophecy of William Penn

CHAPTER SIX • *The Capitol's Fine & Decorative Arts*

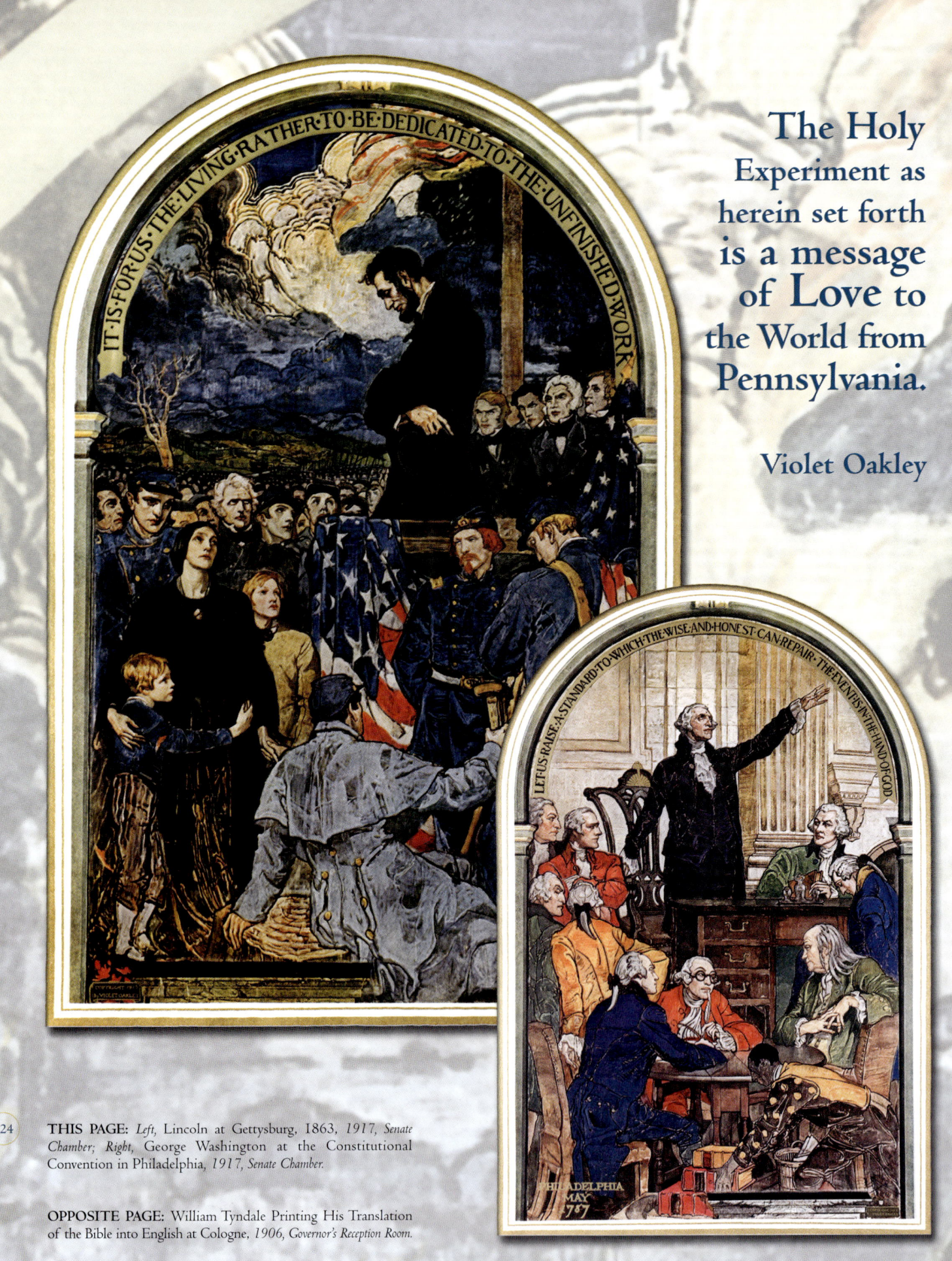

> The Holy Experiment as herein set forth is a message of Love to the World from Pennsylvania.
>
> — Violet Oakley

THIS PAGE: *Left,* Lincoln at Gettysburg, 1863, *1917, Senate Chamber; Right,* George Washington at the Constitutional Convention in Philadelphia, *1917, Senate Chamber.*

OPPOSITE PAGE: William Tyndale Printing His Translation of the Bible into English at Cologne, *1906, Governor's Reception Room.*

the colony. Violet was very strong in her conviction about wanting to trace Pennsylvania's history of religious tolerance and the ideals of social freedom and justice inherited from Penn for the reception room murals. Eventually, both Huston and Governor Stone acquiesced to her designs after they reviewed her preliminary studies that were presented before the Capitol Building Commission. When the frieze was complete in 1906, Oakley's fourteen murals for the reception room were some of the first to be installed in the Capitol. Though they were sent to Harrisburg prior to the October 4 dedication, they were not yet in place due to finishing touches in the reception room. The thirteen murals were unveiled on November 27, 1906 before a large crowd. With her work complete, Oakley found other commissions to occupy her time, but with the passing of Edwin Austin Abbey in 1911, Samuel B. Rambo, Superintendent of Public Grounds and Buildings, offered Oakley the opportunity to create murals for the unfinished Senate and Supreme Court Chambers. She began her new contract in 1912 working on both commissions concurrently, although the Senate took precedence. After more research and work, the

SUPREME COURT CHAMBER:

The Opening of the Book of the Law
- Divine Law: Key-Note
- The Scale of the Law: The Octave
- The Golden Age: Law of Nature
- Themis: Greek Idea of Revealed Law
- The Decalogue: Hebrew Idea of Revealed Law
- The Beatitudes: Christian Idea of Revealed Law
- Code of Justinian: Law of Reason
- Blackstone's Commentaries: Common Law
- The Spirit of William Blackstone: Common Law
- Commentaries: Common Law
- Penn as Law-Giver: Law of Reason
- Supreme Court of the State: Law of Nations
- Supreme Court of the Nation: Law of Nations
- Supreme Court of the World: International Law
- Disarmament: International Law
- The Spirit of Law: Purification & Enlightenment

CHAPTER SIX • *The Capitol's Fine & Decorative Arts*

"I WANT YOU TO PERCEIVE the borders of her garments—the trailing of her veils whenever you look upon the sapphire of the sea… when you hear the sound of rushing water she is there; her voice is in the murmuring of the ice floe. She is the whiteness of dazzling snow; the showers upon the grass; the blue of all mountains and hills… 'HER PRICE IS ABOVE RUBIES' for she is THE WISDOM OF LOVE."

– VIOLET OAKLEY AT *UNITY* DEDICATION

Senate murals on the front wall, *Unity* and *The Creation and Preservation of the Union,* were dedicated on February 12, 1917. The two Quaker legends at the back of the Chamber were dedicated on January 20, 1919.

After the completion of the Senate murals, Violet devoted her attention to the Supreme Court Chamber, and for these paintings she chose to illustrate what she saw as the evolution of law, from its earliest beginnings to the present. The Supreme Court murals are Violet's most allegorical and they also best illustrate her ideological journey as a painter committed to the ideals of world peace. She chose to represent law as movement up a musical scale, beginning with the painting *Divine Law,* which she said was both the Alpha and the

International Understanding and Unity Supreme Manifestation of Enlightenment Prophecy of William Penn, *1917, Senate Chamber.*

CHAPTER SIX • *The Capitol's Fine & Decorative Arts*

Supreme Court Chamber Murals by Violet Oakley

Omega. The frieze continues around the room proceeding from the paintings *The Law of Nature* and *International Law*, before returning to the *Keynote*. Violet fervently believed that her vision of the evolution of law, as depicted in the Supreme Court Chamber, would lead to eventual world peace. The murals in the court chamber were installed and dedicated on May 23, 1927. Overall Violet Oakley had become the one artist to work over a quarter century, creating forty-three murals for the Capitol building.

Literature in Stone: The Hundred Year History of the Pennsylvania State Capitol

> "THE
> PEOPLE DESIRE
> PEACE
> BY THE OVERCOMING
> OF EVIL, BY THE
> DEAFEAT
> OF
> SINISTER FORCES."
>
> WOODROW WILSON

THIS PAGE: *Top*, William Penn as Law Giver-Law of Reason, *1927, Supreme Court Chamber*; *Bottom*, Christ and Disarmament-International Law, *1927, Supreme Court Chamber.*

OPPOSITE PAGE: Divine Law-Key Note, *1927, Supreme Court Chamber.*

CHAPTER SIX • *The Capitol's Fine & Decorative Arts*

ROLAND HINTON PERRY, 1870–1941

Artist Roland Hinton Perry is the man who sculpted the statue *Commonwealth* on top of the Capitol's dome. Often referred to incorrectly as Ms. Penn, *Commonwealth* is the most visible piece of Capitol artwork as she is able to be seen from miles around Harrisburg. Perry was commissioned by Huston in 1904 to execute a drawing that the architect had done of this allegorical figure. Using a series of steam hoists, the bronze figure was lifted to the top on the dome and installed on May 25, 1905.

Roland Hinton Perry

According to Huston, she represents "the symbolic embodiment of the Commonwealth of Pennsylvania." The statue weighs three tons and the figure alone stands fourteen-feet-six-inches tall. Adding the large gilded ball at the base, the entire sculpture stands over eighteen feet high.

Perry was a master of both painting and sculpture, and he began his studies at the Art Students League in New York City at the age of sixteen. Three years later he traveled to Paris to study with Paul Delance at the Academie Delecluse. He entered the École des Beaux-Arts in 1890 as the only American student admitted that year. Perry remained in Paris for six years, producing both paintings and sculpture. Returning to the United States, he was commissioned to sculpt bas reliefs at the Library of Congress. He also created a frieze for the New Amsterdam Theater in New York City. Perry is also credited with two monuments at Gettysburg National Military Park—the statue of Brigadier General George Greene on Culp's Hill, and Brigadier General James Wadsworth on McPherson's Ridge. In all, Perry designed and created over thirty major pieces of art, and he continued to work prolifically until his death on October 27, 1941.

LITERATURE IN STONE: THE HUNDRED YEAR HISTORY OF THE PENNSYLVANIA STATE CAPITOL

THIS PAGE: *Several views of* Commonwealth *during her restoration celebration, 1998.*

OPPOSITE PAGE: *Roland Hinton Perry, undated.*

CHAPTER SIX • *The Capitol's Fine & Decorative Arts*

North Corridor Murals

CAPITOL WORK

NORTH CORRIDOR
- Amish Farming 1730-40
- Lumber ca. 1880
- Coal ca. 1880
- Drakes First Oil Well, Titusville 1859
- Blacksmith Shop 1880
- Country Store 1867-70
- Steel
- Philadelphia Commerce early 1800
- Canal Boat 1835
- Ship Building, Philadelphia 1760-70
- Railroads and Telegraph 1838
- Digging Tunnel - Turnpike 1840
- Turnpike boom - Conestoga Wagon 1828
- John Fitch's Steamboat 1787

Vincent Maragliotti

VINCENT MARAGLIOTTI, 1888–1978

There were other artists at the time who were offered commissions for work on the new Capitol building. One of these artists was John White Alexander, who was commissioned to complete murals for the north hyphen lunettes, opposite those of Van Ingen. However, Alexander said that he was both too busy and too ill at the time to accept the commission and turned it down. The lunettes in the north hyphen were actually left undecorated until the early 1970s, when artist Vincent Maragliotti, who was living in the Harrisburg area, was offered the commission. Maragliotti chose to depict scenes of Pennsylvania's commercial and transportation history on the walls.

Maragliotti was a native of Italy and had emigrated to the United States at age seventeen. He studied architecture and fine arts at the National Academy of Design and the Cooper Union Art College of New York. Maragliotti was noted for his decorations in hotels and theaters throughout the east coast. He painted murals in the Copley Plaza Hotel in Boston, the Waldorf-Astoria and Biltmore Hotels, and the Strand, Roxy, Majestic, and Shubert theaters in New York City.

THIS PAGE: *Maragliotti at work in his studio, undated.*

OPPOSITE PAGE: *A. Drakes First Oil Well, Titusville 1859; B. Steel; C. Canal Boat 1835; All installed 1972 in north corridor, D. Self-portrait by Vincent Maragliotti, undated.*

CHAPTER SIX • *The Capitol's Fine & Decorative Arts*

In the mid-1920s, Maragliotti was at work on the Lexington Avenue synagogue when he was introduced to architect William Gehron. Impressed with Maragliotti's work, Gehron asked him "to supervise and direct the decorations of the public areas in the South Office Building of the Capitol group in Harrisburg…"[5] Maragliotti would eventually work in every building in the Capitol Complex, in creating new murals, repairing, and cleaning artwork from the 1920s through the 1970s. This included the Barnard sculptures and the Abbey and Oakley murals. In 1965 he painted a large mural on the second floor of the newly created William Penn Memorial Museum, (now the State Museum of Pennsylvania). He died at his home in Summerdale, Pennsylvania in 1978.

The famous artist Mary Cassatt was offered a commission for the Capitol, which she accepted. Cassatt's task was to produce a few small paintings for the Ladies Lounge on the second floor, adjoining the Lieutenant Governor's suite. Cassatt eventually completed both of these paintings, but promptly refused to sign a contract with John Sanderson, the furnishing contractor for the Capitol. Cassatt claimed in the newspapers of the time that she was approached by a politician who demanded a kickback of half her commission. Cassatt's stature at the time was such that she immediately resigned her commission and sold the two paintings privately. One of Cassatt's paintings, intended for the Capitol's Ladies' Lounge was purchased by the Westmoreland County Museum, in Westmoreland County, Pennsylvania. A study for this particular mural is located at the Speed Art Museum in Louisville, Kentucky. The other Cassatt work intended for the Capitol is still in private hands.

THIS PAGE: *Top,* Country Store 1867-70, *Vincent Maragliotti, 1970, North corridor; Bottom,* Mother and Two Children, *Mary Cassatt, 1901.*

OPPOSITE PAGE: *Top,* Vincenzo Alfano, undated; *Bottom,* Putti *located on pediment in the Capitol rotunda.*

Vincenzo Alfano

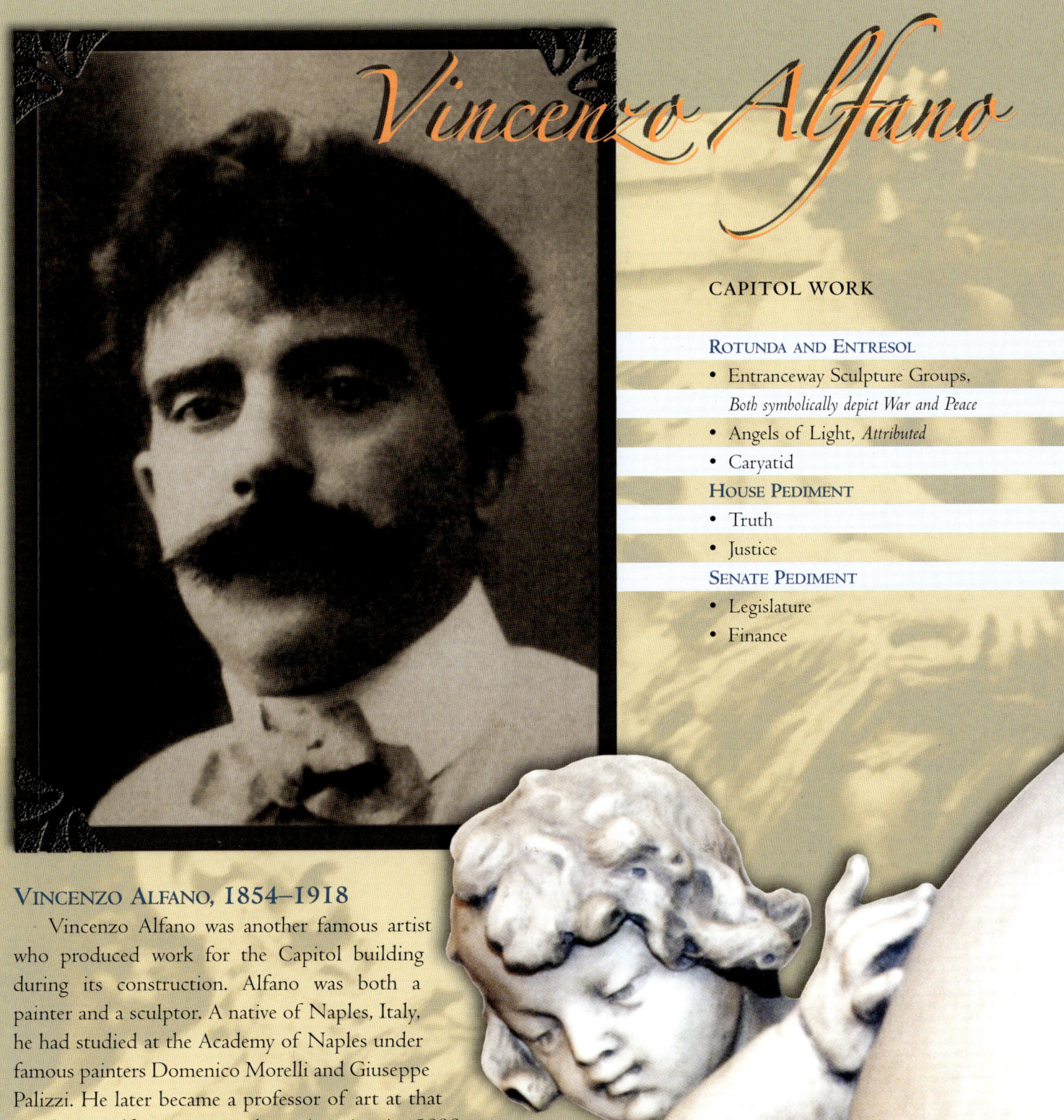

CAPITOL WORK

ROTUNDA AND ENTRESOL
- Entranceway Sculpture Groups, *Both symbolically depict War and Peace*
- Angels of Light, *Attributed*
- Caryatid

HOUSE PEDIMENT
- Truth
- Justice

SENATE PEDIMENT
- Legislature
- Finance

VINCENZO ALFANO, 1854–1918

Vincenzo Alfano was another famous artist who produced work for the Capitol building during its construction. Alfano was both a painter and a sculptor. A native of Naples, Italy, he had studied at the Academy of Naples under famous painters Domenico Morelli and Giuseppe Palizzi. He later became a professor of art at that Academy. Alfano emigrated to America in 1898, attracted largely by commissions from the growing American Renaissance movement, which enticed numerous Italian artists. Alfano took up residence in New York and taught at the New York Industrial Museum. In 1902 he was given his Capitol commission, which was to execute sculptural groups for the two entranceways inside the building's main vestibule. The figures are

Capitol Sculpture by Vincenzo Alfano

- A. Entranceway north sculpture group.
- B. Entranceway south sculpture group.
- C. Angel of Light, Attributed to Vincenzo Alfano, Rotunda.
- D. Pediment sculpture, Second floor House Chamber portal.
- E. Putti figures on pediment of entresol doorway.
- F. Caryatid, Entresol.

Literature in Stone: The Hundred Year History of the Pennsylvania State Capitol

allegorical representations located above the door pediments. The north group represents the early Commonwealth and its contact with Native Americans. The south group represents a Commonwealth enriched by arts and sciences. A theme of war and peace through which society has progressed are also espoused in both of the works.

From Huston's designs, Alfano also modeled the allegorical figures over the pediments at the second floor entrances to the House and Senate Chambers. The figures over the House represent "Truth" and "Justice," and those over the Senate "Legislature" and "Finance." The groups were inspired by Michelangelo's *Medici Tombs* for the New Sacristy in Florence, and similar motifs that were in the Paris Opera House. Alfano also carved the marble caryatids, globe, and cherubs located at the Entresol floor of the grand staircase, along with the sculpted plaster heads of famous Pennsylvanians present in the north and south hyphen corridors. In addition, the pediments over both the House and Senate Chamber's second floor entrances were produced by Alfano. The two large plaster *Angels of Light* gracing the newel posts of the grand staircase may also have been sculpted by Alfano, or possibly by a contemporary of his, Louis Milione of Philadelphia. Unfortunately, the original artist for these pieces remains unknown.

CHAPTER SIX • *The Capitol's Fine & Decorative Arts*

Donald R. MacGregor

Donald R. MacGregor & Company

Throughout the building there are many areas of ornate stenciling, Greek keys, acanthus designs, and elaborate decorative elements that were artistically a statement of Joseph Huston's design. While other artists dealt with the fine arts and specific Pennsylvania topics, the decorative elements in the building were contracted to the Donald MacGregor firm of Philadelphia.

Donald MacGregor (1870–1930), the principal in the firm, had studied art at the Pennsylvania Academy of the Fine Arts under William Merritt Chase. He in turn completed several murals within the building. One is on the ceiling of the Lieutenant Governor's Ladies Reception Room, entitled *Venus and Two Loves*. The other murals that MacGregor produced are at the light court ends of each hyphen corridor and these are titled the *Four Seasons*. In addition the painters on MacGregor's staff were responsible for all the gold and aluminum leafing, stenciling and glazing work, and highly ornate decorative painting throughout the building— a truly massive undertaking. Without the creative work of the MacGregor firm, the beauty of the Capitol would not be unified with its architectural surroundings. Their work blends all of the building's elements, creating a harmony of art.

Capitol Work

Corridors and Chambers
- Stencil and Decorative Finishing

North and South Light Court
- Four Seasons

Lieutenant Governor's Reception Room
- Venus and Two Loves

Donald MacGregor's Capitol Murals

A. Spring and Summer
B. Autumn and Winter
C. Venus and Two Loves

Alfred Godwin

ALFRED GODWIN

The Capitol's green and gold hemispheric opalescent glass dome in the Supreme Court Chamber was created by Alfred Godwin of Philadelphia. Godwin emigrated from England in 1874 where he had received his training in stained glass. In 1891 he ran an advertisement in the directory listing his shop address at 1325 Market Street, Philadelphia. He also produced windows for several churches including the former Presbyterian Church on Market Square in Philadelphia. It is surmised that Godwin also created the ochre stained glass windows in the rotunda's upper dome, the light court skylights, the light court lunette openings on the Capitol's fifth floor, and the decorative ceiling glass in the House and Senate galleries.[6] All of the glasswork in these areas, along with the leaded glass skylights on the fourth floor are indicative of Godwin's style of work.

CAPITOL GLASSWORK

THIS PAGE: *Left, Supreme Court glass dome; Right, Decorative stained glass at top of light court.*

OPPOSITE PAGE:
A. *Rotunda dome glass window.*
B. *Supreme & Superior Court.*
C. *Light court from first floor.*
D. *Light court skylights.*

CHAPTER SIX • *The Capitol's Fine & Decorative Arts*

Henry-Bonnard Bronze Company

HENRY-BONNARD BRONZE COMPANY

The exterior ornate bronze work for the building was all done by the Henry-Bonnard Bronze Company of New York, under the supervision of bronze master Eugene F. Aucaigne. Huston was introduced to Aucaigne through George Grey Barnard, who had contact with the company because they had produced his famous sculpture, *The Hewer*. After Huston had drawn the original sketches and studies, Henry-Bonnard, with Aucaigne at the helm, created the large bronze doors at the Capitol's west entrances, along with the monumental light standards topped with an eagle at the main entrance. They did the majority of the large-scale ornate bronze work in the building. All the light standards on the first floor of the Capitol, the second floor rotunda balcony, the Supreme Court Chamber, and the Governor's Reception Room were produced by Bonnard Bronze. The House Chamber originally had standards most likely also produced by the Henry-Bonnard firm, but were removed as they took up too much space on the floor, hampering legislative activities.

The second floor balcony grills at the post office areas, and the grills over the House and Senate entrance doors, along with the ballustrate railings emblazoned with eagles on the fourth floor balcony, were also created by the Henry-Bonnard company.

A. Supreme and Superior Court light standard.
B. Detail of rotunda light standard.
C. Aucaigne astride an eagle standard that graces the front steps of the Capitol, ca. 1905. (Notice the plaster mold for bronze entranceway doors at right.)
D. West entrance bronze doors.
E. South wing bronze doors.
F. Worker stands beside rotunda light standard, ca. 1905.

Pennsylvania Bronze Company

Pennsylvania Bronze Company

The Pennsylvania Bronze Company was founded in Philadelphia in 1902 by John Sanderson in an effort to win the bronze contract for the Capitol building. It furnished all the ornate bronze light fixtures within the building, including the chandeliers and sconces in the House, Senate, and Supreme Court Chambers, the large lanterns at all three of the Capitol's west entrances, and the pumpkin ball fixtures throughout the building. Many of the company's top craftsmen were former employees of the Sterling Bronze Company of New York City—a premier manufacturer of the finest cast and hand-chased fixtures. Several of the fixtures for the Capitol were gold plated, especially for ornate areas, such as the Governor's Reception Room. Others were coated with a gold-tinted lacquer. The Capitol's ornate bronze fixtures are all representative of the best bronze foundries of the day and do much to heighten the grandeur of the building.

THIS PAGE: *Entrance lantern, South hyphen corridor.*

OPPOSITE PAGE:
A. *Pumpkin Ball light, South hyphen corridor.*
B. *Governor's Reception Room chandelier.*
C. *View of the House Chamber showing chandeliers and wall sconces.*
D. *Supreme and Superior Court chandelier.*

CHAPTER SIX • *The Capitol's Fine & Decorative Arts*

Additional BRONZE Pieces

A. *Eagle grill, Rotunda second floor above chamber vestibules.*
B. *Eagle grill in fourth floor balcony.*
C. *Governor's Reception Room light standard.*
D. *Senate Chamber light standard.*
E. *Rotunda second floor balcony light standard, by Henry-Bonnard Co.*

LITERATURE IN STONE: THE HUNDRED YEAR HISTORY OF THE PENNSYLVANIA STATE CAPITOL

FIGUREHEAD CAPITALS

The first floor corridor capitals represent the vast mixture of countries that have formed the Commonwealth. Below each figure's portrait is the national foilage or flower from their individual homeland.

F. Benjamin Franklin - AMERICAN
Multi-talented figure in American history. Some of his accomplishments include signing the Declaration of Independence, publishing *Poor Richard's Almanac*, serving as postmaster of Philadelphia, founding the first American fire insurance company, serving as an American ambassador to France, and numerous inventions like the lightning rod, the Franklin stove, and bifocal glasses.

G. Daniel Boone - AMERICAN
He was born in Berks County, Pennsylvania. First to attempt colonizing Kentucky.

H. Oneida Chief Swatane - NATIVE AMERICAN
Representative of the "Five Nations" invoved in treaties with land purchases between settlers and Native Americans between 1728–1748. Served as a viceroy of government to tributary tribes from Shamokin, now Sunbury, Pennsylvania.

CHAPTER SIX • *The Capitol's Fine & Decorative Arts*

248

Plaster Capitals
in the Capitol

A. **David Rittenhouse - DUTCH**
Astronomer, mathematician, and clock maker. Member of the convention that formed the State Constitution of Pennsylvania.

B. **Daniel Hayes Agnew - FRENCH**
Born in Lancaster County with Hugenot descent. Famous physician and surgeon at the University of Pennsylvania, most known for his inventions and medical writings.

C. **Heinrich Melchoir Mühlenberg - GERMAN**
He was an organizer of the Lutheran Church in U.S.

D. **George Keith - SCOTTISH**
Converted Quaker who did much to spread the doctrine. He came to the Americas and served as Surveyor General for New Jersey.

E. **James Logan - IRISH SCOTCH**
Cofounder of Philadelphia with William Penn. Remained in the state spending his time as a public servant and author.

F. **David Jones - WELSH**
Clergyman of early Baptist church in U.S., served as a chaplain in Revolutionary War. He specifically served under General Anthony Wayne.

G. **Gustavus Hesselius - SWEDISH**
Earliest painter and organ bulder in America. Received first public commission by a U.S. resident.

H. **Count Casimir Pulaski - POLISH**
Joined Revolutionary army as a volunteer and was appointed by Congress as a brigadier-general three days later. Became leader of a light horse and cavalry division at Valley Forge called Pulaski's Legion.

I. **Tedyuscung - NATIVE AMERICAN**
Born in Delaware, he joined the Moravian Indian Mission and was baptized into their faith. He left shortly afterward to address the grievances of his people by settlers. He helped negotiate a short-lived peace treaty to resolve the conflict.

CHAPTER SIX • *The Capitol's Fine & Decorative Arts*

Capitol Complex, 1938.

C·H·A·P·T·E·R
SEVEN

The Capitol Complex & The City Beautiful Movement

EVEN before the new Pennsylvania Capitol was in the planning stages, civic-minded residents of the city of Harrisburg were convinced that the city had to implement progressive changes tantamount to its stature as a capital city, necessitated by what they saw as horrible conditions of living. Following the devastating Hills Capitol fire in February 1897, Harrisburg slowly began to transform from a mud-encrusted, filth-strewn industrial town, into a more beautiful city, both out of necessity and as a result of the presence of two unique individuals, Mira Lloyd Dock and J. Horace McFarland. To understand the origins of modern Harrisburg, one must begin just prior to the turn of the twentieth century.

Before the great fire that consumed the old Hills Capitol, government officials and burghers of both the city and state had been impressed by the architectural designs displayed at the 1893 World's Columbian Exposition in Chicago.[1] To this end, they had planned and built the Italianate Executive, Library, and Museum Building adjacent to the Capitol in 1893–94.[2] The burning of the Hills Capitol, while at first considered a travesty for the state legislature, became a blessing and a steppingstone that enabled the building of a new, more modern Capitol and fueled the beautification movement in Harrisburg. Several of Harrisburg's leading citizens had unique and far-reaching ideas about how to clean up their city.

| 1907 | The first PA State Farm Show is held in Harrisburg. |

| 1912 | 1,595 people die when the supposedly unsinkable Titanic hits an iceberg in the North Atlantic. |

| 1920 | "The Human Fly" climbs to the top of the State Capitol building twice to raise money for charity. He completed the task once using ropes and a second time with no mechanical assistance. |

| | The first commercial broadcast station in the world begins in Pittsburgh with KDKA. The station begins broadcasts on November 2. Radio very quickly becomes a fixture in people's homes across the country. |

| | The 19th Amendment finally guarantees women the right to vote. |

| 1927 | At 7:52 A.M. on May 20, Charles Lindbergh's plane The Spirit of St. Louis takes off from Roosevelt Field on Long Island, NY. Over 33 hours later the plane lands at Le Bourget Aerodrome in Paris. Lindbergh had traveled 3,500 miles and had not slept in 55 hours. |

| 1929 | On October 29, the stock market crashes with 16.9 million shares traded in a single day. By the end of November investors had lost over $100 billion in assets, and the market would finally bottom out in 1932, the bleakest year of the Great Depression. |

| 1931 | Governor Gifford Pinchot begins a massive campaign of road building and paving in the Commonwealth after his 1930 campaign promise to "get the farmer out of the mud." During the Depression road construction became a significant public works project and was an important means of providing relief work for many who were unemployed. |

THIS PAGE: *Mira Dock, undated.*

OPPOSITE PAGE: *A view of the Susquehanna riverbank during the early twentieth century.*

When compared to modern standards of living, parts of the city of Harrisburg in the late nineteenth century would seem uninhabitable. Sewage contaminated unpaved streets and the Susquehanna River, making diseases common and recurrent. Homes and businesses butted against each other as earlier construction methods hindered upward growth. City planning had not yet been professionalized and

When compared to modern standards of living, parts of the city of Harrisburg in the late nineteenth century would seem uninhabitable.

far-reaching, large-scale city planning models were limited in their scope. As a result, city streets were a century old and many were too narrow to accommodate the newest innovation in transportation—the automobile. The shores of the Susquehanna were "sewage-encrusted,"³ owing in part to low water levels in the summer, and the lack of a suitable pumping station or filtration plant as these pipes fed river water directly into city homes. Beginning at the turn of the new century, Harrisburg native Mira Lloyd Dock publicly challenged these conditions and set out to motivate public sentiment in support of changing them.

Mira Dock was a well-educated and traveled woman. She represented, like some of her contemporaries the "new woman"—college-educated with an eye for civic change and social activism. Certainly, her birth in

[Dock's] speech confronted these elite Harrisburg residents' treatment of *"the Susquehanna as a sewer and its banks as a dumping ground for filthy garbage."*

1853 to one of Harrisburg's more reputable and wealthy families allowed her increased ability to obtain schooling and pursue her own interests above that of most women of the time. Dock was a forty-seven-year-old spinster in 1900 when she presented a speech to the Harrisburg Board of Trade on December 20. Her speech, titled "The City Beautiful," or "Improvement Work at Home and Abroad," was the great impetus for Harrisburg's city improvement.⁴ According to a newspaper article published on December 21, 1900,

Literature in Stone: The Hundred Year History of the Pennsylvania State Capitol

"Members of the Board of Trade who heard Miss Dock went from the auditorium with new ideas, and, it is hoped, with new aspirations for the city's good."

her speech confronted these elite Harrisburg residents' treatment of "the Susquehanna as a sewer and its banks as a dumping ground for filthy garbage."[5] Dock illustrated that these conditions need not be tolerated, let alone continue, by showing the audience slides of other cities that would no longer allow such an unhealthy environment to exist. Dock's world travels provided her with examples of beautified American and European cities, and she appealed to civic pride and interurban competitive spirit that played on the theme of organic social unity. She reminded her audience that the social classes were interdependent and that working-class people and their children needed locations of beauty and recreation areas as much, if not more, than anyone else.[6]

THIS PAGE: *Looking north from Walnut Street, April 10, 1904.*

OPPOSITE PAGE: *Top, Poplar and South Streets toward the Capitol, April 15, 1909; Bottom, An example of the city's cramped conditions.*

1934 — Clyde Barrow and his companion, Bonnie Parker, were shot to death by officers in an ambush staged near Sailes, in Bienville Parish, Louisiana. At the time of their deaths they were believed to have committed 13 murders and a string of burglaries and robberies from Louisiana to New Mexico.

1940 — Pennsylvania opens the first high-speed, multi-lane highway in the country—the Pennsylvania Turnpike. Originally connecting Harrisburg and Pittsburgh, the Turnpike was eventually extended to Philadelphia and northeastern Pennsylvania.

1940s — With the surprise attack by Japan on Pearl Harbor, the nation begins to mobilize for war. Over 1.25 million Pennsylvanians, or about one-eighth of the population, served in the armed forces during World War II. Approximately one out of every seven members was a Pennsylvania citizen. Over 130 generals and admirals came from Pennsylvania and the state's mills and factories contributed immensely to the Allied war effort and the eventual defeat of the Axis powers.

1946 — ENIAC, the world's first electronic digital computer is unveiled at the University of Pennsylvania. It contained 17,468 vacuum tubes, over 5 million hand solders, and weighed approximately 27 tons. It was put to use by the U.S. Army at Aberdeen Proving Ground in Maryland in 1947.

1950 — IN THE YEAR 1950…
U.S. Population: 151,684,000
Total Unemployed: 3,288,000
Life Expectancy: Women 71.1; Men 65.6
Average Salary: $2,992
Cost of a loaf of bread: 14¢

1953 — Ethel and Julius Rosenberg are executed for treason after having been convicted of stealing U.S. atomic bomb secrets and giving them to the Soviet Union.

James Watson and Francis Crick discover the double-spiral helix structure of DNA. They are later awarded the Nobel Prize in Medicine for their discovery.

A primary concern was to filter the Susquehanna's drinking water supply, which was contaminated and reaching the level of "MUNICIPAL MURDER."

Dock's goal was to motivate Harrisburg residents, especially the middle and upper class residents, who had the means to make the changes. According to the *Harrisburg Telegraph*, "members of the Board of Trade who heard Miss Dock went from the auditorium with new ideas, and, it is hoped, with new aspirations for the city's good."[7] These influential community leaders began immediately to actively pursue city beautification. The process of municipal improvement for Harrisburg was not an overnight task. Over the next thirty years, drastic improvements raised

LITERATURE IN STONE: THE HUNDRED YEAR HISTORY OF THE PENNSYLVANIA STATE CAPITOL

Harrisburg's overall standard of living, but in 1900, no master plan for installing sewers, paving streets, or enhancing Harrisburg's natural beauty was adopted.

Due to the benevolence and motivation of Mr. J. V. W. Reynders, owner of the Harrisburg Steel Company, a fund was established to obtain "expert advice upon the Harrisburg difficulties and their remedies…"[8] In the following ten days, $5 thousand was raised from sixty prominent citizens. This remarkable effort continued to fuel the impetus for city beautification. As a result, the Harrisburg League for Municipal Improvements was created. Engineers were commissioned to examine and propose solutions for Harrisburg's unique situation. Their results were published as *Proposed Municipal Improvements for Harrisburg, Pennsylvania*.[9] The report proposed that a city-wide beautification movement needed the support of the majority of citizens, as the proposed plan would entirely alter the city's landscape. Streets would be paved, the sewage from the Susquehanna was to be cleaned up, and a more ordered architectural and municipal system would develop throughout the city.

THIS PAGE: *Capitol from 4th and Walnut Streets, October 13, 1917*

OPPOSITE PAGE: *J. Horace McFarland, undated.*

CHAPTER SEVEN • *The Capitol Complex & the City Beautiful Movement*

VANCE C. MCCORMICK WAS ELECTED AS MAYOR OF HARRISBURG, and under his progressive administration, "the city was cleaned up, morally and physically."

After 1906, the new granite-clad Capitol did much to elevate civic pride. If grandiose public architecture was to be present, the cityscape should in turn mirror this. In addition, the city elites, who were learning the ills of improper sanitation, quite possibly took action "out of their own fear" of sickness and disease.[10] Harrisburg City Beautiful advocates typified the national stereotype, which was composed largely of upper to middle class white males—save for Mira Dock.[11] Dock's contemporary within the Harrisburg movement was Juniata County native J. Horace McFarland, president of the American Civic Association. According to an incident described by McFarland, landlords opposed the proposed improvements, as the cost and lack of personal property rights were prohibitive.[12] However, many were swayed after they realized the increase in property values would allow them to regain their initial investments, a point that McFarland used to argue in favor of the improvements.

Despite minor opposition, legislation was proposed and approved for the Board of Public Works to spend monies for municipal improvements. A primary concern was to filter the Susquehanna's drinking water supply, which was contaminated and reaching the level of "municipal murder."[13] A proposed solution was the erection of a small dam in the Susquehanna.

On a broader scope, city planning was a major component of the City Beautiful movement. Beginning with the 1893 World's Columbian Exposition in Chicago, a new model for the clean and orderly city design gained popular appeal. The new Beaux-Arts architectural style received accolades at the Exposition, and its popularity was accelerated through the designs of the New York architectural firm of McKim, Mead, and White. This movement combined ancient Greek and Roman forms with Renaissance ideas in an eclectic mix. During the late 1800s and early 1900s many American architects were schooled at the legendary École des Beaux-Arts in Paris. Returning to America, the architects fused Beaux-Arts architecture into the American landscape. This clean, elegant architecture was a perfect complement to municipal improvement. The City Beautiful movement blended these elements into a successful campaign.

THIS PAGE: *View west from Peristyle, World's Columbian Exposition, 1893.*

OPPOSITE PAGE: *Top, Pennsylvania display at the Columbian Exposition, 1893; Bottom, Vance McCormick, ca. 1925.*

CHAPTER SEVEN • *The Capitol Complex & the City Beautiful Movement*

1955 *Brown vs. Board of Education reverses previous United States Supreme Court decision Plessy vs. Ferguson declaring that "separate educational facilities are inherently unequal" and all schools are ordered to desegregate.*

1957 *The Soviet Union launches the world's first man-made satellite named Sputnik. The launch does much to ignite the space race between the U.S. and the Soviet Union.*

1962 *Rachel Carson publishes* Silent Spring *which awoke much of America to the dangers of pesticides, like DDT, along with other environmental hazards.*

The Cuban Missile Crisis brings the U.S. as close to nuclear war as it has ever come.

1963 *President John F. Kennedy is assassinated in Dallas, Texas.*

1973 *The official end of the Vietnam War. A total of 23,500 troops were withdrawn from South Vietnam.*

1977 *Steve Jobs and Steve Wozniak found Apple Computer, Inc. The Apple II becomes the world's first personal computer and retails for $1,290.*

1979 *The most significant accident at a U.S. nuclear power plant occurs at Three Mile Island, Middletown, Pennsylvania.*

1985 *21 tornadoes touch down in Pennsylvania causing $300 million worth of damage and 65 deaths.*

1986 *The* Challenger *space shuttle explodes during lift off and all seven crew members are killed.*

THIS PAGE: *Looking north from Walnut Street to 4th Street, October 15, 1917.*

OPPOSITE PAGE: *Looking west from State Street Bridge to Capitol, October 17, 1917.*

Despite the construction of the new state Capitol, the city itself appeared even farther behind in civic planning. The Capitol was a glorious culmination of sophisticated grandeur. There was a direct contrast between the structure rising on Capitol Hill and the surrounding squalor. The new Capitol, however, served as a significant advocate for the City Beautiful movement in Harrisburg.

In 1902 Vance C. McCormick was elected as mayor of Harrisburg, and under his progressive administration, "the city was cleaned up, morally and physically."[14] With the initial approved expenditure in 1902, the city planned for the "improvement of the water supply, the sewerage (sic.) system, the construction of a dam in the Susquehanna River, parks and park improvement, and paving the intersections of streets."[15] In 1906, $400 thousand was loaned for the "reconstruction of the Mulberry Street viaduct, extension and improvement of the sewerage (sic.) system, paving of street intersections, and paving of non-assessable property."[16] By 1907 Harrisburg saw a major transformation and "was becoming one of the cleanest cities in the United States."[17]

LITERATURE IN STONE: THE HUNDRED YEAR HISTORY OF THE PENNSYLVANIA STATE CAPITOL

In 1910 more city improvements were planned and loans were issued totaling $641 thousand. This included improvement of the condition of Paxtang Creek, paving intersections of streets, intercepting sewers along the Susquehanna River, and the construction of a bridge across the Reading Railroad on Thirteenth Street.[18] By the end of the first decade of the twentieth century, Harrisburg had indeed changed much of its built landscape.

Not to be outdone by the city, officials of the state were also beginning their campaign to improve and expand the area of state-owned property surrounding the Capitol building. Beginning in 1911, with the creation of the Capitol Park Extension Commission, the state began to purchase property east of the Main Capitol Building, for the planned expansion of state offices.[19] In the following five years, the state acquired twenty-seven acres "bounded by Third Street on the west, North Street to the north, Seventh Street on the east and Walnut Street on the south."[20]

With adequate room to expand the Capitol Complex buildings, a plan could now be developed to accommodate the expansion of government offices. New York architect Arnold Brunner was chosen to design this Capitol Expansion project. Brunner was well-versed in the City Beautiful movement as a proponent of the Beaux-Arts. The proposed expansion project that he designed reflected the values of this movement of white buildings, symmetry, and classical order. His plan was vast in scale and would eliminate the area of tightly packed slums between the Capitol and the State Street bridge, known as Harrisburg's eighth ward.

CHAPTER SEVEN • *The Capitol Complex & the City Beautiful Movement*

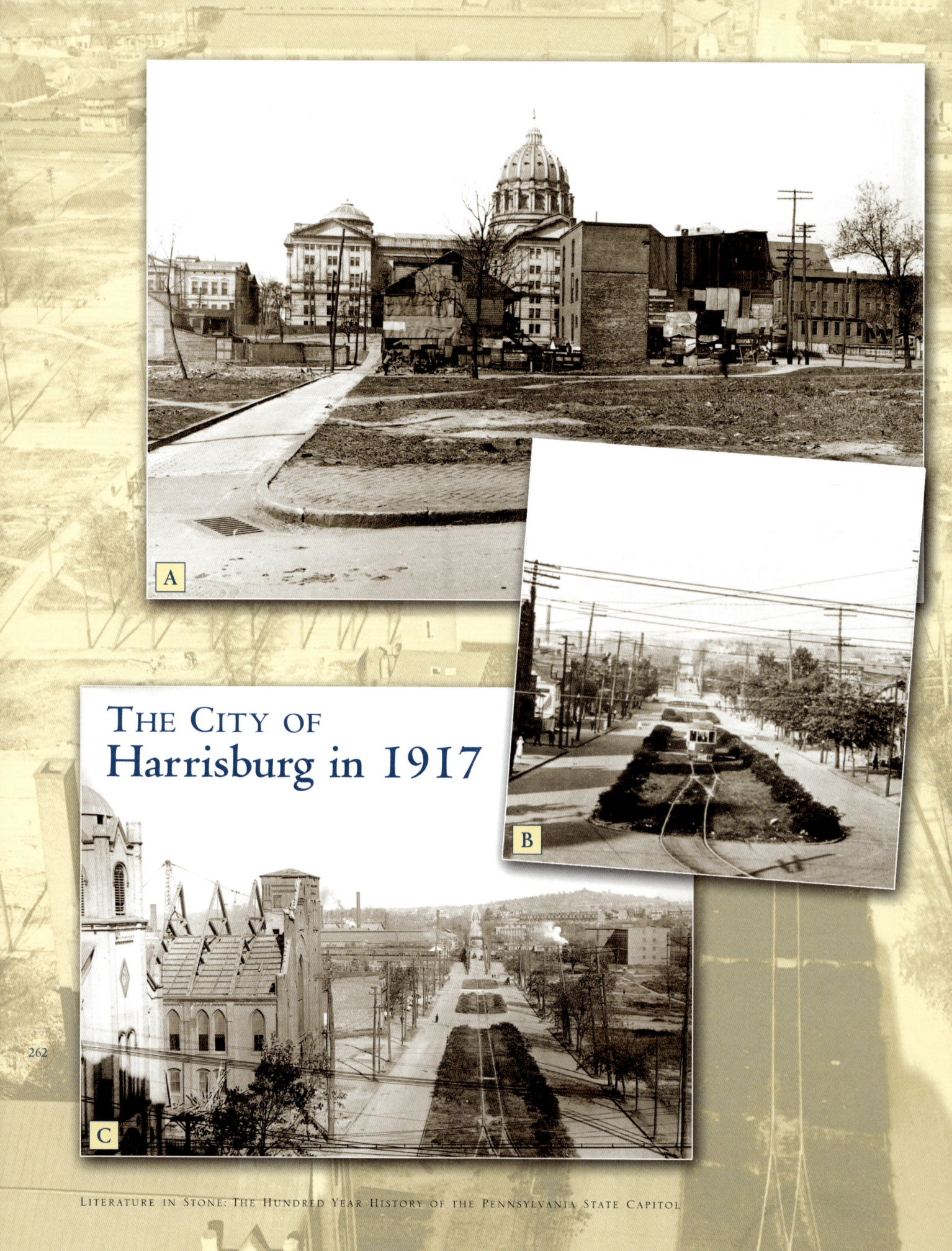

The City of Harrisburg in 1917

In the eyes of proponents for the demolition, the area housed poor immigrants, bred crime, and had more wooden buildings than any other ward in the city. Consequently, it presented an unattractive view of the Capitol's east façade. In Brunner's plan, this area was to be completely razed, redeveloped, and transformed into a pleasant area that reflected the modern city, and accentuated the eastern approach to the Capitol.

More city improvements were instituted in 1914 with $300 thousand loaned for "sewers, bridges, [the] footwalk on Market Street, [a] comfort station in Market Square, apparatus for [the] fire department, [a] municipal asphalt repair plant, playgrounds, park" and like improvements.[21]

In 1917 another $60 thousand was loaned for "improving [the] fire department by purchase of motor-driven apparatus and remodeling fire houses for housing of these."[22] In 1920, $190 thousand was loaned for "improving the sewers, street

THIS PAGE: *Capitol Park Extension, Looking east from the Capitol dome, October 16, 1917.*

OPPOSITE PAGE:
A. *Looking west from Filbert Street to the Capitol, April 5, 1917.*
B. *Trolley on State Street.*
C. *East State Street from Capitol, October 16, 1917.*

CHAPTER SEVEN • *The Capitol Complex & the City Beautiful Movement*

The City of Harrisburg in 1917

Literature in Stone: The Hundred Year History of the Pennsylvania State Capitol

paving and for a municipal bathing beach."[23] Much of these improvements are still visible today on City Island, originally called Island Park.

The improvements outlined in Brunner's official plan for the Commonwealth were approved by the State Capitol Park Extension Committee. In 1921 a loan was approved in the amount of $250 thousand for "rearranging Third and Walnut Streets and for the opening of Front Street from Herr to Calder Streets."[24] This was followed by an $800 thousand loan over the next two years, for the extension of Capitol Park and municipal improvements to accommodate the growing city. Items included in this were the "enlargement of the water supply and the building of a third reservoir."[25]

THIS PAGE: *West State Street from Capitol dome, October 17, 1917.*

OPPOSITE PAGE:
A. *North Street east from 3rd Street, October 11, 1917.*
B. *Harrisburg's National Hotel, undated.*
C. *From North and Filbert Streets looking northwest toward the Capitol, April 15, 1909.*
D. *East panoramic view from Capitol, June 1917.*

THE BRUNNER PLAN made radical far-sweeping changes to how the public would approach and envision the Capitol Complex buildings.

LITERATURE IN STONE: THE HUNDRED YEAR HISTORY OF THE PENNSYLVANIA STATE CAPITOL

In 1923 the improvements continued with $285 thousand loaned "for building a municipal incineration plant, continuation of sewers, and street paving." Two years later in 1925, $330 thousand was loaned "for walls at Island Park" and an upgrade of the bathing beach.[26]

The Capitol Park Extension

The Commonwealth's Department of Public Grounds and Buildings knew even as the Capitol was being constructed that the space and size of the building was still inadequate to house the growing state bureaucracy.[27] By the end of the second decade of the new century, it was determined that another building had to be erected to house state offices, particularly those of the expanding Education Department.

In 1916 the Board of Commissioners of Public Grounds and Buildings called a meeting with Brunner. After the meeting Brunner was charged with developing both landscape and building plans for all of the new Capitol Park Extension. Brunner developed his preliminary landscape sketches in 1917 and a large model of all of the Capitol area was commissioned and put on display in the main rotunda

THIS PAGE: *Sydney Ross and William Gehron's plan for the* Soldiers' and Sailors' Memorial Bridge, *1917.*

OPPOSITE PAGE: *Capitol Park Extension: Top, Looking west from Walnut and Short Streets, January 5, 1918; Bottom, Capitol botanical conservatory ca. 1917.*

CHAPTER SEVEN • *The Capitol Complex & the City Beautiful Movement*

Eventually five wooden frame barrack-like structures would be built behind the Main Capitol Building, in the area now occupied by the East Wing.

in May of 1920. The Brunner plan made radical far-sweeping changes in how the public would approach and envision the Capitol Complex buildings. The overarching theme of the plan was symmetry. Four new buildings were to be built on parallel lines on the eastern side of the Main Capitol, and a new road, Commonwealth Avenue was to be created and widened from what was originally Harrisburg's Aberdeen Street. Brunner described his plan as "one of the largest [of its kind] being undertaken in the United States."[28] Prior to the construction of the first permanent building within the extension, work was begun on the first of several "temporary" buildings behind the Main Capitol, meant to house agencies that had outgrown their spaces. Eventually five wooden frame barrack-like structures would be built behind the Main Capitol Building, in the area now occupied by the East Wing.

THE SOUTH OFFICE BUILDING

In 1920 excavation was undertaken for the South Office Building, now the Speaker K. Leroy Irvis Office Building. Costing $3.25 million, the South Office Building was completed and dedicated in 1923. It held the Departments of Health, Education, Teacher Training and Certification, and the State Board of Education, along with the Superintendent, Deputy Secretaries, and support personnel for the Education Department. The first floor of the building also housed a reference library and an auditorium, which Brunner said was "the first of its kind provided for any state's use."[29]

In 1925 Arnold Brunner died, leaving his plan for the Capitol Complex largely unfinished. In fact the South Office Building was the only one of Brunner's designs to be constructed. However, architects William Gehron and Sydney Ross were hired to complete Brunner's footprint for the Capitol Complex, and though they made modest changes to the overall scheme, they were mostly guided by the framework that Brunner had begun.

The North Office Building

Some four years after the completion of the South Office, construction began on the North Office Building. The new North Office was largely a mirror image of the façade of the South when its construction was completed in 1929. Though appearing the same, the North and South Office Buildings are unique for their artwork and decorative elements. In keeping with Huston's vision for the Main Capitol, they integrate artwork into their design, though obviously not to the level that Huston achieved in the Main Capitol.

The lobby of the South Office Building has two murals by artist Edward Trumbull, entitled *Penn's Treaty with the Indians* and *The Industries of Pennsylvania*. The North Office has a lobby containing a floor map of the highways of the Commonwealth and numerous city seals. The exterior of the buildings actually do vary when examined closely. The earlier South Office is Neoclassical in style, but the North Office's exterior sculpture, along with the bronze doors at the building's east end, display the first vestiges of Art

THIS PAGE:
A. *Capitol Park from Third and Walnut Streets, ca. 1930. (Notice the South Office Building on the right.)*
B. *Portion of Penn's Treaty with the Indians, Edward Trumbull, 1921, South Office Building.*
C. *Labor workers lunette, Edward Trumbull, 1921, South Office Building.*

OPPOSITE PAGE: *Capitol Complex layout, 1920s. (Notice the barrack-like temporary structures on the east side of the building.)*

CHAPTER SEVEN • *The Capitol Complex & the City Beautiful Movement*

Deco within the Capitol Complex. The granite sculpture and doors were created by sculptor Lee Lawrie.

In 1925 Arnold Brunner died, leaving his plan for the Capitol Complex largely unfinished.

During the time of the construction of the North and South Offices, the state was acquiring more land from the city of Harrisburg, largely due to the demolition of the city's eighth (and later fourth) wards. As part of the City Beautiful movement in Harrisburg, this section was slowly reclaimed by the city, and sold to the Commonwealth as complex buildings were added. Harrisburg's old eighth ward was originally bounded by Fourth Street directly in the rear of the Capitol and the Pennsylvania Railroad to the east. The area eventually acquired by the

THIS PAGE: *Top, Foyer to the North Office Building, ca. 1928; Bottom, Star lamp post that was created for the* Soldiers' and Sailors' Memorial Bridge *across State Street east of the Capitol.*

OPPOSITE PAGE: *Southeast view behind Capitol building, which was to be expanded into the Capitol Complex, 1920s.*

LITERATURE IN STONE: THE HUNDRED YEAR HISTORY OF THE PENNSYLVANIA STATE CAPITOL

An interesting anecdote occurred in 1929 with the discovery of numerous bronze chandeliers, which were uncovered in the sub-basement of the Main Capitol Building. The Harrisburg Telegraph stated that approximately 100 tons of light fixtures had been found in a locked room in an "obscure" area of the sub-basement. The fixtures were declared outdated and sold for scrap metal. Architect Joseph M. Huston later verified that the removed lights included four small chandeliers that blocked the Abbey murals once installed in the House Chamber, as well as light standards that were removed for obstructing the floor traffic patterns in the chamber.

THE NEW STRUCTURE was called the *Soldiers' and Sailors' Memorial Bridge* and was dedicated in 1930 to servicemen of the Commonwealth who had died in all previous American wars.

Commonwealth also stretched from Walnut to just beyond Forster Streets.

The next task in the Commonwealth's campaign of buildings was to remove the old railroad overpass on east State Street and replace it with a more substantial bridge approaching the complex from the east. Plans for the bridge actually began in 1919, but construction went slowly due to limited legislative appropriations. The bridge would be a large four-lane structure, which would cross not only the railroad tracks but much of lower Harrisburg, including Cameron Street. Large Art Deco eagle pylons, designed by Gehron and Ross, and sculpted by Lawrie, fringed the bridge's western side. The new structure was to be called the *Soldiers' and Sailors' Memorial Bridge* and was dedicated in 1930 in honor of all the Commonwealth's servicemen and women who had died in previous American wars. A special museum room in the first floor area of the

THIS PAGE: *The* Soldiers' and Sailors' Memorial Bridge, *1930s.*

OPPOSITE PAGE: *Western entrance to the Capitol, 1930s.*

The Capitol's West Façade

THIS PAGE:
A. Front steps before 1930s alterations, 1917.
B. One of two fountains that adorned early Capitol grounds, undated. (Notice the Hartranft statue directly in front of the Capitol's entrance.)
C. Moving the Hartranft statue to its current location in front of the Speaker Matthew J. Ryan Building, 1927.

OPPOSITE PAGE: *Left, Perspective drawing of Capitol Park, designed by Arnold W. Brunner, 1923; Right, Capitol park lamp post sketch, 1923.*

THE PEOPLE'S FORECOURT

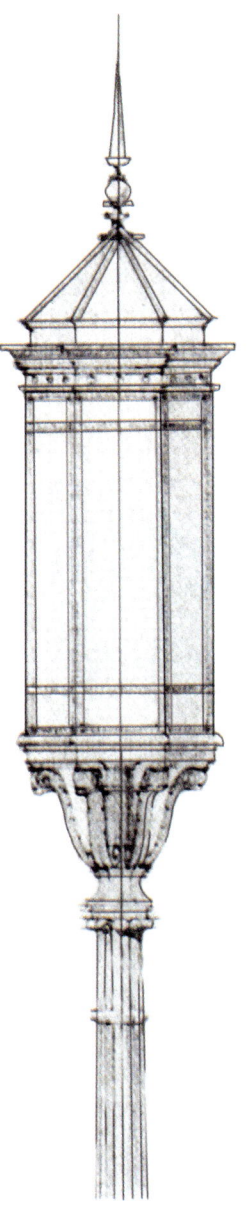

pylons was planned, but unfortunately never completed. Brunner, like Huston before him, had also planned a bridge for the western side of State Street, crossing the Susquehanna, which would have given the Capitol building almost two miles of direct approach both east and west, but this bridge was never completed.[30]

Instead of the large bridge across the Susquehanna, the western façade of the Main Capitol would have a grand staircase rising from Third Street to the Capitol's parking deck. The steps had a platform area in the middle for use as a rostrum area. On blocks of granite surrounding the steps are quotations by some of Pennsylvania's most famous individuals including John Peter Muhlenburg, Benjamin Franklin, Thaddeus Stevens, Andrew Curtin, and others. On the eastern side of the building, Brunner had designed a grand forecourt and fountain (by artist Carl Milles), which he termed, "the people's forecourt." In Brunner's mind the unification of all his buildings was to enlighten and inspire all citizens who may visit the Capitol. The people's forecourt was designed for speeches and gatherings at the state level—a place where the people of the Commonwealth could come to overlook their grand public buildings.

The Commonwealth, however, looked more toward utility than beauty and Brunner's large fountain and "people's forecourt" were never completed in his lifetime. Instead in the late 1920s, the Commonwealth built parking lots between the North and South Office Buildings, adjacent to the temporary structures and also began excavating for a third massive building to house the state's growing Executive and Education Departments.

The Education Building

The new building, called the Education Building (now known as the Forum Building), was finished and dedicated on November 4, 1931. Some of the artists

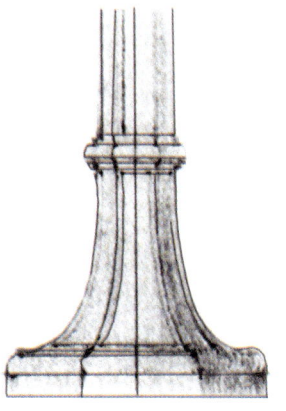

CHAPTER SEVEN • *The Capitol Complex & the City Beautiful Movement*

Forum [Education] Building Construction, late 1920s. The building was finished and dedicated in 1931.

A. Coffer medallions and chandeliers in the foyer ceiling of the Forum Building.
B. Detail of character from Forum Building entrance door.
C. Detail of character from Forum Building entrance door.
D. Carved artwork from columns in Forum Building foyer.

LITERATURE IN STONE: THE HUNDRED YEAR HISTORY OF THE PENNSYLVANIA STATE CAPITOL

THE EDUCATION BUILDING

…was lauded throughout the United States as one of the MOST AMBITIOUS undertakings in PUBLIC EDUCATION in years.

and architects of the structure were on hand at the dedication ceremonies on November 4, including Eric Gugler, C. Paul Jennewein, and Lee Lawrie, along with architects Gehron and Ross, and Capitol artist Violet Oakley.[31] The Education Building cost $5.5 million to complete. The structure is 472 feet long and contains more than eight acres of floor space. At the time of its completion it had 250 rooms, library capacity for more than one million books, and a beautiful auditorium. In addition it was lauded throughout the United States as one of the most ambitious undertakings in public education in years.

The design of the Education/Forum Building also incorporates art with the architecture and function of the building. In the vestibule leading to the main lobby, sculptors C. Paul Jennewein and Harry Kreis created sculptures depicting the sources of mankind's knowledge. Likewise on the ten jambs leading to the lobby are sculptures of man's mind and body that have lead the march of civilization. Within the main lobby artist Vincent Maragliotti painted thirteen horizontal beams with dozens of figures representing all types of learning.

The ceiling of the new 3,000-seat auditorium was decorated with amazing paintings of the zodiacal signs and constellations. On the sides of the walls are large mural paintings of maps of the world at different historical time periods, which were produced by a young studio artist named George Nakashima, who was working for Eric Gugler and Richard Brooks at the time. The murals, coupled with the ceiling and other Art Deco styled elements, make the Forum Auditorium truly unique.

THIS PAGE: *Detail of door sculpture, Lee Lawrie, undated.*

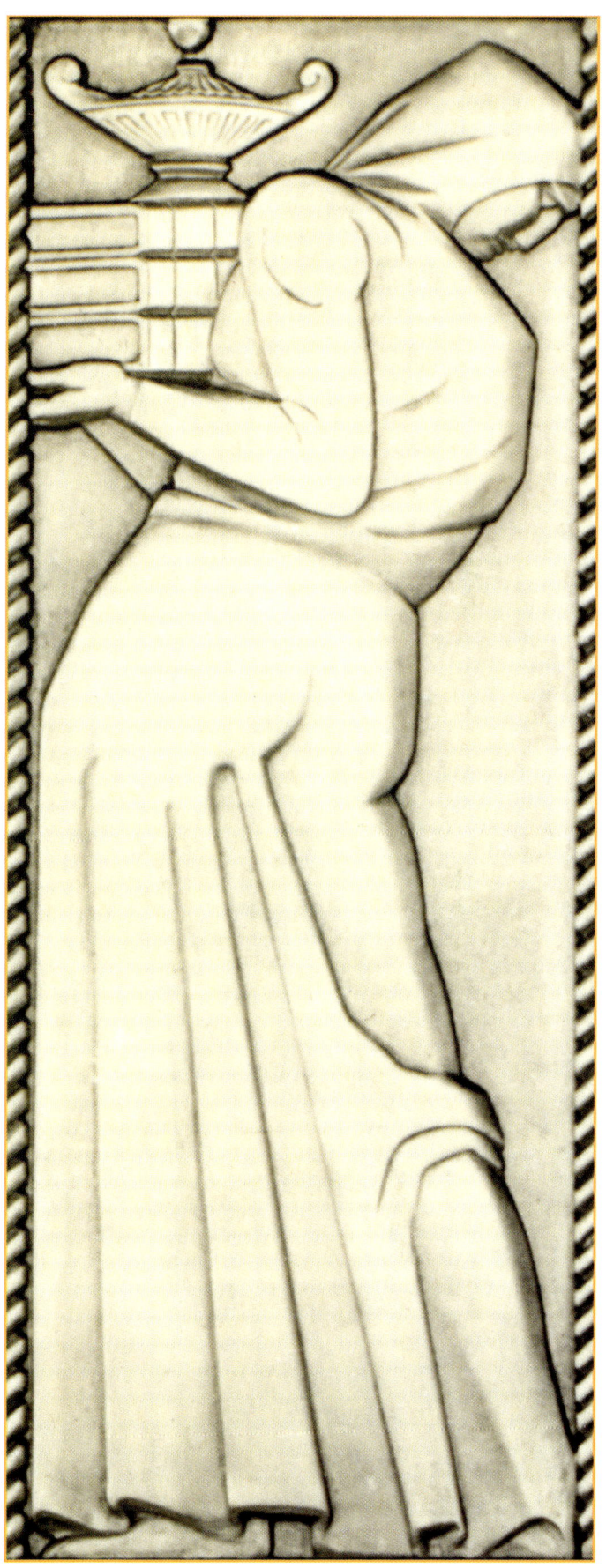

CHAPTER SEVEN • *The Capitol Complex & the City Beautiful Movement*

THIS PAGE: *Top, Detailed layout of ceiling mural for Forum Building auditorium, Eric Gugler, 1930; Bottom, Forum Building, 1931.*

OPPOSITE PAGE: *Top, Auditorium in the Forum Building, undated; Bottom, Carved artwork from columns in Forum Building foyer.*

Literature in Stone: The Hundred Year History of the Pennsylvania State Capitol

CHAPTER SEVEN • *The Capitol Complex & the City Beautiful Movement*

THE FINANCE BUILDING

A. Finance Building door, Carl Milles.
B. Etched glass light sconce in Finance Building foyer.
C. Etched glass light sconce in Finance Building foyer.
D. Details from Milles doors, Finance Building.

LITERATURE IN STONE: THE HUNDRED YEAR HISTORY OF THE PENNSYLVANIA STATE CAPITOL

The Finance Building

The last of the main complex buildings to be built was the Finance Building, which was begun in the latter days of the Great Depression in mid-1937 and completed in 1939, just prior to World War II. The cost of the building was approximately $4.65 million. As a result of the Depression, much of the money to fund the construction project came via the Works Progress Administration, along with many of the workers who assisted in the construction. Sculptors Lee Lawrie and C. Paul Jennewein designed the frieze for the building and sculptor Carl Milles was contracted to create six sets of bronze doors for the structure. Sculptor Ulysses Richie designed the brass interior elevator doors, which each depict a different type of currency. Artists Eugene Savage and Vincent Maragliotti were contracted to paint several ceiling and wall murals within the building. Upon completion, the Finance Building was the last structure actually constructed as an original part of the Brunner plan. However, there were several other items that Brunner had planned that were modified before they were built.

> "In a somewhat ABSTRACT FORM and with a certain amount of REALISM, I have tried to convey the idea of the birth, or the CREATION, of a state (Pennsylvania) INTO BEING: from its EARLY, WILD, UNCULTIVATED LIFE to present, cultivated, industrious and PROGRESSIVE STATE and finally the light to illuminate THE PATH OF THE FUTURE." - LEE LAWRIE *In describing his work in the Finance Building.*

The "People's Forecourt," and the "Court of Honor," which were two items that Brunner had originally wished to see constructed, took different forms in later years. The area that Brunner wished to call "the Court of Honor," took the form of Soldiers' and Sailors' Grove—an area to honor all those killed in foreign wars. Whereas the original court was supposed to have two large fountains designed by Carl Milles.

In 1980 the Department of General Services (DGS) contracted the firm of Celli-Flynn Associates, of Pittsburgh, to design the Capitol East Wing extension. On December 2, 1987 the new East Wing was dedicated. The wing occupies 929,000 square feet, along with a tiered parking garage for 840 vehicles beneath the structure. The design, though varying from Brunner's original People's Forecourt, was intended to harmonize and unify the existing Capitol Complex

Education: Achievement and Failure, Eugene Savage, 1940, Finance Building, Library ceiling mural.

CHAPTER SEVEN • *The Capitol Complex & the City Beautiful Movement*

THIS PAGE: *Capitol western façade, 1994.*

OPPOSITE PAGE: *Capitol Complex showing East Wing, 2000.*

buildings. In 1987 DGS also hired architectural firm Day and Zimmerman (now Vitetta) as the consulting architectural firm for all projects dealing with the historic fabric of the Main Capitol Building. The new East Wing served an important function by relieving some of the cramped conditions that had plagued the Main Capitol over the years. Additionally, with the completion of the fountain and terraced public space, the plan for Pennsylvania's Capitol Complex was complete, with only minor variations.

In the end, there can be no doubt that architect Arnold Brunner achieved his ultimate goal of unity, utility, and beauty within Pennsylvania's Capitol Complex. When examined from afar, each building seems much like the others in terms of their overarching Neoclassical style, which ultimately complements the earlier Main Capitol. However, when examined closely and on an individual basis, the buildings are each unique in their own rights. Each has artwork by many gifted artists, in different styles, but they all work together to form the campus of monumental public buildings that Brunner had intended—one of the largest, most ambitious, and most successful campaigns of civic governmental planning ever undertaken in the United States.

As a whole the entire Capitol Complex stands as what Arnold Brunner had termed… "ONE OF THE LARGEST, MOST AMBITIOUS" and most successful campaigns of CIVIC GOVERNMENTAL PLANNING ever undertaken in the United States.

CHAPTER SEVEN • *The Capitol Complex & the City Beautiful Movement*

E. A. Abbey mural restoration in rotunda, 1984.

C·H·A·P·T·E·R
EIGHT

The People's Building:
A Preservation Journey

EVEN before restoration began, the Pennsylvania Capitol could not hide its inner beauty. It is and has always been the people's building. The story of Pennsylvania and what it meant to be a Pennsylvanian were etched from floor to ceiling. Whether William Penn's search for liberty, the birth of religious tolerance, pivotal battles fought on Pennsylvania's soil, natural wonders, or the pulse of labor and industry—these stories were apparent to anyone who looked past the suspended ceilings and fluorescent lights.

Still, the building had suffered many indignities, reaching its lowest point in terms of neglect by 1980. Decades of alterations had concealed and even destroyed artistic marvels. Occupants of the Capitol decorated according to their personal tastes or eclectic penchant. Staffers despaired of their dreary spaces. Maintenance workers could not find electrical junction boxes. Repairs were expedient, and renovations were often without reverence to the historic value of the building structure. Without a coordinating body no far-reaching plan guided changes to ensure continuity.

The Capitol's working conditions were crowded as well. Five legislators might share an attic office (explaining at least one of the one-hundred fire and safety violations placed on the building). Kurt Zwikl, one of the first members of the Capitol Preservation Committee, occupied an office that was once a closet, "but at least it was private," he recalled.

PRESERVATION FORERUNNERS

A. The Capitol's Tercentenary Celebration. From left: Kermit Roosevelt, Governor Dick Thornburgh, Chairman Joseph Pitts, Paul Vathis (photographer), October 1981.
B. Cake cutting at Tercentenary Celebration. From left: President Pro Tempore Henry Hager, Governor Dick Thornburgh, Speaker Matthew J. Ryan, 1981.
C. Speaker Matthew J. Ryan at podium, 1981.
D. Special guests at the Tercentenary Celebration. From left: Ginny Thornburgh, Kermit Roosevelt, Walter Baran, Mary Roosevelt, 1981.
E. Members of the 87th Pennsylvania Civil War Regiment receive citations during Tercentenary event, 1981.
F. Committee By-Laws Chairman Kurt Zwikl speaking at Tercentenary event, 1981.

STEWARDSHIP over the building and its treasures was **nonexistent**. Something had to change, and **a fortunate series of events finally sparked change.**

Anyone trying to conduct government affairs or constituent business was constrained by the cramped, dreary, and sometimes hazardous conditions.

By 1980 working conditions were intolerable, and stewardship over the building and its treasures was nonexistent. Something had to change, and a fortunate series of events finally sparked change. Governor Dick Thornburgh pledged to build a Capitol extension to relieve overcrowding and improve safety. House Speaker Matthew J. Ryan and Minority Leader K. Leroy Irvis had long discussed the need for preservation, and now, they could use their role as bipartisan leaders to make it happen. Pennsylvania maintained the momentum gained from its featured role in the nation's bicentennial birthday bash, and in 1981, the State celebrated its own milestone birthday—its three hundredth. That tercentenary year coincided with the Capitol's seventy-fifth anniversary.

At a birthday party for the Commonwealth in the Capitol rotunda, complete with a sheet cake depicting Pennsylvania, members of the executive, legislative, and judicial branches pledged their support for preservation. Maybe they had no choice, since Edwin Austin Abbey's rotunda murals, waterlogged and mildew-caked, loomed overhead. At this party however, no single entity—not the governor or legislators—could claim sole credit for Pennsylvania's contributions to American history. They also understood that all shared equally in the burden of the Capitol's deterioration—likewise, they could share equally in the glory of its restoration.

Matt Ryan took the lead. His passion for preservation dated years before to the sight of a marble fireplace butchered to suit a legislator's decorating tastes. The Capitol didn't belong to individual legislators, he believed, but to the people of Pennsylvania and their children and grandchildren. In 1981 Ryan and Irvis implemented a House of Representatives Resolution forming the Tercentenary Committee. Key players were in place, including Chairman Joseph Pitts, Republican House member from Chester County, and Vice Chairman Kurt Zwikl, Democrat from Lehigh County. Committee members saw the Commonwealth's 300th birthday and Capitol preservation

D

E

F

CHAPTER EIGHT • *The People's Building: A Preservation Journey*

in the same light—as vehicles for interpreting and promoting the Commonwealth's heritage. It was time, one member wrote, to reverse the damage inflicted on the building by "neglect, thieves, and remodelers." Members embraced core principles designed to ensure the Capitol's integrity—preserve, restore, reconstruct, make safe, and when needed, build anew.

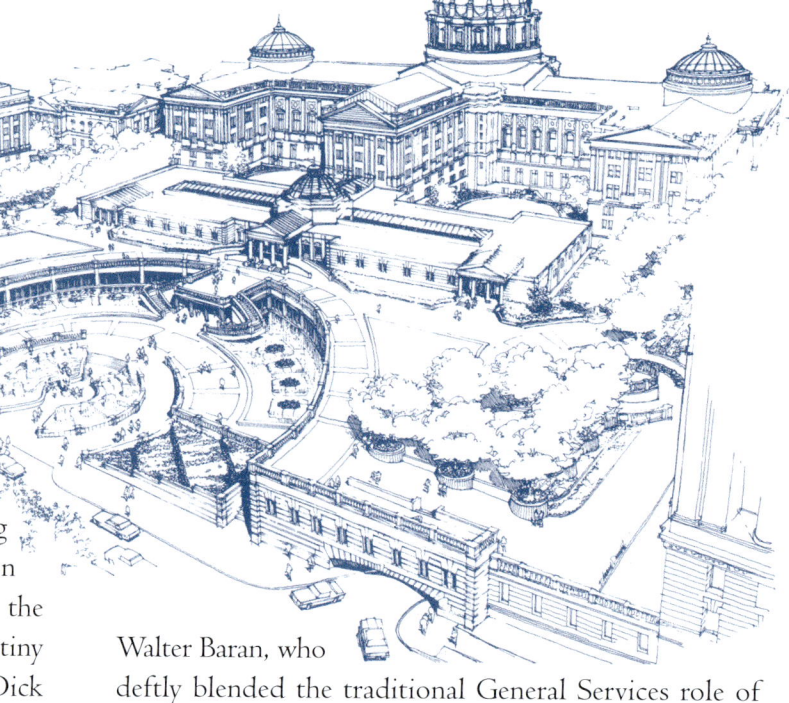

The "build anew" part was pivotal to launching preservation. Construction of a Capitol extension had been considered for decades, but who had the gumption to disrupt lawmakers and brave the scrutiny of penny-pinching skeptics? Finally, Governor Dick Thornburgh looked out a back window, saw delivery trucks maneuvering in a cramped parking lot, and decided he might as well take the heat. He assigned the project to Department of General Services Secretary Walter Baran, who deftly blended the traditional General Services role of plant maintenance and safety enforcement with new concepts such as historic preservation and professional construction management. With more space, intentionally designed to complement the 1906 Capitol, General Services brought the legislature up to code in terms of safety and up to speed technologically. "At the East Wing's dedication, I said the most beautiful part of the building was its innards—the phones, the air conditioning," Baran recalled. With legislators working in a business-like atmosphere and stretching their cramped muscles in all this new space, the preservation-minded among them seized the chance to save the fading jewel known as the Main Capitol.

They were treading in unknown territory. Few states were restoring their capitols then, and only a handful could offer lessons for Pennsylvania. Matt Ryan insisted that the Commonwealth needed what many states lacked—an institutional body to oversee restoration and advocate for upkeep and against that bureaucratic standby, deferred maintenance. Two other pivotal ideas took hold when Ruthann Hubbert-Kemper, the effort's first staffer and future director of the Capitol Preservation Committee, consulted with Clement Conger then White House curator. Make sure committee membership is bipartisan, he advised, and seat professional preservationists with the elected officials.

Together, they could balance preservation and offset politics. Both recommendations made their way into the legislation that officially created the Capitol Preservation Committee (CPC) in 1982.

Under the new law, the Committee's fifteen members would include four each from the Senate and House, three gubernatorial appointees, one Supreme Court appointee, the Secretary of the Department of General Services, and the Pennsylvania Historical and Museum Commission's Executive Director (plus the secretary of the now-defunct State Art Commission). A state budget line item would fund restoration projects and operating expenses, while a trust fund replenished through donations and sales of commemorative items would finance special projects, such as art and furniture acquisitions. The young Committee faced enormous challenges, the first of which was creating a comprehensive plan for preservation and maintenance.

The first works of art to be conserved were the Abbey rotunda murals. The Committee's first chair, state Representative (and later Congressman) Joseph Pitts, remembered seeing plaster deposits seeping through the "big, visionary murals." They had been affixed to the rotunda's plaster walls, which subjected them to decades of moisture seeping through the Capitol's dome. The building, designed as a frame for displaying magnificent artwork, succumbed to

THIS PAGE: *Top, Restoration of the rotunda murals; Bottom, Conservators remove mural from wall.*

OPPOSITE PAGE: *Top, Rendering of East Wing extension plan, 1983; Bottom, Governor Dick Thornburgh portrait, Governor's Office.*

CHAPTER EIGHT • *The People's Building: A Preservation Journey*

SUCCESSFUL PRESERVATION required more than enthusiasm for the building's artistry. The effort had to be bipartisan, or it would retire to the dusty shelf reserved for stalled government initiatives.

neglect and misguided use through years of deferred maintenance. Although the need for emergency repairs was obvious, there was no instruction manual for the job. "We were flying blind, a little bit," Pitts commented. Committee members had to consider the qualifications of contractors consulted for the job—

and, this being politics, maybe their ulterior motives, Pitts said. With preservation architect Day & Zimmerman and Associates (now Vitetta), the Committee developed criteria to gauge bidders' readiness for the specialized jobs ahead, and the internationally renowned conservation firm of Biltmore, Campbell, and Smith won the rotunda contract.

Even then the next steps required careful deliberation. "We had to decide whether to take the murals down and transport them somewhere, or to lay them down on the scaffold floor and work on them right there," Pitts said. "We opted to do the work right there in the Capitol, because there was less opportunity for havoc."

As a very public effort in the heart of the Capitol, the project changed minds and attitudes about the value of preservation. There had been apprehension about the preservation idea at first—a few grumblings about the Committee's seeming power to dictate colors and decor in individual offices—but most people had not given it much thought. Then a scaffold rose 220-feet high, like a skyscraper inside the rotunda. Before the eyes of administration officials, legislators, staff, and visitors, the Abbey murals were saved, and in two years, the whole rotunda metamorphosed from grimy to glorious. Spectators saw the rotunda as it was meant to be seen, as a Progressive-era tribute to government's civilizing influence. If the rotunda can look like this, they wondered, why can't the rest of the building? In short, people caught the preservation bug.

At the same time, citizens rallied around Pennsylvania's historic collection of Civil War battle flags, hundreds of them disintegrating in six rotunda display cases. Hubbert-Kemper found a conservator who would treat any flag, no matter how badly damaged—and some were practically dust—for $1,000. At that price, many individuals, families, re-enactment groups, and civic clubs could afford to sponsor a flag's conservation. And they did, intertwining their names with flags that bore blood stains and powder burns from places like Antietam, Fredericksburg, and Gettysburg. They visited the Committee's lab in Harrisburg to see "their" flags being conserved and experienced a tangible link to Pennsylvania's Civil War history.

PRESERVATION PROGRESS

Governor Dick Thornburgh was among the many who marveled at the Capitol's beauty, before and during restoration. He remembered "just going through the building, walking through it, walking on the Mercer tile floor, seeing the marvelous *Apotheosis* in the House, Violet Oakley's murals in the reception room."

"It was staggering," he said. "That's why it's a Capitol preservation effort, rather than a Capitol refurbishing." But like other officials involved, he understood that successful preservation required more than appreciation of the building's artistry. The effort had to be bipartisan, or it would retire to the dusty shelf reserved for stalled government initiatives. As Judge James R. Kelley of Westmoreland County, then a member of the Senate and the Capitol Preservation Committee's first vice chairman, recalled, "When one is charged with such a responsibility, party had no dominant position. It's a question of everybody pulling the oars at the same time in the same direction."

The Capitol Preservation Committee's comprehensive makeup may explain its longevity and success. Legislators and executives consider and balance political concerns. The Department of General Services manages the complicated physical plant and life safety upgrades.

THIS PAGE:
A. *Decorative stencil restoration by Richard Humbert, 2000.*
B. *Restoring ornate swan design on north light court ceiling by Diane Porterfield, 2000.*
C. *Exposure of original stencil in public hallway, 2003.*
D. *Artisans working in public corridor, 2000. From left, Diane Porterfield, Elaine Gleason, Shawn Vennell, and Jeff Johnson.*

OPPOSITE PAGE: *Top, Chairman Joe Pitts and Madgi Sidarous of Universal Builders Supply reviewing rotunda scaffold drawings, 1984; Bottom, Scaffold for rotunda restoration, 1985.*

CHAPTER EIGHT • *The People's Building: A Preservation Journey*

THIS PAGE: *Left, Modern sprinklers that have been cleverly hidden within the Capitol's decor, 2006; Right, Workers from Albert Michaels Conservation aluminum leaf corridor barrel vault, 1996.*

OPPOSITE PAGE: *Top, Conservator Elaine Kenny polishes a marble balustrade, 1997; Bottom, From left: Eugene DiOrio, Ruthann Hubbert-Kemper, Beatrice Garvan, John Bowie, Robert Glenn with Chief Justice John Flaherty seated on restored Supreme Court chair, 2000.*

Preservationists provide expert guidance, from their knowledge of period decorative arts to their experience in balancing preservation ideals with the needs of a modern working office space. Committee members advise Committee staff and review proposals from contractors. They love to poke around in the Capitol's dark spaces and climb scaffolds to see artisans at work stenciling a ceiling, or carefully concealing a new sprinkler head in an old plaster rosette.

All Committee members—from preservationists to politicians—see themselves as ambassadors for Capitol restoration, and all speak highly of Capitol Preservation Committee staff. "As museum professionals, they're guided by an overriding ethic of preserving as much intact as possible, and that includes finishes, materials, and the character of the space," said John Bowie, architect, historic preservationist, and Committee member since 1995. "Then they spend an awful lot of their time being incredibly creative. They figure out ways of solving problems—running wires in hidden locations and placing sprinklers in cornice sections where they won't see them. They're working within the parameters of preservation of the Capitol as an artifact, and at the same time, making sure it's state of the art."

Always, the Capitol Preservation Committee hewed to the integrity of Joseph Huston's grand design. He envisioned and created a seamless blend of architecture, art, and decor meant to project the highest ideals of government. Many Committee members have the expertise to understand Huston's motives and the turn-of-

"As museum professionals, they're guided by an overriding ethic of preserving as much intact as possible, and that includes finishes, materials, and the character of the space…"

Always, the Capitol Preservation Committee hewed to the integrity of Joseph Huston's grand design. He envisioned and created a seamless blend of architecture, art, and decor meant to project the highest ideals of government.

the-century trends driving his vision. "It's just like doing a period room in a museum," said Committee member Beatrice Garvan, curator emerita of the Philadelphia Museum of Art and an expert in American decorative art. "My job is asking tough, artsy questions. I think I'd know if I saw something that was really wrong. You just get to know period style. Some of those offices, at first, were awful. People thought they were doing period, but it was just awful. It's not just a learned skill out of books, but it's an accumulation of things—archives and textiles. And then we get the information out to the public. We get an explanation of the work, so when it comes time to explain to the outside world—the people who are funding it— we can say more than, 'It's pretty, isn't it?'"

Hyman Myers, (FAIA) witnessed it all from the beginning as chief restoration architect for the Historic Preservation Studio at Vitetta, the Committee's preservation architect. Much of Vitetta's early work happened behind the scenes—unheralded things like ductwork and dome moisture remediation—or enhancing modern-day efficiency while preserving the original feel, but to Myers, the building's remarkable qualities were immediately apparent. "We had never worked on a building which had so much artwork integrated into the architecture," Myers said. "I knew about the Mercer Tile Works in Doylestown, but I walked up the main hall and thought, 'Holy cow, can there be a bigger installation of these tiles in America?'"

Myers is the kind of architect who can wax poetic about the aesthetics of building expansion joints, but with his

CHAPTER EIGHT • *The People's Building: A Preservation Journey*

eye for beauty, he recognizes the combination of vision, design, materials, and craftsmanship that formed a masterpiece. Pennsylvania's Capitol is like no other statehouse.

"Most capitols have a dome, wings, grand stairs, a columned entrance," said Myers, who estimated that Pennsylvania's $13 million Capitol would cost about $2 billion today. "They're all about the same. The general layman sees this icon and says, 'Oh that's a capitol building.' This building was designed to integrate into that icon building the great art of Pennsylvania, and that is so different. This is not just materials. This is philosophy and history, all in the form of artwork. This building tells a proud story, and that story is the history of Pennsylvania. If you learn to read the Capitol's iconography, you learn about Pennsylvania. It becomes magical. It becomes a trip in history."

In Huston's plan, everything had its place and proportion. Even the knobs in unseen doors circling the dome bear the state seal. Enormous, sub-basement piers support the rotunda with the majesty of Aztec temples. Learning to read Huston's signals has been the life work of Joe Sorrentino, the Vitetta historic preservation project architect who has overseen nearly every detail of restoration for the Committee. To find an answer when there is a question about the cut of a molding or the color of a glaze, one reads all the room's elements. "If you need a precedent for some detail, you can go to another place in that building and find it," Sorrentino said. Work there long enough, and be willing to get dirty enough, and even the great mysteries solve themselves, such as: Whatever happened to the Huston building's predecessor, the Cobb Capitol? Sorrentino and a colleague were once crawling behind the Senate Chamber walls, through the oily grit from the days of coal heat, when they were astounded to encounter inner walls hung with decorative canvas and gold capitals—the Cobb Capitol encased in Huston's edifice.

The Capitol's non-architectural elements, every piece of furniture and every ornate drape, also had a place in Huston's scheme, but they often were moved to other state offices or found their way into private homes. So, even before the Committee's official creation, curator and preservationist Hubbert-Kemper was scouring Harrisburg's scariest storage places—including places dripping with actual stalactites—for the pieces that originally adorned the

THIS PAGE: *Top, Joe Sorrentino, architect, (Center) watches as contractors John Young (Left) and Jeff Proctor (Right) of C. A. Lindman, Inc. remove the west entry granite steps, 2005; Bottom, Hyman Myers, architect, addressing crowd at Committee event, 2000.*

OPPOSITE PAGE: *Interstitial space in ceiling above Senate Chamber ceiling, 1995. (Notice golden capital from 1898 Cobb Capitol building).*

"…This building tells a proud story, and that story is the history of Pennsylvania. If you learn to read the iconography, you learn about Pennsylvania. It becomes magical. It becomes a trip in history."

Capitol's public spaces and private offices. Her first major find: The original House Speaker's chair, surviving in an offsite sub-basement, and recognized from a vintage photo. Other reclaimed pieces have included crystal globes tossed into the Capitol's old coal bin, and a Supreme Court justice's ornate chair, reclaimed with Committee member Garvan's help, from a private owner in the Lehigh Valley.

While they protected artistic integrity, Capitol Preservation Committee members and staff also resurrected memories of the artisans and officials who created the building. It started with a visit from Kermit Roosevelt at the tercentenary ceremony. His presence evoked the scene of his grandfather, President Theodore Roosevelt, addressing the throng at the 1906 Capitol dedication ceremony and declaring, "It is the handsomest building I've ever seen." Since then, descendants of major figures in Capitol history have been honored guests at events, such as the 2004 cornerstone-laying commemoration that positioned a Governor Pennypacker re-enactor beside Huston's look-alike grandson, as well as his granddaughter.

The proud graffiti of long-ago workers often resurfaces during restoration. One man may have had the holidays in mind when he inscribed on the House Chamber ceiling, "Wm L Williams Decorator Boston Mass. Decem 1905 God bles you all today." For Hubbert-Kemper, such inscriptions reveal the Capitol's true meaning. "It has always been about the people who built this building," she said. "They're not

The ·Stately·
Commonwealth
of Pennsylvania

THIS PAGE: *Top, Placement of restored* Commonwealth *statue, 1998; Bottom, Pennies recovered from underneath the statue, recovered in 1997.*

OPPOSITE PAGE: *Kevin Snoke with Wohlsen Construction, Ruthann Hubbert-Kemper, Paul Clymer, Merle Ryan, Gary Crowell, and Mitchell Haas, 1998.*

wealthy. They're the working class. It speaks to everyone in Pennsylvania. Pennsylvania is a diverse state, and a diverse people built the Capitol."

The Capitol Preservation Committee maintains ties to the descendants of those workers as well. Two days before the dome-topping statue *Commonwealth* was airlifted for restoration, Hubbert-Kemper heard from a woman whose grandfather, Jacob B. Authur, had always said he placed coins under the statue's base. Did his grandchildren believe the tall tale? The woman admitted they were skeptical. But after the airlift, a helicopter crewman approached Hubbert-Kemper and told her to hold out her hand. In it, he placed three antique coins. When the restored *Commonwealth* made her debut, who better to lead the unveiling than Mitchell Haas, the nine-year-old great-grandson of the worker who placed the coins at her feet?

Sorrentino believes that Pennsylvania's statehouse is one of the most accessible and just-plain-used Capitols, in part because the restoration has seamlessly blended priceless art with technological upgrades "that would stack up with any new building." People have always done business here. Some even left their marks for later preservationists to find, such as tobacco stains from a time when gentlemen rode the open, iron-grated elevators and treated the shafts like giant spittoons. Sorrentino looked over the rotunda from outside the

A. A ripped canvas wall needing repair; B. A worn corner edge detracts from the appearance of the mahogany floor moulding; C. An area of a marble step needs to be repaired.

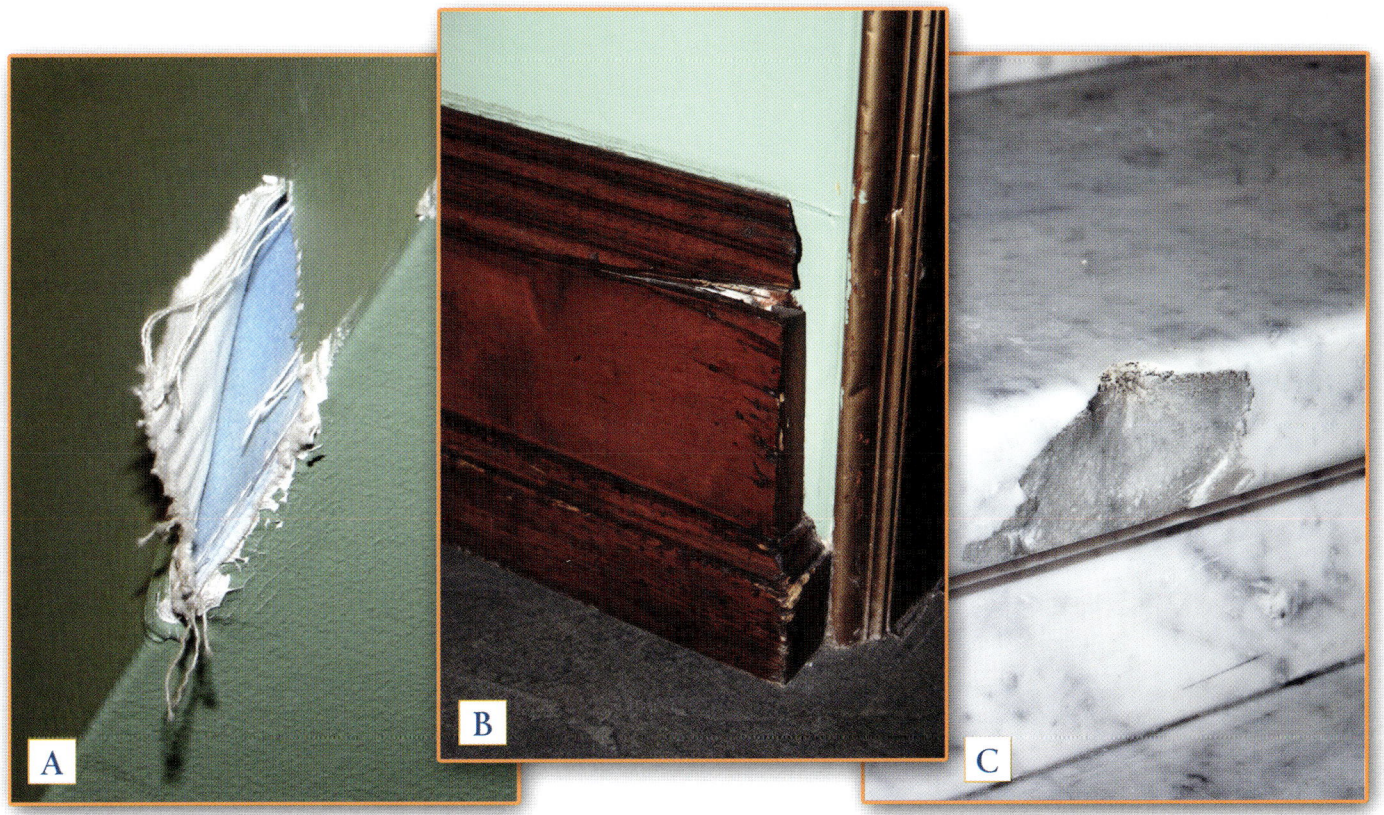

CHAPTER EIGHT • *The People's Building: A Preservation Journey*

THIS PAGE: *Top, Representative Paul Clymer (Left) and Speaker Matthew J. Ryan at the Ryan Building Rededication Ceremony, 1999; Bottom, Elizabeth Kennedy of John Canning Studio gold leafs House Chamber pediment.*

OPPOSITE PAGE: *The Committee accepts the National Trust for Historic Preservation Honor Award from Henry Jordan and Mary Werner De Nadai, 1995. From left, Back row: Diane Kessler, Carrie Forry Roush, Kji Kelly, Sue Ellison, Elana Maynard, Senator Gibson Armstrong, Robert Glenn, Charlie Wilson, Gary Crowell; Front row: William Faulhaber, Representative Fred Belardi, Ruthann Hubbert-Kemper, Representative Joseph Pitts, Henry Jordan, Mary Werner De Nadai, Eugene DiOrio, Senator Allyson Schwartz, Representative Paul Clymer.*

Supreme Court Chamber—his favorite room—and said, "In the annals of American architecture, this building is one of the gems that can have its rightful place in the American portfolio." He looked at the people below, seeming small in the heroic scale of the space. "It's their house," he said. "The place they go to gather, voice opinions and disagreement, and to celebrate as well."

The restoration process spanning nearly twenty-five years began with a simple but groundbreaking idea: create a legal entity to oversee Capitol preservation. The process began with the mechanism of planning and contracting. It progressed through more than fifty individual projects that restored the Capitol's grandeur while making Pennsylvania a national leader in Capitol preservation. Finally, it is intent on ensuring a lasting legacy.

The Ongoing Journey

During one of his final visits to the building before succumbing to cancer in 2003, Matt Ryan spoke of his beloved Capitol with Hubbert-Kemper. She told him about the Committee's latest restoration project, the Mexican War Monument, and how beautiful the marble angel high atop the column now looked after its cleaning.

"That angel will be me one day, with an eye on the Capitol, watching over this building to see that it is protected," he told Hubbert-Kemper. "I want the Preservation Committee to keep it nice for generations to come." And then he quipped, "Or I will come back to haunt the place."

Nearing its hundredth anniversary in 2006, the Pennsylvania Capitol, in a sense, is fully restored. But the work of the Capitol Preservation Committee continues, just as Ryan envisioned. In 2003 the Committee started a database detailing its work, to leave a complete record for tomorrow's Capitol conservators.

The first preservationists had to puzzle through the work of earlier renovators. What materials did they use? What methods? Finding answers required testing, knowledge of past preservation techniques, educated guesses, and old-fashioned detective work. Future preservationists will not have that problem, because the Capitol Preservation Committee's database records materials, manufacturers, techniques, and contractors involved in every project. "In the future, people who come behind us will have it all indexed, well photographed, with information accessible at their fingertips," Bowie said. "They'll know what we did and why." Myers, a nationally known historic preservation architect, said that no one else has ever done such meticulous documentation. "It's never done," he said.

The database covers the spectrum of preservation, from initial restoration through the maintenance projects that are performed according to a schedule and strict standards. From the beginning, Matt Ryan insisted that vigilant maintenance infuse the preservation plan, and in 1995, the National Trust for Historic Preservation recognized the Committee's stewardship with its National Trust for Historic Preservation Honor Award.

Can dull, old maintenance be award-winning? Yes, said Hubbert-Kemper. "When we first started maintenance, people asked why we were up there. Had something gone wrong in the restoration?" she said. "Now, they understand that scaffold is part of summer maintenance. Why spend $100 thousand when you can spend $1,000 on a wash and wax? It's a wise use of public funds, and it shows that we take pride in the building. People say, 'I was here twenty years ago and couldn't get over the difference.' We don't want to see the same problems reappear in another twenty years. Without ongoing preservation maintenance, there would be problems all over again."

Architect Myers tells a parable about people who, installed in a beautifully restored office, want a microwave. They call Sam the maintenance guy, who brings in any old microwave and runs a power line. The next day, someone figures they want an extra telephone, and soon, somebody else shoehorns in some additional lighting, but the lighting doesn't look very nice, so they surround it with a dropped ceiling. The moral of the story: it's easy to backslide. Changes that could have been done carefully are, instead, careless. "If you suspend your effort and nobody's watching and

CHAPTER EIGHT • *The People's Building: A Preservation Journey*

nobody's maintaining, then you're back where you started," Myers said. "It starts with a microwave and ends with a dropped ceiling." When somebody is watching, said Myers' Vitetta colleague Sorrentino, then building caretakers "will not bend to the whims of fashion. Fashion will go but history will remain."

The idea of maintenance has taken root institutionally, in the same way that Capitol preservation became a mindset. Throughout the Capitol, staffers alert CPC staff to problems they see. Cleaning crews and restorers bring in family members to show off their work. Legislators and staffers decorate their offices with prints, models, and ornaments from the Capitol Preservation Committee's gift shop, proceeds of which are used to procure lost relics of the Capitol. Taxpayers agree that preservation dollars are responsibly spent. The Capitol, and its beautification, belongs to everyone.

From his congressional office, looking back on his time as chairman, Joe Pitts said that he is most proud of the structure created to guard preservation efforts. "We established a Committee and made a structure and effort that's ongoing," he said. "There are a hundred different projects that are well managed—all the maintenance and documentation. Just to see this concerted effort on the part of the administration and legislature, that's gratifying."

In the end, what difference can a building make in the way government conducts itself? All the difference in the world, say Committee members and the pioneers of preservation. It comes down to pride in the building, which translates to pride in being a Pennsylvanian. "It makes everyone who serves in that building stand a little taller," said Thornburgh. "It's an incentive to observe good government practices. It's awe-inspiring to new legislators and new governors. It really impresses a sense of history and sense of responsibility."

An exalted building, restored to magnificence, can tell the story it was meant to tell, said Representative Paul Clymer, Capitol Preservation Committee chairman since 1997. To Clymer, and

LITERATURE IN STONE: THE HUNDRED YEAR HISTORY OF THE PENNSYLVANIA STATE CAPITOL

> "Step back for a minute and appreciate what it's all about, what it means to be a Pennsylvanian. Learn what we're about and how William Penn's holy experiment has been successful. We have a better life because of the self-government that he envisioned."
>
> —Representative Paul Clymer

to generations of people devoted to preserving a splendid Capitol, the ideals that gave birth to a Commonwealth are wrought in marble and stone, paint and gold leaf, leather and tile.

"Step back for a minute and appreciate what it's all about, what it means to be a Pennsylvanian," Clymer said. "Learn what we're about and how William Penn's Holy Experiment has been successful. We have a better life because of the self-government that he envisioned."

In 1906 a building rose in gilded-age splendor. Later years took their toll, but in 1982, the building began a restorative journey that would become an ongoing model of preservation that continues today. In 2006 when citizens of the Commonwealth who visit and work there feel ownership in something magnificent, the Pennsylvania Capitol is once again, what it was always meant to be—truly the People's Building.

Contributing Writer **M. Diane McCormick**
President
HISTORIC HARRISBURG ASSOCIATION

THIS PAGE: *Representative Paul Clymer, Chairman, 2001.*

OPPOSITE PAGE: *Top, Jeff Johnson repairs water damaged area on Governor's Office ceiling, 1999; Middle, Eric Malatestenic stencils the ceiling in a first floor office, 2002; Bottom, Contractors from Bob Smith company removing non-historic glass from House Gallery, 1995.*

CHAPTER EIGHT • *The People's Building: A Preservation Journey*

Literature in Stone: The Hundred Year History of the Pennsylvania State Capitol

A Review of the Capitol Preservation Committee's Projects

Pennsylvania's Civil War Battle Flags

Since its inception in 1982, the Capitol Preservation Committee has conducted numerous successful restoration and conservation projects within the Main Capitol Building and at times other Capitol Complex buildings. One of the Committee's first projects was the conservation of the Commonwealth's collection of Civil War battle flags (previously located in the Capitol). The exceptionally fragile conditions of the flags, and the fact that the cases had no environmental controls, alerted the Committee to the need for a complete removal and conservation of all the Civil War colors. A flag sponsorship program, coupled with an appropriation from the General Assembly, allowed the Committee to completely conserve all 390 flags in-house, along with twenty-two Spanish American War flags. The Committee was also the first entity in the nation to hold a Civil War flag symposium—bringing together historians, re-enactors, and textile conservators for serious discussion and scholarship. The successful conservation of these historic colors, one of the first state-owned flag collections in the nation to undergo in-house conservation, presented an opportunity for the

THIS PAGE: *Top, Conservator Marta Rothrock arranges fragmented pieces of a flag; Bottom left, Engineer Frank Ciccone creates a door opening mechanism for the flag case, November 1999; Bottom right, one of six flag cases in Capitol rotunda.*

OPPOSITE PAGE: *A. Conserved Civil War battle flags; B. Workers removing flags from rotunda case for conservation; C. Civil War Flag returned to Pennsylvania, 2003.*

CHAPTER EIGHT • *The People's Building: A Preservation Journey*

THIS PAGE: *Left, Textile conservator Mary Ashton vacuum cleaning Civil War flag; Right, Humidification table used for flag treatment.*

OPPOSITE PAGE:
A. *Rotunda Abbey mural restoration: Mural panel mounting by Biltmore, Campbell, Smith Company.*
B. *Scaffold network used to reach murals.*
C. *Detail of moisture damage to murals.*
D. *Dome moisture monitoring reader.*
E. *Infill for damaged mural.*
F. *Tubes used to remove murals from walls.*

Committee to document the colors through the publication of a two volume set of books, titled *Advance the Colors! Pennsylvania Civil War Battle Flags.* The Committee continues to offer tours of the collection to the public, many of whom are genealogists, Civil War re-enactors, or descendants of a soldier who want to view their ancestor's regimental flag.

ROTUNDA MURAL RESTORATION

The next, and possibly most visible Committee project, was the restoration of the rotunda murals and interior dome. During a week-long rainstorm in the early 1980s, problems within the dome became apparent as Edwin Austin Abbey's *Spirit of Light* lunette mural became water-soaked. As a result of the infiltration, a five-foot-by-six-foot section of canvas peeled from the plaster wall and collapsed over onto itself, hanging by only several inches of canvas. Saturated bricks bulged from the plaster wall, and scaffold was hastily erected to salvage the soaked and torn mural. In May 1984 the Committee funded a conservation project for all of the rotunda murals which also included cleaning and repainting the entire rotunda. By January 1985 a 220-foot-high aluminum tower comprised of two working decks was erected in the main rotunda. The scaffold had to be freestanding and was designed with four support towers, which could not be pinned into the interior marble walls.[1] Structural shoring for the massive weight of the tower required bracing in the basement and sub-basement areas for this one-of-a-kind structure.

Concurrent with the mural project, the Committee funded a three-phase dome restoration and waterproofing project to address the damage and water saturation. Monitoring sensors were installed into the lunette walls to track moisture levels, and today this system continues to provide readings on a regular basis. A moisture alert warning system was also placed in the tunnel around the dome, and this system is activated if moisture ever breaches the walls.

The large rotunda murals were removed from the deteriorated and water-soaked walls through the innovative use of a custom-designed device designed both to roll

CHAPTER EIGHT · *The People's Building: A Preservation Journey*

Literature in Stone: The Hundred Year History of the Pennsylvania State Capitol

the canvas and hold the enormous weight of the murals. Once unrolled, the conservators consolidated layers of paint that had flaked from the canvas, effectively re-adhering the paint to the canvas. When the conservation was finished, the murals were each mounted onto a marouflage panel that was placed inches away from the still wet lunette wall, which needed time to dry. When the scaffold was removed, nearly two years later, the rotunda space was the first public area of the building to be restored. This project was unique for the Committee, in that it made international art news history for its innovative method used in removing the murals from the wall and the processes used for consolidating the delaminated paint.

ROTUNDA Restoration

A. *A fisheye view of the completely restored rotunda, 1986.*
B. *Artisan Richard Jones reapplying gold leaf to capital, Rotunda.*
C. *The Capitol dome as seen from the first floor rotunda.*
D. *Conservation cleaning rotunda marble by Albert Michaels Conservators, 1985.*
E. *Enormous plastic drop cloths are in place during the cleaning of the rotunda marble, 1992.*
F. *Angel of Light deteriorated plaster hand.*
G. *Vestibule marble statues at main entrance to rotunda being poulticed, 1991.*
H. *Repair and repainting of plaster newel post Angel of Light statue.*

CHAPTER EIGHT • *The People's Building: A Preservation Journey*

Light Court Restoration

The William Brantley Van Ingen murals in the first floor south hyphen corridor were restored and the Vincent Maragliotti murals in the north hyphen were cleaned at the same time as the massive rotunda project. In March 1991 the Committee approved funding for the restoration of the first floor areas of the south light court and the first floor hyphen corridors. During the paint analysis a discovery was made on the ceiling in the first floor south corridor. Under a coat of 1950s battleship gray paint was a beautiful design of swans intertwined in an intricate foliate design. The original 1906 designs, such as Greek keys on the ceilings of the corridors, and palmette leaf stencils on the walls from the first through fourth floors, were also restored.

During the mid-1980s the Capitol Preservation Committee also funded the compilation of a *Documentary History and Historic*

A. Completed Senate light court.
B. Swan stencil design discovered on Senate first floor ceiling.
C. Ernel Martinez paints new stencil onto wall following template.
D. Elaine Gleason paints moulding in light courts.
E. Finished north light court ceiling.
F. Light court prior to restoration.
G. Jeff Johnson gold leafs a capital.
H. Rachel Boles cleans glass from a light fixture.

Literature in Stone: The Hundred Year History of the Pennsylvania State Capitol

CHAPTER EIGHT • *The People's Building: A Preservation Journey*

PRESERVING the Moravian Tile Floor

A. Damaged tiles in a mosaic.
B. Technician Pat McBride from Masonry Preservation Group grouts replacement tiles.
C. Workers maintain the tile floor with special conservation cleaning products.
D. Technicians Ivan Castro (Left) and Joe Paciocco mix grout color to fill in damaged areas of a mosaic.

OPPOSITE PAGE: Top, A worker removes damaged tiles so they can be replaced; Bottom, Stained glass windows from House Chamber before and during restoration.

Literature in Stone: The Hundred Year History of the Pennsylvania State Capitol

Structure Report for the Main Capitol Building. The four volume set, titled *The Pennsylvania Capitol: A Documentary History,* includes research on the history of the building, 1906 photos of rooms, existing conditions for all rooms when the building was constructed, and alterations to the spaces over the years. The labor-intensive *Historic Structure Report* contains as-built measured drawings and gives specific details of the historic and modern conditions of the building, such as paint analysis, fixtures, and furniture, along with providing a photograph of every room. Preservation policy and maintenance is also identified in the *Historic Structure Report.* These books help to chronicle and identify a vast majority of research material that is available on the Main Capitol, Capitol Complex, and its historic landscape.

Moravian Tile Floor Preservation

Since the Capitol's completion, damage, wear, and modifications have taken a toll on the Mercer tile floor, the largest collection of artwork in the Capitol. In 1986 the Committee first began contracting with the Moravian Pottery and Tile Works in Bucks County for replacement tiles for those in the tiled floor that had fractured beyond repair. Through subsequent years, comprehensive surveys of both the mosaics and the field tiles have been undertaken, along with preventive measures such as weekly conservation cleaning and techniques employed to maintain the tiles. An intensive study of the tile floor was conducted and recommendations were developed to maintain deteriorated and damaged tiles within the floor. All replacement tiles are still manufactured at Mercer's original factory, the Moravian Pottery and Tile Works in Doylestown, Pennsylvania. The tile project continues today as part of the Committee's cyclical maintenance program.

Van Ingen Stained Glass Windows

Of all the stained glass that decorates the Capitol, the House and Senate chamber windows are unique. The windows in these two chambers are comprised of four layers of opalescent glass with hand painted features. This multi-layered construction is what gives the windows their depth of color. The fourteen Van Ingen stained glass windows that adorn the House Chamber were removed in 1988 for off-site restoration. Plywood cutouts filled the spaces in the chamber until the windows were reinstalled over the summer recess of 1989. Restoration of the first two Senate windows, *Railroads* and *Peace,* was conducted in 1990. One by one, the

remaining eight Senate windows were restored and all had been reinstalled by the end of the summer recess of 1992.

House Chamber Restoration

In early 1989 restoration of all five of Edwin Austin Abbey's House Chamber murals began. Deterioration of the murals was due in part to particulate degradation, such as smoking in the chamber, which is no longer allowed. The uneven application of the white lead adhesives used to originally attach the murals to the wall had caused flaking and pigment loss within the murals. This problem was corrected through consolidation, and the removal of dirt from the murals which revealed the beautiful colors that Abbey had originally used in these works. It was also discovered during the restoration that Abbey had painted the large *Hours* ceiling mural on a circular wheel in his London studio, as the drips of paint were in a circle on the canvas.

In 1994 the House Gallery underwent complete reconstructive restoration to reverse prior non-historic interventions. The project was completed and the gallery re-opened to the public in 1995. In 1998 the Committee began restoration of the ceiling and walls within the House Chamber, which was done in conjunction with the placement of sprinkler heads and electrical upgrades by the Department of General Services. The House at this time installed wiring for laptop computers at each member's desk. The House anterooms at the rear of the chamber including the vestibule, lounge, and telephone room were also restored. The Committee also restored every mahogany desk in the Chamber during the course of this project.

Additionally, the massive bronze chandeliers within the chamber were missing many of their crystal beads, which infill the bronze frames. The small chandeliers

THIS PAGE: *Top, Removing stained glass windows from House Chamber by Cummings Studio, 1999; Bottom, Scaffold erected in House Chamber, 1999.*

OPPOSITE PAGE: *House Chamber*
A. *Scaffold is erected to the* Hours *mural, 1989.*
B. *Conservator Richard Pelter working on* Apotheosis *mural, 1989.*
C. *Art conservator Barney Lamar restores* Penn's Treaty *mural, 1989.*
D. *Stephen Pacovsky (Left) and Eric Goodman examine stained glass ceiling section for House gallery, 1996.*

CHAPTER EIGHT • *The People's Building: A Preservation Journey*

House Chamber
RESTORATION

A. Professional decorator John Canning checks paint samples for original color.
B. Installation of carpet in chamber.
C. Inpainting by artist Michael Deluco to cornice.
D. Worker restoring House chandelier.
E. House Chamber desks being upgraded for computers by C. E. White Enterprises.
F. Completed restored House Chamber, 1999.
G. Rewiring crystal beading for chandelier.
H. Applying gold leaf to balcony plaster element by Elizabeth Kennedy.

LITERATURE IN STONE: THE HUNDRED YEAR HISTORY OF THE PENNSYLVANIA STATE CAPITOL

CHAPTER EIGHT • *The People's Building: A Preservation Journey*

Following World War II, the Federal government had a surplus of battleship gray paint, which was offered free to various states for their use. Consequently, the House Chamber walls and many of the buildings' ornate corridors and spaces had been painted in this color. Paint analysis revealed the original paint color for the chamber and the walls, and they were then repainted to match the original blue and gold color scheme. The paint analysis revealed the same tonality in both the walls and the murals, which was architect Huston's overall plan. Fortunately, the gold leaf in the chamber had not been over-painted and needed only to be conservation cleaned.

Lieutenant Governor's Suite Restoration

In 1989 restoration work was also undertaken in the three second floor rooms of the Lieutenant Governor's suite. Conservation began with Donald MacGregor's *Venus and Two Loves* ceiling mural, which had sustained water damage from leaking water pipes on the floor above. An ornate foliated design surrounding the mural, which had been discovered during the paint analysis, was also recreated. A most unusual historic paint finish was discovered on the walls—the use of air brush techniques designed to create a gold spatter effect over the vibrant green wall paint.

During the time of the restoration several unique pieces of historic furniture, designed exclusively for the Lieutenant Governor's private office, were discovered in an office building on Front Street in Harrisburg. A leather sofa and several club-style chairs shown in the 1906 Capitol photographs and also identified in the original furniture line drawings of Joseph Huston, were restored and returned to the Lieutenant Governor's office. Additionally in 1999, the original Lieutenant Governor's desk was discovered at a State surplus sale at the Farm Show building. This was also recovered, restored, and returned to its original location in the Lieutenant Governor's office.

originally had 18,000 beads and the large ones had approximately 81,000. The contractors used silver-coated copper wire, which increased reflectivity and was the same method used when the beads were originally strung on the framed panels.

During the project within the Lieutenant Governor's office, an infiltration of water from a broken pipe caused damage to the ceiling of the Governor's private office. This emergency restoration project included plaster repairs to the ornate strapwork ceiling. Paint analysis

A. Corner view of the restored Lieutenant Governor's Office, 1989.
B. Member's office after restoration.
C. Conservator John Rita applying glazed finish to Governor's Office ceiling, 1989.

OPPOSITE PAGE: *Top, Bob Devera and crew remove bronze light standard elements for restoration; Bottom, Electricians rewiring light standard.*

CHAPTER EIGHT • *The People's Building: A Preservation Journey*

showed that the fleur-de-lis had originally been aluminum leafed. This leafing was re-applied during the restoration and the entire original color scheme, including the leafing, was then coated in a glaze with a stippled effect.

Maintaining the Capitol Bronze Work

In 1990 the Committee began restoration work on all of the Capitol's exterior bronze sculptures. The John Frederick Hartranft equestrian statue adjacent to the Speaker Matthew J. Ryan Office Building, the Boies Penrose monument in Capitol Park, and the three sets of bronze doors and the two light standards at the Capitol's main entrance all underwent conservation treatment. Environmental degradation, corrosion, sulfide crusts, and Pennsylvania's harsh winter weather conditions contributed to the deterioration of the bronze. All the pieces were repaired, washed, degreased, and treated with corrosion inhibitor and a protective coating.

Additionally several interior bronze fixtures were conserved during the same time. These included the three rotunda figures of Oliver, Stewart, and Curtin and the lantern light fixtures at the entrance porticos. All of the Capitol's bronze has since been added to the Committee's cyclical preservation maintenance schedule. The bronze sculptures and doors are surveyed for surface imperfections, open joints, and cracks annually. Necessary repairs are undertaken and the bronzes are then cleaned and coated with wax, which helps to mitigate harmful environmental effects.

Barnard Statuary Conservation

In 1991–92 the Committee began a study of George Grey Barnard's statue groups at the Capitol's main entrance. The soft Carrara marble used in the groups is highly susceptible to Pennsylvania's freeze/thaw cycles and other harmful environmental conditions. In 1996 the statues were removed from their pedestals for an intensive restoration project conducted in a building on the Capitol's grounds.

THIS PAGE: *Top, Technician cleaning entrance light standard; Bottom, Application of missing features to Barnard sculpture by conservator Mark Rabinowitz.*

OPPOSITE PAGE:
A. *Robert Marshall applying protective wax to equestrian bronze sculpture.*
B. *Conservation cleaning details of Hartranft sculpture.*
C. *Summer maintenance to bronze light standard.*
D. *West entry bronze doors receive protective coating treatment.*

CHAPTER EIGHT • *The People's Building: A Preservation Journey*

Literature in Stone: The Hundred Year History of the Pennsylvania State Capitol

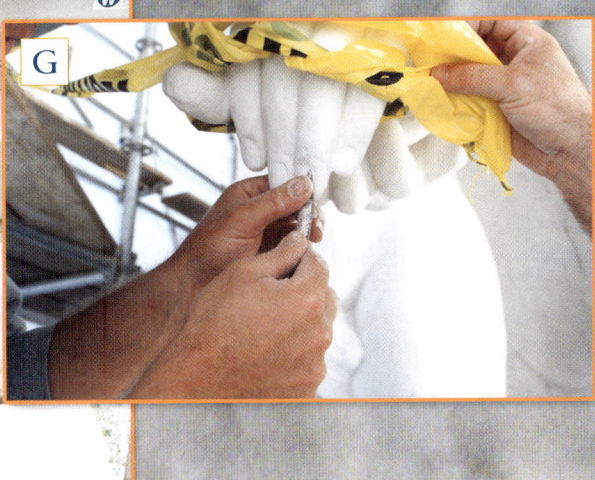
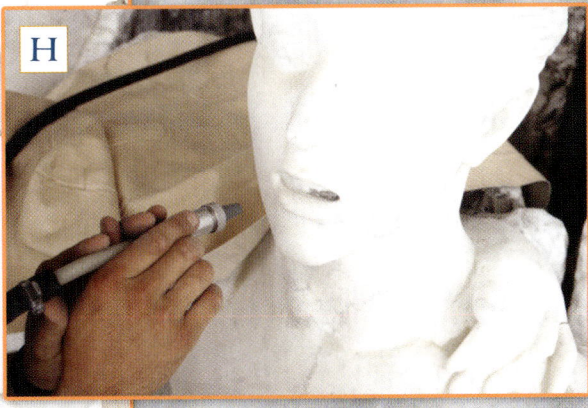

BARNARD
MONUMENTS
Cyclical Maintenance Project
Contracted by C. A. Lindman in association with Conservation Solutions, Inc.

A. Conservator replacing missing carved elements.
B. Injection treatment at cracks.
C. Creating mold for carving replacement marble pieces.
D. Correcting damaged features.
E. Detailed treatment to head.
F. Creating support cavity between groups.
G. Marble reapplication of fingers.
H. Repair to facial features.
I. Applying protective moisture barrier over support cavity.

CHAPTER EIGHT • *The People's Building: A Preservation Journey*

Literature in Stone: The Hundred Year History of the Pennsylvania State Capitol

The Barnard groups are the most fragile pieces of exterior artwork that the Committee maintains. Many decades ago, prior to CPC's establishment, these statuary groups underwent successive detrimental treatment campaigns. During one such unfortunate campaign they were actually sandblasted, which removed the honed surface and made the already fragile marble more porous, allowing for increased water infiltration. In another treatment, the porous marble was sealed with a superficial waterproofing material that did not permit the marble to breathe. As a result, cracks in the marble became increasingly problematic. The Committee began a yearly program of preservation maintenance to treat the statues with sacrificial coatings and consolidant injections that serve to protect the underlying stone from the continuing onslaught of atmospheric and environmental conditions.

Violet Oakley Mural Restoration

In October 1991 conservation of Violet Oakley's murals in the Governor's Reception Room and the Supreme Court Chamber had been completed. The Senate Chamber murals were included in the following year's conservation schedule. In the summer of 1992, Violet Oakley's large Senate mural *Unity* was conserved completing the restoration work on all of Oakley's work in the Capitol. Also, a paint analysis was undertaken in the Supreme Court Chamber to determine the 1906 color and a secondary paint color discovered through documentation. Violet Oakley had recommended to the Justices of the Court and the Board of Public Grounds and Buildings that they change the color of the room to complement her murals, to which the Board agreed in correspondence with Oakley. Therefore, the Committee repainted the walls and ceiling to match Violet's 1927 paint scheme, rather than return the room to its 1906 pre-mural appearance.

In the summer of 1993 the Committee began the restoration of the Senate Majority Caucus Room, Senate Library, and the

THIS PAGE: *Top, Restored Supreme and Superior Court Chamber; Bottom, Moisture damaged wall in court before restoration.*

OPPOSITE PAGE:
A. *Painting conservator from Arthur Page Conservation repairing canvas.*
B. *Reverse side of painting stretcher prior to restoration treatment.*
C. *Restored feature on* Disarmament *mural.*
D. *Conservators removing mural panel stretcher from wall.*
E. *Canvas repairs to* Blackstone *painting.*

Senate Chamber
RESTORATION

A. *Chamber chandeliers are rebeaded.*
B. *Conservator Julie Riker applies gold leafing to Senate gallery railing.*
C. *Workers stain door moulding for Senate entrance.*

OPPOSITE PAGE: *Top, Elaine Kenny and Alan Capriotti applying gold leaf to columns; Bottom, The completed Senate Chamber, 1992.*

Senate Chamber and gallery. The scope of work for these projects included restoration of decorative elements, electrical upgrades, and some structural enhancements. During this same time, restoration of all decorative plaster and wood surfaces was undertaken in the anterooms adjacent to the Senate Chamber. As with the House Chamber, much of the gold leaf on the Senate Chamber ceiling only needed to be conservation cleaned, saving much of the original 1906 decorative work. Unfortunately the balconies, which were originally gold leafed in 1906, had been painted over during the 1950s. The conservators regilded these during the restoration. All other painted surfaces were analyzed to determine the historic colors that were selected by Abbey

CHAPTER EIGHT • *The People's Building: A Preservation Journey*

A. Capitol basement following restoration, 2005.
B. Basement prior to restoration.
C. Basement hallway after being restored, 2005.
D. Example of the disarray of electrical wiring in the Capitol prior to any utility upgrades.
E. Sign from original Capitol construction before, during, and after conservation.
F. Staining HVAC enclosure Room 138, 1997.
G. Senate conference room after restoration.
H. Senate office after being restored.

LITERATURE IN STONE: THE HUNDRED YEAR HISTORY OF THE PENNSYLVANIA STATE CAPITOL

and Huston and repainted to match the 1906 green and gold scheme. By August 1994, the Senate restoration project was completed.

In 1997 implementation of the master plan for the Capitol was begun. This multi-year project by the Department of General Services included repairs to the building's envelope, mechanical, electrical, life safety and Americans with Disabilities Act (ADA) upgrades, and general renovations. The building's occupants were relocated to swing space while their respective areas were under reconstruction. Subsequently this multi-phased project progressed throughout all the floors of the Capitol, concluding with the basement in 2005.

During this project many discoveries were made, such as when a small piece of canvas was removed from a wall on the Senate side, a paper broadside from the Donald A. MacGregor Company was discovered glued directly to the plaster wall. The sign warned that any workman leaving before 12 o'clock or 5 o'clock would be discharged from his position. The Committee hired a paper conservator to clean, in situ, areas of loss and replicate the original notice. Afterwards, the sign was framed, and the canvas and paint were applied around the original poster. This stands as an example of the types of writing and graffiti that were revealed and are still present

CHAPTER EIGHT • *The People's Building: A Preservation Journey*

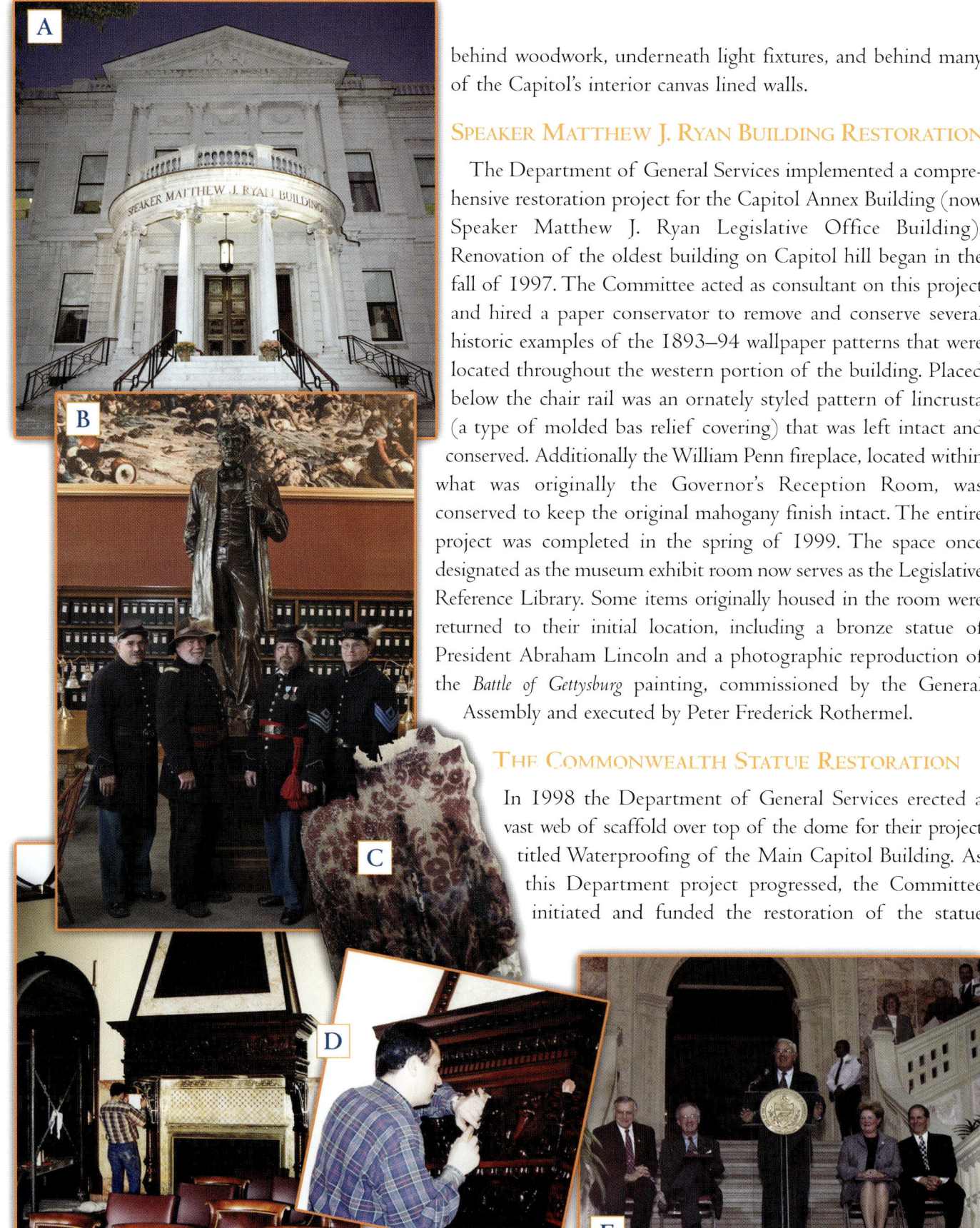

behind woodwork, underneath light fixtures, and behind many of the Capitol's interior canvas lined walls.

Speaker Matthew J. Ryan Building Restoration

The Department of General Services implemented a comprehensive restoration project for the Capitol Annex Building (now Speaker Matthew J. Ryan Legislative Office Building). Renovation of the oldest building on Capitol hill began in the fall of 1997. The Committee acted as consultant on this project and hired a paper conservator to remove and conserve several historic examples of the 1893–94 wallpaper patterns that were located throughout the western portion of the building. Placed below the chair rail was an ornately styled pattern of lincrusta (a type of molded bas relief covering) that was left intact and conserved. Additionally the William Penn fireplace, located within what was originally the Governor's Reception Room, was conserved to keep the original mahogany finish intact. The entire project was completed in the spring of 1999. The space once designated as the museum exhibit room now serves as the Legislative Reference Library. Some items originally housed in the room were returned to their initial location, including a bronze statue of President Abraham Lincoln and a photographic reproduction of the *Battle of Gettysburg* painting, commissioned by the General Assembly and executed by Peter Frederick Rothermel.

The Commonwealth Statue Restoration

In 1998 the Department of General Services erected a vast web of scaffold over top of the dome for their project titled Waterproofing of the Main Capitol Building. As this Department project progressed, the Committee initiated and funded the restoration of the statue

Commonwealth, which graces the top of the Capitol's dome. Condition analysis of the statue indicated that most of the sixteen steel bolts holding *Commonwealth* to its base had deteriorated, along with cracks that were visible in the bronze base and at several locations on the statue. A decision was made to completely remove the statue from the dome using a skycrane helicopter. The statue was sent to a conservation studio to be completely restored. After repairs and cleaning of the statue, a primer was applied to the metal and approximately 7,500 sheets of 23.75-karat gold leaf were applied to the statue, which was then covered with a protective wax coating. In September 1998 *Commonwealth* was again lifted by helicopter and re-attached to the dome.

Also during the summer of 1998 the Committee, utilizing the Department of General Services scaffold, conducted an inspection review of the dome ribs. Due to alterations and multiple weatherproofing decades ago, the dome had lost much of its original grandeur. The dome had been covered in decorative terra cotta tile that was removed during the 1930s. The exposed ribs were then covered with lead in an attempt to keep moisture out. The lead was covered in gold leaf, which over time had deteriorated. After investigative research, the Committee found a product that would coat the lead ribs with a golden color but was guaranteed to last longer and cost less than gold leaf. The coating was applied

A. *Speaker Matthew J. Ryan Building, 1999.*
B. *Civil War re-enactors in the Legislative Reference Library, 2004.*
C. *Old wallpaper found inside Ryan Building.*
D. *Craftsman Renalto Tavecchio carving wood on the William Penn fireplace located in the Ryan Building, 1999.*
E. *Ryan Building rededication event, October 1999. From left, Representative Paul Clymer, Senator Robert Jubelirer, Speaker Matthew J. Ryan, First Lady Michele Ridge, and Brent Glass, Executive Director of PHMC.*
F. *Removal of* Commonwealth, *December 1997.*
G. Commonwealth *during restoration, 1998.*
H. *Detail of damage in statue's features, 1998.*
I. *Before and after treatment of dome ribs, 1998.*

CHAPTER EIGHT • *The People's Building: A Preservation Journey*

to the lead covered elements that surround and highlight the yellow-green Ludowici tile.

Senate Water Damage

On Valentine's Day 1999, a Capitol police officer noticed water leaking under a doorway on the first floor north corridor. After closer examination, it was discovered that a flange on a free-standing cooling unit located in the storage area under the Senate Gallery had failed. This caused flooding in several rooms from the second floor down to the basement with an estimated twenty-six thousand gallons of water. Multiple emergency projects were immediately issued by the Committee and General Services to repair the damage. Large dehumidifiers ran for months through a massive and continuous effort to extract the water that had saturated plaster, woodwork, and furnishings. Many of the first floor Senate hyphen rooms that had been flooded contained suspended ceilings that were completely destroyed and needed to be removed. Upon their removal unique decorative plaster strapwork ceilings were uncovered in each of these rooms. A decision was made by the Senate to undertake a complete restoration to facilitate the already ongoing master plan upgrades at this opportune time. General Services implemented the utility and life safety upgrades and the Committee brought in teams of conservators to restore the woodwork and decorative finishes. Despite the extensive damage, the emergency project progressed rapidly, and the rooms were soon reoccupied.

Committee Initiatives

On the eve of the new millennium the Committee began looking toward the 2006 one-hundredth anniversary of the building's dedication. In 1999 it began a series of annual

A. Art conservators repair water damaged Maragliotti mural, 1999.
B. Removing damaged decorative canvas from caucus room ceiling, 1999.
C. Gretchen Strang repairing plaster Greek key element, 1999.
D. Capitol cornerstone re-enactment ceremony, 2004. From left: Tilda and Stanley Hunting (grandchildren of Joseph Huston), Representative Paul Clymer, Lieutenant Governor Knoll, and Ronald Boice as Governor Pennypacker.
E. Capitol artist Violet Oakley tea and lecture event, 2001.
F. Capitol Preservation Committee ornaments.
G. Rotunda exhibit display case, 2001.

holiday ornaments focusing on different architectural and artistic elements within the building. Also, the Committee's annual project reports highlighted previous Pennsylvania Capitol buildings and events such as the 1901 design competition and the building's construction. Committee events also began to highlight restoration projects and the talented artists and artisans who originally worked on the Capitol. The rotunda exhibit cases showcased historic occurrences that were taking place while the Capitol was being built. In June 2001 the Committee held an exhibition opening with a formal tea in the rotunda followed by a lecture in the Senate Chamber honoring the life and work of artist Violet Oakley. Subsequent exhibitions focused on additional Capitol artists and architectural aspects of the building.

CHAPTER EIGHT • *The People's Building: A Preservation Journey*

Literature in Stone: The Hundred Year History of the Pennsylvania State Capitol

In 2001 the Committee restored all fifty-seven of the Governors' portraits housed in the suite of offices occupied by the Governor and staff. The portraits, which start with William Penn and proceed to the most current Governor, had all become dirty and faded from humidity, smoke, soot, and the effects of time.

The Governor's Reception Room

In 2003 the most prominent project was the restoration of the Governor's Reception Room including the oak woodwork, ceiling, grandfather's clock, and all furnishings, along with the installation of a replica carpet. A scrap of the original rug had been saved in the 1960s when the original thread-bare rug was discarded. This small piece was given by a foresighted employee of the Governor's office to the State Museum. The original rug in the room was made in Berlin, Germany and at the time was reputed to be the largest loomed rug in the world. After reviewing several options on how to replicate the design on a loom large enough to accommodate such an unusually wide and long single piece, the Committee was fortunate to find a Pennsylvania company that could reproduce the carpet. The new replica carpet was financed through donations given to the Capitol Preservation Committee in memory of the late Speaker Matthew J. Ryan. The successful rehabilitation of the Governor's Reception Room in September 2003 marked the completion of restoration within the last major public room in the Main Capitol Building.

Restoring the Governors' Portraits Collection

THIS PAGE: *Top, Governor Benjamin Franklin portrait, Governor's Office; Bottom, Portraits (From left) Governor William Bigler, Governor David R. Porter, Governor John Penn, Governor's Office.*

OPPOSITE PAGE:
A. *Conservator John Rita removes a portrait from the Governor's anteroom for restoration work, 2000.*
B. *Examination of painting for damages.*
C. *Alan Capriotti touches up the woodwork around the portraits.*
D. *Governor Joseph Reed portrait, Governor's Office.*
E. *Before and after restoration detail of a portrait.*

CHAPTER EIGHT • *The People's Building: A Preservation Journey*

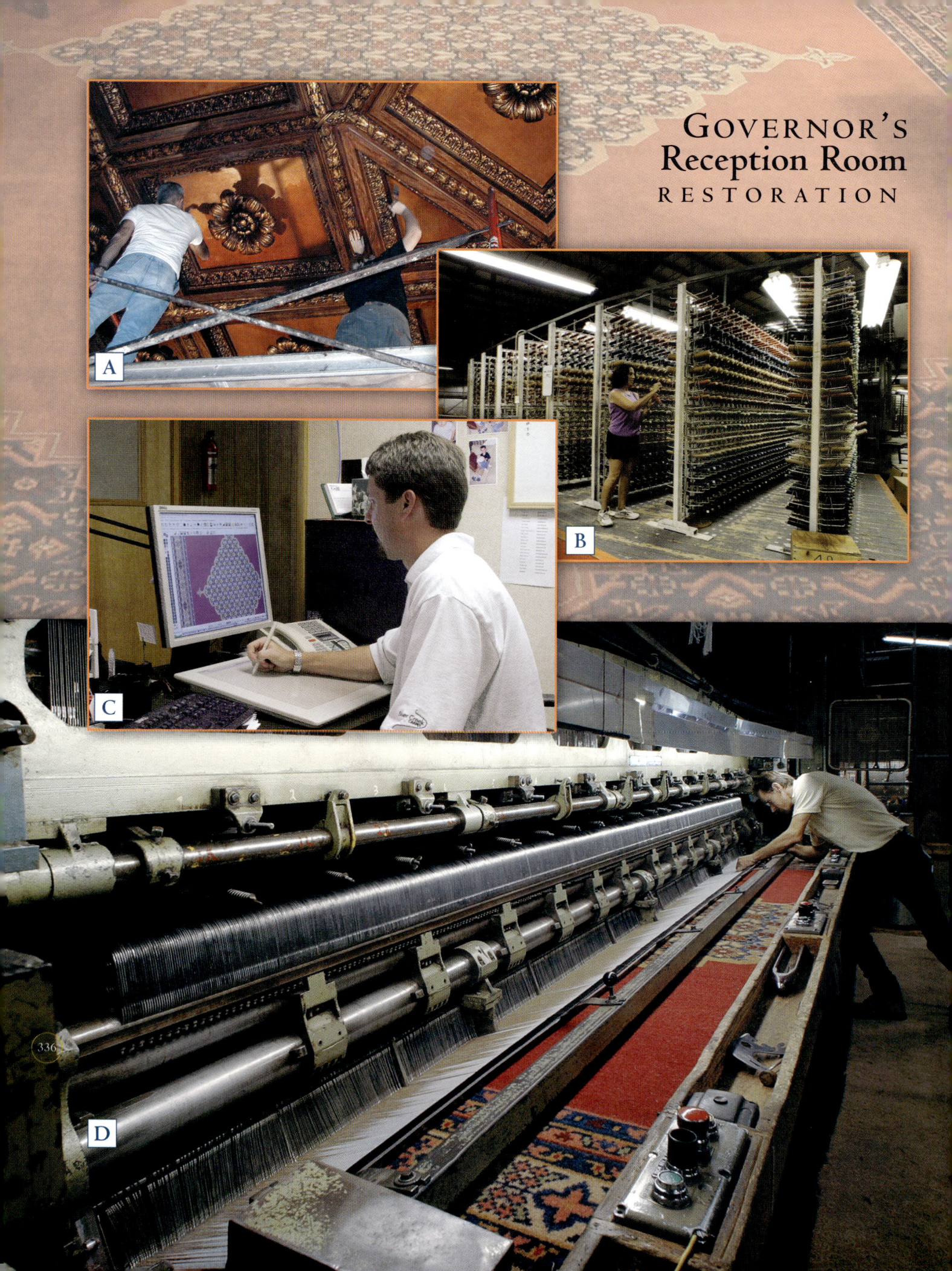

Governor's Reception Room
RESTORATION

A. Conservation of ceiling finishes.
B. Loading spools of yarn for the Bloomsburg Carpet loom.
C. Designer uses CAD software to plan the large carpet for the room.
D. Looming carpet at the Bloomsburg Carpet mill.
E. Reception room after restoration, 2003.
F. Shawn Vennell applies finish to light standard in reception room.
G. Reception room grandfather clock during and after restoration.

CHAPTER EIGHT • *The People's Building: A Preservation Journey*

House Majority Caucus Room RESTORATION

A. Majority Caucus room after restoration, 2002.
B. Workers from Wohlsen Construction Company remove old finish on woodwork.
C. Conservator John Rita cleans stencil work to restore its original luster.
D. Scaffold erected during restoration of the room.

House Majority Caucus Room

The House Majority Caucus room project began in the spring of 2001. From 1906 until the mid-1920s the room was used as a caucus room. However, in 1926 the Treasury Department that occupied the suite of rooms across the hall had run out of usable space and took occupancy of the room. Treasury removed the dais and other decorative elements along the west wall and reinforced the floor to accommodate their massive vault. The caucus members relocated to the third floor center wing area. In 1940, with the movement of the Treasury to the newly constructed Finance Building, the room was returned to use as a caucus room, but few modifications conformed to the 1906 look of the room. In 2001 the Committee conserved the State Coat of Arms mural originally painted on the room's west wall in 1939. A portion of the original 1906 dais railing, which had been discovered in the storage tunnel under the State Street bridge, was also re-installed in the room. The original stencil pattern for the wall was replicated and installed on new canvas, which

was then adhered to the walls overtop of the original painted over finish. This process allows for the original finish to be uncovered in the future when technology allows for safe removal of the overpaint from the original finish. The Committee also undertook restoration work in the staff office of the Speaker of the House in 2002. Originally used as the House Library, the room was modified into the Speaker's office in 1939. The Committee's project consisted of restoration of the woodwork, metal balcony, bookcases, and circular metal staircase, along with ceilings, walls, and other decorative elements within the room.

Cleaning the Capitol Dome

The cleaning of the Capitol dome structural cavity was one of the more unique projects that the Committee has undertaken. It was the first time that this interstitial space had been professionally cleaned since the Capitol was finished in 1906. The project resulted in the removal of more than two thousand pounds of dirt and debris that had accumulated in the space. In addition, numerous artifacts were found and preserved, such as a copy of George M. Cohan's poem and later song, *Harrigan*, which is contemporary to the 1906 time period. A paintbrush, silver spoon, bottles, and period product wrappers were also found. This project gave an interesting look into almost one-hundred years of history based solely upon what workmen at the Capitol had occasionally dropped within the dome's interstitial space.

Speaker's Office Suite

THIS PAGE:
A. Speaker's staff office after restoration, 2003.
B. Technician from Conservation Solutions, Inc. cleaning bronze spiral staircase, 2003.
C. Renato Tavecchio from John Canning Studio repairs mahogany woodwork, 2003.

OPPOSITE PAGE: Top, 1906 items collected from the interstitial space in dome during cleaning, 2002; Middle, Rick Wagner staining woodwork in 139 office, 2003; Bottom, Office prior to restoration.

CHAPTER EIGHT • The People's Building: A Preservation Journey

MEXICAN WAR Monument

A. Annual inspection of the monument checking for weather damage.
B. Conservator from C. A. Lindman applying replicated eagle head, 2002.
C. Application of biocide, 2002.
D. View of the Mexican War above Capitol Park, 2002.

LITERATURE IN STONE: THE HUNDRED YEAR HISTORY OF THE PENNSYLVANIA STATE CAPITOL

Mexican War Monument Preservation

Work on the 1868 Mexican War monument was initially conducted in 1992 to stabilize the large base supporting the columnar base. These emergency repairs were conducted to ensure that a high wind would not topple the entire monument. However, it was not until 2001 that the first year of a five year pre-cyclical restoration of the Mexican War monument began. The monument was originally erected on a small mound adjacent to the Speaker Matthew J. Ryan Legislative Office Building. With the original construction of this building in 1893, this monument was moved to its current location in south Capitol Park. The initial stages of the project incorporated a cleaning of the marble with a non-ionic detergent biocide and water. This removed lichen and biological growth that had accumulated on the monument. Areas of loss and weathered marble were treated with special conservation consolidants that help to slow detrimental environmental effects over time. All mortar joints were raked out and repointed. Stainless steel pins were inserted to stabilize a crack in the capital. Lastly two missing eagle heads were replicated and re-attached. The monument will undergo periodic cyclical maintenance treatment by the Committee's conservators to slow the effects of biological growth and to monitor the expansion of cracks in the stone as the monument weathers.

Ongoing Maintenance

As more and more rooms were restored, the Committee's major works have transitioned from restoration to long-term preservation maintenance, to ensure that over time these areas will retain their present state, instead of deteriorating and making future costly campaigns of restoration necessary. As a result, the Committee began in July 2004 to prepare a comprehensive preservation maintenance manual for the entire Capitol building. This manual will contain information on what was used to restore all aspects of the building. It will contain information on chemical agents, paints, stone conservation, tile maintenance,

Left, Clock contractor Quentin Johnson installing clock face, 2002; Right, Two post-conservation clocks.

database to catalog damage and maintenance to the artifacts of the Capitol. The Committee is also in the ongoing process of cataloging historic and project photographs digitally, allowing them to be indexed, cataloged, easily searched and retrieved, making them an invaluable tool for ongoing preservation.

Over the course of the twenty-four years that the Committee has been undertaking restoration, there have been numerous individuals without which success would have been greatly impeded. They were the packrats of the last one hundred years—those individuals who had the foresight to notice that an artifact or original piece of Capitol furniture or a clock was leaving the building. In the course of the past century the Capitol has changed much and some of its artwork, furniture, and artifacts have gravitated to the four corners of the state. Fortunately, some pieces were returned and many still remain. Without people saving these items, or the generosity of those who returned them, much of the Capitol would be devoid of these historical articles. The citizens of the Commonwealth are likewise indebted to forward-thinking House leaders Matthew J. Ryan and K. Leroy Irvis and Senate leaders Henry Hager and Edward P. Zemprelli who, through bipartisan effort, implemented the preservation efforts of the Capitol.

and information on the restoration of all decorative and design elements. Foremost in any restoration is continuing preservation maintenance. With the committee's comprehensive maintenance manual, combined with all the final reports for each Committee project, questions that arise in the future will have the benefit of these records as a reference. With these tools available, the maintenance manual and final reports will make future preservation more productive and not a matter of trial and error.

As part of the cohesive maintenance master plan, a list of maintenance items is prepared annually, with emergency repairs addressed as they arise. Committee staff also began monitoring restoration and repair of historic clocks, furniture, and artwork within the building through the use of Past Perfect museum software, a

Preservation often mirrors life—change being the only constant. Assessing preservation in terms of a building the size of the Capitol, change is always a definite. Different methods and techniques will arise in the future, the needs of individuals and agencies will change, priorities in state government will vary, populations will ebb and flow—but one thing is certain, fiscal responsibility indicates that periodic cyclical maintenance over time is more effective than successive non-unified campaigns of often detrimental renovation. Unified efforts at sustaining a regular and preservation-based maintenance plan will ensure that all Pennsylvanians can be proud to walk the halls of their state Capitol.

As more and more rooms were restored, THE COMMITTEE'S MAJOR WORKS HAVE TRANSITIONED FROM RESTORATION TO LONG-TERM PRESERVATION MAINTENANCE, to ENSURE that over time these areas WILL RETAIN THEIR PRESENT STATE instead of quickly deteriorating and making future and costly campaigns of restoration necessary.

THIS PAGE: *Left,* Literature in Stone *by Joseph M. Huston; Right, 1920s scrapbook and photographs donated to the Committee by William H. Thomas.*

OPPOSITE PAGE: *Capitol dome lit up at sunset, 1989.*

On the morning of January 5, 1903, Joseph Huston arrived at the Capitol just as construction of the building was beginning. In the piers of one of the main dome pillars, far in the sub-basement, he buried a copy of his personal writing, entitled *Literature in Stone.* The following is a small excerpt of what the design of the Pennsylvania State Capitol meant to Joseph Huston:

Call architecture what you will, frozen music, stony religion or philosophy, or absolute beauty shining through sensuous stone, yet it is literature in stone, writing in its own way of the rural home of the laborer and of the abode of prelate of Rome. It is as broad as human life and as deep as the human soul. And whether architecture basks in the attire of the Chinese, or in the mouths of the Greeks, it touches the keynote of the souls of all peoples, and makes mankind one.[2]

The continued preservation of the Capitol building will allow future generations to stare upward in awe at Pennsylvania's incomparable "Palace of Art."

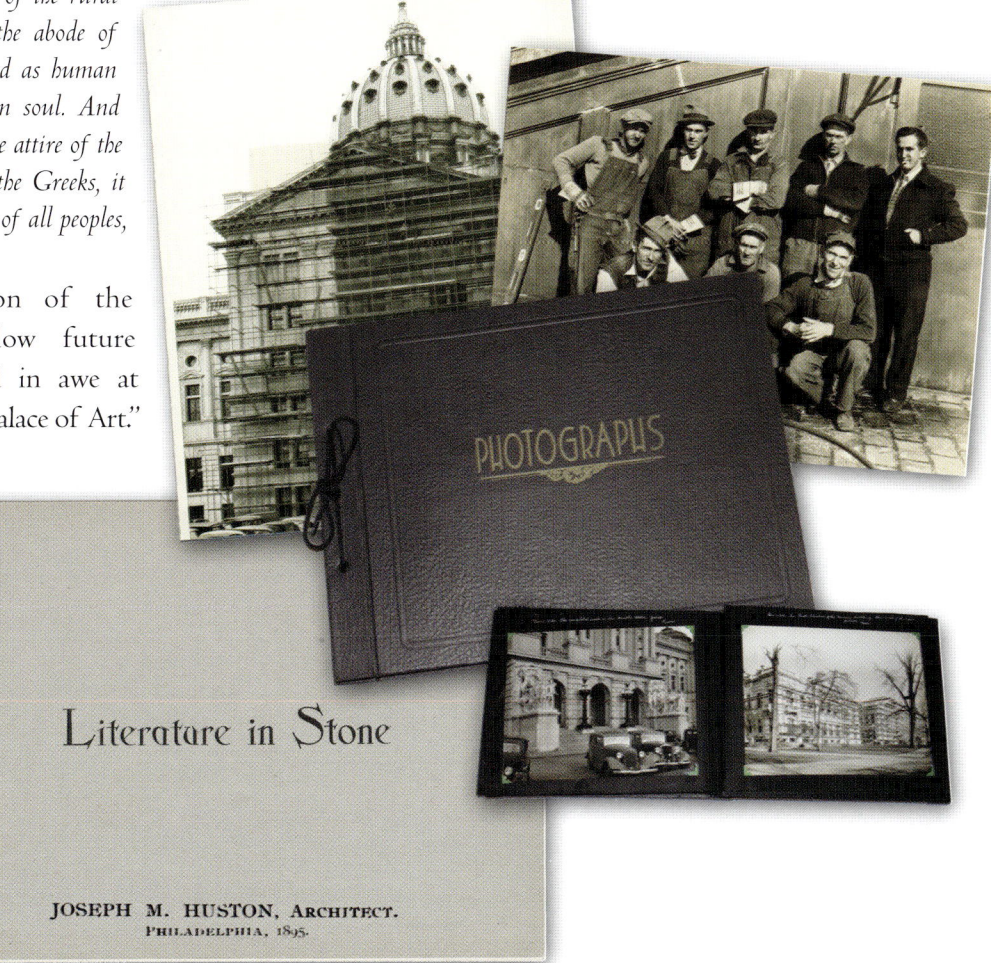

CHAPTER EIGHT • *The People's Building: A Preservation Journey*

End Notes

Introduction:
Our Legacy from William Penn

1. Although there have been numerous studies of Penn's life and career in the past 50 years, there has been only one strong biography, Catherine Owen Peare's *William Penn* (Philadelphia, 1956). Peare's work was written before the Penn papers were published, and a contemporary reader will best be able to discover Penn's life by reading the biographical and analytical entries in Mary Maples Dunn and Richard S. Dunn, eds., *The Papers of William Penn*, vols. 1–4, and Edwin B. Bronner and David Fraser, eds., vol. 5 (Philadelphia, 1981–87). Hereafter cited as *Papers*, this edition is the source for this brief essay.

2. Known as the Penn-Mead trial, Penn wrote up his version of it in *The Peoples' Ancient and Just Liberties Asserted* (London, 1670).

3. *An Essay Towards the Present and Future Peace of Europe* (London, 1693).

4. *Papers*, vol. 2, 84.

5. *Papers*, vol. 2, 100.

6. *Papers*, vol. 2, 127–28.

7. The process occupies more than one hundred pages in *Papers*, vol. 2, 135–38.

8. The plan may be seen in *Portrait of the City of Philadelphia*, *Papers*, vol. 2, 515. The plan was drawn by Thomas Holme, Penn's surveyor.

9. *Papers*, vol. 4, 104–110.

Chapter 1:
Pennsylvania's Early Capitols

1. William Penn Tercentenary Committee, *Remember William Penn, 1644–1944* (Harrisburg: Commonwealth of Pennsylvania), 86–87. Hereafter cited as *Remember William Penn*.

2. Henry Russell-Hitchcock and William Seale, *Temples of Democracy: The State Capitols of the U.S.A.* (New York: Harcourt Brace, 1976), 59.

3. William Wyman Colson and Lewis Slifer Shimmell, eds. *The State Capitol of Pennsylvania, Harrisburg, Nineteen Hundred and Six* (Harrisburg: Telegraph Printing Company, 1907), 14–16.

4. Colson and Shimmell, 15.

5. Ibid.

6. Colson and Shimmell, 16.

7. Colson and Shimmell, 18.

8. Colson and Shimmell, 26.

9. *The Pennsylvania Capitol: A Documentary History*, vol. II (Harrisburg: Prepared by Heritage Studios for the Capitol Preservation Committee, 1988), 661. Hereafter cited as *Pennsylvania Capitol*.

10. *Pennsylvania Capitol*, 33. There is some disparity as to what happened to the original furniture from Independence Hall. Various sources say some was burned in 1778 by the British, some was sold on each successive move, and some did indeed make the trip to Harrisburg, most notably the "Sun" chair and the Philip Syng inkwell, which were later returned by the Commonwealth to Independence Hall National Historic Site. The original General Assembly collection, along with the 1739 Assembly Bible ordered by Benjamin Franklin remained in Harrisburg and are now part of the Commonwealth's Rare Books collection.

11. For a breakdown of the costs of these two structures, see *Journal of the Senate*, 1811–12, 66.

12. *Pennsylvania Capitol*, 22.

13. It is interesting to note that this is the derivation of the original term "Main Capitol" as these first two buildings were built almost a decade before the construction of a primary building. The term is still used today to denote the offices of the current Main Capitol.

14. *Pennsylvania Capitol*, Figure 3, p. 19a, *illus*.

15. Ibid., 22.

16. Ibid., 5.

17. Henry Russell-Hitchcock and William Seale, 60.

18. Hubertis Cummings, "Stephen Hills and the Building of Pennsylvania's First Capitol," in *The Capitols of Pennsylvania* (n.p., n.d.), 15. Reprinted from *Pennsylvania History* 20, 4 (1953), 420. Also interesting to note that both Mills and Strickland were assistants to famous architect, Benjamin Henry Latrobe.

19. Ibid., 24.

20. Ibid., 14.

21. Governor's message to the Senate and House of Representatives, December 3, 1918, quoted in Colson and Shimmel, 38.

22. Hubertis Cummings, "Stephen Hills and the Building of Pennsylvania's First Capitol," in *The Capitols of Pennsylvania* (n.p., n.d.), 15. Reprinted from *Pennsylvania History* 20, 4 (1953), 420.

23. The Historic American Buildings Survey (HABS) has the elevation and first floor plans available online at http://memory.loc.gov/cgi-bin/query/D?hh:10:./temp/~ammem_QU52:: [Cited March 1, 2006].

24. *Pennsylvania Capitol*, 25–26.

25. "Contract by Stephen Hills architect for building the State Capitol…" JJ 290 B, RG-13, Pennsylvania State Archives. Also available in the *Journal of the House of Representatives of the Commonwealth of Pennsylvania*…(Harrisburg: James Peacock, 1820), 61–65.

26. Colson and Shimmel, 46.

27. Until 1873, the head of the Senate was called the Speaker. In that year the office was abolished and the President Pro Tempore replaced it.

28. Cummings, 29–30.

29. The University of Virginia has an online account of Dicken's American Notes and Pictures from Italy available online at http://www.people.virginia.edu/~jlg4p/dickens/amnotes/dks9.html [Cited March 1, 2006].

30. Tanner's Alley in back of the Hills Capitol was one of the stops on the railroad.

31. *Pennsylvania Capitol*, 32.

32. Colson and Shimmel, 47. This extension originally held numerous museum artifacts, the original Assembly collection. "An Hour Among the Battle Flags," *The Harrisburg Daily Journal*, September 22, 1873.

33. Colson and Shimmel, 49. The Executive, Library, and Museum Building, as it was known when created, was built from 1893–94. It later became known as the Capitol Annex Building and is now the Speaker Matthew J. Ryan Legislative Office Building. It remains the oldest of the State Capitol Complex Buildings still in existence.

34. For a wonderfully researched, in-depth look at the Hills Capitol Fire, consult Robert M. Houseal, Jr's booklet "The Pennsylvania Statehouse Fire."

35. Houseal, 14.

Chapter Two:
The Cobb Capitol

1. *Harrisburg Telegraph*, February 3–4, 1897.

2. Houseal, 22–23.

3. *Harrisburg Patriot*, February 4, 1897.

4. *Pennsylvania Capitol*, 55.

5. Boyer subsequently resigned his Speakership on January 17, 1898, perhaps because he did not openly support the return of the capital to Philadelphia and thereby knew he would be voted out by the Philadelphia members.

6. *Pennsylvania Capitol*, 56. See also Russell-Hitchcock and Seale. This must have been a mistake as there are several early colonial state houses that do survive, and the style of the Hills Capitol was actually Federal.

7. *Harrisburg Patriot*, February 3, 1897.

8. Ibid.

9. Since Haywood and Mylin's terms were about to expire, they were replaced on the commission by Beacom and McCauley, who succeeded, respectively, the former officials offices.

10. McKim, Meade, and White apparently turned down the invitation and Cope and Stewardson replaced them.

11. *Pennsylvania Capitol*, vol. II, 740.

END NOTES

12. *Report of the Capitol Building Commission, 1898*, 67. To alleviate confusion between both the 1898 and 1901 Building Commissions, *Report of the Capitol Building Commission, 1898*, indicates the Cobb Capitol Commission, while *CBC Minutes* denotes the 1901 or present Capitol Commission.

13. *Report of the Capitol Building Commission, 1898*, 17.

14. Colson and Shimmel, 55–56. Also *Harrisburg Patriot*, August 10, 1898.

15. *Report of the Capitol Building Commission, 1898*, 34–35.

16. *Report of the Capitol Building Commission, 1898*, 19.

17. From the *London Architect*, quoted in the *American Architect and Building News*, June 11, 1898.

18. George E. Reed, ed. Pennsylvania Archives "*Papers of the Governors, 1897–1902*," Fourth Series, 343–44.

Chapter Three:
The Huston Capitol: Inspiration, Design, and Construction

1. Colson and Shimmel, 59.

2. Ibid., 58.

3. *The Legislative Record*, June 11, 1901, 3130.

4. *Minutes of the Capitol Building Commission*, August 24, 1901. Hereafter cited as *CBC Minutes*.

5. *Capitol Investigation Commission Report*, 230. Hereafter cited as *CIC Report*.

6. *CBC Minutes*, December 28, 1901.

7. In 1896 the firm would be renamed Furness and Evans.

8. For a look at the formation of this idea in Huston's mind, consult the 1892 pamphlet *Literature in Stone*. Though a privately published work, it discusses the need for monumental public architecture in America, as Huston envisioned even prior to his European trips.

9. William R. Ware, *Harrisburg Capitol Competition Report*, December 24, 1901, Huston Papers, Pennsylvania Capitol Preservation Committee (CPC).

10. Bernard R. Green to the Capitol Building Commission, July 22, 1902, *CIC Report*, RG-25, PA State Archives.

11. Most of the debris from the building was taken to Hargest's Island (now City Island) and dumped along the north western sides.

12. Stanford B. Lewis, Diary Extracts, Huston Papers, Pennsylvania CPC.

13. Ibid.

14. Huston, *Specifications*, 25-26.

15. *Pennsylvania Capitol*, vol. II, 770.

16. *Harrisburg Telegraph*, July 11, 1903.

17. Huston to Board of Commissioners of Public Grounds and Buildings, March 2, 1903, in the *New York Audit Company Report*, Part III, 21-23.

18. *CIC Report*, 262.

19. Governor Pennypacker and other state officials were in St. Louis at the 1904 World's Fair. The trowel to be used by the Governor was originally inscribed May 3, 1904 but the date of the ceremony was changed to May 5th to allow Pennsylvania's dignitaries time to return.

20. *Pennsylvania Capitol*, vol. II, Appendix III, 3–6.

21. *Pennsylvania Capitol*, vol. II, Appendix III, 3–5.

22. Colson and Shimmel, 66–67.

23. Huston to Gerwig, April 21, 1904, Historical Society of Pennsylvania.

24. *Harrisburg Telegraph*, September 10, 1904.

25. Colson and Shimmel, 67.

26. *Pennsylvania Capitol*, vol. I, 204.

27. In 1998 when the helicopter lifted the statue *Commonwealth*, these three pennies were discovered. The story became more intriguing when the Committee received a call from a private citizen who had heard the statue was to be removed. She remarked that her grandfather had said he was on of the workers who helped install the statue and had placed pennies at its base to commemorate the event.

28. *Pennsylvania Capitol*, vol. II, 771.

29. *CIC Report*, 249.

CHAPTER FOUR:
Capitol Dedication: October 4, 1906

1. *Harrisburg Patriot*, October 3–5, 1906. Most state papers covered the dedication of the Capitol with great interest and much detail. While individual papers chose to publish varying details, two of the best resources for information on the overall dedication are the *Harrisburg Patriot* and the *Philadelphia Press*. Various other papers such as the *Harrisburg Telegraph* and the Philadelphia *North American* published supplements devoted specifically to the dedication ceremonies.

2. *Harrisburg Patriot*, October 5, 1906

3. *Harrisburg Patriot*, October 4, 1906.

4. Ibid.

5. Ibid.

6. *Harrisburg Telegraph*, October 3, 1906.

7. *Harrisburg Patriot*, October 3, 1906.

8. *Harrisburg Patriot*, October 4, 1906.

9. Ibid.

10. *Harrisburg Patriot*, October 3, 1906.

11. *Harrisburg Patriot*, October 4, 1906.

12. *Harrisburg Patriot*, October 5, 1906.

13. *Harrisburg Star Independent*, October 4, 1906.

14. *Harrisburg Patriot*, October 5, 1906.

15. Ibid.

16. Ibid.

17. Ibid.

18. Ibid.

19. Ibid.

20. Ibid.

21. Ibid.

22. *Philadelphia Inquirer*, October 5, 1906.

23. Ibid.

24. Ibid.

25. Though was no "official" national anthem at the time, the song played was most certainly the popular *Star Spangled Banner*, which became the official U.S. anthem in 1931.

26. *North American*, Philadelphia, October 4, 1906.

27. *Philadelphia Inquirer*, October 5, 1906.

28. Ibid.

29. Ibid.

30. *Philadelphia Inquirer*, October 5, 1906.

31. *Harrisburg Telegraph*, October 4, 1906.

32. Ibid.

33. *Harrisburg Patriot*, October 8, 1906.

34. *Harrisburg Star Independent*, October 4, 1906.

35. *Harrisburg Patriot*, October 6, 1906.

36. Ibid.

37. Ibid.

38. Ibid.

39. Ibid.

40. *Harrisburg Patriot*, October 5, 1906.

CHAPTER FIVE:
The Capitol Graft Scandal

1. Owen Wister, "The Keystone Crime" in *Everybody's Magazine*, vol. XVII, no. 4, October 1907, 437.

2. Paul B. Beers, *Pennsylvania Politics Today and Yesterday: The Tolerable Accommodation* gives an interesting and in-depth look at Guilded Age party politics within Pennsylvania during the Quay/Penrose period.

3. *Pennsylvania Capitol*, 443. The cost for the buildings construction did come in under the budgeted appropriation of $4 million, the furnishing of the building ran another $8.5 million.

4. *Pennsylvania Capitol*, 445.

5. *Pennsylvania Laws*, no. 416, July 18, 1901.

6. *CIC Report* in the *House Journal* (1909), 290–292. See also Thomas B. Cochran (Compiler), *Smull's Legislative Handbook and Manual of Pennsylvania* (Harrisburg: 1897), 61.

7. Samuel W. Pennypacker, *The Desecration and Profanation of the Pennsylvania Capitol* (Philadelphia: William J. Campbell, 1911), 13. Hereafter cited as *Desecration and Profanation*.

8. *General Appropriations Act of 1903*.

9. Ibid.

10. *Pennsylvania Capitol*, 446.

11. Ibid., 447.

12. *New York Audit Company Report*, Part III, *Records of the Capitol Investigation Commission*, RG-25, Pennsylvania State Archives, Harrisburg, PA, 54.

13. *CIC Report*, 291.

14. *New York Audit Company Report*, Part III, 63–64.

15. *Pennsylvania Capitol*, vol. II, 448.

16. *Desecration and Profanation*, 12.

17. Charles H. Darlington, "Pennsylvania's Palace of Graft," *World's Work* (July–August 1907), 9241.

18. *New York Audit Company Report*, Part III, 71. See also Hampton L. Carson, *Report of the Attorney General in re. Capitol Investigation* (Harrisburg: 1907), 16, 275.

19. Harold J. Howland, "A Costly Triumph," *The Outlook* 85 (1907), 207.

20. Wister, 444.

21. *New York Times*, March 24, 1907.

22. Wister, 437.

23. *Philadelphia Press*, September 18, 1906. See also Samuel W. Pennypacker and William P. Snyder, "The State Capitol at Harrisburg," (Harrisburg: September 26, 1906), in pamphlet volume 767, no. 11, Pennsylvania State Library.

24. Carson, 87–90.

25. *Desecration and Profanation*, 43.

26. Carson, *Report of the Attorney General*, 85–86. Also *CIC Report*, 290.

27. *Public Ledger*, Philadelphia, December 27, 1906.

28. *Pennsylvania Capitol*, 456.

29. *New York Audit Company Report*, Part I, 9.

30. *CBC Minutes*, June 9, 1904; *New York Audit Company Report*, Part I, 45.

31. *CIC Report*, 258–265.

32. The Capitol Building Commission and not the Board of Commissioners of Public Grounds and Buildings was solely in charge of the Capitol's construction. Therefore Public Grounds and Buildings was out of its jurisdiction in awarding a contract for a fifth floor for the building, but both entities are blameworthy since the Building Commission did acquiesce.

33. *New York Audit Company Report*, Part III, 178.

34. *CIC Report*, 224–225.

35. *New York Times*, April 10, 1907.

36. *Pennsylvania Capitol*, 472.

37. *CIC Report*, 380.

38. Henry Russell-Hitchcock and William Seale, 50.

39. Ibid., 49.

40. *Philadelphia Press*, September 19, 1907; *New York Times*, September 19, 1907.

41. *Philadelphia Press*, January 28, 1908; *New York Times*, January 28, 1908.

42. *Philadelphia Press*, February 29 and March 1, 1908; *New York Times*, March 14, 1908.

43. *Philadelphia Press*, December 19, 1908; *New York Times*, December 12 and December 19, 1908.

44. *Harrisburg Patriot*, May 14, 1909; Philadelphia *North American*, May 14, 1909; *New York Times*, May 14, 1909.

45. Henry Russell-Hitchcock and William Seale, 46.

46. *New York Times*, April 30, 1910.

47. *Philadelphia Press*, May 24, 1911.

48. Ibid.

49. George R. Barnett (editor), Dauphin County Report, volume 13, p. 274; *New York Times*, May 24, 1911; *Philadelphia Press*, March 21, March 26, 1911; *Harrisburg Telegraph*, May 23, 1911.

50. *Harrisburg Patriot*, January 10, 1912.

51. Wister, 448.

Chapter Six:
The Capitol's Fine & Decorative Arts

1. John Calvin to Mr. W. B. Van Ingen, February 9, 1904. Copy in Capitol Preservation Committee office.

2. Mercer, Henry Chapman, *Guide to the Tiled Pavement in the Pennsylvania Capitol* (Doylestown: Privately Printed, 1908), [Reprinted by the Capitol Preservation Committee, 1998], Introduction, 1.

3. *Pennsylvania Capitol*, vol. II, 759.

4. *Pennsylvania Capitol*, vol. II, 335.

5. Ibid., vol. II, 756.

6. Ibid., vol. II, Appendix III, 3–3.

Chapter Seven:
The Capitol Complex and the City Beautiful Movement

1. Pennsylvania Capitol Preservation Committee, *The Executive, Library and Museum Building: A Capitol Treasure Celebrates 100 Years, 1894-1994* (Harrisburg, Pennsylvania CPC, 1994), 8–9.

2. Ernest Morrison, *J. Horace McFarland: A Thorn for Beauty* (Harrisburg, Pennsylvania Historical and Museum Commission, 1995), 5.

3. J. Horace McFarland, *The Awakening of Harrisburg: Some Account of the Improvement Movement Begun in 1902; with the Progress of the Work to the End of 1906* (Philadelphia: National Municipal League, 1907), 5.

4. *Harrisburg Telegraph*, December 21, 1900.

5. William H. Wilson, *The City Beautiful Movement*, (Baltimore, Johns Hopkins Press, 1989), 130. It is believed by the author to be the first time that the phrase "City Beautiful" was used to describe the movement.

6. *Harrisburg Telegraph*, December 21, 1900.

7. Ibid.

8. McFarland, 2.

9. McFarland, 3.

10. "City Beautiful Movement" *American Studies at the University of Virginia*. Available at http://xroads.virginia.edu/~CAP/CITYBEAUTIFUL/city.html [Cited March 1, 2006].

11. Ibid.

12. McFarland, 5.

13. Ibid., 6.

14. Ibid., 15.

15. George P. Donehoo, *A Brief Description of the Capitol at Harrisburg, Pennsylvania: With an Outline of the State Government* (Harrisburg: Commonwealth of Pennsylvania, 1923), 180–181.

16. Ibid., 181.

17. "City Beautiful Movement" *American Studies at the University of Virginia*. Available at http://xroads.virginia.edu/~CAP/CITYBEAUTIFUL/city.html [Cited March 1, 2006].

18. Donehoo, 181.

19. "The Finance Building, 1939-1989," pamphlet, published by the Commonwealth of Pennsylvania in Commemoration of the Finance Building's 50th anniversary.

20. Donehoo, 181.

21. Ibid.

22. Ibid.

23. Ibid.

24. Ibid.

25. Donehoo, 181–82.

26. Ibid.

27. For more information, refer to Pennsylvania Capitol, "Attic Contract," 186–192.

28. *Minutes, Board of Public Grounds and Buildings*, December 11, 1917, Pennsylvania State Archives, RG-20.

29. *Minutes, Board of Public Grounds and Buildings*, Capitol Park Extension Plan, Pennsylvania State Archives, RG-20.

30. *Pennsylvania Capitol*, 685. See also *Commonwealth of Pennsylvania Education Building* (Harrisburg: J. Horace McFarland Company, 1932).

31. *Harrisburg Telegraph*, December 6, 1929.

Chapter Eight:
The People's Building: A Preservation Journey

1. The tower was erected by the same company and crew that had previously provided the work for the statue of liberty in New York harbor.

2. *Literature in Stone*, privately published by Joseph M. Huston, 1900.

APPENDIX I

Past and Present CPC Members

Appell, Jr., Louis J.
    Governor's Appointee
    2003–Present

Argall, David G., Representative
    2003–Present

Armstrong, Gibson E., Senator
    1993–Present

Baran, Walter L., Secretary
    Department of General Service
    1982–1986

Belardi, Fred, Representative
    1987–Present

Bodack, Leonard J. Senator
    1989–2002

Bowie, John R.
    Governor's Appointee
    1996–Present

Breene, Samuel A., Esquire
    Judicial Appointee
    1982–1984

Brown, Denise Scott
    Governor's Appointee
    1982–1987

Brown, James, Secretary
    Department of General Services
    1987–1987

Caltagirone, Thomas R., Representative
    1985–1987

Chappell, Emma
    Judicial Appointee
    1995–1996

Clymer, Paul I., Representative
    1991–Present

Creedon, James P., Secretary
    Department of General Services
    2005–Present

Crowell, Gary, Secretary
    Department of General Services
    1995–2001

Cunningham, Donald, Secretary
    Department of General Services
    2003–2005

Darr, Thomas B.
    Judicial Appointee
    2003–Present

DeWeese, H. William, Representative
    1993–1996

Dickey, John M., FAIA
    Governor's Appointee
    1982–1990

DiOrio, Eugene
    Governor's Appointee
    1995–2003

Franco, Barbara, Executive Director
    PA Historical & Museum Commission
    2004–Present

Gallery, Leslie M.
    Governor's Appointee
    1989–1994

Garvan, Beatrice
    Governor's Appointee
    1996–Present

Gedid, John
    Judicial Appointee
    1996–2002

Glass, Brent D., Executive Director
    PA Historical & Museum Commission
    1987–2002

Glenn, Robert L., Secretary
    State Art Commission
    1983–1989

Haughwout, John L., Secretary
    State Art Commission
    1982–1983

Itkin, Ivan, Representative
    1997–1999

Jannetta, David L., Secretary
    Department of General Services
    1988–1994

Jones, Renee
    Judicial Appointee
    1984–1994

Kelley, James R., Senator
    1982–1988

Logan, Kelly Powell, Secretary
    Department of General Services
    2001–2002

Mellow, Robert J., Senator
    1989–1990

Moore, William J., Senator
    1983–1988

Mowery, Harold, Senator
    1995–2004

O'Pake, Michael A., Senator
    2003–Present

Peterson, John E., Senator
    1989–1990

Pitts, Joseph R., Representative
    1982–1996

Price, Philip, Jr., Senator
    1982–1984

Punt, Terry L., Senator
    1993–1994

Real, William A.
    Governor's Appointee
    1989–1994

Romanelli, James A., Senator
    1982–1984

Ryan, Matthew J., Speaker
    1997–2002

Schwartz, Allyson, Senator
    1991–1997

Shumaker, John, Senator
    1982–1992

Snyder, Richard, Senator
    1985–1987

Sturla, P. Michael, Representative
    1999–Present

Tise, Larry, Executive Director
    PA Historical & Museum Commission
    1982–1987

Vance, Patricia H., Senator
    2005–Present

Wambach, Peter C., Representative
    1982–1992

Wenger, Noah W., Senator
    1991–1992

Wesley, John, Acting Executive Director
    PA Historical & Museum Commission
    2003–2003

Wozniak, John N., Senator
    1998–Present

Wright, James L., Jr., Representative
    1982–1990

Zemprelli, Edward P., Senator
    1985–1988

Zwikl, Kurt D., Representative
    1982–1984

Appendix II

Contractor, Sub-Contractors, and Suppliers

The Capitol Building Commission awarded the general construction contract for the Capitol to George F. Payne and Company on September 30, 1902. Payne subcontracted much of the work to the firms listed below. In 1904 the Board of Commissioners of Public Grounds and Buildings awarded the "special furnishings" contract to John H. Sanderson of Philadelphia. This contract included furnishings, decorating, and additional construction work. Sanderson subsequently sublet the construction and decorating elements of his contract to Payne and Company, which passed the additional work along to its subcontractors. Sanderson employed additional subcontractors for the furnishings.

An alphabetical listing of individual firms associated with the Capitol's construction and the specific trade or material they supplied.

American Bridge Company of New York; Pencoyd, Pennsylvania—*Structural steel*
American Car and Foundry Company; Wilmington, Delaware—*Interior woodwork*
William M. Anderson; Philadelphia, Pennsylvania—*Plumbing work*
Armstrong and Conkling; Philadelphia, Pennsylvania—*Terra cotta tile for the dome*
Art Metal Construction Company; Jamestown, New York—*Metal furniture*
Assembled Tile and Slab Company; Pittsburgh, Pennsylvania—*Glass mosaic frieze bands for the rotunda*
Atlas Portland Cement Company; New York City, with manufacturing operations in Northampton and Coplay, Pennsylvania—*Cement*
Automatic Mail Delivery Company—*Mail chutes*
Joseph Bechtel and Son; Philadelphia, Pennsylvania—*Bricklaying and foundation masonry*
Bigelow Carpet Company; Boston, Massachusetts—*Carpets*
Bigler and Company; Harrisburg, Pennsylvania—*Brick*
Carl Buchholtz; Hoboken, New Jersey—*Wrought iron and brass work (andirons)*
Buehler and Lauter; New York City, New York—*Cast plaster work and modeling; exterior architectural carving, modeling for woodwork, modeling of chandeliers cast by the Henry-Bonnard Bronze Company for the House and Senate chambers.*
C and C Electric Company; New Jersey—*Direct-current generators for the power plant*
W. H. Crook; Williamsport, Pennsylvania—*Lumber*
Derby Desk Company; Somerville, Massachusetts—*Desks and swivel chairs*
John A. Dubs; Philadelphia, Pennsylvania—*Umbrella tubs*
James Edwards and Company; New York City, New York—*Furniture*
Etter Erecting Company; Philadelphia, Pennsylvania—*Erected the structural steel skeleton of the Capitol*
Charles J. Field's Sons; Philadelphia, Pennsylvania—*General hardware*
Filbert Paving Company; Philadelphia, Pennsylvania—*Concrete flooring work, paving work*
Robert C. Fisher Company; New York City, New York—*Interior marble work*
Bertram G. Galbraith; Harrisburg, Pennsylvania—*Lime and cement*
Henry Gilbert and Son; Harrisburg, Pennsylvania—*General hardware*
Alfred Godwin; Philadelphia, Pennsylvania—*Stained glass (with the exception of the oculi windows in the House and Senate Chambers)*
Joseph Goldsmith; Harrisburg, Pennsylvania—*Furniture*
Hall and Carpenter; Philadelphia, Pennsylvania—*Bronze-plated cast iron registers*
Harrisburg Foundry and Machine Company; Harrisburg, Pennsylvania—*Four engines to drive the generators of the sub-basement power plant*
Harrisburg Planing Mill Company; Harrisburg, Pennsylvania—*Finish woodwork, particularly windows and window frames, door and door frames*
Henry-Bonnard Bronze Company; New York City, New York—*Bronze doors for the entrances on the west side (Third Street); bronze light standards for the rotunda, House (later removed), Senate, and Supreme Court Chambers, Governor's Reception Room, and light courts; ornamental grills*
E. Howard Clock Company; Boston, Massachusetts—*Clocks*
Hummelstown Brownstone Company; Hummelstown, Pennsylvania—*Foundation stone*
International Manufacturing and Supply Company; Philadelphia, Pennsylvania—*Furniture*
Johnson Service Company; Milwaukee, Wisconsin—*Thermostatic regulation system*
E. Keeler and Company; Williamsport, Pennsylvania—*Boilers for the Capitol heating plant*

Keller, Pike and Company; Philadelphia, Pennsylvania—*Installed electrical equipment and electrical wiring throughout the Capitol*
Keystone Plaster Company; Philadelphia, Pennsylvania—*Plaster*
J. B. King and Company; New York City, New York—*Wall plaster*
Francis D. Kramer and Son; Philadelphia, Pennsylvania—*Interior woodwork*
Lloyd and Company; Philadelphia, Pennsylvania—*Oak parquet flooring*
David A. MacGregor and Brother; Philadelphia, Pennsylvania—*Decorating work and painting*
Marble and Shattuck Chair Company; Cleveland, Ohio—*Capitol furniture*
Meade Roofing and Cornice Company; Philadelphia, Pennsylvania—*Skylights and roofing materials*
Henry C. Mercer; Doylestown, Pennsylvania—*Moravian tile mosaic floor in the first floor corridors and rotunda*
Merritt and Company; Philadelphia, Pennsylvania—*Steel lath*
Joseph S. Miller and Company; Philadelphia, Pennsylvania—*Tile work*
F. Mohr and Company; New York City, New York—*Furniture*
Montello Brick Company; Reading, Pennsylvania—*Brick*
Morse, Williams and Company; Philadelphia, Pennsylvania—*Elevators*
S. Musser—*Light fixtures for the attic*
National Fire Proofing Company; Philadelphia, Pennsylvania—*Terra cotta blocks for floor arches and wall partitions*
Palmer and Embury; New York City, New York—*Furniture*
Charles F. Parsons Company; New York City, New York—*Granite setting of exterior walls*
Paxtang Electric Company; Harrisburg, Pennsylvania—*Light fixtures for the attic*
George F. Payne and Company; Philadelphia, Pennsylvania—*General contractor*
Penn Construction Company; Marietta, Pennsylvania—*Agent for Art Metal Construction Company to supply metal filing cabinets*
Penn Erecting Company; Philadelphia, Pennsylvania—*Setting of structural steel*
Pennsylvania Bronze Company; Philadelphia, Pennsylvania—*Bronze lighting fixtures*
Phoenix Glass Company; Monaca, Pennsylvania—*Cut and engraved glass for lighting fixtures*
Piccirilli Brothers; New York City, New York—*Pointing of Barnard statues, modeling for other sculptural work*
Pittsburgh Plate Glass Company; Philadelphia, Pennsylvania—*Furnished windows and miscellaneous items*
S. F. Prentzel; Philadelphia, Pennsylvania—*Safes*
J. W. and C. H. Reeves; Philadelphia, Pennsylvania—*Plain and ornamental plastering*
William F. Remppis Company; Philadelphia and Reading, Pennsylvania—*Ornamental ironwork and staircases*
John A. Roebling's Son Company; Trenton, New Jersey—*Wire rope for the elevators*
William L. Russell; Philadelphia, Pennsylvania—*Interior woodwork*
John H. Sanderson; Philadelphia, Pennsylvania—*Contractor for major furnishings and decorating which included furniture, carpets, bronze, and white metal electric fixtures, finish woodwork, parquetry floors, thermostatic regulators, painting, ornamental plastering, and other items of construction, furnishing, and decoration*
Sargent and Company; New Haven, Connecticut—*Hardware including custom state seal door handles*
Robert Scott Engineering Company; Philadelphia, Pennsylvania—*Installed steam heating, plumbing, and ventilating systems*
W. & J. Sloane Company; New York City, New York—*Carpets and drapery.* Sub-contractor, **McGee Carpet Company;** Bloomsburg, Pennsylvania—*Wilton loomed, wall-to-wall carpets, arabesque and domestic patterns and Berlin area rugs from Germany*
Stiffel and Freeman Company; Philadelphia, Pennsylvania—*Safes*
A. B. Tack—*Window shades*
Thonet & Brothers; New York City, New York—*Chairs*
United Ice and Coal Company; Harrisburg, Pennsylvania—*Excavation*
Vermont Marble Company; Vermont—*Marble for the rotunda*
Vulcanite Paving Company; Philadelphia, Pennsylvania—*Concrete sub floors*
Charles S. Weakley and Company—*Rugs*
Williams and Brothers Company; Philadelphia, Pennsylvania—*Iron castings and turnbuckles, supports for the four ton light fixtures produced by the Pennsylvania Bronze Company*
James G. Wilson Manufacturing Company; Norfolk, Virginia—*Wood parquet flooring*
A. Wilt and Sons Company; Philadelphia, Pennsylvania—*Interior woodwork and composition work, this firm built the rostra in the House and Senate Chambers and the caucus rooms*
Wood-Mosaic Flooring Company; Rochester, New York—*Wood parquet flooring*
Woodbury Granite Company; Hardwick, Vermont—*Granite for the exterior walls*

APPENDIX III

THE ROTUNDA

Edwin Austin Abbey, four murals located in the lunettes, installed June 1908 by Charles L. Hesselbach and Sons, New York, New York, each 38' x 22'.

Science Revealing the Treasures of the Earth (West Wall)—Pennsylvania's natural resources, represented through a heroic allegorical figure of coal mining guided by the winged figures representing, Science, Fortune, and Abundance.

The Spirit of Vulcan (North Wall)—The steel mills of Pennsylvania were Abbey's inspiration for this mural. The Roman god Vulcan is cast against the workers highlighted by the glow of flaming steel.

The Spirit of Religious Liberty (East Wall)—Beautiful allegorical maidens guide those seeking religious refuge to the new colony of Pennsylvania in this lunette by Abbey. This mural also represents the state's shipbuildig industry of which Abbey conducted extensive research of period vessels to assure accuracy in his work.

The Spirit of Light (South Wall)—This mural expresses the dichotomous message of Pennsylvania in bringing light to the world. The mural depicts actual production of illumination through the drilling of oil for lamps and also spiritually through the message of founder, William Penn.

Edwin Austin Abbey four rondel murals, installed in the tondos June 1908 by Charles L. Hesselbach and Sons, New York, New York, each 14' round.

Religion—The symbolic figure of Religion stands in conquest over a serpent and flanked by a classical altar and torch. The quote in the background is from English martyr Hugh Latimer. "For religion, pure religion, I say, standeth not in wearing of a monk's cowl, but in righteousness, justice, and well doing."

Art—In her left hand the allegorical figure of Art holds a model of the Pantheon. The quote is from the Greek philosopher Plotinus. "Art deals with things forever incapable of definition, and that belong to love, beauty, joy, and worship, the shapes, powers, and glory of which are forever building, unbuilding and rebuilding in each man's soul, and in the soul of the whole world."

Science—Standing on a serpent, the quote is taken from the Temple of Isis in Egypt. "I am what is, what shall be, what hath been. My veil hath been disclosed by none. The fruit which I have brought forth is this. The sun is born."

Law—The allegorical figure of justice, blindfolded and bearing a scale and sword, appears astride a serpent. The quote is from Alexander Hamilton. "Justice is the end of Government. It is the end of Civil Society. It ever has been, ever will be pursued until it is obtained or until Liberty be lost in the pursuit."

THE HOUSE CHAMBER

Edwin Austin Abbey, *The Apotheosis of Pennsylvania*, Installed 1911, by Hesselbach, 35' x 35'.

Abbey's Apotheosis mural is the largest single mural in the Capitol building. The mural depicts the Genius of State seated underneath a dome, with the important sons of Pennsylvania arranged at her feet. The highest tiers are occupied by explorers and pioneers, next colonial intellectual and religious leaders, and on the bottom right (facing the mural) are leaders important in science and industry, and the bottom left, (facing view) important military leaders. In 1930 artist Arpad Kallos added the second drummer boy in the mural and filled the void left when a canopy was removed.

Penn's Treaty, Installed 1911 by Hesselbach190, 12' x 24'.

This painting modeled after Benjamin West's Penn's Treaty with the Indians depicts the founder with Indians all of whom are shown underneath the great tree where the treaty is said to have taken place. The attire for both Penn and the Indians was meticulously researched by Abbey, who was consummately concerned with historical details.

The Declaration of Independence, Installed 1911, 12' x 24'.

This painting to the right side of the *Apotheosis* (when facing the mural) was the only mural that was left incomplete at the time of Abbey's death. Abbey had postponed finishing the painting because he was waiting for archaeological data about the precise location of David Rittenhouse's observatory, which was adjacent to Independence Hall. As a result, the mural was finished by his assistant Ernest Board under the supervision of Abbey's friend and neighbor John Singer Sargent.

The Hours, Installed 1911 by Hesselbach, 24' circular.

> The final piece of artwork created specifically for the House was called *The Hours*. This area above the chamber was originally to have a stained glass dome but a change order for the "attic contract" to add a fifth floor to the building made the dome impossible to build. Therefore, Joseph Huston asked Abbey to create an additional mural for the ceiling space to fill the area where the dome was originally to have been.

The Camp of the American Army at Valley Forge, February 1778, 12' 6" x 6'.

> This mural was completed by Abbey in 1910 and originally placed in the Senate Chamber as a companion to a Civil War scene that was never completed beyond some preliminary sketches. After Abbey's death in 1911 the mural was moved to the House Chamber to allow completion of the Senate Chamber by a single artist, Violet Oakley.

In addition, it was discovered that Abbey had produced the two angels holding garlands present in the Senate Chamber as well as the cartoon sketches used by the plasterers and decorators in both the House and Senate Chambers. Abbey and Huston collaborated on the color schemes for the spaces where his art was to be installed.

THE SENATE CHAMBER
The Creation and Preservation of the Union

Violet Oakley, North Wall, Panel 9. *International Understanding and Unity: Supreme Manifestation of Enlightenment*, Installed February 1917, 9' x 44'.

> Oakley reportedly based her primary mural for the Senate Chamber on a Madonna of Mercy, a figure emanating from the years of the black plague and found in many churches in northern Italy. The figure of Unity, Violet stated, is a testament to the world that the power of peace and love is stronger than the power of war. The Unity figure and river is painted in electrifying blues. To the left of the figure are soldiers beating swords into plowshares and on the right are the slaves of the world being set free.

North Wall, Panel 7. *The Armies of the Earth Striving Together to Take the Kingdom of Unity by Violence*, 11' 4" x 13' 8".

North Wall, Panel 8. *The Slaves of the Earth—Driven Forward and Upward by Their Slave-Drivers, Greed, Ignorance and Fear*, 11' 4" x 13' 8".

The Creation and Preservation of the Union, Installed February 1917.
North Wall, Panel 3. *Troops of the Revolution: Washington Marching through Philadelphia*, 10' 4" x 12' 4".

North Wall, Panel 4. *The Constitutional Convention*, 16' 4" x 10'.

North Wall, Panel 5. *Troops of the Civil War: General George Gordon Meade and Pennsylvania Soldiers in camp before Gettysburg*, 10' 4" x 12' 4".

North Wall, Panel 6. *Lincoln at Gettysburg—The Preservation of the Union*, 16' 4" x 10'.

The Quaker Legends, Installed January 1919.

South Wall, Panel 1. *The Little Sanctuary in the Wilderness—Illustrating the Quaker Legend of the Latchstring*, 7' 10" x 12' 6".

South Wall, Panel 2. *The Slave Ship Ransomed*, 7' 10" x 12' 6".

THE SUPREME AND SUPERIOR COURT CHAMBER
The Opening of the Book of the Law

Violet Oakley, *Divine Law, Love and Wisdom*, Entire frieze installed May 1927.

Plate I, *The Keynote, Divine Law…Love and Wisdom*, 10' x 11'.

Plate II, *The Octave*, 10' x 4' 6".

Plate III, *The Golden Age: Law of Nature*, 10' x 8'.

Plate IV, *Themis…Greek Idea of Revealed Law*, 10' x 8'.

Plate V, *The Decalogue…Hebrew Idea of Revealed Law*, 10' x 8'.

Plate VI, *The Beatitudes…Christian Idea of Revealed Law*, 10' x 8'.

Plate VII, *Code of Justinian…Law of Reason*, 10' x 8'.

Plates VIII and X, *Commentaries*, 10' x 4' 6".

Plate IX, *The Spirit of William Blackstone*, 10' x 11'.

Plate XI, *William Penn as Lawgiver*, 10' x 8'.

Plate XII, *Supreme Court of the State…Law of Nations*, 10' x 8'.

Plate XIII, *Supreme Court of the Nation…Law of Nations*, 10' x 8'.

Plate XIV, *Supreme Court of the World…International Law*, 10' x 8'.

Plate XV, *Christ and Disarmament…International Law*, 10' x 8'.

Plate XVI, *The Spirit of the Law—Purification and Enlightenment*, 10' x 8'.

THE GOVERNOR'S RECEPTION ROOM
The Founding of the State of Liberty Spiritual

Violet Oakley, *The Holy Experiment*, Installed November 24, 1906.

South Wall, panel 1, a. and b. *William Tyndale Printing his Translation of the Bible into English at Cologne, 1525 and Smuggling the First Volumes of the Testament into England*, 1526, 6' x 10' 4".

South Wall, panel 2, a. and b. *The Burning of the Books at Oxford in the Attempt to Stop "The New Learning" and The Execution of William Tyndale*, 6' x 11' 10".

South Wall, panel 3, a. and b. *The Answer to Tyndale's Prayer and Anne Askew Before the Lord Chancellor*, 6' x 11' 10".

South Wall, panel 4, *Culmination of Intolerance and Persecution in the Civil War: Development of the Puritan Idea*, 6' x 10' 4".

West Wall, panel 5, *George Fox Upon his Mount of Vision*, 6' x 6' 6".

West Wall, panel 6, *William Penn Student at Christ-Church, Oxford, 1600s*, 6' x 6' 6".

North Wall, panel 7, *Penn Meets the Quaker in the Field—Preaching at Oxford*, 6' x 13'.

North Wall, panel 8, *Admiral Sir William Penn Denouncing and Turning his Son from Home*, 6' x 9' 6".

North Wall, panel 9, a., b., c., *Penn's Arrest While Preaching at Meeting, Penn Condemned to Prison at Newgate, Writing in Prison, "The Great Case of Liberty of Conscience,"* 6' x 19'.

North Wall, panel 10, *Penn Liberated*, 6' x 9' 6".

North Wall, panel 11, *Penn's Vision*, 6' x 13'.

East Wall, panel 12, *Achievement of his Purposes: The Charter of Pennsylvania Receives the King's Signature*, 6' x 6' 6".

East Wall, panel 13, *Penn's First Sight of the Shore of Pennsylvania*, 6' x 6' 6". Documents reveal that Oakley and Huston developed colors for the large Berlin rug to compliment the murals for the room.

THE LADIES' LOUNGE

The original Ladies' Lounge, located on the second floor above the rotunda, was decorated in Louis XV style furnishings, complete with tapestry panels and a vintage marble fireplace imported from France. It was used solely as the Ladies' Lounge until recent decades as it has become the staff office for the Lieutenant Governor.

Donald MacGregor—MacGregor painted this mural on the ceiling of the Ladies' Lounge.

Venus and Two Loves, 1907, 14' round.

THE NORTH AND SOUTH LIGHT COURTS

Donald MacGregor—

The Four Seasons—Spring, Summer, Winter and Fall, 9'3" H x 3' W at bottom x 8' W at top. These murals are located at the North and South Light Court entrances to the hyphen corridors on the first floor of the building.

SOUTH HYPHEN CORRIDOR

Murals progress from the rotunda south, from right to left.

William Brantley Van Ingen, 1907, 5' x 15'.

The Ephrata Sisters, Lancaster County—Spinning and carding wool.

William Tenant, Sr.,—Scots Irish professor teaching ministerial candidates at Log College, near the fork of Neshaminy Creek, Bucks County, Pennsylvania.

Mennonite Sister, "Pendelavium"—semi-annual feet-washing.

Peter Miller—Transcribing the Declaration of Independence into seven different languages.

Quaker Sisters—Worshipping at a meeting house.

Landing of the Sara Maria—First German settlers in the new world who established Germantown.

A Rosicrucian Monk worshipping at the cave of Johann Kelpius—Wissahickon Creek, Philadelphia.

Burning of the Bonfires—To celebrate "Christus" an old English custom.

Moravian woman—teaching the Bible to the Indians.

Open air Baptism by Immersion—The Dunkards.

Moravian Trombone Quartet—Bethlehem, Pennsylvania.

Old Swedes Church—Swanson and Christian Streets, Philadelphia, erected in 1702.

Printing of the Bible on the Sauer Press.

Daniel Pastorius, founder of Germantown—circulating petitions for the abolition of slavery.

SOUTH HYPHEN CAPITAL CASTS

These plaster relief capitals depict the faces of famous Pennsylvanians. They are gilded in 24-karat gold leaf.

Vincenzo Alfano

NORTH HYPHEN CORRIDOR

Murals progress from the first floor of the rotunda proceeding north, from right to left.

Vincent Maragliotti—1970–73, 5' x 15'.

Amish Farming, 1730–40.

Lumber, ca. 1880.

Coal, ca. 1880.

Drakes First Oil Well, Titusville 1859.

Blacksmith Shop 1880.

Country Store 1867–70.

Philadelphia Commerce early 1800.

Canal Boat 1835.

Ship Building, Philadelphia 1760-70.

Railroads and Telegraph 1838.

Digging Tunnel–Turnpike 1840.

Turnpike Boom–Conestoga Wagon 1828.

John Fitch's Steamboat 1787.

Steel.

NORTH HYPHEN CAPITAL CASTS

These plaster relief capitals depict the faces of famous Pennsylvanians. They are gilded in 24-karat gold leaf.

Vincenzo Alfano

APPENDICES

APPENDIX IV

Dedication Day Speeches

Theodore Roosevelt's Speech

It is a very real pleasure for me to attend these ceremonies at the capital of your great State. In every great crisis of our government the attitude of Pennsylvania has been of crucial importance, as the affectionate nickname of "Keystone State" signifies. Pennsylvania has always looked warily before she leaped, and it was well that she should do so. But having finally made up her mind, in each great crisis of our national history, her weight has been cast unhesitatingly upon the right side, and has been found irresistible. This was true alike at the time of the Declaration of Independence, at the time of the adoption of the Constitution, and during the terrible years when the issue was the preservation of the Union.

Pennsylvania A Great State

Pennsylvania's soil is historic. It was within Pennsylvania's borders that the contest opened which was to decide whether the valiant soldiers of France would be able to bar this continent against the domination of the people of the English-speaking colonies. It was on Pennsylvania's soil that the Declaration of Independence was signed and the Constitutional Convention held. It was in Pennsylvania that Washington wintered at Valley Forge, and by keeping his army together during that winter definitely turned the scales in our favor in the contest for independence. It was again on Pennsylvania's soil at Gettysburg that the tide turned in the Civil War.

In the composition of her people, moreover, Pennsylvania has epitomized the composition of our Union; for here many Old World races have mingled their blood to make that new type, the American. Finally, in all branches of the public service, in peace and in war, the native or adopted citizens of Pennsylvania have attained the highest eminence.

I do not, however, come here today to speak only of the past, and still less to appeal merely to state pride. We can show that the past is with us, a living force, only by the way in which we handle ourselves in the present, and each of us can best show his devotion to his own state by making evident his paramount devotion to that Union which includes all the States.

The study of the great deeds of the past is of chief avail in so far as it incites us to grapple resolutely and effectively with the problems of the present. We are not now menaced by foreign war. Our Union is firmly established. But each generation has its special and serious difficulties; and we of this generation have to struggle with evils springing from the very material success of which we are so proud, from the very growth and prosperity of which, with justice, we boast. The extraordinary industrial changes of the last half century have produced a totally new set of conditions under which new evils flourish; and for these new evils new remedies must be devised.

Some of these evils can be grappled with by private effort only; for we never can afford to forget that in the last analysis the chief factor in personal success, and indeed in national greatness, must be the sturdy, self reliant character of the individual citizen. But many of these evils are of such a nature that no private effort can avail against them. Those evils, therefore, must be grappled with by governmental action. In some cases this governmental action must be exercised by the several states individually.

Must Increase Federal Power

In yet others it has become increasingly evident that no efficient state action is possible, and that we need through executive action, through legislation, and through judicial interpretation and construction of law, to increase the power of the federal government.

If we fail thus to increase it, we show our impotence and leave ourselves at the mercy of those ingenious legal advisers of the holders of vast corporate wealth, who, in the performance of what they regard as their duty, and to serve the ends of their clients, invoke the law at one time for the confounding of their rivals and at another time strive for the nullification of the law, in order that they themselves may be left free to work their unbridled will on these same rivals, or on those who labor for them, or on the general public.

In the exercise of their profession and in the service of their clients, these astute lawyers strive to prevent the passage of efficient laws and strive to secure judicial determination of those that pass which shall emasculate them. They do not invoke the constitution in order to compel the due observance of law alike by rich and poor, by great and small; on the contrary, they are ceaselessly on the watch to cry out that the constitution is violated whenever any effort is made to invoke the aid of the national government, whether for the efficient regulation of railroads, for the efficient supervision of great corporations, or for efficiently securing obedience to such a law as the national eight hour law and similar so-called "labor statutes."

The doctrine they preach would make the Constitution merely the shield of incompetence and the excuse for governmental paralysis; they treat it as a justification for refusing to attempt the remedy of evil, instead of as the source of vital power necessary for the existence of a mighty and ever-growing nation.

Praises Reform in Pennsylvania

Strong nationalist though I am, and firm though my belief is that there must be a wide extension of the power of the national government to deal with questions of this kind, I freely admit that as regards many matters of first-rate importance we must rely purely upon the states for the betterment of present conditions. The several states must do their duty or our citizenship can never be put on a proper plane. Therefore, I most heartily congratulate the people of the State of Pennsylvania on what its legislature, upon what its government, has accomplished during this present year. It is a remarkable record of achievement.

Through your legislature you have abolished passes; you have placed the offices of the Secretary of the Commonwealth and the Insurance Commission upon an honorable and honest basis of salary only by abolishing the fee system; you have passed a law compelling the officers and employees of great cities to attend to the duties for which they are paid by all the taxpayers, and to refrain from using the power conferred by their offices to influence political campaigns; you have prohibited the solicitation or receiving of political assessments by city employees; you have by law protected the State Treasury from depredation and conserved the public moneys for use only in the public interest; you have by a law for the protection of the elective franchise made tampering with the ballot boxes and the casting of illegal votes so difficult as in all probability to be unprofitable; you have provided a primary election law which guarantees to the voters free expression in the selection of candidates for office; you have by law regulated and improved the civil service systems of your greatest cities; and finally, you have passed a law containing a provision which I most earnestly hope will in substance be embodied likewise in a law by the Congress at the coming session—a provision prohibiting the officers of any corporation from making a contribution of the money of that corporation to any candidate or any political committee for the payment of any election expenses whatever.

More Legislation Needed

It is surely not too much to say that this body of substantive legislation marks an epoch in the history of the practical betterment of political conditions, not merely for your state, but for all our states. I do not recall any other state legislature which, in a similar length of time, has to its credit such a body of admirable legislation. Let me, however, most earnestly urge that your legislature continue this record of public service by enacting one or two additional laws. One subject which every good citizen should have at heart above almost all others is the matter of child labor. Everywhere the great growth of modern industrialism has been accompanied by abuses in connection with the employment of labor which have necessitated a complete change in the attitude of the state toward labor.

This is above all true in connection with the employment of child labor. In Pennsylvania you have made a beginning, but only a beginning, in proper legislation and administration on this subject; the law must if necessary be strengthened, and it must be rigorously enforced. The national government can do but little in the matter of child labor, though I earnestly hope that that little will be permitted to be done by Congress. The great bulk of the work, however, must be left to the state legislature; and if our state legislatures would act as drastically and yet as wisely on this subject of child labor as Pennsylvania has acted within the present year as regards the subjects I have enumerated above, the gain would be literally incalculable and one of the most vital needs of modern American life would at least be adequately met.

So much for the state. Now for the nation; and here I can not do better than base my theory of governmental action upon the words of one of Pennsylvania's greatest sons, Justice James Wilson. Wilson's career has been singularly overlooked for many years, but I believe that more and more it is now being adequately appreciated; and I congratulate your state upon the fact that Wilson's body is to be taken away from where it now rests and brought back to lie, as it should, in Pennsylvania soil. He was a signer of the Declaration of Independence.

He was one of the men who saw that the Revolution, in which he had served as a soldier, would be utterly fruitless unless it was followed by a close and permanent union of the states; and in the Constitutional Convention, and in securing the adoption of the Constitution and expounding what it meant, he rendered services even greater than he rendered as a member of the Continental Congress, which declared our independence; for it was the success of the makers and preservers of the Union, which justified our independence.

He believed in the people with the faith of Abraham Lincoln; and coupled with his faith in the people he had what most of the men who in his generation believed in the people did not have; that is, the courage to recognize the fact that faith in the people amounted to nothing unless the representatives of the people assembled together in the national government were given full and complete power to work on behalf of the people. He developed, even before Marshall, the doctrine (absolutely essential not merely to the efficiency but to the existence of this nation) that an inherent power rested in the nation, outside of the enumerated powers conferred upon it by the Constitution, in all cases where the object involved was beyond the power of the several states and was a power ordinarily exercised by sovereign nations.

State and Nation Must Co-operate

In a remarkable letter in which he advocated setting forth in early and clear fashion the powers of the national government, he laid down the proposition that it should be made clear that there were neither vacancies nor interference between the limits of state and national jurisdiction, and that both jurisdictions together composed only one uniform and comprehensive system of government and laws; that is, whenever the states can not act, because the need to be met is not one of merely a single locality, then the national government, representing all the people, should have complete power to act. It was in the spirit of Wilson that Washington and Washington's lieutenant Hamilton acted and it was in the same spirit that Marshall construed the law.

It is only by acting in this spirit that the national judges, legislators and executives can give a satisfactory solution of the great questions of the present day—the question of providing on behalf of the sovereign people the means which will enable the people in effective form to assert their sovereignty over the immense corporation of the day. Certain judicial decisions have done just what Wilson feared; they have, as a matter of fact, left vacancies, left blanks between the limits of possible state jurisdiction and the limits of actual national jurisdiction over the control of the great business corporations. It is the narrow construction of the powers of the national government which in our democracy has provided the chief means of limiting the national power to cut out abuses and which is now the chief bulwark of those great moneyed interests which oppose and dread any attempt to place them under efficient governmental control.

Many legislative actions and many judicial decisions which I am confident time will show to have been erroneous and a damage to the country would have been avoided if our legislators and jurists had approached the matter of enacting and construing the laws of the land in the spirit of your great Pennsylvanian, Justice Wilson—in the spirit of Marshall and of Washington. Such decisions put us at a great disadvantage in the battle for industrial order as against the present industrial chaos. If we interpret the Constitution in narrow instead of broad fashion, if we forsake the principles of Washington, Marshall, Wilson and Hamilton, we as a people will render ourselves impotent to deal with any abuses which may be committed by the men who have accumulated the enormous fortunes of today, and who use these fortunes in still vaster corporate form in business.

The legislative or judicial actions and decisions of which I complain, be it remembered, do not really leave to the states power to deal with corporate wealth in business. Actual experience has shown that the states are wholly powerless to deal with this subject, and any action or decision that deprives the nation of the power to deal with it, simply results in leaving the corporations absolutely free to work without any effective supervision whatever; and such a course is fraught with untold danger to the future of our whole system of government, and, indeed, to our whole civilization.

Must Control Big Fortunes

All honest men must abhor and reprobate any effort to excite hostility to men of wealth as such. We should do all we can to encourage thrift and business energy, to put a premium upon the conduct of the man who honestly earns his livelihood and more than his livelihood, and who honestly uses the money he has earned.

But it is our clear duty to see, in the interest of the people, that there is adequate supervision and control over the business used of the swollen fortunes of today, and also wisely to determine the conditions upon which these fortunes are to be transmitted and the percentage that they shall pay to the government whose protecting arm alone enables them to exist. Only the nation can do this work. To relegate it to the states is a farce, and is simply another way of saying that it shall not be done at all.

For More Power at Washington

Under a wise and farseeing interpretation of the interstate commerce clause of the Constitution, I maintain that the national government should have complete power to deal with all of this wealth which in any way goes into the commerce between the states—and practically all of it that is employed in the great corporations does thus go in. The national legislators should most scrupulously avoid any demagogic legislation about the business use of this wealth, and should realize that it would be better to have no legislation at all than legislation couched either in a vindictive spirit of hatred towards men of wealth or else drawn with the recklessness of impracticable visionaries. But, on the other hand, it shall and must ultimately be understood that the United States government, on behalf of the people of the United States, has and is to exercise the power of supervision and control over the business use of this wealth—in the first place, over all the work of the common carriers of the nation, and in the next place over the work of all the great corporations which directly or indirectly do any interstate business whatever—and this includes almost all of the great corporations.

Federal Government's Strides

During the last few years the national government has taken very long strides in the direction of exercising and securing this adequate control over the great corporations, and it was under the leadership of one of the most honored public men in our country, one of Pennsylvania's most eminent sons-the present Senator, and then Attorney General, Knox—that the new departure was begun. Events have moved fast during the last five years; and it is curious to look back at the extreme bitterness which not merely the spokesmen and representatives of organized wealth, but many most excellent conservative people then felt as to the action of Mr. Knox and of the administration.

Financiers Predicted Panic

Many of the greatest financiers of this country were certain that Mr. Knox's Northern Securities suit, if won, would plunge us into the worst panic we had ever seen. They denounced as incitement to anarchy, as an apology for socialism, the advocacy of policies that either have now become law or are in fair way of becoming law; and yet these same policies, so far from representing either anarchy or socialism, were in reality the antidotes to anarchy, the antidotes to socialism.

To exercise a constantly increasing and constantly more efficient supervision and control over the great common carriers of the country prevents all necessity for seriously considering such a project as the government ownership of railroads—a policy which would be evil in its results from every standpoint.

A similar extension of the national power to oversee and secure correct behavior is the management of all great corporations engaged in interstate business will in similar fashion render far more stable the present system by doing away with those grave abuses which are not only evil in themselves but are also evil because they furnish an excuse for agitators to inflame well-meaning people against all forms of property, and to commit the country to schemes of wild, would-be remedy which would work infinitely more harm than the disease itself.

The government ought not to conduct the business of the country; but it ought to regulate it so that it shall be conducted in the interest of the public. Perhaps the best justification of the course which in the national government we have been pursuing in the past few years, and which we intend steadily and progressively to pursue in the future, is that it is condemned with almost equal rancor alike by the reactionaries—the Bourbons on one side, and by the wild apostles of unrest on the other. The reactionary is bitterly angry because we have deprived him of that portion of his power which he misuses to the public hurt; the agitator is angered for various reasons, including among others the fact that by remedying the abuses we have deprived him of the fulcrum of real grievance, which alone renders the lever of irrational agitation formidable.

Have Accomplished Much

We have actually accomplished much. But we have not accomplished all, nor anything like all, that we feel must be accomplished. We shall not wait; we shall steadily follow the path we have marked out, executing the laws we have succeeded in putting upon the statute books with absolute impartiality as between man and man, and unresting in our endeavor to strengthen and supplement these by further laws which shall enable us in more efficiency and more summary fashion to achieve the ends we have in view.
Vital Questions in Congress

During the last few years, Congress has had to deal with such vitally important questions as providing for the building of the Panama Canal, inaugurating the vast system of national irrigation in the states of the Great Plains and the Rocky Mountains, providing for a Pacific cable, and so forth. Yet in addition to these tasks, some of which are of stupendous importance, Congress has taken giant strides along the path of government regulation and control of corporations; the interstate commerce law has been made effective in radical and far-reaching fashion, rebates have been stopped, a pure food law has been passed, proper supervision of the meat packing business provided, and the Bureau of Corporations established—a bureau which has already done great good, and which can and should be given a constantly increasing functional power.

The work of legislation has been no more important than the work done by the Department of Justice in executing the laws, not only against corporations and individuals who have broken the anti-trust or interstate commerce law, but against those who have engaged in land frauds. Scores of suits, civil and criminal, have been successfully undertaken against offenders of all kinds—many of them against the most formidable and wealthy combinations in the land; in some the combinations have been dissolved, in some heavy fines have been imposed, in several cases the chief offenders have been imprisoned.

Americans Should Look Ahead

It behooves us Americans to look ahead and plan out the right kind of civilization, as that which we intend to develop, from these wonderful new conditions of vast industrial growth. It must not be, it shall not be, the civilization of a mere plutocracy, a banking house, Wall Street syndicate civilization; nor yet can there be submission to class hatred, to rancor, brutality, and mob violence, for that would mean the end of all civilization. Increased powers are susceptible of abuse as well as use; never before have the opportunities for selfishness been so great, nor the results of selfishness so appalling; for in communities where everything is organized on a merely selfish commercial basis, such selfishness, if unchecked, may transform the great forces of the new epoch into powers of destruction hitherto unequaled.

We need to check the forces of greed, to insure just treatment alike of capital and of labor, and of the general public, to prevent any man, rich or poor, from doing or receiving wrong, whether, this wrong be one of cunning or of violence.

Much can be done by wise legislation and by resolute enforcement of the law. But still more must be done by steady training of the individual citizen. In conscience and character, until he grows to abhor corruptions and greed and tyranny and brutality and to prize justice and fair dealing.

The men who are to do the work of the new epoch must be trained so as to have a sturdy self-respect, a power of study insistence on their own right, and with it a proud and generous recognition of their duties, a sense of honorable obligation to their fellows, which will bind them, as by bands of steel, to refrain in their daily work at home or in their business from doing aught to any man which cannot be blazoned under the noonday sun.

Governor Stone's Address

The Capitol building was constructed by authority of the Act of Assembly approved July 18, 1901, which appropriated four million dollars for the removal of the old buildings and the construction of the new. This act vested the authority of construction in a commission of five persons who were to have the building completed by the first day of January, 1906. Honorable William H. Graham, of Allegheny, Pennsylvania; Honorable W. P. Snyder, of Chester County, Pennsylvania; Honorable N. C. Schaeffer, of Lancaster, Pennsylvania; Mr. Edward Bailey, of Harrisburg, Pennsylvania and myself constituted this commission. Our first meeting was held on August 20, 1901, at which time I became the president of the commission, Mr. Edward Bailey, treasurer; Mr. E.C. Gerwig, of Allegheny, Pennsylvania, secretary; Honorable Robert K. Young, of Wellsboro, Pennsylvania, solicitor, and T. Larry Eyre, of West Chester, Pennsylvania, superintendent.

Advertisements were inserted in the leading newspapers of the state, asking architects to submit plans and specifications, the commission agreeing to give to the architect whose plans and specifications should be adopted, five per cent commission on the cost of the building for supervision of its construction; and the architects submitting the five next best plans in the opinion of the commission were to receive $1,000 each.

Professor W. R. Ware, a professor of architecture in the Columbia University, and a man whose reputation as a judge of architecture is not excelled in this country, was employed to pass upon the plans and specifications submitted by the architects in response to our advertisements. All knowledge of the name of the architects presenting plans and specifications was withheld from Professor Ware and the commission. These plans and specifications were known from the time they came into the possession of the commission by number.

After thorough and complete examination of the ten sets of plans and specifications submitted, Professor Ware reported to the commission that they could safely select any one of four different sets of plans. The commission then, without knowing whose plans they were, decided upon a certain set of plans which they adopted, and it was after this decision had been made that they became aware that the chosen plans had been submitted by Joseph M. Huston, of Philadelphia.

We then employed Bernard H. Green, superintendent of the Congressional Library at Washington, D.C., a man who had supervised the construction of many buildings for the government, as an assistant and adviser to the commission. Mr. Huston with Mr. Green's assistance, then worked out the specifications in detail, and advertisements were inserted in the leading newspapers of the country, calling for bids by contractors, to furnish all the material and construct the building in accordance with the plans and specifications. Six bids were submitted. The lowest bidder was George F. Payne and Company, of Philadelphia, and they being otherwise satisfactory and furnishing the necessary bond required by law, were awarded the contract.

A little more than a year was consumed in the preparations of specifications in making different examinations and tests of granite, and by the bidders in examination of plans and specifications, before the contract was executed.

The history of the construction of this building is generally known to the people of the State, as the newspapers have made frequent reference to it in their columns.

The commission met once a month, at which meetings the contractor, the architect and Mr. Green made reports as to the condition and progress of the work. We have had our allotted number of strikes, several accidents and a number of delays, caused by the weather, the failure of sub-contractors to deliver materials and from other causes. The building was substantially completed some weeks before the time specified in the law.

The law under which the building was constructed contemplated a completed building, ready for occupancy. We found that in addition to the money necessary for that purpose, we could spare one hundred and ninety thousand dollars for decorations. Contracts were therefore made with Miss Violet Oakley, George Gray Barnard, and Edwin A. Abbey for mural paintings and sculpture.

The amount paid and to be paid to the contractors, George F. Payne's company is $3,522,638; the amount to Miss Violet Oakley is $20,000; the amount to George Gray Barnard, $100,000; the amount to Edwin A. Abbey is $70,000; the architect's commission amounts to $185,631; the amount paid to competing architects is $5,000. The expenses of the commission, including salaries to employees, amounts to $50,839, leaving in the hands of the commission $45,890. A further expenditure of money will be necessary in placing in the building the sculpture and paintings contracted for and not yet completed, and probably other small items. What this amount will be cannot be determined at present, but there will be from thirty to forty thousand dollars unexpended, which will be turned back to the state by the commission.

Such in brief is the history of the construction of this building. The building speaks for itself and it is very gratifying to the commission to find that it is generally accepted and approved by the people of the State. We claim no special credit for the work. We have simply done the best we could with the money appropriated, and the acceptance and approval of our work, by the people, is our sufficient reward.

The commission has not stinted the work in time nor attention in any particular. The members have been prompt and regular in their attendance at all meetings. They have manifested great interest and zeal and I do not believe they could have given any more attention to the building or taken any greater interest in it, if it had been their own.

The commission has been harmonious from its first meeting. There have never been any serious disputes or jealousy or bitterness or strife. Upon frequent occasions there have been differences of opinion as to action, but when differences were voted upon, the minority has readily acquiesced and accepted the situation, and done just as much to carry out the wishes of the majority as if they had been their own.

The selection of the architect and contractors was exceedingly fortunate. They have been imbued with the same zeal and the same interest and have done their best. And the same may be said of the officers of the commission; and I doubt very much whether Mr. Green took any greater interest in the construction of the Congressional library, or any government building, than he has in this.

This occasion does not justify me in making any extended remarks. Having briefly made a report of our work, my mission is ended. And now, in behalf of the commission, I tender to you sir, as Governor of the State, the building, and hope that it will not only meet with your approval, but the approval of all the people of our State.

Governor Samuel W. Pennypacker's Speech*

*There are variations between the speech that the newspapers printed and the speech that the Governor delivered to the crowd on dedication day. The following text is a transcription of the speech that Pennypacker held in his hands on dedication day, courtesy of Pennypacker Mill's, his home in Montgomery County, Pennsylvania. The text actually contains watermarks from the rain that was falling as the Governor spoke.

The Capitol is much more than the building in which the Legislature holds its sessions, the courts sit in judgment, and the executive exercises his authority. It is a concrete manifestation of the importance and power of the State, and an expression of its artistic development. Intelligent observers who look upon the structure and the ornamentation, are enabled to divine at what stage in the advance of civilization the people have arrived, and to determine with sufficient accuracy what have been their achievements in the past, and what are their aspirations for the future.

The Commission charged with the duty of erecting this Capitol, and those who have had responsibility in connection with it, have felt that in architecture and appointments the outcome ought to be worthy of the Commonwealth. They have not forgotten the essential and unique relation which Pennsylvania has borne to the development of our national life, that in her first capitol the government of the United States had its birth, that during the ten years of the early and uncertain existence of that government she gave it a home, that since its origin what has ever been accepted as the "Pennsylvania idea" has been the dominant political principle of its administration, and that its present unparalleled material prosperity rests finally, in large measure, upon the outcome of her furnaces and mines. Nor have they forgotten that the thought of William Penn, enunciated over two centuries ago, and rewritten around the dome of this Capitol, has become the fundamental principle of our national constitution, acknowledged now by all men as axiomatic truth.

There is a sermon which the many Americans who hie hither in the future years to study chaste art expressed in form, as today they go to the Parthenon and St. Peter's, to the cathedrals of Antwerp and Cologne, will be enabled to read in these stones of polished marble and hewn granite. When Moses set out to build "an altar under the hill and twelve pillars", he beforehand "wrote all the words of the Lord". Let us take comfort in the belief that in like manner this massive and beautiful building, which we have in our later time erected, will be for an example and inspiration to all of the people, encouraging them in pure thoughts and inciting them to worthy deeds. Let us bear in mind the injunction of the far seeing founder of the Province, which made it indeed, as he hoped, the seed of a nation, "that we may do the thing that is truly wise and just".

On behalf of the Commonwealth, as its chief executive, I accept this Capitol, and now with pride, with faith, and with hope, I dedicate it to the public use and to the purposes for which it was designed and constructed.

(On the reverse side, handwritten by Governor Pennypacker it states:)
"Paper from which I read my address at the dedication of the Capitol Oct. 4. 1906"

Mayor Edward Z. Gross' Proclamation

Proclamation—To the People of the City of Harrisburg

Whereas, The dedication of the new Capitol of the Commonwealth of Pennsylvania will take place in this city on Thursday, the fourth day of October, A.D. 1906, the President of the United States, Theodore Roosevelt, being present and assisting in that most important ceremony, now, therefore, I, Edward Z. Gross, Mayor of the City of Harrisburg, do enjoin upon the citizens of Harrisburg and the strangers within our gates to assist in promoting the success of the occasion by observing the following directions:

First—Closing of all places of business after 10:30 A.M., at least until after the departure of the President at 3 P.M.

Second—Wearing the official commemorative medal on the left breast and liberally displaying the National flag, the President's flag and the flag of the State of Pennsylvania.

Third—Complying readily and cheerfully with the instructions of those in authority in order that all the events of the day may proceed promptly.

Given under my hand and the seal of the City of Harrisburg, in the County of Dauphin, and State of Pennsylvania, this first day of October, in the year of our Lord, one thousand nine hundred and six.

APPENDIX V

LIST OF THE MEMBERS OF SPECIAL COMMISSIONS

Capitol Building Commission
Governor William A. Stone, Pittsburgh—Former Governor
Edward Bailey, Harrisburg—Banker
William H. Graham, Pittsburgh—Congressman
Nathan C. Shaeffer, Lancaster—
    Superintendent of Public Instruction
William P. Snyder, Chester County—Auditor General
Thomas Lawrence Eyre, West Chester—Superintendent of
    Public Grounds and Buildings
Edgar C. Gerwig—Personal Secretary to Governor Stone
Robert K. Young, Wellsboro—Attorney

Officers of the Building Commission
President—William A. Stone
Secretary—Edgar C. Gerwig
Treasurer—Edward Bailey
Attorney—Robert K. Young
Superintendent—Thomas L. Eyre

Capitol Dedication Commission
Governor Samuel W. Pennypacker—President
President Pro Tempore of the Senate, William C. Sproul
Speaker of the House, Henry R. Walton
Senator John E. Fox—Dauphin County
Auditor General William P. Snyder
State Treasurer William L. Mathues
    (succeeded by Treasurer William H. Berry)
Thomas Lynch and Thomas M. Jones—Secretaries

CAPITOL DEDICATION COMMISSION

The Capitol Dedication Commission, whose labors so successfully carried the dedication to a fine finish, was created by an act of the Legislature of 1905, which provided that it should be composed of the members of the Commission of Public Grounds and Buildings, and three members of the General Assembly, to be appointed by the Governor.

The Governor appointed the presiding officers of the Senate and House, President Pro Tempore William C. Sproul of Delaware County, and Speaker Henry R. Walton, of Philadelphia. In addition, he recognized the work that Senator John E. Fox, of Harrisburg, had done in securing the legislation for the reception of the new Capitol and appointed Senator Fox as the other legislative member. These three appointees, along with Governor Pennypacker, Auditor General Snyder and State Treasurer Mathues made up the commission. The commission met in February 1906 and was organized by the election of Governor Pennypacker as president and Thomas J. Lynch and Thomas M. Jones as secretaries.

The commissioners and the secretaries, beginning in February 1906, carefully planned details of the dedication. State Treasurer Berry succeeded Mr. Mathues on the commission in May. Meetings were held at the Governor's Office in the Capitol and at the office of Speaker Walton, in Philadelphia, and slowly but surely, the plans were perfected until everything was done that could be done to make the dedication a success.

Appendix VI

Professionals, Contractors and Sub-Contractors

We are grateful for the many individuals that have played a role in the restoration and preservation of the Pennsylvania Capitol during the past two decades. A special thank you is extended to all the dedicated people who worked on hundreds of projects and to those who continue to provide their expertise and diligent attention in the ongoing preservation and maintenance of the building.

This list is not all-inclusive as there were many unsung heroes who labored on numerous projects under other companies and subcontractors that played a valuable role in the preservation efforts of the Capitol. In addition, the Department of General Services' Bureau of Facility and Maintenance Management who provide the daily security protection, routine utility, and custodial services are to be commended in their vigilant service to the Capitol building and grounds. Our highest praise and appreciation are extended to you all.

A.G. Mauro Co.
Advanced Communications
Advanced Composite Products, Inc.
Albert Michaels Conservation, Inc.
Alexander Building Construction, LLC
Allweins Carpet
Analytical Laboratory Services, Inc.
Armstrong World Industries
Ball & Ball
Benetec Associates
Berrett Conservation Studio
Biltmore Campbell Smith Restoration
Bink Architectural Partnership
Bloomsburg Carpet Company
Bob Smith Contractors
Bob's Refinishing
Brian O'Connell Architects
Brinjac, Kambic, Consulting Engineers
C & D Waterproofing
C & J Carpet Co.
C. A. Lindman
C. E. White Enterprises
Caretti Inc.
Carlisle Syntec Incorporated
Cathedral Stone
Celli Flynn Brennan & Turkall Architects
CH Briggs
Conestoga Tile
Conewago Precast Building Systems
Conservation Tech. Assoc.
Conservation Solutions, Inc.
Crenshaw Lighting
Crescent Brass
Crescent Iron Works

Cumberland Woodcraft Co.
Cumberland Stained Glass
Cummings Stained Glass Studio
Cumulus Communications
Daedalus, Inc.
Dan Peter Kopple & Associates
Dauphin Electric
Delmhierst Instrument Co.
Desso Carpet
Dieter Goldkuhle Stained Glass
Diversified Lighting Assoc.
Duraclean Solutions
E. C. Snyder, Inc.
Environmental Interiors
Eshenauers Fuels, Inc.
Essis & Sons Carpet
E-V Air Tight Calking
Ewing's Wood Floors
Farfield Company
F. E. Ciccone & Company
Felber Ornamental Plastering Corp.
Fire Protection Industries, Inc.
Forbo Flooring, Inc.
G. R. Sponaugles
Gancom
Ganflec Architects & Engineers
Gannett Fleming, Inc.
Gatter & Diehl
Glen-Geary Corporation
Gold Leaf Studios, Inc.
H. F. Lenz
H2L2 Architects
Harrisburg Decorating Company
Harvey Stern & Co.

Professionals, Contractors and Sub-Contractors *Continued*

Haverstick-Borthwick Co.
Hayles & Howe
Heritage Studies
Herre Bros.
Hershocks Inc.
Hickock Manufacturing Co.
Hillier Group
Houck & Co., Inc.
Hunt Commercial Photography
IMR
Integra Graphics
Integrated Conservation Resources
Interface Flooring Systems
International Fine Art Conservation Studios, Ltd
Inter-State Tile & Mantel Co., Inc.
J. C. Budding Co.
Jewelry & Clock Works
John Blatteau Associates
John Canning Company
John G. Waite Associates
John Milner Architects
John Rudy Photography
Keast & Hood Company
Keystone Preservation Group
Klemm Reflector Co.
Koroseal Interior Products Group
Kreilick Conservation
L. R. Costanzo
Lanier
Lederach Assoc.
Lesher Inc. Marble and Granite
Librandis Machine Shop, Inc.
Lobar Inc.
Ludowici Tile Co.
Lutron Electronics
Marianna Thomas Architects
Mascaro Construction Co.
Masland Carpets Inc.
Masonry Preservation Group
Melillo Consulting
Moravian Pottery & Tile Works
Moreland Studios, Inc.
W. Brown Morton, III., Architectural Preservationist
National Park Service
New England Pewter
New Holland Concrete
New Roots, Inc.
Nitterhouse Concrete Products
Noble Preservation Services

Norcam
Norton Art Conservation
Novingers Inc.
NRB (USA), Inc.
Office Center
Old Mill Cabinet Shop
Olin Conservation Inc.
Oswald Sewer Service
Otis Elevator Co.
PA Environmental Remedial Contracting Services
PA Public Television Network
Page Conservation, Inc.
Patent Construction Systems
Paul W. Zimmerman Foundries
Perfido Weiskopf Architects
Picture Perfect Productions
Pipe Data View Services
Pocobene Conservation Studio
Post & Schell, P. C.
Powers & Co.
PPL Electric Utilities
Preservation Services, Inc.
Prosoco Inc.
R. Alden Marshall & Sheila A. Grimes
Rathgeber/Goss Associates
Bernie Rabin, Painting Conservator
Remco, Inc.
Reynolds Construction Management
Richart Graphics
Rogele Company
Roman Mosaic Tile Co.
Safeway Steel Scaffolds
Saxe Woodwork
Scalamandre
Secco
Shea & Latone Inc.
Constance Silver, Painting Conservator
Simplex/Grinnell
Slough Flooring
Spencer Industries Inc.
Stained Glass Conservation Studio
Stambaugh Metal, Inc.
Structural Maintenance Systems, Inc.
Surtech Industries Inc.
Swishers Cleaning
Terminix Company
The Brass Wheel Antiques
The Gilders Studio
The Restoration Clinic
Theatre Solutions, Inc.

Tom Venturella Studio
Tremco
Tuckey Restoration, Inc.
Ullmann Glass
Unified Industries Inc.
Universal Building Supply
Vitetta
W. G. Tomko
Wenrich Painting, Inc.
Wert Bookbinding, Inc.
Wohlsen Construction Company
Woodcock Electric Service, Inc.
Woodlore Builders Studio
Wyatt Inc.
Yale Electric

BIBLIOGRAPHY

PUBLISHED BOOKS

Edwin Austin Abbey, 1852-1911: An Exhibition Organized by the Yale University Art Gallery. New Haven: Yale University Art Gallery, 1974.

Aitken, Robert I., et. al. *Arnold W. Brunner and His Work.* New York: Press of the American Institute of Architects, 1926.

Alumni Record, Class of 1892, Triennial Record. Princeton UP.

Andrews, Wayne. *Architecture in Chicago and Mid-America: A Photographic History.* New York: Harper and Row, 1973.

Architectural and Art Contracts: The Capitol, Commonwealth of Pennsylvania. [privately printed by friends of Joseph M. Huston, ca 1906–7].

Art Work of Harrisburg. Chicago: W. H. Parish Publishing Co., 1892.

Art Work of Harrisburg. Chicago: The Gravure Illustration Co., 1914.

Art Work of Harrisburg, Lancaster and York. Chicago: The Gravure Illustration Co., 1901.

Barton, Michael. *Life by the Moving Road: An Illustrated History of Greater Harrisburg.* Woodland Hills, CA: Windsor Publications, 1983.

Beers, Paul B. *Pennsylvania Politics Yesterday and Today: The Tolerable Accomodation.* University Park: Pennsylvania State University, 1980.

———. *Profiles of the Susquehanna Valley: Past and Present Vignettes of its People, Times and Towns.* Harrisburg: Stackpole Books, 1973.

Boyd, Andrew and W. Harry Boyd [comp]. *"The Patriot" Harrisburg City Directory…1872-73.* Philadelphia: 1872.

Breeskin, Adelaide Dohme. *Mary Cassatt: A Catalogue Raisonné of the Oils, Pastels, Watercolors, and Drawings.* Washington, DC: Smithsonian Institution Press, 1970.

Caffin, Charles Henry. *Handbook of the New Capitol of Pennsylvania.* Harrisburg; Mount Pleasant Press, 1906. Reprinted by the Capitol Preservation Committee, 2002.

Chamberlain, General Joshua L. [Editor-in-Chief] *Universities and Their Sons.* 5 Volumes. Boston: R. Herndon Co., 1898–1900.

Class of 1892, Fortieth Record. Princeton UP, 1932.

Cochran, Thomas B., ed. *Smull's Legislative Hand Book and Manual of the State of Pennsylvania…* Harrisburg: Clarence M. Busch, State Printer, 1897.

Commemorative Biographical Encyclopedia of Dauphin County. Chambersburg, PA: J. M. Runk and Co., 1896.

Craven, Wayne. *Sculpture in America.* New York: Thomas Y. Crowell Co., 1968.

Dickson, Harold E. *George Grey Barnard: Centenary Exhibition, 1863–1963.* University Park, PA: Pennsylvania State University Library and Harrisburg: Pennsylvania Historical and Museum Commission, 1964.

Dictionary of American Sculptors. Poughkeepsie, NY: Apollo, 1984.

Donehoo, George Patterson. *A Brief Description of the Capitol at Harrisburg, Pennsylvania with an Outline of the State Government.* Harrisburg: 1923.

———. *Harrisburg and Dauphin County: A Sketch of the History of the Past Twenty-Five Years, 1900-1925.* 2 vols. Dayton, OH: National Historical Association, 1925.

———. *Harrisburg, The City Beautiful, Romantic and Historic.* Harrisburg: E.J. Stackpole, 1927.

Drexler, Arthur, ed. *The Architecture of École des Beaux Arts.* New York: Museum of Modern Art, 1977.

Edgell, G.H. *The American Architecture of Today.* New York and London: Charles Scribner's Sons, 1928.

Egle, William Henry. *History of the Counties of Dauphin and Lebanon, in the Commonwealth of Pennsylvania…* Philadelphia: Everts and Peck, 1883; reprinted 1977.

Ellis, Franklin. *History of Lancaster County, Pennsylvania…* Philadelphia: Everts and Peck, 1883.

Federal Writers Project. *Illinois: A Descriptive and Historical Guide.* Revised edition. Chicago: A. C. McClure and Co., 1947.

Fielding, Mantle. *Dictionary of American Painters, Sculptors, and Engravers.* New York: James F. Carr, 1965.

Fifteenth Year Book, 1892. New York: The Grafton Press, 1907.

Gemmill, Helen Hartman. *E. L., The Bread Box Papers, A Biography*. Philadelphia: Dorrance and Co., 1983.

Hitchcock, Henry Russell and William Seale. *Temples of Democracy: The State Capitols of the U.S.A.*. New York and London: Harcourt, Brace Jovanovich, 1976.

Historical and Illustrated Sketch of Lancaster. Lancaster, PA: E. J. Phelps, 1987.

Howard. E., Clock Co. *E. Howard: The Man and the Company*. Boston: F. Earl Hackett, 1962.

Hughes, Tom. *Networks of Power*. Baltimore: Johns Hopkins UP, 1984.

Industrial and Commercial Resources of the City of Harrisburg. Harrisburg: Board of Trade, 1887.

Innes, Lowell. *Pittsburgh Glass, 1791-1891: A History and Guide for Collectors*. Boston: Houghton Mifflin, 1976.

Jordy, William H. *American Buildings and Their Architects: Progressive and Academic Ideals At the Turn of the Twentieth Century*. Garden City, NY and New York: Anchor Press/Doubleday, 1976.

Kelker, Luther R. *History of Dauphin County, Pennsylvania*. 2 vols. Chicago: Luther Publishing Co., 1907.

Kilburn, Francis R. *A Brief History of the City of Lancaster...* Lancaster, PA: Pearsol and Geist, 1870.

Klein, H. M. J. ed. *Lancaster County, Pennsylvania: A History*. 4 vols. New York: Lewis Historical Publishing Co., 1924.

———. *A Century of Education at Mercersburg, 1836–1936*. Mercersburg, PA: 1936.

Klein, Philip S. and Ari Hoogenboom. *A History of Pennsylvania*. Second and Enlarged Edition. University Park and London: The Pennsylvania University Press, 1980.

Larkin, Oliver W. *Art and Life in America*. Revised edition. New York: Holt, Rinehart and Winston, 1960.

Laverty, George Lauman, M.D. *History of Medicine in Dauphin County, Pennsylvania*. Harrisburg: Dauphin County Medical Society and the Telegraph Press, 1967.

Locomotive Sketches, With Pen and Pencil, Or Hints and Suggestions to the Tourist Over the Great Central Route from Philadelphia to Pittsburgh, With Numerous Illustrations. Philadelphia: J.W. Moore, 1854.

Loose, John W. W. *The Heritage of Lancaster*. Woodland Hills, CA: Windsor Publications, 1978.

Lowe, David. *Chicago Interiors: Views of a Splendid World*. Chicago: Contemporary Books, 1979.

Lucas, E. V. *Edwin Austin Abbey, Royal Academician: The Record of His Life and Work*. New York and London: Charles Scribner's Sons, 1921.

Lynes, Russell. *The Art-Makers*. New York: Dover, 1982.

Mercer, Henry Chapman. *The Tiled Pavement in the Capitol of Pennsylvania*. 1908. Revised and edited by Ginger Duemler. State College, PA: Pennsylvania Guild of Craftsmen, 1975. Revised with a new foreword by Vance Koehler, Capitol Preservation Committee, 1998.

Miller, Herman P. and W. Harry Baker. (compilers). *Smull's Legislative Hand Book and Manual of the State of Pennsylvania*. Harrisburg: J. L. L. Kuhn, 1919, annual.

Mombert, J. I. *An Authentic History of Lancaster County*. Lancaster: J. E. Barr & Co., 1869.

Montgomery, Florence A. *Textiles In America, 1650-1870*. New York: W. W. Norton and Co., 1984.

Morgan, George H. *Annals of Harrisburg*. Harrisburg: 1858.

———. *Annals of Harrisburg*. Harrisburg: 1906.

Morrison, Ernest. *J. Horace McFarland: A Thorn for Beauty*. Harrisburg: Commonwealth of PA, Historical and Museum Commission, 1995.

Oakley, Violet. *The Founding of the "State of Liberty Spiritual:" Representing the Triumph of the Idea of Liberty of Conscience in the "Holy Experiment of Pennsylvania."* Harrisburg: Mount Pleasant Press, 1906.

———. *The Holy Experiment: A Message to the World from Pennsylvania, Series of Mural Paintings...In the Governor's Reception Room and in the Senate Chamber of the State Capitol at Harrisburg*. Philadelphia: 1922.

———. *The Holy Experiment: Our Heritage from William Penn, 1644–1944*. Philadelphia: Cogslea Studio Publications, 1950.

———. *Law Triumphant Containing "The Opening of the Book of Law" and "The Miracle of Geneva."* Philadelphia: Biddle-Deemer Printing Co., 1932.

Opitz, Glenn B., ed. *Dictionary of American Sculptors*. Poughkeepsie, NY: Apollo, 1984.

Orwig, Joseph Ray. *The Harrisburg Visitors' Guide, 1876, For the Use of Strangers Visiting the City, Containing a Descriptive "Tour of the City and Capitol Buildings"...*Harrisburg: Patriot Publishing Co., 1876.

Pennsylvania's New Capitol at Harrisburg. Harrisburg: Press of the Harrisburg Telegraph, ca. 1906.

Pennsylvania State Capitol Guide Book. Harrisburg: Bernard C. Dunn Estate and the Telegraph Press, ca. 1929.

Pennypacker, Samuel W. *The Desecration and Profanation of the Pennsylvania Capitol.* Philadelphia: William J. Campbell, 1911.

Placzek, Adolf F. ed. *Macmillan Encyclopedia of Architects.* New York: The Free Press, 1982.

Postcard Views of Harrisburg, Pennsylvania. Various printers, ca. 1902–1912.

Proske, Beatrice Gilman. *Brookgreen Garden Sculpture.* Murrill's Inlet, S. C.: Trustees of Brookgreen Garden, 1968.

Riddle, William. *The Story of Lancaster: Old and New.* Lancaster, PA: Self-published, 1917.

Roshon, J. W. *The New Capitol at Harrisburg, PA.* Brooklyn, NY: Albertype Co. 1906.

Rubenstein, Charlotte Streifer. *American Women Artists: From Early Indian Times to Present.* Boston: G. K. Hall and Co., 1982.

Rupp, Daniel. *The History and Topography of Dauphin, Cumberland, Franklin, Bedford, Adams, Perry, Somerset, Cambria and Indiana Counties...* Lancaster: Gilbert Hills, 1848.

———. *History of Lancaster County...* Lancaster: Gilbert Hills, 1844.

Sauers, Richard A. *Advance the Colors: Pennsylvania Civil War Battle Flags.* 2 vols. Harrisburg: Pennsylvania; Capitol Preservation Committee, 1987, 1992.

Schuyler, Montgomery A. "A Critique of the Works of Adler and Sullivan, D. H. Burnham and Co., and Henry Ives Cobb." In *Great American Architects* Series, Nos. 1–6, May 1895-July 1899. New York: The Architectural Record Co., ca. 1900. Reprint ed., New York: DeCapo Press, 1977.

Scott, Joseph. *A Geographical Description of Pennsylvania.* Philadelphia: 1806.

Shimmel, Lewis Slifer and William Colson, eds. *The State Capitol of Pennsylvania, Harrisburg, Nineteen Hundred and Six.* Harrisburg: The Telegraph Printing Co., 1907.

Smith, Isreal Clare. *Lancaster and Its People...* Lancaster, PA: D. S. Stauffer, 1892.

Sobel, Robert and John Raimo. *Biographical Dictionary of the Governors of the United States, 1789–1978.* 4 vols. Westport, CT: Meckler Books, 1978.

Steffens, Lincoln. *The Shame of the Cities.* New York: McClure and Phillips & Co., 1904; republished, New York: Hill and Wang, 1957.

Steinmetz, Richard H. *This Was Harrisburg: A Photographic History.* Harrisburg: Stackpole Books, 1976.

Sweet's Indexed Catalogue of Building Construction for the Year 1906. New York: Architectural Record Co., 1906.

Taft, Lorado. *The History of American Sculpture.* New York: MacMillan Co., 1930; republished 1980.

Tatman, Sandra L. and Roger W. Moss. *Biographical Dictionary of Philadelphia Architects: 1700–1930.* Boston: G.K. Hall and Co., 1985.

Warner, William F. *Old Lancaster: Tales and Traditions.* Lancaster: William F. Warner, 1927.

Who's Who In America. Volume 18, 1934–35. Chicago: A. N. Marquis Co., 1934.

Wilson, Richard Guy, et. al. *The American Renaissance: 1876–1917.* New York: The Brooklyn Museum, 1979.

Withey, Henry F. and Elsie Withey. *Biographical Dictionary of American Architects.* Los Angeles: Hennesy and Ingalls, 1970.

Wood Jerome H. *Conestoga Crossroads: Lancaster, Pennsylvania, 1730–1970.* Harrisburg, PA: Historical and Museum Commission, 1979.

Government Documents

Barnett, George R. ed. *The Dauphin County Reports...* vol. 13. Harrisburg: Warren O. Foster, 1910.

[Capitol Building Commission]. *Programme of a Competition for the Selection of an Architect for a New Capitol Building to be Erected by the Commonwealth of Pennsylvania in Harrisburg.* Harrisburg: State Printer, 1897.

Capitol Building Commission. *Report of the Capitol Building Commission Created by the Act of April 14 A. D. 1897...Presented to the General Assembly March 16, 1899.* Harrisburg: State Printer, 1899.

Capitol Graft Cases. 3 vols. n.p., ca. 1911.

Capitol Investigation Commission. "Report of the Capitol Investigation Commission." August 16, 1907, in *House Journal,* 1909, pp. 221–385.

Carson, Hampton L. [compiler]. *Report of the Attorney General in Re Capitol Investigation.* [Harrisburg], 1907.

Commonwealth of Pennsylvania, Bureau of Publications. *Pennsylvania Manual: Formerly Smull's Legislative Handbook.* Harrisburg: 1927-Annual.

Combined History of Senate and House Bills, Sessions of 1969 and 1970. Harrisburg: Secretary of the Senate and Clerk of the House, biennial.

House Journal…, 1827–28. 2 vols. Harrisburg: State Printer, 1828.

Journal of the House of Representatives of the Commonwealth of Pennsylvania, for the Session Begun at Harrisburg on the Third day of January, 1905. Part I. Harrisburg, State printer, 1905.

Laws of the General Assembly of the Commonwealth of Pennsylvania. Harrisburg, biennial.

Legislative Record. Harrisburg: State Printer, biennial.

Pennsylvania Capitol Preservation Committee. *The Pennsylvania Capitol: A Documentary History.* Harrisburg: Heritage Studios, 1987.

Hubbert-Kemper, Ruthann and Jason Wilson, eds. *A Sacred Challenge: Violet Oakley and the Pennsylvania Capitol Murals.* Harrisburg: Pennsylvania Capitol Preservation Committee, 2002.

Pennsylvania Commission For Legislative Modernization. *Toward Tomorrow's Legislature.* Harrisburg, 1969.

Pennsylvania Constitutional Convention. *Debates of the Pennsylvania Constitutional Convention of 1967-1968.* 2 vols. Harrisburg, 1968.

Pennsylvania General Assembly, Commission in charge of the dedication ceremonies of the Barnard Statues. *Dedication Ceremonies of the Barnard Statues, State Capitol Building, Harrisburg, Penna., October the fourth, Nineteen hundred and eleven.* Harrisburg, 1912.

Reed George, ed. *Papers of the Governors, 1897–1902.* Pennsylvania Archives. 4th Series. Harrisburg: State printer, 1902.

Schaffer, William I. [State Reporter]. *Pennsylvania State Reports. Vol. 232, Containing Cases Decided by the Supreme Court of Pennsylvania. May Term 1911.* New York: The Banks Law Publishing Co., 1912.

Smull, William P. *Rules and Decisions of the General Assembly of Pennsylvania, Legislative Directory, Together With Useful Political Statistics, Lists of Post Offices, County Officers, &c.* Harrisburg: State Printer. 1875-Annual. Titles and compilers vary; after 1896 title was *Smull's Legislative Hand Book and Manual of the State of Pennsylvania.* Compiled by Thomas B. Cochran.

Maps

(18th Century) Pennsylvania Department of Internal Affairs. "A Connected Draft of Twelve Tracts of land Situated…Whereon is Located the City of Harrisburg…" Harrisburg: 1904. Held by the Pennsylvania State Archives.

(1785–1808) "Original Plot of the Borough of Harrisburg, With Additions From 1785 to 1808." Held by the Pennsylvania State Archives.

(1795) Foster, Thomas. "Manuscript Parchment Draft of Harrisburg." unpublished, 1795. Copy in Rare Books Section, Pennsylvania State Library.

(1841) *A Plan of the Borough Of Harrisburg.* Harrisburg: ?, 1841.

(1850) Sidney, J. C. *Plan of the Borough of Harrisburg, Dauphin County, Penna.* Philadelphia: Moody, 1850.

(1858) Southwick, J. *Map of Dauphin County.* Philadelphia: Wm. J. Barker, 1858.

(1860) Hage, Hother. *Map of the City of Harrisburg in Dauphin County, Pennsylvania, As Laid Out Under the Direction of the Commissioners for the City Survey in 1860 & 1861.* Philadelphia: R. L. Barnes, 1860.

(1862) Beers, S. N. and F. W. *Map of Dauphin County.* Philadelphia: A Pomeroy, 1862.

(1871) Hopkins, G. M. and Cunningham, L. *Map of the City of Harrisburg, Dauphin County, PA…*Philadelphia: H. S. Converse and G. M. Hopkins, 1871.

(1875) *Combination Atlas Map of Dauphin County, Pennsylvania.* Philadelphia: Everts & Stewart, 1875.

(1885) Baist, G. William. *Map of Harrisburg, Dauphin County, Pennsylvania.* Philadelphia: J. L. Smith, 1885.

(1889) Roe, Frederick B. *Atlas of the City of Harrisburg, Dauphin County, Pennsylvania, Compiled and Drawn from Official Plans and Actual Surveys…* Frederick B. Roe, 1889.

(1901) *Atlas of the City of Harrisburg, Dauphin County, Pennsylvania, Made from Plans, Deeds, Surveys.* Harrisburg: Harrisburg Title Company, 1901.

Pamphlets

Bell, John C. *Address of Honorable John C. Bell, Attorney General of the State of Pennsylvania, upon the occasion of the dedication of the Barnard statues at the State Capitol Building, Harrisburg, PA.* [Harrisburg]: [1911].

Board of Commissioners of Public Grounds and Buildings. *The State Capitol at Harrisburg.* [Harrisburg]: 1906. In pamphlet vol. 767, Pennsylvania State Library.

Board of Commissioners of Public Grounds and Buildings. *The State Capitol at Harrisburg.* [Harrisburg]: n.d. In pamphlet vol. 1308, Pennsylvania State Library.

Civic Club of Harrisburg. *Dedication of the Market Street Entrance to the City of Harrisburg, PA.* [Harrisburg]: n.p., 1906.

Furness, Evans & Co. *An Open Letter from Furness, Evans & Co. to the Philadelphia Chapter of the American Institute of Architects.* Philadelphia: Allen, Lane & Scott, printer, 1897.

Guide to the Microfilm of the Papers of Henry C. Mercer and the Records of the Moravian Pottery and Tile Works. Doylestown, PA: Bucks County Historical Society, 1985.

Oakley, Violet. *The Founding of the 'State of Liberty Spiritual.'* Harrisburg: Mount Pleasant Press, ca. 1906.

Proceedings at the Dedication of the Market Street Entrance to the City of Harrisburg, PA. Harrisburg: Family of Henry McCormick, 1906.

Periodicals

American Architect and Building News 88 (1905): 34; 90 (1906): 105–106, 113–114, 137, 167–168, 194–198, 201; 91 (1907): 2, 105, 114, 121–122, 130, 138, 238, 245–246; 92 (1907): 9, 11–12.

American Institute of Architects. *Journal of the Proceedings.* American Institute of Architects: 1866-Annual.

Architecture and Building (September 25, 1897).

Architecture and Builders Journal (January 1903).

"George Grey Barnard, Sculptor," *Harper's Weekly* 46 (August 23, 1902): 1133–1134, 1155.

Blackaby, James R. "The Carpet of History." *Mercer Mosaic: The Journal of the Bucks County Historical Society* 3, 5 (September-October 1986): 128–132.

Caffin, Charles H. "The New Capitol of Pennsylvania." *World's Work* 13 (November 1906-April 1907): 8195–8210.

Coleman, Caryl. "An Appreciation." *Architectural Record* 22 (1907): 455–456.

Cotissoz, Royal. "Abbey's Latest Mural Paintings." *Scribner's Magazine* 44, 6 (December 1908): 655–668.

———. "Abbey's Last Mural Paintings." *Scribner's Magazine* 51, 1 (January 1912): 1–16.

Cummings, Hubertis. "Pennsylvania's State Houses and Capitols." *The Capitols of Pennsylvania,* n.p., n.d. [Reprinted from *Pennsylvania History* 20, 4 (1953)].

———. "Stephen Hills and the Building of Pennsylvania's First Capitol." *The Capitols of Pennsylvania.* [Reprinted from *Pennsylvania History* 20, 4 (1953)].

Darlington, Charles H. "Pennsylvania's Palace of Graft." *World's Work* 14 (May-October 1907): 9237–9242.

"Description of the State Capitol of Pennsylvania, now building at Harrisburg." *Analectic Magazine* 2, 1 (July 1820): 46–52.

Dickson, Harold. "The Origins of the Cloister." *Art Quarterly* 28, 4 (1965).

Downes, William Howe. "Mr. Barnard's Exhibit at Boston." *World's Work* 46 (November 1908-April 1909): 11267–11269.

"Free-Standing Scaffold Covers State Capitol Dome." *Construction Methods* (August 1945): 70–72.

Harry T. Everett. "Is Pennsylvania's New Capitol a Palatial Monument to Fraud?" *Harper's Weekly* 50 (November 30, 1906): 1560–1563.

"Harrisburg Views and Description." *Ballou's Pictorial Drawing-Room Companion.* 1857.

"Heavy Sheet Lead Construction Applied to Dome of Pennsylvania State Capitol Building." *Lead* 15, 2 (March-April 1945): 2–3.

"Henry Ives Cobb." *Pencil Points,* May 1931.

Howland, Harold J. "A Costly Triumph." *The Outlook* 85 (January 26, 1907): 193–210.

Independent, The 62 (March 28, 1907): 743–744; 63 (September 26, 1907): 717; 70 (January 26, 1911): 209–210.

Mills, Sally. "What the Triptych Means." *Vassar Quarterly* 80, 3 (Spring 1984): 23–25.

Morris, Harrison S. "Miss Violet Oakley's Mural Decorations." *The Century Magazine* 70 (May-October 1905): 265–268.

Nation, The, 86, 2234 (April 23, 1908): 384.

"The New Capitol, St. Paul." *Architectural Record* 10 (1900–1901): 280–282.

Oakley, Violet. "The Vision of William Penn: Mural Paintings in the Capitol of Pennsylvania." *The Capitols of Pennsylvania*. n.p., n.d. [Reprinted from *Pennsylvania History* 20, 4 (1953)].

Outlook, The 84 (September-December 1906): 347–348; 86 (May-August 1907): 126–127, 934–935; 87 (September-December 1907): 146–147.

"The Pennsylvania Capitol." *Through the Ages* 3, 3 (July 1925): 10–18.

Pennypacker, Isaac A. "A Brief for Pennsylvania's Capitol and Its Builders." *Harper's Weekly* 50, 2610 (December 29, 1906): 1888–1890.

"Pipe Scaffold for Repair of Big Dome." *Engineering News-Record* (August 16, 1945): 10–11.

Pratt, Henry C. "Architecture of the World's Fair." *Brush and Pencil*. vol. xiv, pp. 135–159.

Schroder, J. L. "George Grey Barnard: The Cloisters and the Abbey." *Metropolitan Museum of Art Bulletin* 37, 1 (Summer 1979).

Sturgis, Russell. "Mr. Van Ingen's Lunettes in the Harrisburg State House." *Scribner's Magazine* 41, 4 (April 1907): 509–512.

———. "Miss Oakley's Pictures in the Harrisburg State House." *Scribner's Magazine* 41, 5 (May 1907): 637–640.

Thaw, Alexander Blair. "George Grey Barnard, Sculptor." *World's Work*. 5 (December 1902): 2837–2852.

Twombley, Mary. "George Grey Barnard: His Statues for the Pennsylvania Capitol." *World's Work* 17 (November 1908-April 1909): 11256–11267.

"William B. Van Ingen, Mural Painter." *Architectural Record* 13 (1903): 323–334.

Wister, Owen. "The Keystone Crime." *Everybody's Magazine* 14, 4 (October 1907): 435–448.

Young, Mahroni Sharp. "George Grey Barnard and the Cloisters." *Apollo* 189 (November 1977).

THESES

Cohen, Zara. "A Comprehensive History of the State House of New Jersey and Recommendations for its Continuation as a Historic Site." M.A. thesis, Neward State College, May 1969.

Deibler, Dan Grove. "An Architectural Competition: A Capitol Offense." M.A. thesis, University of Virginia, 1974.

Pattee, Sarah Lewis. "The Pennsylvania State Capitol Grounds: A Plan for Development." M. A. thesis, Pennsylvania State College, 1918.

TRADE CATALOGS

Derby and Kilmer Desk Company. *Tenth Illustrated Catalogue and Price-List of the Derby Roll-top Desks*. Boston, 1889.

Edwards Joseph and Co. *Illustrated Catalogue of the New and Improved "Cataract" Centrifugal Pump*. New York: post-1882.

Howard, E., Watch & Clock Company. *Price List of Hall Striking Clocks*. Boston: [1887].

Kramer, Francis D., Co. *Art Catalogue*. Philadelphia: 1880.

Marble and Shattuck. *High Grade Chairs*. 1922.

———. *Fine Office Chairs For Every Commercial Requirement: Catalogue No. 58*. Cleveland, OH: [ca. 1937].

Phoenix Glass Company. *Catalogue of Gas and Electric Globes, and Other Lighting Fixtures*. Monaca, PA: 1893, 1901.

———. *Electric Globes, Shades, etc. of All Kinds*. Catalogue 16. Pittsburgh: 1904.

Pyne Press, The. *Pennsylvania Glassware: 1870–1904*. Princeton, NJ: The Pyne Press, 1970.

MANUSCRIPT COLLECTIONS—COLLECTIONS HOUSED IN HARRISBURG

Dauphin County Court, Clerks Office. Records of the Dauphin County Court of Common Pleas. September Term, 1907.

Pennsylvania Capitol Preservation Committee. Joseph M. Huston Personal Papers.

Pennsylvania Department of General Services. Bureau of Space and Facilities Management, Bureau of Technical Support, State Arts Commission.

Pennsylvania Historical and Museum Commission. Archives and Manuscripts Division.

MG-8	Pennsylvania Collection
MG-75	Joseph M. Huston Collection.
MG-145	Daniel H. Hastings Collection.
MG-152	S. Emerson Bolton Collection.
MG-171	Samuel W. Pennypacker papers.

Unaccessioned—Gilbert Seltzer Collection: This collection contains the papers of Capitol Complex Architect William Gehron, along with information on Arnold W. Brunner and the development and expansion of Capitol Park.

RG-13	PHMC, Division of Land Records.
RG-20	Department of Property and Supplies.
RG-25	Records of Special Commissions. The Capitol Investigation Commission.
RG-26	Department of State Records. Secretary of the Commonwealth files.

Manuscript Collections— Not Housed in Harrisburg

Historical Society of Pennsylvania. Collection of Violet Oakley's journals and sketches.

Library Company of Pennsylvania. Holds a significant collection of William Rau photographs of the Capitol, and several renderings by Huston of projected Capitol interiors.

Library of Congress. Prints and Photographs Division. Numerous photographs of the Capitol and its dedication.

Mary Baker Eddy Library, Boston. Collection of Violet Oakley's letters and illustrations.

Mercer Museum and Spruance Library. Personal Papers. Correspondence, 1899–1928.

Metropolitan Museum of Art, The Cloisters Library. George Grey Barnard Correspondence and Collections.

Pennsylvania Academy of the Fine Arts. Large collection of Violet Oakley's original art and artifacts.

Pennsylvania State University Library. Huston, Joseph M. "Specifications of Capitol Building for the Commonwealth of Pennsylvania, Harrisburg, Penna." Harrisburg, Capitol Building Commission, 1902.

Philadelphia Athenaeum. Holds a significant number of drawings from the 1897 and 1901 Capitol design competitions. Henry Cobb's and Joseph Huston's 1897 drawings.

Philadelphia Museum of Art. George Grey Barnard Papers, Violet Oakley Scrapbooks and various works.

Princeton University Archives. Records of the Class of 1892.

Records of the Moravian Pottery and Tile Works. Order Books 2 and 3, 1900–1904; Kiln records, 1900–1909; Ledgers, 1904–1915.

Royal Academy of Art, London. Collection of Edwin Austin Abbey's art.

Smithsonian Institution. Archives of American Art. Violet Oakley Papers; George Grey Barnard Correspondence.

Woodmere Art Museum. Large collection of Violet Oakley's art and artifacts.

Yale University Art Gallery. Manuscripts and Archives. Largest collection of Edwin Austin Abbey's art and documents in the United States.

INDEX

Boldface page numbers refer to illustrations and artwork.

A

Abbey, Edwin Austin, 109, 118, 121, 197, **198**, 199, 201, 203, 225, 234, 289, 306
Abbey, Gertrude (Mrs. Edwin Austin), 201
Académie Delecluse, 230
Act of 1810, 33, 37
Act of 1901, 47
Agnew, Daniel H., **246**, 247
Albert Michaels Conservators, 294, 309
Alden and Harlow, 73
Alexander, John White, 233
Alfano, Vincenzo, **235**, 237
    artwork of,
        angel of light, **236**
        caryatid, **237**
        pediment sculpture, **237**
        puttis, **235**, **237**
        sculpture groups, **236**
American Civic Association, 258
American Institute of Architects (AIA), 76, 89
American's with Disabilities Act, (ADA), 329
Annex Building, (See Executive, Library and Museum Building)
Apotheosis of Pennsylvania, (Abbey), **201**, 293
Armstrong, Gibson, **301**
Arthur Page Conservation, 325
Art, (Abbey), **202**
Art Institute of Chicago, 204
Arthur, Jacob, 299
Aucaigne, Eugene F., **242**
Audit Company of New York City, 180, 183–84
Autumn and Winter, (MacGregor), **239**

B

Bailey, Edward, 87, 89
Baker and Dallett, 77
Baran Walter, 290
Barnard, George Grey, 109, 197, **204–205**, 207, 210, 234
    sculptures, 197, 204, **205–10**
        restoration of, **320**, **322–23**
Beaver, Governor James A., 210
Bechtel, Joseph, 103
Belardi, Fred, **301**
Benjamin Franklin bridge, 95
Berry, William H., 133, **174–75**, 177–78, 184
Bigler, Governor William, **335**
Bloomsburg Carpet, **336–37**
Board of Commissioners of Public Grounds and Buildings, 67, 111, 118, 121, 123, 170–71, 173, 183–84, 186, 189, 194, 267
Board, Ernest, 201
Bob Smith Contractors, **302**
Boice, Ronald, **333**
Boileau, Wallis, 189
Boles, Rachel, **309**
Bonnát, Leon, 211
Boone, Daniel, 245
Boston Public Library, 199
Bowie, John, 294, 301
Boyer, Henry K., 67, 70, 73, 76
Bright, John Irwin, 222
Brooks, Richard, 279
bronze, (restoration of), 320
Brothers of Ephrata, (Van Ingen), **213**
Brunner, Arnold W., 261, 267, 270, 283–84
    plan of Capitol Complex, 263, 265, 267–69, 275
Bryan, George, 41
Burden of Life: The Broken Law, (South Group, Barnard), **205**, **209**
Burning of the Books at Oxford, (Oakley), **196**

C

C. A. Lindman, 296, 323, 342
C. E. White Enterprises, 316
Caffin, Charles H., 139
Calder, Alexander, 93
Calvin, John, 213
Cameron, Simon, 165, **166**
Campbell, William, 116
Camp Curtin, (See Harrisburg, Camp Curtin)
Camp of the American Army at Valley Forge, February, 1778, (Abbey), **199**
Canal Boat 1835, (Maragliotti), **232**
Canning, John, **316**
capital,
    debate over, 29–30, 32, 69–70
    Harrisburg, 32–33
    Lancaster, 29
    Philadelphia, 26, 29, 30
Capitol Building,
    Cobb Capitol, (1898–1901), 66, 67
        architect, (See Cobb, Henry Ives)
        construction, 76, **78–80**, 81
        dedication, 81, **82**
        design competition, 73–77
        design, **71–72**, **74**, 77–79
        groundbreaking, 80–81
        interior, **83**

reaction to, 81–83
Hills Capitol, (1822–1897), **22**, **37–38**, **43**, **48**, **52**, **57**, **73**
   architect, (See Hills, Stephen)
   construction, **40–41**, **42–43**, 48
   dedication, **49**
   design competition, 38-39
   design, 37, 42, 48, 296
   fire, 60–65, 68–70
   interior, **41**, **44–47**, **54–55**
   legislation passed within, 52
   notable visitors, 49–50
   significance of, 37–38, 40
Huston Capitol, (1902-present)
   architect, (See Huston, Joseph Miller) **123**, **133**, **137**, **159–60**, **250**, **257**, **261**, **268**, **272**, **274**, **284–85**, **344**
   construction, 84, 103, **104–106**, 107–109, **110–19**, 120–23
      deaths during, 116–17
   cornerstone, 113
   dedication,
      ceremonies, 147, 152, 155–56
      Citizens Committee, 143, 161–62,
      Colored Citizens Reception Committee, 129
      Finance Committee, 129
      Publicity Committee, 126
      Music Committee, 126
   design competition, **88–89**, 90–93
   design, **96**, 98–99, **100–102**, **109**
   dome, (cleaning of), 340
   furniture designs, **166**, **170**, **172–73**, **178–79**, **190**
   graft scandal,
      cartoons, **174–76**, **181**, **184–85**, **187–88**, **192**, **195**
      hearings, 185–86, 189
      indictments, 189
      investigation of, 177–78, 183, (See also Audit Company of New York and Capitol Investigation Commission)
      Pennypacker's response to, 178, 180
      press coverage of, 174–77, 193
      purchasing system, 171–74
      trials, 190, 193
   interior, **130**, **132**, **148**, **164**, **171**, **182**, **191**
   House Chamber, **91**, **121**, **134–36**
   rotunda, **98**
   Senate Chamber, **144–45**
   Supreme Court Chamber, **240**
   labor disputes, 112
Capitol Building Commission, 71, 75–77, 81–82, 86–91, 98–99, 108–109, 121, 123, 142, 147 167, 170, 183–84, 186, 194, 225
Capitol Complex, 250, 261, 268–70, 273, 275, 284–85, 290
Capitol Dedication Committee, 127, 142
Capitol Investigation Commission, 120, 180, 183–86, 189
Capitol Park, 55, **58**, 79, **108**, 113, **120**, 136, 141,**158–59**, 269
   Extension Commission, 55, 261, **262–63**, 265, **266**, 267, **271**
   formation of, 33

Harris grant, 30
Capitol Preservation Committee, 294–96, 305
   creation of, 287, 290–91
   cyclical maintenance, 299–300, 343–44
   dome restoration, 331–32, 340
   events, 332–33
   rotunda restoration, 292, 306
Caprioti, Alan, **326**, **334**
Carlisle Indian School, 156
Carrere, John M., 73
Carson, Hampton L., 121, 178, **180**
Cassel, H. Burd, **186**, 189
Cassatt, Mary, 234
Castro, Ivan, **312**
Celli-Flynn Associates, 283
Central Pennsylvania Traction Company, 132
Chase, William Merritt, 238
Christ and Disarmament—International Law, (Oakley), **229**
Ciccone, Frank, **305**
City Beautiful movement, 253, 259, 261, 270
Civil War,
   flags, 57, **304–306**
   projects, 292–93, 305–306
Clark, Alfred Corning, 204
Clarkson, Robert G., 80
Clifford, John, 79
Clyde, John C., 81
Clymer, Paul, **299**, **300–301**, 303, **330**, **333**
Cobb, Henry Ives, **75**, 77–83, 85–86, 89, 95
Commonwealth, (statue), **119**, 121, 160–61, 230–**31**, 298, 299, **331**
   restoration of, 330–31
Conservation,
   of flags, 292–93, **304–306**
Conservation Solutions, 323, 341
Cook, Walter, 73
Cope and Stewardson, 73, 77
Country Store 1867–70, (Maragliotti), **234**
Crain, Richard M., 41
Crowell, Gary, **301**
Curtain, Andrew, 275

D

Darlington, Frederick W., 80
Darlington, Rev. James Henry, 152
Dauphin County,
   courthouse, as first capitol, 33, **36**, 49
   formation of, 30
Declaration of Independence, 27
Dedication,
   Barnard statues, **207**, 210
   Hills Capitol, 49
Delance, Paul, 230
Delaney, John, 70

De Nadai, Mary Werner, **301**
Deluco, Michael, **316**
Dewey Arch, 95
Dickens, Charles, 50
Dillingham, John H., 147
Divine Law—Key Note, (Oakley), **228**
Dixon, Dr. Samuel, 157
Dock, Mira Lloyd, 251–**52**, 253, 255–56, 258
Drakes First Oil Well, Titusville 1859, (Maragliotti), **232**

E

1897 design competition, 73, 75–77
Eakins, Thomas, 211
Eastern State Penitentiary, 193
East Wing Expansion, 268, 283–84, 290
École des Beaux Arts, 204, 230
Education Building, (See Forum Building)
Elkins, William L., 107
Ellison, John B., 93
Ellison, Sue, **301**
Ephrata Community Spinning and Carding, (Van Ingen), **215**
Erb, Abraham T., 81
Executive, Library and Museum Building, 56, 57, **59**, 63, 251, 284, **330**
Eyre, Thomas L., 88

F

Faulhaber, William, **301**
Finance Building, **282**, 283
Findlay, Governor William, 39–41
Flaherty, John, **295**
Forum Building, 275, **276–281**
Fox, John, 86
Franklin, Benjamin, 245, 275, **335**
Fridy, Sam Matt, 190, **193**
Frost, Charles S., 77
Furness, Frank, 75–77, 93
Furness and Evans, 73, 77
Furness and Sons, 93, 95

G

Garvan, Beatrice, **295**, 297
Gehron, William, 234, 269, 273, 279
General Assembly of Pennsylvania, 57, 61, 71, 81, 83, 85
    move to Harrisburg, 37–38
    move to Lancaster, 31–32
George Washington at the Constitutional Convention in Philadelphia, (Oakley), **224**
Gerwig, Edgar C., 88, 90
Gibson, John Bannister, 41
Glass, Brent, **330**
Gleason, Elaine, **293**, **309**
Glenn, Robert, **295**, **301**
Gobin, John P. S., 155

Godwin, Alfred, 241
    artwork of, **240–241**
Governor's office, (restoration) 318–20
Governor's portraits, 335
Governor's Reception Room, (restoration), 335
Grace Methodist Episcopal Church, 67, **68–69**, 75
Grady, John C., 61
Graft scandal, (See Huston Capitol, graft)
Graham, William H., 87
Graydon, William, 41
Green, Bernard R., 98–99, 103, 109, 122, 183
Green, Elizabeth Shippen, 223
Gross, Edward Z., 129, 142
Gugler, Eric, 279

H

H. B. Marshall, (Firm of), 73
Haas, Mitchell, **299**
Hager, Henry, **288**, 344
Hamilton, Andrew, 25–26
Hardenbergh, E. B., 189
Harding and Gooch, 73, 77
Harris, Frank G., 177, 189
Harris, John, Jr., 29–30, 32, 40
Harris, John, Sr., 32, 40
Harris, Robert, 33, 36
Harrisburg, 29–30, **32–35**, 49
    Board of Public Works, 258
    Board of Trade, 253, 256
    Camp Curtin, 52
    City Island, 160, **253**, 265
    during dedication, **140**, **146**, **154**
    fire companies, 61–63
    League for Municipal Improvements, 257
    Light, Heat, and Power Company, 158
    Old 8th Ward, 270
    Opera House, 67, **129**
    Steel Company, 257
    streets of, **250**, **254–55**, **260–62**, **264–65**
Hartzell, Ralph, 150
Hastings, Governor Daniel, 67, **70–71**, 73, 75–76, 79–81, 85
Hays, Frank, 93
Hays, William C., 90
Haywood, Benjamin, 73
Henry-Bonnard Bronze Company, **242–44**
Hesselius, Gustavus, **247**
Hiester, Governor Joseph, 49
Hills Capitol, (See Capitol Building, Hills)
Hills, Stephen, 36–49
Hinckley, Cornelius T., 53
Hitchcock, Henry-Russell, 37

Hoelle, Lucas A., 116
Hours, (Abbey), **203**
House Chamber, (restoration), 314, 318
House Majority Caucus Room, (restoration), 339–40
Houseal, Robert M., Jr., 61
Hoy, H. H., 156
Hoyer, George, 33
Hubbert-Kemper, Ruthann, 290–91, 294, **295**, 296, **299**, 300, **301**
Humbert, Robert, **293**
Hunting, Stanley, **333**
Hunting, Tilda, **333**
Huston, Joseph M., 77, **97**, 107, 121–**22**, 146
    biography of, 91, 93, 95
    construction of Capitol, 103, 108–109, 111, **113**, 121
    design for Capitol, 90–91, 98, 118, 173, 269
    graft involvement, 171, 173, 178, 184, 186, 189–90
        sentence, 193–94
    Literature in Stone, **345**
    relationship with Building Commission, 99, 103, 109
    selection of artists, 198–99, 206, 216, 220, 222–23, 225, 230, 242, 269
Huston, Samuel, 95, 103, 190, 194
Hutchison, Joseph B., 141
Hutton, Addison, 90

I

Independence Hall,
    construction of, **26–28**
    sale of, 38
International Understanding and Unity: Supreme Manifestation of Enlightenment Prophecy of William Penn, (Oakley), **226–27**
Irvine, Frank, 189
Irvis, Speaker K. Leroy, **vii, viii, ix,** 289

J

Jenkins, Hale, 150
Jennewein, C. Paul, 279, 283
Jennings, William, 129
Johnson, Dr. F. C., 157
Johnson, George, 116
Johnson, Jeff, **293**, **302**, **310**
Johnson, Philip H., 80
Johnson, Quentin, **342**
Jones, David, **246**, 247
Jones, Richard, **309**
Jordan, Henry, **301**
Jubelirer, Robert, **330**

K

Kauffman, Meyer, 117
Kearsley, Dr. John, 25
Keith, George, **246**, 247
Kelley, James, 293

Kelley, William J., 80
Kelly, Kji, **301**
Kemble, William H., 166
Kennedy, Elizabeth, **300**, **317**
Kenny, Elaine, **295**, **326**
Kessler, Diane, **301**
Keyworth, Charles A., 120
King Charles II Signs the Charter of Pennsylvania, (Oakley), **18**
Kinsman, Charles F., 189
Klingerman, Edward, 138
Kneeling Youth, (Barnard), **210**
Knoll, Lieutenant Governor Catherine Baker, **333**
Knox, Philander C., 150, 152
Kreis, Harry, 279
Kunkel, Judge George, 189

L

La Farge, John, 211
Lafayette, Marquis de, 49–50
Laird, Warren P., 71, 76
Lancaster,
    courthouse, **31**
    as capital city, 31–32
Lathrop, Francis, 211
Lavelier, James C., 39
Law, (Abbey), **200**
Lawrence, Elizabeth, 217
Lawrence, Thomas, 25
Lawrie, Lee, 270, 273, 279, 283
LeFever, Hippolyte, 206
Legend of the Latchstring, (Oakley), **223**
Lewis, Stanford B., 95, 98–**99**, 103, **108**, **118**, 189–190
Liberty Bell, 26–27
Lieutenant Governor's Office, (restoration), 318.
light courts, (restoration), 310
Lincoln, President Abraham, 50, 210
Lincoln at Gettysburg, 1863, (Oakley), **224**
Lindy, Erasmus, 39
Lochman, Rev. Dr. George, 49
Logan, James, **246**, 247
Louisburg, (See Harrisburg)
Love and Labor: The Unbroken Law, (North Group, Barnard), **208**
Lyon, Lieutenant Governor Walter, 68, 70
Lyter, Albert, 116

M

MacClay, William, 32–33, 37, 55
MacGregor, David A. (& Brother), 112, 329
MacGregor, Donald R. (& Company), 112, 238
MacGregor, Norman, 112
Makin's schoolhouse, 25
Malatestenic, Eric, **302**
Maragliotti, Vincent, **233**–34, 279, 310

Marshall, W. T., 70
Martin, Richard, 31
Martinez, Ernel, **309**
Mason, John, 49
Masonry Preservation Group, 312
Maynard, Elana, **301**
Mathues, William L., 177, **186**, 189–90
Matthew J. Ryan Legislative Office Building, (restoration), 330
McBride, Pat, **312**
McCarrell, Samuel J. M., 61, 67, 73
McCleod, A. A., 93
McClure, Alexander K., 80
McCormick, Henry C., 80, 158.
McCormick, James, 158
McCormick, Vance, **258**, 260
McFarland, J. Horace, 126, 251, **256**, 258
McKim, Charles Follen, 198
McKim, Mead and White, 199, 259
McKinley, President William, 95
Mercer, Henry Chapman, **216**–17, 219–20, 313
    mosaics,
        Automobile, **220**
        Blast Furnace, **220**
        Candle Dipper, **219**
        Elk, **218**
        Grey Squirrel, **218**
        Indian Paddling Canoe, **221**
        Milking the Cow, **221**
        Penn's Treaty, **221**
        Raccoon, **218**
        Scythe, **217**
        Shelling Corn, **221**
Merritt and Company, 112
Mexican-War monument, (See also monuments), 343
Michelangelo, 237
Mifflin, Governor Thomas, **30**, 31
Milione, Louis, 237
Miller, Herman, 57, 61, 90, 93
Milles, Carl, 275, 283
Mills, Robert, 37, 39, 41
monuments,
    Boies Penrose, 320
    Hartranft, **321**
    Mexican War, 56, 300, **342**
    Quay statue, **167**
Moravian Tile Floor, (preservation of), 313
Morelli, Domenico, 235
Morris, Anthony, 25
Morse, Wilbur, 157
Morgan, George, 55
Mother and Two Children, (Cassatt), **234**
Mühlenberg, Heinrich Melchior, 246, 247
Muhlenburg, John Peter, 275

Myers, Hyman (FAIA), 295, **296**, 301–302
Mylin, Amos, 73

N
Nakashima, George, 279
National Academy of Design, 233
National Trust for Historic Preservation, 301
Neiderer, John G., 189
North and South Executive Buildings (old), 37, **54**, 69
North Office Building, 269–**70**, 275

O
Oakley, Violet, 197, 203, 210, **222**–23, 225, 228, 234, 279
    mural restoration, 325, 327
Olmstead, Marlin E., 155, 162
Osterling, Fred J., 90

P
Pacioco, Joe, **312**
Palizzi, Giuseppe, 235
Palmer, James A., 80
Paris Opera, 98, 237
Pass and Stowe, 26–27
Patterson, John D., 70
Payne, George F., 103, 106–107, **108**–109, 113, **118**, 120–21, 123, 177, 186, 189–90, **193**
Peabody and Sterns, 73, 77
Peale, Charles Willson, 29
Penn, William, 16–**19**, **20**–21, 32, 223, 287, 303
    Charter of Privileges, 21, 23–26
    early life, 16–17
    founding of PA, 18–19
    frame of government, 18–19, 21
    General Assembly, (first), 23–24
    imprisonment, **17**
    legacy of, 21
    religious philosophy, 17, 19
Penn as Law Giver, (Oakley), **19**
Penn's First Sight of the Promised Land, (Oakley), **20**
Penn's Treaty, (Abbey), **21**
Penn's Treaty with the Indians, (Trumbull), **296**
Penn's Vision, (Oakley), **16**
Pennsylvania,
    charter of, 19
    Constitution of 1873, 71, 165
    first state house, (See Independence Hall)
    Historical and Museum Commission, 291
    Main Line of Public Works, 52
    State Art Commission, 291
    State Library, 56
    State Museum, 234
Pennsylvania Academy of the Fine Arts, 198, 211, 238
Pennsylvania Bronze Company, 189, **244**, **248**–49

Pennsylvania Construction Company, 186
Pennsylvania Railroad, **51**, 63
Pennypacker, Governor Samuel W., 103, 109, 113, 122, 127, 142–43, **147**, 166, 174, **177**–78, 180, 189–90, 210, 223, 297
    campaign materials, **168–69**
Penrose, Senator Boies, 150, 165, **167**, 194
Perry, Roland Hinton, **230**
Piccirilli Brothers, 210
Pitts, Joseph, **288–89**, 291, **292**, **301–302**
Porter, Governor David R., **335**
Porterfield, Diane, **293**
Prince of Wales, Edward, 50
Pulaski, Count Casimir, **247**
Pyle, Howard, 223

Q
Quaker legend murals, 223, 227
Quaker meeting houses, **24–25**
Quay, Matthew Stanley, 165, **167**, 194

R
Rambo, Samuel B., 109, **120**, 187, 225
Reading of the Declaration of Independence, (Abbey), **202**
Redfield, Edward, 93
Reed, Governor Joseph, **334**
Reynders, J. V. W., 257
Richardson, William F., 155
Richie, Ulysses, 283
Rising Sun chair, 33
Rita, John, **334**
Rittenhouse Commission, 30
Rittenhouse, David, 30, **246–47**
Roberts, Owen, 103, **108**, 116, 120
Rodin, Auguste, 210
Roosevelt, Kermit, **288–89**, 297
Roosevelt, President Theodore, **124**, 127, 129, 142–43, 146–47, **150–51**, **152–53**, **156**, 158, 210, 297
Rorke, Allen B., 80–81
Ross, Sydney, 269, 273, 279
Rothrock, Marta, **305**
rotunda, (restoration of), 292, 306–309
Roush, Carrie Forry, **301**
Ryan, Speaker Matthew J., **ix**, **x**, **xi**, **288**-90, **300–301**, **330**
Ryan, Merle, 299

S
Sacred Heart Catholic Church, 126
Saint-Gaudens, Augustus, 199
Sanderson, John H., 106–107, 112–13, 118, 173–75, 177–78, 184, 186, 189–90, 193–94, 197, 234, 248
Sargent, John Singer, 201
Savage, Eugene, 283
Saylor, Henry D., 61

Schwartz, Allyson, **301**
Schwartz, Charles, 81
Schuessele, Christian, 198, 211
Scotch-Irish Teaching Theology, (Van Ingen), **215**
Scotland Soldiers' Orphans School, 156
Senate Chamber, (restoration of), 327
Senate Library, **56**, 325
Senate Majority Caucus Room, (restoration of), 325
Senate water damage, 332
Shumaker, James M., 120, 177, 186, 189–90
Seale, William, 37
Shaeffer, Nathan C., 87
Sidarous, Madgi, **293**
Simonton, John W., 73
Smith, Jessie Wilcox, 223
Snoke, Kevin, **299**
Snyder, Governor Simon, 32-33, 38
Snyder, William P., 87, 133, 177, 184, 189–90
Soldiers' and Sailors' Memorial Bridge, **267**, **273**
Soldiers' Grove, 283
Sorrentino, Joe, **296**, 299–300, 302
South Office Building, 268–70, 275
Speaker K. Leroy Irvis Building, (See South Office Building)
Speaker Matthew J. Ryan Legislative Office Building, (See Executive, Library and Museum Building)
Spirit of Religious Liberty, (Abbey), **202**
Spirit of the Vulcan, (Abbey), **200**
Spring and Summer, (MacGregor), **239**
Steel, (Maragliotti), **232**
St. Peter's Basilica, 95, 98
state arsenal, Stephen Hills design, 40
stained glass, (restoration of), 313–14
Sterling Bronze Company, 248
Stevens, Thaddeus, 275
Stoll, Dr. G. B., 157
Stone, Governor William A., 85–**86**, 87–88, 98, 121, **147**, 225
Storm, Charles K., 189
Stuart, Governor Edwin S., 120, 180, **183**, 186
Strang, Gretchen, **332**
Strickland, William, 39
Strickler, Jacob, 31
Swatane, Oneida Chief, 245
Syng inkwell, 33

T
Taft, Lorado, 209
Tedyuscung, Delaware Chief, **247**
tercentenary, 289
Thomas, C. Wesley, 69
Thompson, Charles H., 129
Thornburgh, Governor Richard, **288–89**, **290**, 293, 302
Tiffany, Louis Comfort, 211
Todd, Moses Hampton, 189

Trimble and Stevens, 90
Trombone Choir in the cupola of the Moravian Church at Bethlehem, (Van Ingen), **215**
Trumbull, Edward, 269
    artwork of, **269**

U
Universal Builder's Supply, 293

V
Van Ingen, William Brantley, **211**, 213, 215, 310
    stained glass windows,
        Abundance, **134**
        Architecture, **144**
        Commerce, **135**
        Glass Blowing, **145**
        Justice, **134**
        Liberty, **214**
        Natural Gas, **214**
        Petroleum, **214**
        Railroads, **145**
        Religion, **212**
        Steam Engineering, **214**
        Steel and Iron, **214**
Vennel, Shawn, **293**, **337**
Venus and Two Loves, (MacGregor), **239**
Vitetta, 284, 292, 295–96, 302
Vorhees, Charles, 62, 85

W
Ware, William H., 89–90, 93, 98
Warner, James, 73, 76, 90
Warwick, Charles F., 70
Washington, President George (vignette), **53**
Weakley, C. S. (& Company), 126
Webster, Daniel, 50
Weiss, John Fox, 126
Wetter, Charles G., 103, 106, **108**, 121, **186**, 189
Widener, Peter A. B., 106
William Penn as Law Giver—Law of Reason, (Oakley), **229**
William Penn Memorial Museum, (See Pennsylvania, State Museum)
William Tyndale Printing His Translation of the Bible into English at Cologne, (Oakley), **225**
Williams, William L., 297
Wilmot, David, **50**, 52
Wilson, Charlie, 301
Wilson, James, 152
Windrim, James Hamilton (father), 57
Windrim, John Torrey (son), 57
Wister, Owen, 194
Wolfe, Leroy J., 158
Woodbury Granite Company, 103

Wooley, Edmund, 26
World's Columbian Exposition, 77, 251, **259**
    Pennsylvania Building, **258**
Works Progress Administration, (WPA), 283
Wright, Thomas, 213

Y
Yerkes, Charles T., 213
Yingel, Edith, 157
Young, Robert K., 88, 108

Z
Zeigler, George, 33
Zemprelli, Edward P., 344
Zwikl, Kurt, 287, **289**–90

Photography Credits

ABBREVIATIONS KEY:

CPC   Capitol Preservation Committee
HABS   Historic American Buildings Survey, Library of Congress, Washington, D. C.
HSP   Historical Society of Pennsylvania, Philadelphia
LC   Library of Congress, Prints and Photographs Division (unless otherwise noted)
LCP   The Library Company of Philadelphia
PPM   Pennypacker Mills, County of Montgomery, Schwenksville, Pennsylvania
PSA   Pennsylvania State Archives, Harrisburg
SMP   State Museum of Pennsylvania, Harrisburg

α denotes photography by Brian Foster
ϕ denotes photography by Brian Hunt
Δ denotes photography by John Rudy

Page numbers in the photographic section are in boldface type. On a page with more than one illustration, the credits correspond to illustrations clockwise from top left.

Title Page CPCϕ. **ii** CPC. **iii** PSA. **vi** PSA.• Athenæum of Philadelphia. • LCP. **vii** PA House of Representatives Archives. **viii** Pennsylvania House of Representatives. **ix** PA House of Representatives Archives. **x** CPC. **xi** Pennsylvania House of Representatives. **xii** Source unknown. **xiii** SMPϕ. • PSA. • PSA. **xiv** CPC. **xv** CPCϕ. • CPCϕ. • CPCϕ. • CPCϕ.

Introduction: **16** CPCϕ. **17** CPCϕ. **18** CPCϕ. **19** CPCϕ. **20** CPCϕ. **21** CPCϕ.

Chapter 1: **22** SMPϕ. **24** HSP "A view of the Bank Meeting House, Front Street" #Bb 862 Ev15#64. • HSP "Buildings in which the first Assembly was convened" #Bb 862 B756 #20. **25** Athenæum of Philadelphia. **26** LC # LC-USZC2-6374. **27** Independence National Historical Park. • HABS Delineated by Alan L. Wieskamp. **28** LC, Geography and Map Division #G3824.P5 1752.S3. **29** Detail from *"View of Harrisburg..."* LC, Geography and Map Division #G3824.H3A3 1855.W5. **30** Detail from *"View of Harrisburg..."* LC, Geography and Map Division #G3824.H3A3 1855.W5. **31** Lancaster County Historical Society. • CPCΔ. **32–33** Detail from *"View of Harrisburg..."* LC, Geography and Map Division #G3824.H3A3 1855.W5. • CPCΔ. **34–35** LC, Geography and Map Division #G3824.H3A3 1855.W5. **36** Dauphin County Historical Society. **37** Source unknown. **38** CPC. **39** CPCΔ. **40** HABS Delineated by F. E. Loescher. **41** State Library of Pennsylvania. • Courtesy of Kathy Baker. **42** PSA. • PSA. **43** SMPϕ. **44** SMPϕ. **45** Courtesy of Kathy Baker. • Detail from *"View of Harrisburg..."* LC, Geography and Map Division #G3824.H3A3 1855.W5. **46** SMPϕ. **47** State Library of Pennsylvania. • Detail from *"View of Harrisburg..."* LC, Geography and Map Division #G3824.H3A3 1855.W5. **48** Courtesy of Kathy Baker. **49** Dauphin County Historical Society. **50** LC #USZ62-132936. • PSA. **51** LC #LC-USZ62-57210. • LC #LC-USZ62-57212. • Detail from *"View of Harrisburg..."* LC, Geography and Map Division #G3824.H3A3 1855.W5. • LC # LC-USZ62-57214. **52** PSA. **53** SMPϕ. • SMPϕ. **54** PSA. • SMP. **55** State Library of Pennsylvania. • SMP. **56** SMP. • PSA. **57** LCP. **58** State Library of Pennsylvania. • State Library of Pennsylvania. **59** PSA. • Dauphin County Historical Society. **60** PSA. **61** PSA. **62** PSA. **63** PSA. • PSA. **64** PSA. • Courtesy of William Thomas. **65** PSA.

Chapter 2: **66** PSA. **68** PSA. **69** Dauphin County Historical Society. **70** CPCΔ. **71** Source unknown. **72** Athenæum of Philadelphia. **74** Courtesy of Ted Hanson. • Athenæum of Philadelphia. **75** University of Chicago. **76** PSA. **78** Dauphin County Historical Society. **79** PSA. **80** PSA. **81** Courtesy of Ruthann Hubbert-Kemper. • SMP. **82** SMP. • PSA. **83** Source unknown.

Chapter 3: **84** PSA. **86** CPCΔ. **87** LC. **88** CPCα. **89** Courtesy of Wilbur and Loice Gouker. **90** CPC. **91** LCP. **92** Courtesy of Tony Chibarro. • Witherspoon Building. Source: Moses King. *Philadelphia and Notable Philadelphians* (New York: Blanchard Press, Isaac H. Blanchard Co., 1901), 16. • PSA. • HABS PA, 51-PHILA, 290. • LC # LC-D4-12950. **93** CPC. **94** Courtesy of Russell Harris. • CPCϕ. **95** CPC. **96** Courtesy of Russell Harris. • Courtesy of Russell Harris. • Courtesy of Russell Harris. **97** Courtesy of Russell Harris. • CPCΔ. **98** LCP. **99** CPC.• Avery Architectural and Fine Arts Library. **100** LCP. • CPC. **101** LCP. **102** PSA. **104** PSA. • PSA. • PSA. • PSA. • PSA. • PSA. **105** PSA. **106** PSA. **107** CPC. • CPC. **108** PSA. • PSA. **109** LCP. **110** PSA. • PSA. • PSA. **111** PSA. **112** PSA. **113** PSA. **114** PSA. • PSA. • PSA. • PSA. **115** PSA. **116** PSA. **117** PSA. • PSA. **118** PSA. • PSA. **119** PSA. • CPCϕ. **120** Samuel Rambo. Source: CPC.• PSA. **121** PSA. **122** CPCΔ. **123** PSA.

Chapter 4: **124** PSA. **126** CPC, photographed by Jason Wilson. **127** Courtesy of Ruthann Hubbert-Kemper. **128** PSA. • State Library of Pennsylvania. **129** PPM. • PSA. **130** PSA. • PSA. • PSA. • PSA. **131** CPC. • CPC. • CPC. **132** PSA. • PSA. **133** CPC. **134** CPCϕ. • CPCϕ. • PSA. • PSA. **135** PSA. • CPCϕ. **136** PSA. **137** Dauphin County Historical Society. **138** PSA. **139** PPM. • PPM. • PPM. **140** PSAϕ. **141** Courtesy of Mike Cassidy. **142** PPM. • CPC. **143** "The Star Spangled Banner," LC, Music Division # M1630.3S7M53Case. • LC # LC-USZ62-102880. **144** CPCϕ. • PSA. **145** PSA. • CPCϕ. • CPCϕ. **146** PSA. **147** CPC. • CPCΔ. **148** PSA. • PSA. • PSA. • PSA. **149** PPM. • PPM. • PPM. **150**

LC # LC-USZC206275. **151** CPC.• LC # LC-USZ62-10445. **152** PPM. • SMP. • SMP. **153** CPC. **154** PSAφ. **155** Courtesy of Mike Cassidy. • Courtesy of Mike Cassidy. • Courtesy of Mike Cassidy. • Courtesy of Ruthann Hubbert-Kemper. **156** SMP. • PPM. • SMP. **157** LC # LC-USZ62-119032. **158** CPC. • CPC. **159** CPC. • CPC. **160** CPC. **161** Historic American Sheet Music, "Strolling with My Summer Girl," Music A-2693, Duke University Rare Book, Manuscript, and Special Collections Library. • LC # LC-USZ62-56662. • Historic American Sheet Music, "In the Good Old United States," Music A-5902, Duke University Rare Book, Manuscript, and Special Collections Library. • Historic American Sheet Music, "The Wedding of the Blue and Gray," Music B-165, Duke University Rare Book, Manuscript, and Special Collections Library. **162** PPM. • SMP. • Courtesy of Duane M. Searle. **163** Courtesy of Donald Brown. • CPC. • Courtesy of Donald Brown.

Chapter 5: **164** PSA. **166** PSA. • LC # LC-B8172-1599. **167** CPC.• CPC, photographed by Jason Wilson. **168** PPM. • PPM. • Tricolor ribbon. Source: PPM. • PPM. • PPM. **169** PPM. • PPM. • PPM. • PPM. **170** PSA. • PSA. **171** PSA. • PSA. **172** PSA. **173** PSA. **174** PPM. • CPC. **175** State Library of Pennsylvania. **176** State Library of Pennsylvania. **177** CPC. **178** PSA. **179** PSA. **180** PPM. • CPC. **181** State Library of Pennsylvania. **182** CPC. • CPC. • CPC. **183** CPC. **184** PPM. **185** State Library of Pennsylvania. **186** CPC. • CPC. • CPC. **187** State Library of Pennsylvania. **188** PPM. **190** PSA. • PSA. **191** CPC. • CPC. • CPC. **192** PPM. **193** Courtesy of Captain Winston G. Churchill. • CPC. **195** State Library of Pennsylvania.

Chapter 6: **196** CPCφ. **198** Source: E. V. Lucas, *Edwin Austin Abbey, Royal Academician: The Record of His Life and Work* (New York: Charles Scribner's Sons, 1921), 204. **199** CPCφ. **200** CPCφ. • CPCφ. • CPCφ. **201** CPCφ. **202** CPCφ. • CPCφ. • CPCφ. **203** CPCφ. **204** PSA. **205** CPCΔ. • SMP. **206** PSA. • LCP. **207** PSAφ. • CPC, photographed by Jason Wilson. **208** CPCΔ. • CPCΔ. **209** CPCΔ. **210** PSAφ. **211** Courtesy of Marian H. Van Soest. **212** CPCφ. **213** CPCφ. **214** CPCφ. • CPCφ. • CPCφ. • CPCφ. • CPCφ. **215** CPCφ. • CPCφ. • CPCφ. **216** Bucks County Historical Society, Spruance Library Collectionφ. **217** CPCφ. **218** CPCφ. • CPCφ. • CPCφ. **219** CPCφ. **220** CPCφ. • CPCφ. **221** CPCφ. • CPCφ. • CPCφ. • CPCφ. **222** LC # LC-B2-1250-3. **223** CPCφ. **224** CPCφ. • CPCφ. **225** CPCφ. **226–227** CPCφ. **228** CPCφ. **229** CPCφ. • CPCφ. **230** LC # LC-USZ6-1053. **231** CPCφ. • CPCφ. • CPCφ. **232** CPCφ. • CPCφ. • CPCφ. • CPCφ. **233** Courtesy of Robert Albarino. **234** CPCφ. • Westmoreland Museum of Art. **235** Source: Brush, Edward Hale. "The Work of Vincenzo Alfano." *Brush and Pencil* 16, no. 1 (1905): 3. • CPC. **236** CPCφ. • CPCΔ. • CPCΔ. **237** CPCΔ. • CPCΔ. • CPCΔ. **238** CPCΔ. **239** CPCΔ. • CPCΔ. • CPCΔ. • CPCΔ. • CPCΔ. **240** CPC, photographed by Jason Wilson. • CPCφ. • CPCΔ. • CPCΔ. **241** Administrative Office of Pennsylvania Courts. • CPCΔ. **242** CPCΔ. • CPCΔ. • LCP. **243** CPCΔ. • LCP. • CPCΔ. **244** CPC, photographed by Jason Wilson. • CPCΔ. • CPCΔ. • CPC, photographed by Jason Wilson. **245** CPCΔ. • CPCΔ. • CPCΔ. **246** CPCΔ. • CPCΔ. • CPCΔ. • CPCΔ.

• CPCΔ. • CPCΔ. **247** CPCΔ. • CPCΔ. • CPCΔ. **248** CPCΔ. **249** CPCΔ. • CPCΔ. • CPCφ. • CPCΔ.

Chapter 7: **250** Courtesy of William Thomas, photographed by S. W. Kuhnert. **252** PSA. **253** PSA. **254** PSA. • PSA. **255** PSA. **256** PSA. **257** PSA. **258** CPC. • LC # LC-USZ2-94591. **259** Chicago Historical Society. **260** PSA. **261** PSA. **262** PSA. • PSA. • PSA. **263** PSA. **264** PSA. • PSA. • PSA. • PSA. **265** PSA. **266** PSA. • PSA. **267** CPC. **268** Courtesy of William Thomas, photographed by S. W. Kuhnert. **269** PSA. • CPC, photographed by Jason Wilson. • CPC, photographed by Jason Wilson. **270** PSA. • PSA. **271** PSA. **272** Courtesy of William Thomas, photographed by S. W. Kuhnert. **273** PSA. **274** PSA. • PSA. • PSA. **275** Perspective drawing of Capitol Park, by Arnold Brunner. Source: Price, Matlack. "Capitol Park." *The Architectural Record* 53, no. 4 (1923): 288. • Capitol park lamp post, by Arnold Brunner. Source: Price, Matlack. "Capitol Park." *The Architectural Record* 53, no. 4 (1923): 305. **276–277** PSA. **278** CPCΔ. • CPCΔ. • CPC. • CPCΔ. • CPC. • CPCΔ. **279** CPC. **280** Courtesy of Representative Paul Clymer. • PSA. **281** PSA. • CPCΔ. **282** CPCΔ. • CPCΔ. • CPCΔ. • CPCΔ. **283** CPC. **284** CPCφ. **285** Pennsylvania Senate, photographed by Douglas Gross.

Chapter 8: **286** CPC. **288** CPC. • CPC. • CPC. **289** CPC. • CPC. • CPC. **290** Complex rendering. Source: Department of General Services. • CPCΔ. **291** CPC. • CPC. **292** CPC. • CPC. **293** CPCφ. • CPCφ. **294** CPC. • CPC. • CPC. • CPC. **295** CPC. • CPCφ. **296** CPC. • CPCφ. **297** CPC. **298** CPCφ. • CPCφ. • CPCφ. **299** CPC. • CPC. • CPC. • CPC. **300** CPCφ. • CPC. **301** CPC. **302** CPC. • CPC. • CPC. **303** CPC. **304** CPC. • CPC. • CPC. • CPC. • CPC, photographed by Douglas Gross. **305** CPC. • CPC. • CPC. **306** CPC. • CPC. **307** CPC. • CPC. • CPC. • CPC. • CPC. **308** CPCφ. • CPC. • CPCφ. **309** CPCφ. • CPC. • CPC. • CPC. **310** CPCΔ. • CPCφ. • CPCφ. • CPCΔ. **311** CPCΔ. • CPCΔ. • CPCφ. • CPCφ. **312** CPCα. • CPCα. • CPCα. • CPC. **313** CPCα. • CPC. • CPC. **314** CPC. • CPC. • CPC. **315** CPCφ. • CPCφ. • CPCφ. **316** CPC. • CPC. • CPC. • CPC. • CPCφ. **317** CPCφ. • CPCφ. • CPCφ. **318** CPC. • CPC. **319** CPCα. • CPCα. • CPC. **320** CPC. • CPC. **321** CPC. • CPC. • CPC. **322** CPC. • CPC. • CPC. • CPC. **323** CPC. • CPC. • CPC. • CPC. **324** CPC. • CPC. • CPC. • CPC. • CPC. **325** CPCφ. • CPC. **326** CPC. • CPC. • CPC. **327** CPC. • CPCφ. **328** CPC, photographed by Richard Saiers. • CPCα. • CPC, photographed by Richard Saiers. • CPCα. • CPCα. • CPCα. • CPC. **329** CPCφ. • CPCφ. • CPCΔ. **330** CPCφ. • CPCφ. • CPC. • CPC. • CPC. • Civil War re-enactors. Source: CPCΔ. **331** CPCφ. • CPC. • CPC. • CPC. **332** CPC. • CPC. • CPC. **333** CPC. • CPC. • CPC. • CPCα. • CPCα. • CPCα. **334** CPC. • CPCΔ. • CPC. • CPC. • CPC. **335** CPCΔ. • CPCΔ. • CPCΔ. • CPCΔ. **336** CPC. • CPCΔ. • CPCΔ. • CPC. **337** CPCΔ. • CPC. • CPC. • CPC. **338** CPC. • CPC. **339** CPC. • CPC. **340** CPC. • CPCΔ. • CPCΔ. **341** CPCΔ. • CPCΔ. • CPCΔ. **342** CPC. • CPC. • CPC. **343** CPCΔ. • CPC. • CPCΔ. **344** CPCφ. **345** CPC. • CPC.